William Lowe Bryan, Charlotte Lowe Bryan

Plato the Teacher

Being Selections from the Apology, Euthydemus, Protagoras, Symposium, Phædrus,

Republic and Phædo of Plato

William Lowe Bryan, Charlotte Lowe Bryan

Plato the Teacher

Being Selections from the Apology, Euthydemus, Protagoras, Symposium, Phædrus, Republic and Phædo of Plato

ISBN/EAN: 9783337019457

Printed in Europe, USA, Canada, Australia, Japan

Cover: Foto ©Thomas Meinert / pixelio.de

More available books at **www.hansebooks.com**

PLATO THE TEACHER

BEING SELECTIONS FROM THE APOLOGY, EUTHYDEMUS,
PROTAGORAS, SYMPOSIUM, PHÆDRUS, REPUBLIC,
AND PHÆDO OF PLATO

EDITED WITH INTRODUCTION AND NOTES

BY

WILLIAM LOWE BRYAN, Ph.D.

PROFESSOR OF PHILOSOPHY, INDIANA UNIVERSITY

AND

CHARLOTTE LOWE BRYAN, A.M.

NEW YORK
CHARLES SCRIBNER'S SONS
1897

EDUCATION DEPT.

Copyright, 1897, by
CHARLES SCRIBNER'S SONS

In memory
OF
HENRY BATES
A lover of men

TABLE OF CONTENTS

	PAGE
PREFACE,	ix
GENERAL INTRODUCTION,	xiii
INTRODUCTION TO APOLOGY,	3
APOLOGY,	5
INTRODUCTION TO EUTHYDEMUS,	33
EUTHYDEMUS,	35
INTRODUCTION TO PROTAGORAS,	63
PROTAGORAS,	67
INTRODUCTION TO THE SYMPOSIUM,	105
THE SYMPOSIUM,	107
INTRODUCTION TO PHÆDRUS,	137
PHÆDRUS,	141
INTRODUCTION TO THE REPUBLIC,	181
THE REPUBLIC:	
Book I.,	187
Book II.,	199
Book III.,	227
Book IV.,	251
Book V.,	279
Book VI.,	291
Book VII.,	319
Book VIII.,	342
Book IX.,	373
Book X.,	394
SUGGESTIONS ON THE STUDY OF THE PHÆDO,	413
PHÆDO,	417

PREFACE

PLATO'S fame as a philosopher prevents many from reading him far enough to discover that he is also a teacher of the folk. He is one of very few who can speak at times for the masters alone, and at other times so that the "common people hear him gladly." The historic Socrates drew about him all sorts and conditions of men, from the philosopher to the rake, each by the proper magic; and all sorts and conditions of men may yet feel something of his magic through the dialogues of Plato. To help publish the open secret that Plato speaks with simplicity and charm and power to all of us, is the purpose of this book.

The Apology is placed first as the best possible introduction to the life and spirit of Socrates. The Euthydemus shows Socrates in contrast with the baser Sophists, the Protagoras in contrast with the superior Sophists. The Symposium and Phædrus show philosophically and dramatically Plato's conception of love as the basis of science and of teaching. This is Plato's most important contribution to Education. The Republic gives Plato's entire scheme of education, as determined by the individual and by his social relations. This is an inexhaustible mine of wisdom for the teacher. The Phædo is introduced partly for its own sake and partly because all Plato's thought about the education of man was determined by his conception of the absolute nature and destiny of man.

The introductions to the several dialogues are intended only to give a few suggestive clews which may prove useful to elementary readers. The introduction to the Phædo is an outline for the study of that dialogue.

The notes constitute a dictionary of the biographical, geographical, and mythological terms or references in the text. Scholars will observe that the notes have been written with great reserve. While we have sought the highest accuracy in every line, we have sought no less to exclude all antiquarian lore that would not directly assist the elementary reader to understand the text.

In the preparation of this book the endeavor throughout has been to let Plato speak for himself. The notes and introductions are intended only to elucidate and not to criticise. To prevent possible misunderstanding, however, it may be well to state a few of the more important points in which we do not accept Plato's teaching. (1.) It is scarcely necessary to say that the modern Christian world has outgrown many of Plato's ideas of morality. In criticising these, however, it should be remembered that no one is wholly free from the influence of his age, and that in many things Plato was better than his age. (2.) We prefer actual democracy even to Plato's ideal aristocracy. (3.) We believe that con-

PREFACE　　　　　　　　　xi

tact with the earth through the senses and hands is not, as Plato seems to have believed, a degradation to the soul, but is a spiritual necessity. (4.) We believe that Plato's conception of God and of man's relation to God, far as it is beyond that which is often found among Christians, falls far short of that shown to us by our Lord.

The translation used is that of Jowett (the Charles Scribner's Sons' Edition). In a few cases where Jowett uses a foreign phrase or an expression presenting special difficulty to those unread in the classics, slight alterations have been made.

In the preparation of the notes we have used the Greek text of Plato; Liddell and Scott's Greek Dictionary;* Harper's Classical Dictionary; Johnson's Cyclopædia; Smith's Classical Dictionary; Bulfinch's, Guerber's, and Gayley's Manuals of Mythology; Jowett's Introductions and Analyses; The Index to Jowett's Plato, third edition; Zeller's Plato and the Older Academy; Zeller's Socrates; Grote's History of Greece; Grote's Plato; Bosanquet's Companion to Plato's Republic; Socrates, Talks with Socrates about Life, Talks with Athenian Youth, A Day in Athens with Socrates, published by Charles Scribner's Sons; and Webster's Dictionary, on the pronunciation of proper names.

* Referred to in notes as L. & S.

GENERAL INTRODUCTION

THE ATHENS OF PLATO.

PLATO was born at Athens about 427 B.C. His native city was then at the height of its prosperity. At the beginning of that century the Greek states, often at war with each other, and always jealous of each other, had been forced to unite in a fight for life against the innumerable hordes of the Persian Empire. Athens was foremost in this fight, and when the Persians were finally driven away, she succeeded in placing herself at the head of a powerful league of Greek cities. Accordingly, although the city had been captured and burned by the Persians, she presently became, under the direction of the statesman Pericles, far stronger politically and commercially than ever before. A variety of causes made this period also a golden age for many of the arts. The city had to be rebuilt. This was done under direction of the sculptor Phidias, with a splendor and artistic perfection perhaps never elsewhere equalled. The democratic Athenian government, according to which questions of State were decided in a general assembly of all the people, gave occasion for the development of oratory of the highest order. Finally, in this century, the drama which had gradually developed in connection with the worship of Dionysus, came to classic perfection in the comedies of Aristophanes and the tragedies of Æschylus, Sophocles, and Euripides.

Athens had yet another glory of which some of her citizens were not proud. She had become the principal seat of philosophy. In order to appreciate the state of philosophy at this time, and the feeling of the people toward it, we must give a brief account of the preceding history of philosophy.

GREEK PHILOSOPHY BEFORE PLATO.

The deliberate search after scientific or philosophic truth arose first, so far as we know, about two hundred years before the time of Plato, among the Greeks who lived on the western coast of Asia Minor. There were a dozen Greek cities on that coast and the adjacent islands of the Ægean archipelago, as far back as authentic history runs. These cities were fortunately placed. They had at their back a prosperous country and before them the sea. They developed a great trade all around the Ægean and Mediterranean Seas,—with Tyre and Sidon, with Egypt, and with the widely scattered Greek colonies. They became very rich. But that was not all. By contact with new peoples, they acquired new ideas and the habit of looking out for new ideas. They were without doubt especially indebted to Egypt. Indirectly through Phœnicia, they got from Egypt the alphabet which is substantially the one we use to-day. Besides this invaluable gift, they got from the Egyptians a first lesson in science. The study of the heavenly bodies had been from ancient times part of the religious duty of the Egyptian priests, who therefore had considerable knowledge of astronomy. On account of the yearly overflow of the Nile, it had been necessary to have some method of measuring land in order to re-establish boundary lines. The Egyptians had accordingly some knowledge of geometry. In the course of time Greek travelers acquired this learning. We find, for example, that Thales, a Greek of Miletus, predicted an eclipse of the sun which occurred in 585 B.C.

But, as I have said, these Greeks acquired by their travel, not only new ideas, but also an eager curiosity for more new ideas. They were not at all satisfied to accept the learning of Egypt and of Tyre and Sidon, as they found it. That learning helped to free them somewhat from faith in the myths by which their ancestors had explained all things in heaven and earth, but gave them no sufficient substitute for the old faith. It is, at any rate, certain that about 650 B.C., a few sages in the Ionic cities were beginning to grope toward a *natural* explanation of things. In the movements of the heavenly bodies, for example, where the superstitious saw only the caprice of the gods, they had learned to see an order such that future events could be predicted. This led some of the wiser men to believe that there is an order ruling in nature everywhere. They began to raise questions accordingly, not only about the true length of the year, and the means of measuring time, but also very general questions, such as: What is the world made of? What force has caused it to be generated? What law has ruled in this generation? We have authentic accounts of more than a dozen distinguished men, living between 650 B.C. and the time of Plato's birth (427 B.C.), whose lives were spent in trying to answer questions of this sort.

If you read the answers they were able to make to these questions, ignorantly or carelessly enough, you may think them little better than childish. One said that the world is made of water, which thickens and hardens to make solid bodies, and thins to make air and fire. Another said that the world is made of air; another that it is made of fire; another that it is made of four elements—earth, air, fire, and water. Another said that all things are in eternal motion and that when we think that anything is at rest, our senses deceive us. Another said that all things are eternally at rest and that when we think we see motion, our senses deceive us. One said that all things in nature move by numerical harmony, like the notes of the musical scale. Another said that love and hate are the two forces that bring all things together or keep them apart. More than one of them expressed in some form the belief that the evolution of the world is directed by one supreme intelligence. Many of them expressed views on particular scientific questions which are very similar to those now accepted. So, for example, Anaximander, who lived about 600 B.C., held some views about the structure of the solar system which were more nearly correct than the theories generally accepted down to the time of Copernicus (A.D. 1543). I shall not, however, discuss the value of this early philosophizing further than to say that the more deeply one studies it, the more surely one sees that these men were not fools, and that, in spite of their crudities, some of them were giants of all time. What I wish now to do is to discuss their influence upon the public mind of Greece.

As might be expected, they produced one kind of effect upon the few who paid special attention to them and an altogether different effect upon the general public. Even with the former, the effect was by no means always flattering to the philosophers. Just in the period between the Persian wars and the birth of Plato, a great many of the Greeks who devoted themselves to learning were coming to the conclusion that philosophy was a failure. "The philosophers," they said in substance, "tell us that we cannot trust our senses for the truth of anything, and that we must learn the truth of them. We go to them and find that they contradict one another at every point. The truth is," some went on to say, "there is no truth which is truth always and everywhere. The world is different at every point and is always changing. Men are all different from each other and every one is constantly changing. How can a changing man find anything in a changing world which every other man will always find just so? It is impossible. That is true for each man which he finds true. Let us cease the vain search for a universal and absolute truth. Let us be content to learn how to be practically effective. Let us learn how to fight, how to write, how to speak, how to plead in the courts and before the assembly of the people. Let us acquire skill to get on in the world. There is no other wisdom than this."

The class of men who took substantially this position called themselves Sophists, that is, wise men. Some of them were very talented, very thoroughly schooled in the learning of that time, and very skillful in the practical arts which they professed to teach. They gave special attention to language—that is, to grammar, rhetoric, and oratory. They are given credit for the development of Greek prose style, as it appears, for example, in the orations of Demosthenes, a century later, and indirectly for the development of the same art among the Romans. Some of the Sophists were, of course, inferior. I need only refer to the dialogue Euthydemus, in this volume, to show that some of them were despicably so. Such men cared for nothing but their own advantage, and were, without doubt, gross corrupters of the youth.

Now, the general public did not draw any fine distinctions between the superior Sophists, such as Protagoras, and the baser sort, such as Euthydemus and Dionysodorus. Moreover, the public did not distinguish between the Sophists and the philosophers. Although the philosophers had sought earnestly for the truth, and believed that they had found some truth, while the Sophists believed all such search vain, the Athenian public, intelligent as they were in many things, lumped all men of learning together, and called them Sophists. As a result of this failure to distinguish between men whose views were directly opposed, the public attributed to all of them substantially all the faults they found or suspected in any of them. Some of the philosophers had outgrown the popular religion; the people were accordingly quick to believe that any learned man was an atheist. Some of the Sophists rejected the conventional notions of morals; every scholar was, therefore, readily suspected of being a corrupter of the youth, and if any youth who consorted with scholars turned out badly, his ruin was charged up to the new learning.

The public opinion, with its muddle-headed opposition to the whole movement of science and philosophy, was expressed perfectly in a comedy by the great Athenian, Aristophanes. The story of the play, called "The Clouds," runs as follows: A certain man finds himself in debt, without ability to pay. He is told that there is a school of the Sophists where he can be taught how to argue himself out of all his debts. The school is described, with Socrates as chief teacher. Socrates is represented as engaged in profound investigations on various nonsensical questions about things in heaven and beneath the earth. He is calculating, for example, the distance from one place to another in terms of the foot of a flea. The man is taught how to argue away his debt; but his son gets from the same teachers a lesson which enables him to prove his right to thrash his father. It is easy to see how the average Athenian, who looked and laughed at this play, would lump all the philosophers together, and attribute to each of them, but especially to Socrates, a nonsense and a knavery which would bring the country to ruin.

So far nothing has been said about the real belief and purposes of Socrates or of Plato. What it is necessary to see is the actual situation which they faced.

1. There were the old philosophers, reaching back nearly two hundred years to Thales of Meletus, who had been floundering and struggling toward the truth about nature, without coming to an agreement.

2. There were the Sophists, some of them scholars and gentlemen, some of them ignorant tricksters, who rejected all the foregoing philosophy, and, more or less, also the popular ideas of religion, law, and morals.

3. There were the Athenian people, proud of their military glory, their growing wealth, and their beautiful city, but ignorant of the new learning and hostile to it.

PLATO'S MASTER.

The foregoing pages touch the principal features —political, economic, artistic, philosophical, and social, of the situation in Athens at the time of Plato's birth. One element in the situation has been barely mentioned, Plato's master, Socrates.

Socrates had more influence upon Plato and upon subsequent philosophy than had any of the men or conditions heretofore mentioned. I shall not, however, in this place give an account of his life and teachings. I refrain from doing this solely because those who read this book may become acquainted with Socrates far better, as well as far more delightfully, through the dialogues of Plato that are given

GENERAL INTRODUCTION   xxi

here, than from any biography that could be written about him. Indeed, one main object of this book is just to make those who read it personally acquainted with Socrates. There is, however, one matter of fact, in this connection, which should be thoroughly understood.

Socrates wrote nothing. We know of his life and teachings chiefly through the writings of two of his disciples, Xenophon and Plato. Xenophon probably told the truth about his master as well as he could. But Xenophon was like some of those who heard the teachings of our Saviour—he heard the words, but not their deeper spiritual sense. Plato understood Socrates better than any one else did, and he could have given us, without doubt, a trustworthy picture of his master. The difficulty in getting at the real Socrates through the writings of Plato is this. All Plato's writings are in dialogue. In almost all the dialogues, Plato's own opinions are put into the mouth of Socrates. Plato's own views, however, became in the course of time considerably different from those of his master. It is, consequently, impossible to be sure just how far the speeches of Socrates, in Plato's dialogues, represent the actual opinions of Socrates, and how far they represent opinions acquired by Plato after his master's death. It is, indeed, true that Plato's philosophy was developed out of that of Socrates, and we may be sure that, as a rule, in ascribing his own opinions to Socrates, Plato did not greatly violate the spirit of the master's teaching. It should, however, be understood that the Socrates who speaks in Plato's writings is more or less a dramatic creation.

PLATO'S LIFE.

Of Plato's life and work only the bare outlines will be given here. He was born about 427 B.C., of a wealthy and aristocratic family. He had the best education which the world then afforded, becoming in time master of all branches of learning then known. He was particularly proficient in mathematics. When he was twenty years old, he became the disciple of Socrates, and lived with the master until the death of the latter in 399. Later, he traveled in Egypt, Cyrene, Italy, and Sicily, pursuing philosophic studies. In Sicily he was sold as a slave. After being ransomed, he opened a school of mathematics and philosophy in Athens, where, among others, he had Aristotle for a pupil. Twice, by invitation of Dion, ruler of Sicily, he attempted to apply his political theories to an actual government, but both attempts were failures. His death occurred at Athens, 347 B.C.

No philosophy can be adequately represented by an outline, even if the outline were made by the philosopher himself, because the definite doctrines which can be stated in an outline are always to be understood in connection with the thousand subtle meanings that lie between his lines. There is, however, special reason why Plato cannot be represented by an outline of his philosophy. He was, in fact, far more than a mere philosopher. He was a dramatic artist. He was more than that. He was a lover of men. And in the measure that he was these three—philosopher, dramatist, and lover—he was a teacher.

PLATO THE PHILOSOPHER.

In this place will be given first an account of Plato's central doctrine, and then a view of his attitude toward the life of his day.

The Doctrine of Ideas. Plato's doctrine of ideas varied at different periods of his life. Its established features may be stated as follows:

Every one knows what a common noun is, as tree, horse, stone, etc. A moment's thought will show that common nouns may be arranged in a system. Children recognize some such system in their game of twenty questions, when they ask if the thing you have thought of is material or immaterial; if material, whether it is animal, vegetable, or mineral; if an animal, whether a land animal or a water animal; and so on until they have run down the particular thing or class of things thought of. In any such system the special classes run together into general classes, until at last all run together into one class, say the class *being*, which includes all beings, divine and human, living and dead.

Now Plato believed (1) that corresponding to every common noun there is a real, eternal, and perfect being, in the likeness of which and by the power of which every particular being coming under that class is made; (2) that, corresponding to the system of common nouns, there is a system of such real, eternal, and perfect beings; and (3) that, corresponding to the highest common noun, there is a Highest Being, which is the prime source of all lower beings and so of all things whatever. The real, eternal, and perfect beings corresponding to our common nouns

Plato called *ideas*. He did not, therefore, use the word idea in the sense that we are most accustomed to. The highest idea is God.
Now while he believed that these ideas are pure, holy, and beautiful, he believed that the particular objects which the world that we see is made of—the actual trees, horses, etc.—are only imperfect copies of their ideas, and are, therefore, not at all pure, holy, and beautiful, but just the contrary. The goodness of the ideas and the badness of particular things is the central thought of Plato's philosophy. Man has or may have knowledge of both. With his eyes and ears and other senses he comes into contact with the world of things. With his soul he may know directly the world of ideal being, which culminates in God. Contact with the world through the senses, gives us not true or valuable knowledge, but only the appearance of true wisdom. Contact with the eternal ideal beings, by means of the eye of the soul, gives us the only true and divine wisdom.

To account for the fact that the soul may know the ideal beings,?Plato held that the soul has existed always; that before being born into this earthly life the soul lived in the world of ideal beings; that the soul retains a memory of its former life; that we may recall the knowledge we had in a former life, if we will withdraw our senses from the things of the world and give ourselves to diligent reflection. That is, by diligent reflection, we are able to recall more and more accurately the system of real beings, corresponding to our system of common nouns, and at last we are able to rise in this way to a contemplation of the Highest Idea, that is, God. On this point read the parable given in Book VII. of the Republic.

As we are misled by the senses, when we seek knowledge through them, so we are misled by them in regard to the conduct of individual and social life. The senses are the source of all our sinning. We should die to the body and the things of the body and turn our souls altogether toward the ideal being. By contemplation of and obedience to the ideal being we shall be made more and more good and beautiful in this life, and after death we shall reënter the ideal world where we shall be in the company of perfect souls. As our individual life, so our political life should be wholly directed by the divine truth. This is possible only through the guidance of men who have purified themselves from the world, and by long consecration have come to see the divine truth. That is, the State should be governed by the wisest and best, and all others will find their true interest in obeying them.

Plato's attitude toward the life of his time: Probably very few of those who read this book will accept Plato's doctrine of ideas in the form in which he presented it. However that may be, no one should fail to see that what Plato stood for most centrally, along with the prophets and apostles of every age, was the reality and power of the truth. He believed in the truth; that the truth is one and eternal; that the truth rules all things both great and small in the world and in the lives of men; that men need the truth and no other thing to compass them about in infancy with influences that make for righteousness, and to rise in their souls as clear knowledge and as holy purpose, with their growth into manhood. This central faith in the reality and power of truth determined Plato's attitude toward every important question that met him,—toward the old philosophy, toward the theories and practices of the Sophists, toward the business, art, religion, and politics of his nation, and toward the conduct of his own life. Let us look at each of these points.

Rel. to The Old Philosophers: Plato did not join the Sophists and the general public in scorn of the old philosophers. He believed that their long search for the truth had not been altogether in vain. He believed that some of them were worth the deepest study he could give them. He made extensive and expensive journeys to meet living disciples of the various schools of philosophy. There is a tradition that he paid a sum equal to about $1,600 for one small book on the teachings of Pythagoras. It is at any rate certain that he was a profound student of Pythagoras, of Parmenides, of Heracleitus, and doubtless of other old masters. He was not afraid that such study of his predecessors would affect his own originality. No passage can be recalled which shows that he was jealous of any of his predecessors or anxious to prove his own superiority. In the Theætetus there is a reference to one of the old masters which seems to be not ironical, but characteristic of Plato's genuine reverence for the greater philosophers. "I have a kind of reverence," he says, "for the great leader himself, Parmenides, venerable and awful as in Homeric language he may be called:

GENERAL INTRODUCTION   xxvii

him I should be ashamed to approach in a spirit unworthy of him."

The Sophists? Plato was unceasingly hostile to the doctrines and practices of the Sophists. He clearly saw that the Sophists were not all upon the same level. The best and the worst of them one may become acquainted with in two of the dialogues given in this volume—Euthydemus and Protagoras. Euthydemus and his brother, Dionysodorus, are exhibited as substantially a pair of confidence men. They are ignorant, shallow, unscrupulous tricksters. Their game is the half-grown youth who has much money and little judgment. When they have dazzled and corrupted and robbed the boy, their work is done. In the dialogue, Plato scorches these men with his irony, and holds them up to public shame as mercilessly as Aristophanes did in the comedy their kind to which I have referred.

In the Protagoras we are introduced to Sophists of a very different kind. Protagoras, Hippias, and Prodicus were men who had earned distinction by attainments which are honored in almost all civilized countries. They were masters of the learning and of the arts of the time. Judged by any ordinary standard, the Sophists of this class would receive an honorable if not an eminent place in the history of culture. It is held by some scholars that Plato was not just to them. It is possible that he was not, although, indeed, he shows very clearly that he was by no means ignorant of their many gifts and accomplishments. The reason for his unfailing antagonism to every kind of Sophist is not ignorance of their attainments, as judged by ordinary standards.

He utterly refuses to judge them by ordinary standards. Everything *is* eternally judged by one standard, the absolute truth. Judged by this standard, the most accomplished Sophist stands self-condemned. He does not believe in the absolute truth. He does not seek to know it. He does not seek to obey it. He has no faith in anything except the power of artifice. His learning, since it never leads toward the absolute truth, is " the art of giving, by quibbling criticism, an appearance of knowledge." His rhetoric is not a true but a spurious art, which does not seek to supply true food for the soul, but only to concoct highly spiced dishes which shall pamper and corrupt the people.

Athens. What did Plato think of his own city,— its art, its religion, its politics? If you glance again at the brief account which has been given of the many glories of Athens at that time, or, better, if you become thoroughly acquainted with the history of Athens, you may well think that any Athenian had a right to be proud of his birthplace,—its commercial and political prosperity, its temples, its classic drama, its impressive religious ceremonials. Indeed, if you get to know and love the "glory that was Greece," you may be inclined to anger against any one who would dare to criticise it. Be angry if you will, but Plato, who grew up in the midst of that glory was its remorseless critic. He made his criticisms in the exquisitely graceful Athenian fashion, but in substance they are as stern as if he had been Jeremiah or John Knox. The reason for this severe judgment, as in the case of the Sophists, is that he knows only one standard of judgment, the absolute truth. The paintings, the songs, the stories, the dramas, are full of what is beautiful to the senses, but to the soul they are for the most part ugly and evil. When they tell of the gods and heroes they are full of lies. When they pretend to portray the virtues temperance and courage, they misrepresent and mislead. This influence is for the most part corrupting, and they should all be banished from education and from the State, except such as really lead the soul toward the truth.

In a like spirit Plato criticised the business and political life of his time. The people are wasting their life for that which is not bread. Some want military glory, some want money, some want pleasure. All these wants lead more or less rapidly to ruin in this world and the next. The people need one thing—to be under the power of the truth. They need wise and righteous men, who have, by years of search, come to know the truth, to direct the state and the activities of its citizens. Only in such a state can there be true health and happiness for the people.

PLATO AS DRAMATIST.

I do not call Plato a dramatist merely because he wrote in dialogue. A dialogue is not always dramatic. The speakers may be only masks, through which one hears always the author's voice. Plato himself often writes in this style. In such cases we presently see through the masks and discover that the dialogue is only an essay.

There is proof of Plato's dramatic gift in the

graphic pictures of Greek life which make the setting of his dialogues. But this would have slight importance, if those pictures were found to be only a sort of artistic coating for his philosophical pill.

The justification for calling Plato a dramatist becomes more substantial when one finds a dialogue whose story illustrates the theme discussed. Take, for example, The Symposium. The theme is love. One after another of the banqueters praises love in a new way. At length Socrates unfolds his own view. Suddenly in bursts a crowd of revelers, drowning all discussion and scattering all serious thought. When the leader of the revel learns what the banqueters have been doing, he also will make a speech. But he will choose his own subject. He will make a speech about Socrates. The interruption and the speech are very interesting, but what of that? It would be *interesting* if Bildad, the Shuhite, should comfort Job with a fiddle. Why should Plato, any more than the author of Job, interrupt sublime discourse by a farce? A little closer inspection, however, shows that the interruption is not real, that the subject is not changed, that the debauched revelers and the story which Alcibiades tells of his relations with Socrates, together illustrate the whole range of beastly, human, and divine love which it is the purpose of the dialogue to portray. In the Phædo, Phædrus, and elsewhere, there are other fine examples of Plato's skill in making the story of one spirit with the argument.

But the full justification for calling Plato a dramatist does not rest upon such occasional examples of his art. If this were all, we should only say that

GENERAL INTRODUCTION   xxxi

Plato is a philosopher who sometimes shows that he might have been a dramatist. *Plato is a dramatist because of this: It is never enough for him to know the absolute solution of any problem. He wishes also to know, with the sympathetic imagination, just how men of every sort look at that problem.* In most of his dialogues, not all, Plato somewhere seeks to work his way toward the absolute truth by rigid systematic thinking. There he is purely philosopher. There the dialogue is only form, and the speakers courteously make way for the argument. But in no dialogue is this the only thing done. All sorts and conditions of men are introduced—a slave boy, a confidence man, an ignorant braggart, a rake, a youth eager for learning, a professor of things-in-general, a physician, a poet, a business man, a philosopher—a great range of people, historical and fictitious, representing every phase of the life of his time. These people are not masks. Some of them feel even to us as real as Shakespeare's Mercutio, or Polonius, or Dogberry. Often they are given their way with the argument. Often within the same dialogue first one and then another type of man takes the lead and fixes the plane of the conversation. Now they tussle at the problem like puppy dogs (Republic, VII., 539), Socrates tussling gayly with the rest. Now some one smothers discerning inquiry with a fine oration, and perhaps Socrates matches this with another of the same sort. Now an eager youth plunges courageously into a discussion beyond his depth, and Socrates follows him with joyful applause, often without a hint that there are depths in the problem which the youth has not sounded. In many cases the dialogue ends with the question at issue unsettled. In such cases one sees that Plato's purpose in that dialogue is <u>not to set forth the truth as he sees it, but to show men in struggle for the truth.</u> The former were the achievement of a philosopher; the latter is the achievement of a dramatist whose drama is the whole spiritual journey of mankind. If I may borrow a figure from Pilgrim's Progress, I shall say that Plato, the Philosopher, had sight of the Celestial City; but that Plato, the Dramatist, kept also in view the long way back to the City of Destruction. He knew all the way stations upon that road, how many there are, how far apart, and how in one or another of them— in Vanity Fair, in the Valley of Humiliation, in the Slough of Despond, in the Arbor of the Enchanted Ground—men dance or curse or pray or lie in perilous sleep far from the Celestial City.

PLATO THE LOVER {*wisdom*, *men*}

This title is not a new invention. In several ways Plato distinctly claimed it for himself. For one thing, he called himself *philo-sophos*, lover of wisdom. This title meant two things. It meant for one thing that he would not be called *sophos*, wise. This was not mock humility. In one sense Plato was not humble. He was a proud man. He believed that he had found *the way* toward truth while most men wander blind and helpless in other ways. He believed that he had found some essential truth which the world must accept or perish for lack of. When he had these things in mind, he spoke with the dog-

GENERAL INTRODUCTION   xxxiii

matic authority of a prophet. But just because he saw so far into the truth of things, he saw more clearly than most men ever do, that the whole truth is not to be compassed in this life, that none is Wise but God. And just because he felt so deeply the need of actual truth, to live by, now, he turned from all pretense of wisdom with instinctive hatred. There will be nothing new in this to any one who has learned Plato from his own writings. In most dialogues, the Platonic Socrates is more genuinely docile than his antagonists or disciples. On the day of his death, he warned those about him against letting their love of him add undue weight to his arguments, and bade them withstand him might and main, where he seemed astray.[1]

But the title *philo-sophos* meant more with Plato than a recognition that he was not like God,—wise. Above all things this title meant that he was quite literally a lover of wisdom, that his desire to be wise was a passion. In order to prepare one's self to appreciate Plato's passion for the Absolute Good, one might read some of those passages in the Bible which express the longing of the soul for God. The Psalmist says, " As the hart panteth for the water brooks, so longeth my soul for Thee." " My soul longeth, yea, even fainteth for the courts of the Lord; my heart and my flesh crieth out for the living God." Moses declares that the first and greatest

---

[1] A fashionable amusement of this century is to bait philosophers. It may be that philosophers as a class deserve and need this chastisement. As a rule, however, those who, professing to speak for common sense or for exact science, deride philosophical inquiry into the problems of life, will give you the solution to any such problem while standing on one leg. Such men make queer figures in presence of Socrates.

commandment is "Thou shalt love the Lord thy God with all thy heart, and with all thy soul, and with all thy strength," and to this Christ adds, "and with all thy mind." The emotional tone of these and such passages is characteristically different from that of Plato, but his language is not less strong. One can imagine his quoting and approving all these passages.[1] In the Phædrus and Symposium, Plato represents love as a principle which ranges through many forms from animal passion up to the purest longing for absolute truth. In all its forms it is intense, a mania, an ecstasy. In its highest form, it is holy fire in which the earthly soul is consumed and the heavenly soul is reborn.

But Plato is more than *philo-sophos*, lover of wisdom. With the same intensity and for the same reason he is *phil-anthropos*, lover of men. Love, says the wise woman, Diotima, in the Symposium, is not love of the beautiful and good only. Love is essentially love of "birth in beauty." "Some," she goes on, "beget earthly children, but some are more creative in their souls." "He who in youth has the seeds of temperance and justice implanted in him desires to implant them in others." Above all, when he finds a fair and noble and well-nourished soul, "he is full of speech about virtue and the nature and pursuits of a good man, and he tries to educate him, and they are married by a far closer tie and have closer friendship than those who beget mortal children, for the children who are their com-

---

[1] As nearly as I can characterize the difference, it is this: Plato is not himself so lost in the ecstatic longing which he describes as the Psalmist seems to be.

mon offspring are fairer and more immortal." In such deep fashion would Plato, the pagan, realize the maxim, thou shalt love thy neighbor as thyself.

PLATO THE TEACHER.

Socrates and Plato have universal fame as teachers. Their fame is usually attributed to their development of the so-called Socratic method of teaching. That device requires, therefore, special consideration.

Socrates and Plato believed that the truth is latent in the soul; that to waken this latent truth into clear consciousness is very difficult; that the highest means of achieving this end is systematic reflection; and that systematic reflection in its step-by-step approach to clear knowledge takes naturally the verbal form of a series of questions and answers. They used this device in their own most difficult investigations, and with their most mature disciples. They sometimes used it with less mature disciples, and even with illiterate persons. (So, for example, in a passage from the Meno, much quoted in educational journals, Socrates, by a series of questions, leads an illiterate slave boy to see for himself the truth of a simple geometrical proposition.) They used the device at times ironically, that is, for the purpose of revealing to an antagonist the contradictions between his different assertions. Finally, it is not to be denied that they sometimes used the device in a manner which seems grossly sophistical, and it would be difficult to prove that in all such cases the sophistry is ironical.

The Socratic method, more or less perfectly understood, has had great influence upon professional Pedagogy. In many schools for the professional training of teachers, and in many schools in charge of teachers professionally trained, systematic questioning of this sort is looked upon as ideal teaching; and there is no lack of conscientious endeavor to prepare for use in recitation, series of questions which shall lead the child mind to take the logical steps which given occasions require. One who doubts the value of such systematic questioning may usually be converted by hearing a single typical recitation conducted by a master of the art. The power of such a recitation to touch, move, chasten, and direct the soul is so evident, that if Socrates and Plato had taught us nothing but how to do such work their fame as teachers would be justified.

If, however, systematic questioning were the whole Socratic art, we should be obliged to say that that art stands in unfavorable contrast with many other arts and occupations. For in most arts and occupations, systematic procedure is not the sole or highest ideal. On the contrary, it is the open secret of successful men generally that system must bow to circumstance. A great business man knows that the method of running a railroad and the method of running a kerosene wagon cannot be interchanged with profit to either, and perhaps uses both methods at the same time for the benefit of the same corporation (*e.g.*, The Standard Oil Company). A great lawyer knows well the power of technicality, but also when to leave the little men chopping logic over legal trivialities, and rest his case upon a common sense principle which the highest courts will declare to be the law. A great general conforms to the rules of military science when he is fighting British Regulars, and abandons those rules when he is fighting Indians in ambush. (Compare Washington in the Revolution and Washington at Braddock's Defeat.) A great statesman has a task not unlike that of the teacher. He has to deal with human beings. He has to lead them if he can, from their present position to a higher. He has to instruct, persuade, convert,—achieve with the folk essentially the same things that the teacher has to achieve with the smaller folk. In doing this work he does not underestimate the educational value of formalities, of platforms, statutes, decisions, and executive acts. He knows the power of logical argument in print or on the stump, and indeed the occasional value of Socratic questioning as a weapon in debate. (See, for example, the use of formal questions in the Lincoln-Douglass debate.) But no master statesman wins his place as leader, teacher, father of the folk, by any sort of systematic procedure. He meets men face to face. He looks them through to the marrow. He is subtle as a lover to find the right word or the right silence. He wins men for his idea by winning them for himself. As Tennyson says: "He lays his mind upon them, and they believe in his belief."

In presence of such ideals and achievements among men of affairs, what can be said of systematic Socratic questioning as the sole or highest ideal for teaching? Is there nothing in a child but logical apparatus? Are all the informal ways by which statesmen from Moses to Lincoln have led the folk too informal and unscientific for little folk? Is that surely the best way of "leading the child mind to take the necessary steps," by which you would not dare try to elicit the necessary steps, if you were applying for a position,—or a wife? Whatever the modern professor of didactics may think of these things, it is certain that the power of Socrates himself did not lie wholly in his gift for catechising. He did not cast a spell over the men of his generation—business men, soldiers, politicians, philosophers, and rakes—simply by subjecting them to logical inquisition. If Plato affirmed this of his master, those who know human nature would not believe it. But Plato says nothing of the sort. Let us turn from the hand-books on didactics to Plato for an account of the real Socratic Art.

In Phædrus, 271–272, Plato says that the orator (and the orator in this case is essentially a teacher) should have three degrees of knowledge of the soul.

1. He should know the "true nature of the soul, how she acts or is acted upon." If Plato's philosophy of teaching had stopped here, perhaps he would have supposed that his systematic questioning was the whole art of teaching. But he went farther.

2. The orator or teacher should know the several classes of men, and "why one sort of soul is persuaded by one argument, and another not."

3. He is to become acquainted with men in actual life, and "be able to follow them with all his wits about him, or he will never get beyond the precepts of his masters." He must in this way at last be able,

when confronting an actual man, to say, "This is the man who needs this argument to be convinced of this thing." "When he has attained the knowledge of all this and knows when he should speak, and when he should abstain from speaking, when he should make use of pithy sayings, pathetic appeals, aggravated effects and all the other figures of speech, when he knows the times and seasons of all these things, then, and not till then, is he perfect master of the art."

This wonderfully inclusive Psychology of Education, embracing at the one extreme the essential nature of the soul and at the other the infinitely varied peculiarities of individuals, was not with Plato a mere theory. He practiced the theory even better than he preached it. As I have shown, in speaking of Plato as dramatist and as lover, there are many illustrations of this. Perhaps none of them is better than the Phædrus, taken as a whole. Socrates finds Phædrus full of a youth's enthusiasm for a piece of brilliant rhetoric about love. There is little true insight and no sincerity in the speech, and the prose is not really good. How shall the youth be sobered from his perilous intoxication and given taste for wine of better vintage? How shall he be directed toward the acquisition of true artistic power and how shall he be led into knowledge and reverence for the best thing in the world, which is love. The dialogue as a whole tells how Socrates actually did this. It takes the dialogue as a whole, its story, its arguments, its orations, and the criticisms upon them, its myths, and above all, its free and joyous conversation—it takes all to explain how Socrates went about to win a man.

This is the true Socratic Art. It is determined by the philosophic insight that art must adapt itself not only to the common nature of man, but also to the varying natures, and even to the varying moods of men. It is determined by dramatic insight into the actual ways of the souls addressed. It is determined by a passion as deep as it is tranquil to save the best of the youth into the higher life.

HOW SHALL ONE READ PLATO?

When corn takes in stuff from the soil, the soil is changed into corn, but also the corn is changed by the soil. So when you read Plato, Plato is translated into your way of thinking, but also your way of thinking is influenced by Plato. It is possible for either of these effects to be over-emphasized to the neglect of the other. The secret of right growth is to maintain the right balance between the old which one has and the new which is asking for admission. To find this balance is not easy, but many wise men say that the *first* thing to do with a new book, or anything else worth attention, is to surrender one's self to it as completely as possible. I believe accordingly that I can give no better advice to one who meets Plato for the first time in this volume, than that you should let him talk to you. Imagine that you have wandered into the Athens of 400 B.C. and have come upon Socrates engaged in talk. Join the crowd. Keep still. Try to catch the drift. Do not pigeonhole Socrates the first day. Get acquainted with him as you do with a living man. You will find it useful without doubt to study

Plato's system of thought in the brief outline which is given, or in the fuller accounts which you may find in other books. But if you suppose that any such outline of doctrines can compass the fullness of Plato, you will not understand this or any philosophy in the spirit. With whatever formal devices you study any master-book, the essential condition of becoming really acquainted with it is that you shall live with it in joyful, informal fellowship.

APOLOGY

UNIV. OF
CALIFORNIA

INTRODUCTION

THE defense of Socrates includes an answer to the formal accusations made against him in court, and an answer to those who for years had attacked his reputation. In both cases, the charge is the same in substance,—that he is the enemy of the traditional religion and morality of the State. Those who brought this charge before the court, supported it with false or trivial evidence and arguments. Socrates met these with arguments, which are, in form, nearly upon the same level.

His numerous unofficial accusers, Socrates met partly by an explanation of the popular misunderstanding which identified him with the natural philosophers or with the Sophists, but especially by a declaration of his own mission in life, which was not to deny God but to know and obey the will of God, and not to corrupt but to save men.

In studying the defense of Socrates against his official and unofficial accusers, it should be seen that the conflict was not merely one between a wise and good man and a crowd of ignorant and malicious ones. The real conflict was between the unwritten religious, moral, and social constitution of the Athenian people, and a man who would put everything in that constitution to question with the hope of arriving at a better. Socrates was not many things that his accusers charged,—not a natural philosopher, not a Sophist, not an atheist, perhaps not a disbeliever in the popular mythology, not responsible for the sins of young Athenians whom he had labored to make men of. But the instinct of the Athenians was not substantially wrong in holding him an alien from *their* religion and morality. "I do believe that there are gods," says Socrates in closing his first speech, "and in a far higher sense than any of my accusers believe in them." Because he believed in God, the formal charges against him were false. But because he believed in God in a far higher sense than did his accusers, he and his accusers, the people of Athens, stood in real conflict. They stood for the religion and morals which they had inherited. He stood for a religion and morality based upon deeper insight into the truth. It was a conflict between a people and its prophet. It was a conflict in some respects like that between the orthodox Jews, who would defend their law and their separate nationality against destruction, and Him who came not to destroy but to fulfill. In such a case the question decided is this: Will the people rise from their own view to their prophet's view of the life which is proper for them? At Athens, as at Jerusalem, the people chose for their traditions. Socrates, like our Saviour, rejected of his own, became minister to all mankind.

APOLOGY[1]

How you have felt, O men of Athens, at hearing the speeches of my accusers, I cannot tell; but I know that their persuasive words almost made me forget who I was, such was the effect of them; and yet they have hardly spoken a word of truth. But many as their falsehoods were, there was one of them which quite amazed me: I mean when they told you to be upon your guard, and not to let yourselves be deceived by the force of my eloquence. They ought to have been ashamed of saying this, because they were sure to be detected as soon as I opened my lips and displayed my deficiency; they certainly did appear to be most shameless in saying this, unless by the force of eloquence they mean the force of truth; for then I do indeed admit that I am eloquent. But in how different a way from theirs! Well, as I was saying, they have hardly uttered a word, or not more than a word, of truth; but you shall hear from me the whole truth: not, however, delivered after their manner, in a set oration duly ornamented with words and phrases. No, indeed! but I shall use the words and arguments which occur to me at the moment; for I am certain that this is right, and that at my time of life I ought not to be appearing before you, O men of Athens, in the character of a juvenile orator: let no one expect this of me. And I must beg of you to grant me one favor, which is this,—If you hear me using the same words in my defense which I have been in the habit of using and which most of you may have heard in the agora,[2] and at the tables of the money-changers,[3] or anywhere else, I would ask you not to be surprised at this, and not to interrupt me.

Steph.
17

[1] Defense.
[2] The market-place, corresponding to the Roman forum. Not only was most of the traffic carried on here, but in most Greek cities it was the general meeting-place for social and political purposes.
[3] The bankers did business at tables in the market-place.

For I am more than seventy years of age, and this is the first time that I have ever appeared in a court of law, and I am quite a stranger to the ways of the place; and therefore **18** I would have you regard me as if I were really a stranger, whom you would excuse if he spoke in his native tongue, and after the fashion of his country: that I think is not an unfair request. Never mind the manner, which may or may not be good; but think only of the justice of my cause, and give heed to that: let the judge decide justly and the speaker speak truly.

And first, I have to reply to the older charges and to my first accusers, and then I will go on to the later ones. For I have had many accusers, who accused me of old, and their false charges have continued during many years; and I am more afraid of them than of Anytus[4] and his associates, who are dangerous, too, in their own way. But far more dangerous are these, who began when you were children, and took possession of your minds with their falsehoods, telling of one Socrates, a wise man, who speculated about the heaven above, and searched into the earth beneath, and made the worse appear the better cause. These are the accusers whom I dread; for they are the circulators of this rumor, and their hearers are too apt to fancy that speculators of this sort do not believe in the gods. And they are many, and their charges against me are of ancient date, and they made them in days when you were impressible,—in childhood, or perhaps in youth,—and the cause when heard went by default, for there was none to answer. And hardest of all, their names I do not know and cannot tell; unless in the chance case of a comic poet.[5] But the main body of these slanderers who from envy

---

[4] Anytus (ăn′y-tus): a wealthy Athenian, high in popular favor, the most formidable of the accusers of Socrates. He was a bitter antagonist of the Sophists and hated Socrates especially for having influenced his son to study philosophy. He is said to have gone into exile after the death of Socrates to escape the vengeance of the fickle people. In the dialogue Meno, Anytus, incensed at something Socrates has said, threatens him thus: "I think that you are too ready to speak evil of men; and, if you take my advice I would recommend you to be careful. Perhaps there is no city in which it is not easier to do men harm than to do them good, and this is certainly the case at Athens, as I believe that you know."

[5] Aristophanes (ăr-ĭs-tŏf′a-nēz), 444-388 B.C., greatest of the Greek comic poets, wrote a comedy called The Clouds, in which he ridiculed Socrates, representing him as a visionary thinker and as one who would break down the ancient standards of morality. This comedy, which appeared about twenty-four years before the trial of Socrates, tended to make the general public regard Socrates as a Sophist.

and malice have wrought upon you,—and there are some of them who are convinced themselves, and impart their convictions to others,—all these, I say, are most difficult to deal with; for I cannot have them up here, and examine them, and therefore I must simply fight with shadows in my own defense, and examine when there is no one who answers. I will ask you then to assume with me, as I was saying, that my opponents are of two kinds,—one recent, the other ancient; and I hope that you will see the propriety of my answering the latter first, for these accusations you heard long before the others, and much oftener.

Well, then, I will make my defense, and I will endeavor in the short time which is allowed to do away with this evil opinion of me which you have held for such a long time; and I hope that I may succeed, if this be well for you and me, and that my words may find favor with you. But I know that to accomplish this is not easy—I quite see the nature of the task. Let the event be as God wills: in obedience to the law I make my defense.

I will begin at the beginning, and ask what the accusation is which has given rise to this slander of me, and which has encouraged Meletus[6] to proceed against me. What do the slanderers say? They shall be my prosecutors, and I will sum up their words in an affidavit: "Socrates is an evil-doer, and a curious person, who searches into things under the earth and in heaven, and he makes the worse appear the better cause; and he teaches the aforesaid doctrines to others." That is the nature of the accusation, and that is what you have seen yourselves in the comedy of Aristophanes, who has introduced a man whom he calls Socrates, going about and saying that he can walk in the air, and talking a deal of nonsense concerning matters of which I do not pretend to know either much or little—not that I mean to say anything disparaging of any one who is a student of natural philosophy. I should be very sorry if Meletus could lay that to my charge. But the simple truth is, O Athenians, that I have nothing to do with these studies. Very many of those here present are witnesses to the

---

[6] Meletus (me-lē'tŭs): an obscure young tragic poet, who made the formal accusation against Socrates. He was the least important of the three accusers and is said to have been stoned to death by the people in their revulsion of feeling after the death of Socrates.

truth of this, and to them I appeal. Speak then, you who have heard me, and tell your neighbors whether any of you have ever known me hold forth in few words or in many upon matters of this sort. . . . You hear their answer. And from what they say of this you will be able to judge of the truth of the rest.

As little foundation is there for the report that I am a teacher, and take money; that is no more true than the other. Although, if a man is able to teach, I honor him for being paid. There is Gorgias of Leontium, and Prodicus of Ceos, and Hippias of Elis,[7] who go the round of the cities, and are able to persuade the young men to leave their own citizens, by whom they might be taught for nothing, and come to them whom they not only pay, but are thankful if they may be allowed to pay them. There is actually a Parian philosopher [8] residing in Athens, of whom I have heard; and I came to hear of him in this way: I met a man who has spent a world of money on the Sophists, Callias [9] the son of Hipponicus, and knowing that he had sons, I asked him: "Callias," I said, "if your two sons were foals or calves, there would be no difficulty in finding some one to put over them; we should hire a trainer of horses, or a farmer probably, who would improve and perfect them in <u>their own proper virtue and excellence</u>; but as they are human beings, whom are you thinking of placing over them? Is there any one who understands human and political virtue? You must have thought about this as you have sons; is there any one?" "There is," he said. "Who is he?" said I, "and of what country? and what does he charge?" "Evenus the Parian," he replied; "he is the man, and his charge is five minæ." [10] Happy is Evenus, I said to myself, if he really has this wis-

---

[7] Of these three Sophists, the most famous was Gorgias (gôr'jĭ-as), a native of Leontini in Sicily. One of Plato's dialogues bears his name. He was a great rhetorician and the founder of a school of oratory. He was very popular and received large fees. Prodicus (prŏd'ĭ-kus). Hippias (hĭp'pĭ-as). See Protagoras, note 1.

[8] Evenus (e-vē'nus) of Paros (pā'ros, an island in the Ægean): mentioned in the Phædo as a poet, and in the Phædrus as the inventor of certain rhetorical devices.

[9] Callias (kăl'lĭ-as): an Athenian of noble and wealthy family, and a great admirer of the Sophists. His house is the scene of Plato's Protagoras.

[10] Mina (mī'na); pl. Minæ (mī'nē) or Minas: a sum of money varying in value; in Athens, about $16 or $18.

dom, and teaches at such a modest charge.¹¹ Had I the same, I should have been very proud and conceited; but the truth is that I have no knowledge of the kind, O Athenians.

I dare say that some one will ask the question, "Why is this, Socrates, and what is the origin of these accusations of you: for there must have been something strange which you have been doing? All this great fame and talk about you would never have arisen if you had been like other men: tell us, then, why this is, as we should be sorry to judge hastily of you." Now I regard this as a fair challenge, and I will endeavor to explain to you the origin of this name of "wise," and of this evil fame. Please to attend, then. And although some of you may think that I am joking, I declare that I will tell you the entire truth. Men of Athens, this reputation of mine has come of a certain sort of wisdom which I possess. If you ask me what kind of wisdom, I reply, such wisdom as is attainable by man, for to that extent I am inclined to believe that I am wise; whereas the persons of whom I was speaking have a superhuman wisdom, which I may fail to describe, because I have it not myself; and he who says that I have, speaks falsely, and is taking away my character. And here, O men of Athens, I must beg you not to interrupt me, even if I seem to say something extravagant. For the word which I will speak is not mine. I will refer you to a witness who is worthy of credit, and will tell you about my wisdom —whether I have any, and of what sort—and that witness shall be the God of Delphi.¹² You must have known Chærephon;¹³ he was early a friend of mine, and also a friend of yours, for he shared in the exile of the people,¹⁴ and returned with you. Well, Chærephon, as you know, was very impetuous in all his doings, and he went to Delphi and

---

¹¹ The Sophists Gorgias and Protagoras are said to have received as much as one hundred minæ.
¹² Delphi (dĕl'fĭ), a small city in central Greece, was the seat of one of the most famous oracles. Here Apollo, one of the greatest and most beneficent of the Greek gods, was supposed to inspire his prophetess and through her reveal his will to those who came to consult him. This priestess of Apollo was sometimes called the Pythian prophetess because the ancient name of Delphi was Pytho (pȳ'thō).
¹³ Chærephon (kĕr'e-fon): an enthusiastic admirer of Socrates.
¹⁴ The Peloponnesian War (431-404 B.C), was a conflict between Athens and Sparta in which Athens was defeated. Sparta placed Athens under the control of a Council of Thirty. Under these tyrants Athens suffered many cruelties, one of them being the exile of many of her citizens.

boldly asked the oracle to tell him whether—as I was saying, I must beg you not to interrupt—he asked the oracle to tell him whether there was any one wiser than I was, and the Pythian prophetess answered, that there was no man wiser. Chærephon is dead himself, but his brother, who is in court, will confirm the truth of this story.

Why do I mention this? Because I am going to explain to you why I have such an evil name. When I heard the answer, I said to myself, What can the god mean? and what is the interpretation of this riddle? for I know that I have no wisdom, small or great. What can he mean when he says that I am the wisest of men? And yet he is a god and cannot lie; that would be against his nature. After a long consideration, I at last thought of a method of trying the question. I reflected that if I could only find a man wiser than myself, then I might go to the god with a refutation in my hand. I should say to him, "Here is a man who is wiser than I am; but you said that I was the wisest." Accordingly I went to one who had the reputation of wisdom, and observed him—his name I need not mention; he was a politician whom I selected for examination—and the result was as follows: When I began to talk with him, I could not help thinking that he was not really wise, although he was thought wise by many, and wiser still by himself; and I went and tried to explain to him that he thought himself wise, but was not really wise; and the consequence was that he hated me, and his enmity was shared by several who were present and heard me. So I left him, saying to myself, as I went away: Well, although I do not suppose that either of us knows anything really beautiful and good, I am better off than he is,—for he knows nothing, and thinks that he knows. I neither know nor think that I know. In this latter particular, then, I seem to have slightly the advantage of him. Then I went to another who had still higher philosophical pretensions, and my conclusion was exactly the same. I made another enemy of him, and of many others beside him.

After this I went to one man after another, being not unconscious of the enmity which I provoked, and I lamented and feared this: but necessity was laid upon me,—the word of God, I thought, ought to be considered first. And I said to myself, Go I must to all who appear to know, and find out the meaning of the oracle. And I swear to you, Athenians, by the dog [15] I swear!—for I must tell you the truth—the result of my mission was just this: I found that the men most in repute were all but the most foolish; and that some inferior men were really wiser and better. I will tell you the tale of my wanderings and of the "Herculean" labors, as I may call them, which I endured only to find at last the oracle irrefutable. When I left the politicians, I went to the poets; tragic, dithyrambic,[16] and all sorts. And there, I said to myself, you will be detected; now you will find out that you are more ignorant than they are. Accordingly, I took them some of the most elaborate passages in their own writings, and asked what was the meaning of them—thinking that they would teach me something. Will you believe me? I am almost ashamed to speak of this, but still I must say that there is hardly a person present who would not have talked better about their poetry than they did themselves. That showed me in an instant that not by wisdom do poets write poetry, but by a sort of genius and inspiration [17]; they are like diviners or soothsayers who also say many fine things, but do not understand the meaning of them. And the poets appeared to me to be much in the same case; and I further observed that upon the strength of their poetry they believed themselves to be the wisest of men in other things in which they were not wise. So I departed, conceiving myself to be superior to them for the same reason that I was superior to the politicians.

At last I went to the artisans, for I was conscious that I knew nothing at all, as I may say, and I was sure that they knew many fine things; and in this I was not mistaken, for they did know many things of which I was ignorant, and in this they certainly were wiser than I was. But I observed that even the good artisans fell into the same error as the poets; because they were good workmen they thought that they also knew all sorts of high matters, and this defect in them overshadowed their wisdom — therefore I asked myself on behalf of the oracle, whether I would like to be as I was, neither having their knowledge nor their ignorance, or like

---

[15] An oath, of uncertain, possibly Egyptian origin, often used by Socrates.
[16] The dithyramb was a kind of lyric poem.
[17] Compare Phædrus, 245.

them in both; and I made answer to myself and the oracle that I was better off as I was.

This investigation has led to my having many enemies of the worst and most dangerous kind, and has given occasion also to many calumnies. And I am called wise, for my hearers always imagine that I myself possess the wisdom which I find wanting in others: but the truth is, O men of Athens, that God only is wise; and in this oracle he means to say that the wisdom of men is little or nothing; he is not speaking of Socrates, he is only using my name as an illustration, as if he said, He, O men, is the wisest, who, like Socrates, knows that his wisdom is in truth worth nothing. And so I go my way, obedient to the god, and make inquisition into the wisdom of any one, whether citizen or stranger, who appears to be wise; and if he is not wise, then in vindication of the oracle I show him that he is not wise; and this occupation quite absorbs me, and I have no time to give either to any public matter of interest or to any concern of my own, but I am in utter poverty [18] by reason of my devotion to the god.

There is another thing:—young men of the richer classes, who have not much to do, come about me of their own accord; they like to hear the pretenders examined, and they often imitate me, and examine others themselves; [19] there are plenty of persons, as they soon enough discover, who think that they know something, but really know little or nothing: and then those who are examined by them instead of being angry with themselves are angry with me: This confounded Socrates, they say; this villainous misleader of youth!—and then if somebody asks them, Why, what evil does he practise or teach? they do not know, and cannot tell; but in order that they may not appear to be at a loss, they repeat the ready-made charges which are used against all philosophers about teaching things up in the clouds and under the earth, and having no gods, and making the worse appear the better cause; for they do not like to confess that their pretense of knowledge has been detected—which is the truth: and as they are numerous and ambitious and energetic, and are all in battle array and have persuasive tongues, they have filled your ears with their

---

[18] Socrates was notoriously neglectful of his own private interests.
[19] Compare Republic VII., 539: "They must not be allowed to taste," etc.

loud and inveterate calumnies. And this is the reason why my three accusers, Meletus and Anytus and Lycon,[20] have set upon me: Meletus, who has a quarrel with me on behalf of the poets; Anytus, on behalf of the craftsmen; Lycon, on behalf of the rhetoricians: and as I said at the beginning, I cannot expect to get rid of this mass of calumny all in a moment. And this, O men of Athens, is the truth and the whole truth; I have concealed nothing, I have dissembled nothing. And yet, I know that this plainness of speech makes them hate me, and what is their hatred but a proof that I am speaking the truth?—this is the occasion and reason of their slander of me, as you will find out either in this or in any future inquiry.

24-27

I have said enough in my defense against the first class of my accusers; I turn to the second class who are headed by Meletus, that good and patriotic man, as he calls himself. And now I will try to defend myself against them: these new accusers must also have their affidavit read. What do they say? Something of this sort: That Socrates is a doer of evil, and corrupter of the youth, and he does not believe in the gods of the State, and has other new divinities of his own. That is the sort of charge; and now let us examine the particular counts. He says that I am a doer of evil, who corrupt the youth; but I say, O men of Athens, that Meletus is a doer of evil, and the evil is that he makes a joke of a serious matter, and is too ready at bringing other men to trial from a pretended zeal and interest about matters in which he really never had the smallest interest. And the truth of this I will endeavor to prove.

[By questioning Meletus, Socrates brings out the fact that Meletus himself is careless about the improvement of the youth. In answer to the charge that he corrupts the youth, Socrates shows how inconceivable it is that a man should intentionally injure citizens among whom he has to live and from whom he must expect evil in return as Meletus admits. The declaration of Meletus that Socrates is an atheist is shown to contradict the charge that he is introducing new gods.]

[20] Lycon (lȳ'kon): a rhetorician and orator, said to have been banished for his part in the prosecution of Socrates.

I have said enough in answer to the charge of Meletus: any elaborate defense is unnecessary; but as I was saying before, I certainly have many enemies, and this is what will be my destruction if I am destroyed; of that I am certain; not Meletus, nor yet Anytus, but the envy and detraction of the world, which has been the death of many good men, and will probably be the death of many more; there is no danger of my being the last of them.

"Some one will say: And are you not ashamed, Socrates, of a course of life which is likely to bring you to an untimely end? To him I may fairly answer: There you are mistaken: a man who is good for anything ought not to calculate the chance of living or dying; he ought only to consider whether in doing anything he is doing right or wrong—acting the part of a good man or of a bad." Whereas, according to your view, the heroes who fell at Troy[21] were not good for much, and the son of Thetis above all, who altogether despised danger in comparison with disgrace; and when his goddess mother said to him, in his eagerness to slay Hector, that if he avenged his companion Patroclus, and slew Hector, he would die himself, —"Fate," as she said, "waits upon you next after Hector;" he, hearing this, utterly despised danger and death, and instead of fearing them, feared rather to live in dishonor, and not to avenge his friend. "Let me die next," he replies, "and be avenged of my enemy, rather than abide here by the beaked ships, a scorn and a burden of the earth." Had Achilles any thought of death and danger? For wherever a man's place is, whether the place which he has chosen or that in which he has been placed by a commander, there he ought to remain in the hour of danger; he should not think of death or of anything, but of disgrace. And this, O men of Athens, is a true saying.

Strange, indeed, would be my conduct, O men of Athens, if I who, when I was ordered by the generals whom you chose

---

[21] According to legend, Helen, the beautiful wife of King Menelaus (měn'-e-lā'us) of Sparta, was carried off to Troy during her husband's absence, by Paris, son of King Priam of Troy. Under the leadership of Agamemnon (ăg'a-měm'nŏn) brother of Menelaus, the Greeks went to Troy and besieged the city for ten years before it was finally taken and Helen recovered. This war is the subject of Homer's Iliad. Achilles (a-kĭl'lēz), son of the sea-nymph Thetis (thē'tĭs), was the bravest of the Greek heroes. His friend Patroclus (păt-rŏ'klus) fell by the spear of the Trojan warrior Hector. To avenge this death, Achilles engaged in combat with Hector and slew him.

to command me at Potidæa and Amphipolis and Delium,[22] remained where they placed me, like any other man, facing death,—if, I say, now, when, as I conceive and imagine, God orders me to fulfill the philosopher's mission of searching into myself and other men, I were to desert my post through fear of death, or any other fear; that would indeed be strange, and I might justly be arraigned in court for denying the existence of the gods, if I disobeyed the oracle because I was afraid of death: then I should be fancying that I was wise when I was not wise. For this fear of death is indeed the pretense of wisdom, and not real wisdom, being the appearance of knowing the unknown; since no one knows whether death, which they in their fear apprehend to be the greatest evil, may not be the greatest good. Is there not here conceit of knowledge, which is a disgraceful sort of ignorance? And this is the point in which, as I think, I am superior to men in general, and in which I might perhaps fancy myself wiser than other men,—that whereas I know but little of the world below,[23] I do not suppose that I know: "but I do know that injustice and disobedience to a better, whether God or man, is evil and dishonorable, and I will never fear or avoid a possible good rather than a certain evil." And therefore if you

[22] In the hostilities preceding and during the Peloponnesian War (see note 14), Socrates served as foot soldier in battles at Potidæa (pŏt'ĭ-dē'a) in Macedonia in 432 B.C.; at Delium (dē'lĭ-um) in Bœotia (bē-ō'shĭ-à) in 424 B.C.; at Amphipolis (ăm-fĭp'o-lĭs) in Macedonia, in 422 B.C.
[23] The Greeks believed that the world of the dead was in the depths of the earth. In the most ancient usage, Hades meant simply the world of the dead, inhabited by incorporeal images having the form of the earthly body and following the occupations of the earthly life, but, except by special favor of the gods, without consciousness. Later, Hades was made to include a place for the blessed (Elysium, or the Islands of the Blest), and a place for the damned, Tartarus (tär'ta-rŭs), the inhabitants of both being of course conscious of their states. The Hebrew word Sheol (shē'ŏl) made familiar by its use in the revised version of the English Bible, passed through a somewhat similar change of meaning and in the Septuagint, the ancient Greek translation of the Old Testament, is usually translated by the Greek word Hades. When the authorized version of the English Bible was made in 1611, the word hell still sometimes retained the meaning, the place of the dead, although it had also the meaning, the place of the damned. The word hell was therefore, as a rule, properly used to translate Sheol and Hades. Now that our word hell has lost its general meaning, the place of the dead, it is no longer equivalent to Sheol and Hades; and since we have now no English word for the place of the dead, the revised version of the English Bible simply transfers Sheol (nearly always) and Hades (always) into English spelling. This explanation of a word much used by Plato is made necessary because of the popular misconception that Hades is a mild term for the place of eternal torment.

let me go now, and reject the counsels of Anytus, who said that if I were not put to death I ought not to have been prosecuted, and that if I escape now, your sons will all be utterly ruined by listening to my words,—if you say to me, Socrates, this time we will not mind Anytus, and will let you off, but upon one condition, that you are not to inquire and speculate in this way any more, and that if you are caught doing this again you shall die,—if this was the condition on which you let me go, I should reply: Men of Athens, I honor and love you; but I shall obey God rather than you,[24] and while I have life and strength I shall never cease from the practice and teaching of philosophy, exhorting any one whom I meet after my manner, and convincing him, saying: O my friend, why do you, who are a citizen of the great and mighty and wise city of Athens, care so much about laying up the greatest amount of money and honor and reputation, and so little about wisdom and truth and the greatest improvement of the soul,[25] which you never regard or heed at all? Are you not ashamed of this? And if the person with whom I am arguing, says, Yes, but I do care: I do not depart or let him go at once; I interrogate and examine and cross-examine him, and if I think that he has no virtue, but only says that he has, I reproach him with undervaluing the greater, and overvaluing the less. And this I should say to every one whom I meet, young and old, citizen and alien, but especially to the citizens, inasmuch as they are my brethren. For this is the command to God, as I would have you know; and I believe that to this day no greater good has ever happened in the State than my service to the God. For I do nothing but go about persuading you all, old and young alike, not to take thought for your persons or your properties, but first and chiefly to care about the greatest improvement of the soul. I tell you that virtue is not given by money, but that from virtue come money and every other good of man, public as well as private.[26] This is my teaching, and if this is the doctrine which corrupts the youth, my influence is ruinous indeed. But if any one says that this is not my teaching, he is speak-

---

[24] "We ought to obey God rather than men."—Acts v. 29.
[25] "For a man's life consisteth not in the abundance of the things which he possesseth."—Luke xii. 15.
[26] "But rather seek ye the kingdom of God; and all these things shall be added unto you."—Luke xii. 31.

ing an untruth. Wherefore, O men of Athens, I say to you, do as Anytus bids or not as Anytus bids, and either acquit me or not; but whatever you do, know that I shall never alter my ways, not even if I have to die many times.

Men of Athens, do not interrupt, but hear me; there was an agreement between us that you should hear me out. And I think that what I am going to say will do you good: for I have something more to say, at which you may be inclined to cry out; but I beg that you will not do this. I would have you know, that if you kill such a one as I am, you will injure yourselves more than you will injure me. Meletus and Anytus will not injure me: they cannot; for it is not in the nature of things that a bad man should injure a better than himself. I do not deny that he may, perhaps, kill him, or drive him into exile, or deprive him of civil rights; and he may imagine, and others may imagine, that he is doing him a great injury: but in that I do not agree with him; for the evil of doing as Anytus is doing—of unjustly taking away another man's life—is greater far. And now, Athenians, I am not going to argue for my own sake, as you may think, but for yours, that you may not sin against the God, or lightly reject his boon by condemning me. For if you kill me you will not easily find another like me, who, if I may use such a ludicrous figure of speech, am a sort of gadfly, given to the State by the God; and the State is like a great and noble steed who is tardy in his motions owing to his very size, and requires to be stirred into life. I am that gadfly which God has given the State, and all day long and in all places am always fastening upon you, arousing and persuading and reproaching you. And as you will not easily find another like me, I would advise you to spare me. I dare say that you may feel irritated at being suddenly awakened when you are caught napping; and you may think that if you were to strike me dead as Anytus advises, which you easily might, then you would sleep on for the remainder of your lives, unless God in his care of you gives you another gadfly. And that I am given to you by God is proved by this: that if I had been like other men, I should not have neglected all my own concerns, or patiently seen the neglect of them during all these years, and have been doing yours, coming to you individually, like a father or elder brother, exhorting you to regard virtue; this, I say, would not be like human nature. And had I gained anything, or if my exhortations had been paid, there would have been some sense in that : but now, as you will perceive, not even the impudence of my accusers dares to say that I have ever exacted or sought pay of any one ; they have no witness of that. And I have a witness of the truth of what I say ; my poverty is a sufficient witness.

Some one may wonder why I go about in private, giving advice and busying myself with the concerns of others, but do not venture to come forward in public and advise the State. I will tell you the reason of this. You have often heard me speak of an oracle or sign [27] which comes to me, and is the divinity which Meletus ridicules in the indictment. This sign I have had ever since I was a child. The sign is a voice which comes to me and always forbids me to do something which I am going to do, but never commands me to do anything, and this is what stands in the way of my being a politician. And rightly, as I think. For I am certain, O men of Athens, that if I had engaged in politics, I should have perished long ago, and done no good either to you or to myself. And don't be offended at my telling you the truth : for the truth is, that no man who goes to war with you or any other multitude, honestly struggling against the commission of unrighteousness and wrong in the State, will save his life ; he who will really fight for the right, if he would live even for a little while, must have a private station and not a public one.[28]

32

I can give you as proofs of this, not words only, but deeds, which you value more than words. Let me tell you a passage of my own life, which will prove to you that I should never have yielded to injustice from any fear of death, and that if I had not yielded I should have died at once. I will tell you a story—tasteless, perhaps, and commonplace, but nevertheless true. The only office of state which I ever held, O men of Athens, was that of senator [29]; the tribe Antiochis, which is my

[27] Socrates frequently speaks of this sign or voice. He seems to have regarded it not as a personal divinity, but as a divine influence.
[28] Compare Rep. VI., 496.
[29] At the time of Socrates, Attica, the Athenian State, was divided into ten tribes. The senate consisted of five hundred members, chosen by lot, fifty from each tribe. " Its sittings became constant, with the exception of special holidays. The year was distributed into ten portions called Prytanies—the fifty senators of each tribe taking by turns the duty of constant attendance during one prytany, and receiving during that time the title of The Prytanes (prўt'a-nēz). . . . A further subdivision of the prytany into five periods of seven days each, and of the fifty tribe senators into five bodies of ten

tribe, had the presidency at the trial of the generals who had not taken up the bodies of the slain after the battle of Arginusæ;[30] and you proposed to try them all together, which was illegal, as you all thought afterwards; but at the time I was the only one of the prytanes who was opposed to the illegality, and I gave my vote against you; and when the orators threatened to impeach and arrest me, and have me taken away, and you called and shouted, I made up my mind that I would run the risk, having law and justice with me, rather than take part in your injustice because I feared imprisonment and death. This happened in the days of the democracy. But when the oligarchy of the Thirty[31] was in power, they sent for me and four others into the rotunda,[32] and bade us bring Leon the Salaminian from Salamis,[33] as they wanted to execute him. This was a specimen of the sort of commands which they were always giving with the view of implicating as many as possible in their crimes; and then I showed, not in word only but in deed, that, if I may be allowed to use such an expression, I cared not a straw for death, and that my only fear was the fear of doing an unrighteous or unholy thing." For the strong arm of that oppressive power did not frighten me into doing wrong;

each, was recognized. Each body of ten presided in the senate for one period of seven days, drawing lots every day among their number for a new chairman."—Grote's History of Greece, chap. xxxi.
Part of the business of the senate was to prepare resolutions to be laid before the general assembly of all the citizens, which, in cases like the one referred to by Socrates, had, with the senate, the power of final decision.

[30] Arginusæ (ăr'jĭ-nu̯'sē): a naval battle of the Poloponnesian War, occurring in 406 B.C. Although victorious, the Athenian generals left their dead unburied and abandoned the living on the wrecked vessels. This neglect and cruelty aroused great indignation at Athens. The generals were illegally tried, condemned and executed.

" So intimidated were the Prytanes by the incensed manifestations of the assembly that all of them, except one, relinquished their opposition and agreed to put the question " [as to the guilt and condemnation of the generals in a body]. The single obstinate Prytanis, whose refusal no menace could subdue, was a man whose name we read with peculiar interest, and in whom an impregnable adherence to law and duty was only one among many other titles to reverence. It was the philosopher Socrates; on this trying occasion, once throughout a life of seventy years, discharging a political office, among the fifty senators taken by lot from the tribe Antiochus. Socrates could not be induced to withdraw his protest, so that the question was ultimately put by the remaining Prytanes without his concurrence."—Grote's History of Greece III., chap. lxiv.

[31] See Apology, note 14.

[32] The office of the Prytanes at the Prytaneum (prȳt'a-nē'um) where they also dined at public cost. See Apology, note 43.

[33] Salamis (săl'a-mĭs): an island of the Ægean, near Athens.

and when we came out of the rotunda the other four went to Salamis and fetched Leon, but I went quietly home. For which I might have lost my life, had not the power of the Thirty shortly afterwards come to an end. And to this many will witness.

Now do you really imagine that I could have survived all these years, if I had led a public life, supposing that like a good man I had always supported the right and had made justice, as I ought, the first thing? No indeed, men of Athens, neither I nor any other. But I have been always the same in all my actions, public as well as private, and never have I yielded any base compliance to those who are slanderously termed my disciples,[34] or to any other. For the truth is that I have no regular disciples: but if any one likes to come and hear me while I am pursuing my mission, whether he be young or old, he may freely come. Nor do I converse with those who pay only, and not with those who do not pay; but any one, whether he be rich or poor, may ask and answer me and listen to my words; and whether he turns out to be a bad man or a good one, that cannot be justly laid to my charge, as I never taught him anything. And if any one says that he has ever learned or heard anything from me in private which all the world has not heard, I should like you to know that he is speaking an untruth.

But I shall be asked, Why do people delight in continually conversing with you? I have told you already, Athenians, the whole truth about this: they like to hear the cross-examination of the pretenders to wisdom; there is amusement in this. And this is a duty which the God has imposed upon me, as I am assured by oracles, visions, and in every sort of way in which the will of divine power was ever signified to any one. This is true, O Athenians; or, if not true, would be soon refuted. For if I am really corrupting the youth, and have corrupted some of them already, those of them who have grown up and have become sensible that I gave them bad advice in the days of their youth should come forward as accusers and take their revenge; and if they do not like to come themselves, some of

---

[34] Probably an allusion to Critias, the most unscrupulous and most hated of the Thirty Tyrants, and Alcibiades, a corrupt general and politician, both of whom had in youth associated with Socrates, and for whose evil doing he was sometimes held responsible. See Protagoras, note 1; Symposium, 212 and following.

their relatives, fathers, brothers, or other kinsmen, should say what evil their families suffered at my hands. Now is their time. Many of them I see in the court. There is Crito,[35] who is of the same age and of the same deme [36] with myself; and there is Critobulus [37] his son, whom I also see. Then again there is Lysanias of Sphettus, who is the father of Æschines,— he is present; and also there is Antiphon of Cephisus, who is the father of Epigenes; and there are the brothers of several who have associated with me. There is Nicostratus the son of Theosdotides, and the brother of Theodotus (now Theodotus himself is dead, and therefore he, at any rate, will not seek to stop him); and there is Paralus the son of Demodocus, who had a brother Theages, and Adeimantus the son of Ariston, whose brother Plato is present; and Æantodorus, who is the brother of Apollodorus, whom I also see. I might mention a great many others, any of whom Meletus should have produced as witnesses in the course of his speech; and let him still produce them, if he has forgotten; I will make way for him. And let him say, if he has any testimony of the sort which he can produce. Nay, Athenians, the very opposite is the truth. For all these are ready to witness on behalf of the corrupter, of the destroyer of their kindred, as Meletus and Anytus call me; not the corrupted youth only,—there might have been a motive for that,—but their uncorrupted elder relatives. Why should they too support me with their testimony? Why, indeed, except for the sake of truth and justice, and because they know that I am speaking the truth, and that Meletus is lying.

Well, Athenians, this and the like of this is nearly all the defense which I have to offer. Yet a word more. Perhaps

[35] Crito (krī'tō): a wealthy Athenian, the devoted friend and disciple of Socrates. He is said to have relieved Socrates from the necessity of manual labor. He offered Socrates means of escape from prison. He appears in the Phædo. A dialogue of Plato bears his name.
[36] Each of the ten tribes of Attica comprised a certain number of demes (dēmz) or administrative districts, something like our townships. They were named after persons or places.
[37] Critobulus (krīt' o-bū'lus); Lysanias (ly-sā'nĭ-as); Sphettus (sfĕt'tŭs); Æschines (ĕs'kĭ-nēz); Antiphon (ăn'tĭ-fon); Cephisus (se-fī'sus); Epigenes (e-pĭj'e-nēz); Nicostratus (ni-cŏs'tra-tus); Theosdotides (thē-ŏs'dō-tī'dez); Theodotus (thē-ŏd'o-tus); Paralus (păr'a-lus); Demodocus (dĕ-mŏd'o-cus); Theages (thē-ā'jēz); Adeimantus (ăd'ĭ-măn'tus); Ariston (a-rĭs'ton); Æantodorus (ē-ăn'tō-dō'rus); Apollodorus (ā-pŏl'lō-dō'rus). Of these men Æschines and Epigenes were present at the death of Socrates; See Phædo, 59. Adeimantus appears in the Republic.

there may be some one who is offended at me, when he calls to mind how he himself on a similar, or even a less serious occasion, had recourse to prayers and supplications with many tears, and how he produced his children in court, which was a moving spectacle, together with a posse of his relations and friends; whereas I, who am probably in danger of my life, will do none of these things. Perhaps this may come into his mind, and he may be set against me, and vote in anger because he is displeased at this. Now if there be such a person among you, which I am far from affirming, I may fairly reply to him: My friend, I am a man, and like other men, a creature of flesh and blood, and not of wood or stone,[38] as Homer[39] says; and I have a family, yes, and sons, O Athenians, three in number, one of whom is growing up, and the two others are still young; and yet I will not bring any of them hither in order to petition you for an acquittal. And why not? Not from any self-will or disregard of you. Whether I am or am not afraid of death is another question, of which I will not now speak. But my reason simply is, that I feel such conduct to be discreditable to myself, and you, and the whole State. One who has reached my years, and who has a name for wisdom, whether deserved or not, ought not to demean himself. At any rate, the world has decided that Socrates is in some way superior to other men.

35 And if those among you who are said to be superior in wisdom and courage, and any other virtue, demean themselves in this way, how shameful is their conduct! I have seen men of reputation, when they have been condemned, behaving in the strangest manner: they seemed to fancy that they were going to suffer something dreadful if they died, and that they could be immortal if you only allowed them to live; and I think that they were a dishonor to the State, and that any stranger coming in would say of them that the most eminent men of Athens, to whom the Athenians themselves give honor and command, are no better than women. And I say that these things ought not to be done by those of us who are of

---

[38] Now, I pray, declare
Thy lineage, for thou surely art not sprung
From the old fabulous oak, nor from a rock.
—Bryant's Odyssey, xix. 201.

[39] The earliest poet whose works were known to the Greeks of this period. To him was attributed the authorship of many poems, among them the Iliad and the Odyssey. We have no authentic information about him. His date was probably between 1000 and 850 B.C.

reputation; and if they are done, you ought not to permit them; you ought rather to show that you are more inclined to condemn, not the man who is quiet, but the man who gets up a doleful scene, and makes the city ridiculous.

But, setting aside the question of dishonor, there seems to be something wrong in petitioning a judge, and thus procuring an acquittal instead of informing and convincing him. For his duty is not to make a present of justice, but to give judgment, and he has sworn that he will judge according to the laws, and not according to his own good pleasure; and neither he nor we should get into the habit of perjuring ourselves—there can be no piety in that. Do not then require me to do what I consider dishonorable and impious and wrong, especially now, when I am being tried for impiety on the indictment of Meletus. For if, O men of Athens, by force of persuasion and entreaty, I could overpower your oaths, then I should be teaching you to believe that there are no gods, and convict myself, in my own defense, of not believing in them. But that is not the case; for I do believe that there are gods, and in a far higher sense than that in which any of my accusers believe in them. And to you and to God I commit my cause, to be determined by you as is best for you and me.

There are many reasons why I am not grieved, O men of Athens, at the vote of condemnation. I expected this, and am only surprised that the votes are so nearly equal; for I had thought that the majority against me would have been far larger; but now, had thirty votes [40] gone over to the other side, I should have been acquitted. And I may say that I have escaped Meletus. And I may say more; for without the assistance of Anytus and Lycon, he would not have had a fifth part of the votes, as the law requires, in which case he would have incurred a fine of a thousand drachmæ,[41] as is evident.

And so he proposes death as the penalty. And what shall I propose on my part,[42] O men of Athens? Clearly that

[40] Socrates was probably not speaking exactly, but in round numbers.
[41] Drachma (drăk'ma); pl. Drachmæ (drăk'mē) or Drachmas (drăk'măz): one drachma was the hundredth part of a mina. See Apology, note 10.
[42] "In Athenian procedure, the penalty inflicted was determined by a separate vote of the Dikasts" (officers somewhat like our jurymen) "taken after the verdict of guilty. The accuser having named the penalty which he

which is my due. And what is that which I ought to pay or to receive? What shall be done to the man who has never had the wit to be idle during his whole life; but has been carless of what the many care about—wealth, and family interests, and military offices, and speaking in the assembly, and magistracies, and plots, and parties. Reflecting that I was really too honest a man to follow in this way and live, I did not go where I could do no good to you or to myself; but where I could do the greatest good privately to every one of you, thither I went, and sought to persuade every man among you, that he must look to himself, and seek virtue and wisdom before he looks to his private interests, and look to the State before he looks to the interests of the State; and that this should be the order which he observes in all his actions. What shall be done to such a one? Doubtless some good thing, O men of Athens, if he has his reward; and the good should be of a kind suitable to him. What would be a reward suitable to a poor man who is your benefactor, who desires leisure that he may instruct you? There can be no more fitting reward than maintenence in the prytaneum,[43] O men of Athens, a reward which he deserves far more than the citizen who has won the prize at Olympia[44] in the horse or chariot race, whether the chariots were drawn by two horses or by many. For I am in want, and he has enough; and he only gives you the appearance of happiness, and I give you the reality. And if I am to estimate the penalty justly, I say that maintenance in the prytaneum is the just return.

Perhaps you may think that I am braving you in saying

thought suitable, the accused party on his side named some lighter penalty upon himself; and between these two the Dikasts were called on to make their option—no third proposition being admissible. The prudence of an accused party always induced him to propose, even against himself, some measure of punishment which the Dikasts might be satisfied to accept, in preference to the heavier sentence invoked by his antagonist."—Grote's History of Greece III., chap lxviii.

[43] Prўt'-a-nē'um: a public building in Greek cities. At Athens entertainment was furnished in the Prytaneum at public cost to foreign ambassadors and to citizens whom the State wished to honor.

[44] A small plain in Elis (ē'lis) near the southwestern coast of Greece where, every four years, the chief national festival of the Greeks was celebrated in honor of Zeus. An important part of the festival was the Olympian Games —contests in wrestling, boxing, leaping, spear and quoit-throwing, and races of various kinds. The winners were publicly honored in many ways and received undying fame.

this, as in what I said before about the tears and prayer. But that is not the case. I speak rather because I am convinced that I never intentionally wronged any one, although I cannot convince you of that—for we have had a short conversation only; but if there were a law at Athens, such as there is, in other cities, that a capital cause should not be decided in one day, then I believe I should have convinced you; but now the time is too short. I cannot in a moment refute great slanders; and, as I am convinced that I never wronged another, I will assuredly not wrong myself. I will not say of myself that I deserve any evil, or propose any penalty. Why should I. Because I am afraid of the penalty of death which Meletus proposes? When I do not know whether death is a good or an evil, why should I propose a penalty which would certainly be an evil? Shall I say imprisonment? And why should I live in prison, and be the slave of the magistrates of the year—of the eleven?[45] Or shall the penalty be a fine, and imprisonment until the fine is paid? There is the same objection. I should have to lie in prison, for money I have none, and cannot pay. And if I say exile (and this may possibly be the penalty which you will affix), I must indeed be blinded by the love of life, if I were to consider that when you, who are my own citizens, cannot endure my discourses and words, and have found them so grievous and odious that you would fain have done with them, others are likely to endure me. No indeed, men of Athens, that is not very likely. And what a life should I lead, at my age, wandering from city to city, living in ever-changing exile, and always being driven out! For I am quite sure that into whatever place I go, as here so also there, the young men will come to me; and if I drive them away, their elders will drive me out at their desire: and if I let them come, their fathers and friends will drive me out for their sakes.

Some one will say: Yes, Socrates, but cannot you hold your tongue, and then you may go into a foreign city, and no one will interfere with you? Now I have great difficulty in making you understand my answer to this. "For if I tell

[45] Police commissioners at Athens who had charge of the prisons and the punishment of criminals. Each tribe furnished one member by lot and the eleventh was a scribe.

you that this would be a disobedience to a divine command, and therefore that I cannot hold my tongue, you will not believe that I am serious; and if I say again that the greatest good of man is daily to converse about virtue, and all that concerning which you hear me examining myself and others, and that the life which is unexamined is not worth living—that you are still less likely to believe." And yet what I say is true, although a thing of which it is hard for me to persuade you. Moreover, I am not accustomed to think that I deserve any punishment. Had I money I might have proposed to give you what I had, and have been none the worse. But you see that I have none, and can only ask you to proportion the fine to my means. However, I think that I could afford a mina, and therefore I propose that penalty: Plato, Crito, Critobulus, and Apollodorus, my friends here, bid me say thirty minæ, and they will be the sureties. Well, then, say thirty minæ, let that be the penalty; for that they will be ample security to you.

Not much time will be gained, O Athenians, in return for the evil name which you will get from the detractors of the city, who will say that you killed Socrates, a wise man; for they will call me wise even although I am not wise when they want to reproach you. If you had waited a little while, your desire would have been fulfilled in the course of nature. For I am far advanced in years, as you may perceive, and not far from death. I am speaking now only to those of you who have condemned me to death. And I have another thing to say to them: You think that I was convicted through deficiency of words—I mean, that if I had thought fit to leave nothing undone, nothing unsaid, I might have gained an acquittal. Not so; the deficiency which led to my conviction was not of words—certainly not. But I had not the boldness or impudence or inclination to address you as you would have liked me to address you, weeping and wailing and lamenting, and saying and doing many things which you have been accustomed to hear from others and which, as I say, are unworthy of me. But I thought that I ought not to do anything common or mean in the hour of danger: nor do I now repent of the manner of my defense, and I would rather die having spoken after my manner, than speak in your manner and live. For neither in war nor yet at law ought any man to use every way of escaping death. For often in battle there is no doubt that if a man will throw away his arms, and fall on his knees before his pursuers, he may escape death; and in other dangers there are other ways of escaping death, if a man is willing to say and do anything. The difficulty, my friends, is not in avoiding death, but in avoiding unrighteousness; for that runs faster than death. I am old and move slowly, and the slower runner has overtaken me, and my accusers are keen and quick, and the faster runner, who is unrighteousness, has overtaken them. And now I depart hence condemned by you to suffer the penalty of death, and they too go their ways condemned by the truth to suffer the penalty of villainy and wrong; and I must abide by my award—let them abide by theirs. I suppose that these things may be regarded as fated,—and I think that they are well.

And now, O men who have condemned me, I would fain prophesy to you; for I am about to die, and that is the hour in which men are gifted with prophetic power.[46] And I prophesy to you who are my murderers, that immediately after my death punishment far heavier than you have inflicted on me will surely await you. Me you have killed because you wanted to escape the accuser, and not to give an account of your lives. But that will not be as you suppose: far otherwise. For I say that there will be more accusers of you than there are now; accusers whom hitherto I have restrained: and as they are younger they will be more severe with you, and you will be more offended at them. For if you think that by killing men you can avoid the accuser censuring your lives, you are mistaken; that is not a way of escape which is either possible or honorable; the easiest and the noblest way is not to be crushing others, but to be improving yourselves. This is the prophecy which I utter before my departure to the judges who have condemned me.

Friends, who would have acquitted me, I would like also to talk with you about this thing which has happened, while the magistrates are busy, and before I go to the place at which I must die. Stay then a while, for we may as well talk with one another while there is time. You are my friends, and I should like to show you the meaning of this event which has happened to me. O my judges—for you I may

[46] Compare Phædo, 84-85.

truly call judges—I should like to tell you of a wonderful circumstance. Hitherto the familiar oracle [47] within me has constantly been in the habit of opposing me even about trifles, if I was going to make a slip or error about anything; and now as you see there has come upon me that which may be thought, and is generally believed to be, the last and worst evil. But the oracle made no sign of opposition, either as I was leaving my house and going out in the morning, or when I was going up into this court, or while I was speaking, at anything which I was going to say; and yet I have often been stopped in the middle of a speech, but now in nothing I either said or did touching this matter has the oracle opposed me. What do I take to be the explanation of this? I will tell you. I regard this as a proof that what has happened to me is a good, and that those of us who think that death is an evil are in error. This is a great proof to me of what I am saying, for the customary sign would surely have opposed me had I been going to evil and not to good.

Let us reflect in another way, and we shall see that there is great reason to hope that death is a good, for one of two things: either death is a state of nothingness and utter unconsciousness, or, as men say, there is a change and migration of the soul from this world to another. Now if you suppose that there is no consciousness, but a sleep like the sleep of him who is undisturbed even by the sight of dreams, death will be an unspeakable gain. For if a person were to select the night in which his sleep was undisturbed even by dreams, and were to compare with this the other days and nights of his life, and then were to tell us how many days and nights he had passed in the course of his life better and more pleasantly than this one, I think that any man, I will not say a private man, but even the great king [48] will not find many such days or nights, when compared with the others. Now if death is like this, I say that to die is gain; for eternity is then only a single night. But if death is the journey to another place, and there, as men say, all the dead are, what good, O my friends and judges, can be greater than this? If indeed when the pilgrim arrives in the world below, he is delivered from the professors of justice in this world, and finds the true judges who are said to give judgment there, Minos

[47] Compare Apology, 31.   [48] The king of Persia.

and Rhadamanthus and Æacus [49] and Triptolemus,[50] and other sons of God who were righteous in their own life, that pilgrimage will be worth making. What would not a man give if he might converse with Orpheus [51] and Musæus [52] and Hesiod [53] and Homer [54]? Nay, if this be true, let me die again and again. I, too, shall have a wonderful interest in a place where I can converse with Palamedes,[55] and Ajax [56] the son of Telamon, and other heroes of old, who have suffered death through an unjust judgment; and there will be no small pleasure, as I think, in comparing my own sufferings with theirs. Above all, I shall be able to continue my search into true and false knowledge; as in this world, so also in that; I shall find out who is wise, and who pretends to be wise, and is not. What would not a man give, O judges, to be able to examine the leader of the great Trojan expedition [57]; or Odysseus [58] or Sisyphus,[59] or numberless others, men and women too! What infinite delight would there be in conversing with them and asking them questions! For in that world they do not put a

[49] In the Gorgias, another of Plato's dialogues, Socrates relates the following myth. There was of old a law that the just and holy man should go after death to the Islands of the Blest, but the wicked man should go to Tartarus, the house of punishment. Now, it often happened that a soul went to the wrong place after death. This was because judgment had been passed before death, when the material bodies and garments of the judges and the judged formed a double veil, which prevented clear vision and correct judgment. As a remedy Zeus appointed his three sons, Æacus (ē'a-cus), Minos (mī'nos), and Rhadamanthus (răd'a-man'thus), to become after death judges in the world below, where with naked souls they could pierce the naked souls of the dead, and the judgment would be just.
[50] Triptolemus (trĭp-tŏl'e-mus): a legendary character noted for his piety and beneficence.
[51] Orpheus (ôr'fe-us): a celebrated mythical poet and musician. See Protagoras, note 28.
[52] Musæus (mu-sē-us): a mythological musician, seer, and priest. See Protagoras, note 28.
[53] Hesiod (hē'sĭ-od): a celebrated Greek poet, almost, if not quite, as ancient as Homer. Many works attributed to him are extant.
[54] See Apology, note 39.
[55] Palamedes (păl'a-mē'dēz): a Greek hero of the Trojan War, noted for his wisdom and ingenuity. The Greeks attributed many inventions to him.
[56] Ajax [ā'jăx, son of Telamon (tĕl'a-mon)]: a Greek hero of surpassing strength and stature, second only to Achilles in bravery at the siege of Troy.
[57] See Apology, note 21.
[58] Odysseus (ō-dys'sus): one of the most illustrious Greek heroes of the Trojan War, noted for his courage and cunning. The adventures of his twenty years of wandering on his return from Troy are related in Homer's Odyssey.
[59] Sisyphus (sĭs'ĭ-fus), the legendary builder and King of Corinth.

man to death for this; certainly not. For besides being happier in that world than in this, they will be immortal, if what is said is true.

Wherefore, O judges, be of good cheer about death, and know this of a truth—that no evil can happen to a good man, either in life or after death. He and his are not neglected by the gods; nor has my own approaching end happened by mere chance. But I see clearly that to die and be released was better for me; and therefore the oracle gave no sign. For which reason, also, I am not angry with my accusers or my condemners; they have done me no harm, although neither of them meant to do me any good; and for this I may gently blame them.

Still I have a favor to ask of them. When my sons are grown up, I would ask you, O my friends, to punish them; and I would have you trouble them, as I have troubled you, if they seem to care about riches, or anything, more than about virtue; or if they pretend to be something when they are really nothing,—then reprove them, as I have reproved you, for not caring about that for which they ought to care, and thinking that they are something when they are really nothing.[60] And if you do this, I and my sons will have received justice at your hands.

The hour of departure has arrived, and we go our ways—I to die, and you to live. Which is better God only knows.

[60] " For if a man think himself to be something when he is nothing, he deceiveth himself."—Gal., vi. 3.

EUTHYDEMUS

INTRODUCTION

The Euthydemus is a farce—with a purpose. The clew to the purpose is found in the conversation between Socrates and Crito at the close of the dialogue. Crito was a well-to-do Athenian citizen and a warm personal friend of Socrates. As a citizen, business man, and father, he had the interests and was naturally inclined to share the average opinions of his fellow-citizens. Like other Athenians, he was accordingly inclined to distrust the new breed of men called Sophists, who were turning the world upside down with their teachings. He knew and loved and trusted Socrates, and did not therefore confuse him with the Sophists; but he saw that others did so, and partly for fear on Socrates' account, partly for fear that his sons would be misled and corrupted by the new learning, he came to Socrates with anxious questions and warnings.

The dialogue Euthydemus is intended to show the difference between Socrates and the Sophists in such a way that a wayfaring man, though a fool, should not confuse them. The Sophists have nothing real to teach,—believe in nothing real to teach; Socrates believes unvaryingly in the reality and power of the truth. Their art is word trickery; the art of Socrates is step-by-step approach to the truth. Their purpose is to get the boy's money; Socrates will take no money, but wants to save the boy's life. In spite of these differences,

Grote is doubtless right in saying that if you had asked an Athenian citizen of that time to name one or two Sophists, he would probably have replied, Socrates and Plato, so hard it is to make the public discriminate.

There is a deep pathos in Crito's bewilderment about what to do with his sons. Shall he bring them up as money-makers, ignorant of divine philosophy? Shall he commit them to some of the teachers of the new learning? What shall he do with them? The philosophy of Socrates is there face to face with a real question, not to be evaded. Socrates did not hesitate to reply.

EUTHYDEMUS

PERSONS OF THE DIALOGUE.[1]

SOCRATES, who is the narrator of the Dialogue.
EUTHYDEMUS.
DIONYSODORUS.
CRITO.
CLEINIAS.
CTESIPPUS.

SCENE:—The Lyceum.[2]

Crito. Who was the person, Socrates, with whom you were talking yesterday at the Lyceum? There was such a crowd around you that I could not get within hearing, but I caught sight of him over their heads, and I made out, as I thought, that he was a stranger with whom you were talking: who was he?

Socrates. There were two, Crito; which of them do you mean?

Cri. The one who was seated second from you on the right-hand side. In the middle was Cleinias, the young son of Axiochus, who has wonderfully grown; he is only about the age of my own Critobulus,[3] but he is much forwarder and very good-looking: the other is thin and looks younger than he is.

---

[1] Crito: see Apology, note 35; Euthydemus (ū'thy-dē'mus) and Dionysodorus (dī'o-nȳs'-o-dō'rus): probably merely dramatic characters. "That they correspond to any actual persons at Athens, is neither proved nor probable." Grote's Plato I., p. 536. Ctesippus (tē-sĭp'pus): the principal knowledge we have of this young man is gained from this dialogue. He was present at the death of Socrates, Phædo 59. Cleinias (klī' nĭ-as), son of Axiochus (ăx-ĭ'o-kus), not mentioned elsewhere in Plato.

[2] An enclosure dedicated to Apollo just east of Athens, outside the gate. It was decorated with fountains, buildings, and covered walks. It became the largest of the three great gymnasia of ancient Athens. It was frequented by philosophers and others as a place for retirement and study.

[3] See Apology 33.

Soc. He whom you mean, Crito, is Euthydemus; and on my left hand there was his brother Dionysodorus, who also took part in the conversation.

Cri. Neither of them are known to me, Socrates; they are a new importation of Sophists, as I should imagine. Of what country are they, and what is their line of wisdom?

Soc. As to their origin, I believe that they are natives of this part of the world, and have migrated from Chios to Thurii,[4] they were driven out of Thurii, and have been living for many years past in this region. As to their wisdom, about which you ask, Crito, they are wonderful — consummate! I never knew what the true pancratiast[5] was before; they are simply made up of fighting, not like the two Acarnanian brothers[6] who fight with their bodies only, but this pair are perfect in the use of their bodies and have a universal mode of fighting (for they are capital at fighting in armor, and will teach the art to any one who pays them): and also they are masters of legal fence, and are ready to do battle in the courts; they will give lessons in speaking and pleading, and in writing speeches. And this was only the beginning of their wisdom, but they have at last carried out the pancrastiastic art to the very end, and have mastered the only mode of fighting which had been hitherto neglected by them; and now no one dares look at them; such is their skill in the war of words, that they can refute any proposition whether true or false. Now I am thinking, Crito, of putting myself in their hands; for they say that in a short time they can impart their skill to any one.

272

Cri. But, Socrates, are you not too old? there may be reason to fear that.

Soc. Certainly not, Crito; as I will prove to you, for I have the consolation of knowing that they began this art of disputation which I covet, quite, as I may say, in old age; last year, or the year before, they had none of their new wisdom. I am

---

[4] Chios (kī'os): An island in the Ægean, off the coast of Lydia, colonized by Greeks.

Thurii (thū' rĭ-ĭ): a Greek city in southern Italy.

[5] Pancratiast (from *pan*, all, and *kratos*, strength): strictly, one who took part in the pancratium (păn-krā'shĭ-um), an athletic contest which combined boxing and wrestling.

[6] Acarnania (ăc'ar-nă'nĭ-a): a district on the western coast of Greece whose inhabitants were rude and less civilized than the rest of the Greeks. They were skilled in the use of the sling. The brothers mentioned do not seem to have been widely known.

only apprehensive that I may bring the two strangers into disrepute, as I have done Connus the son of Metrobius,[7] the harp-player, who is still my music-master; for when the boys who also go to him see me going, they laugh at me and call him grandpapa's master. Now I should not like the strangers to experience this sort of treatment, and perhaps they may be afraid and not like to receive me because of this; and therefore, Crito, I shall try and persuade some old men to go along with me to them, as I persuaded them to go to Connus, and I hope that you will make one: and perhaps we had better take your sons as a bait; they will want to have them, and will be willing to receive us as pupils for the sake of them.

Cri. I see no objection, Socrates, if you like; but first I wish that you would give me a description of their wisdom, that I may know beforehand what we are going to learn.

Soc. I will tell you at once; for I cannot say that I did not attend: the fact was that I paid great attention to them, and I remember and will endeavor to tell you the whole story. I was providentially sitting alone in the dressing-room of the Lyceum in which you saw me, and was about to depart, when as I was getting up I recognized the familiar divine sign: [8]so I sat down again, and in a little while the two brothers Euthydemus and Dionysodorus came in, and several others with them, whom I believe to be their disciples, and they walked about in the covered space; they had not taken more than two or three turns when Cleinias entered, who, as you truly say, is very much improved: he was followed by a host of lovers,[9] one of whom was Ctesippus the Pæanian,[10] a well-bred youth, but also having the wildness of youth. Cleinias saw me from the entrance as I was sitting alone, and at once came and sat down on the right hand of me, as you describe; and Dionysodorus and Euthydemus, when they saw him, at first stopped and talked with one another, now and then glancing at us, for I particularly watched them; and then Euthydemus came and sat down by the youth, and the other by me on the left hand; the rest anywhere. I saluted the brothers, whom I had not seen for a long time; and then I said to Cleinias: These two men, Euthydemus and Dionysodorus, Cleinias, are

273

---

[7] Connus (kŏn'nus) ; Metrobius (mē-trō'bĭ-us).
[8] See Apology, 31 and 40.
[9] See Phædrus, note 9.   [10] Pæania (pē-ā'nĭ-a) : a deme of Attica.

not in a small but in a large way of wisdom, for they know all about war,—all that a good general ought to know about the array and command of an army, and the whole art of fighting in armor: and they know about the law too, and can teach a man how to use the weapons of the courts when he is injured.

They heard me say this, and I was despised by them; they looked at one another, and both of them laughed; and then Euthydemus said: Those, Socrates, are matters which we no longer pursue seriously; they are secondary occupations to us.

Indeed, I said, if such occupations are regarded by you as secondary, what must the principal one be; tell me, I beseech you, what that noble study is?

The teaching of virtue, Socrates, he replied, is our principal occupation; and we believe that we can impart it better and quicker than any man.

My God! I said, and where did you learn that? I always thought, as I was saying just now, that your chief accomplishment was the art of fighting in armor; and this was what I used to say of you, for I remember that this was professed by you when you were here before. But now if you really have the other knowledge, O forgive me: I address you as I would superior beings, and ask you to pardon the impiety of my former expressions. But are you quite sure about this, Dionysodorus and Euthydemus? the promise is so vast, that a feeling of incredulity will creep in.

274

You may take our word, Socrates, for the fact.

Then I think you happier in having such a treasure than the great king[11] is in the possession of his kingdom. And please to tell me whether you intend to exhibit this wisdom, or what you will do.

That is why we are come hither, Socrates; and our purpose is not only to exhibit, but also to teach any one who likes to learn.

But I can promise you, I said, that every unvirtuous person will want to learn. I shall be the first; and there is the youth Cleinias, and Ctesippus: and here are several others, I said, pointing to the lovers of Cleinias, who were beginning to gather round us. Now Ctesippus was sitting at some distance from Cleinias; and when Euthydemus leaned forward

[11] King of Persia.

in talking with me, he was prevented from seeing Cleinias, who was between us; and so, partly because he wanted to look at his love, and also because he was interested, he jumped up and stood opposite to us: and all the other admirers of Cleinias, as well as the disciples of Euthydemus and Dionysodorus, followed his example. And these were the persons whom I showed to Euthydemus, telling him that they were all eager to learn: to which Ctesippus and all of them with one voice vehemently assented, and bid him exhibit the power of his wisdom. Then I said: O Euthydemus and Dionysodorus, I earnestly request you to do myself and the company the favor to exhibit. There may be some trouble in giving the whole exhibition; but tell me one thing,—can you make a good man only of him who is convinced that he ought to learn of you, or of him also who is not convinced? either because he imagines that virtue is not a thing which can be taught at all, or that you two are not the teachers of it. Say whether your art is able to persuade such a one nevertheless that virtue can be taught; and that you are the men from whom he will be most likely to learn.

This is the art, Socrates, said Dionysodorus, and no other.

And you, Dionysodorus, I said, are the men who among those who are now living are the most likely to stimulate him to philosophy and the study of virtue?

Yes, Socrates, I rather think that we are.

Then I wish that you would be so good as to defer the other part of the exhibition, and only try to persuade the youth whom you see here that he ought to be a philosopher and study virtue. Exhibit that, and you will confer a great favor on me and on every one present; for the fact is that I and all of us are extremely anxious that he should be truly good. His name is Cleinias, and he is the son of Axiochus, and grandson of the old Alcibiades, cousin of the Alcibiades that now is. He is quite young, and we are naturally afraid that some one may get the start of us, and turn his mind in a wrong direction, and he may be ruined. Your visit, therefore, is most happily timed; and I hope that you will make a trial of the young man, and converse with him in our presence, if you have no objection.

These were pretty nearly the expressions which I used; and Euthydemus, in a lofty and at the same time cheerful tone, replied: There can be no objection, Socrates, if the young man is only willing to answer questions.

He is quite accustomed to that, I replied; for his friends often come and ask him questions and argue with him; so that he is at home in answering.

What followed, Crito, how can I rightly narrate? for not slight is the task of rehearsing infinite wisdom, and therefore, like the poets, I ought to commence my relation with an invocation to Memory and the Muses.[12] Now Euthydemus, if I remember rightly, began nearly as follows: O Cleinias, are those who learn the wise or the ignorant?

The youth, overpowered by the question, blushed, and in his perplexity looked at me for help; and I, knowing that he was disconcerted, said: Don't be afraid, Cleinias, but answer like a man whichever you think; for my belief is that you will derive the greatest good from their questions.

Whichever he answers, said Dionysodorus, leaning forward in my ear and laughing, I prophesy that he will be refuted, Socrates.

While he was speaking to me, Cleinias gave his answer: the consequence was that I had no time to warn him of the predicament in which he was placed, and he answered that those who learned were the wise.

Euthydemus proceeded: There are those whom you call teachers, are there not?

The boy assented.

And they are the teachers of those who learn,—the grammar-master and the lyre-master used to teach you and other boys; and you were the learners?

Yes.

And when you were learners you did not as yet know the things which you were learning?

No, he said.

And were you wise then?

No, indeed, he said.

But if you were not wise you were unlearned?

Certainly.

You then, learning what you did not know, were unlearned when you were learning?

---

[12] Originally, nymphs of springs whose waters were thought to inspire song; then goddesses of song, music, poetry, the drama and all fine arts.

The youth nodded assent.

Then the unlearned learn, and not the wise, Cleinias, as you imagine.

At these words the followers of Euthydemus, of whom I spoke, like a chorus at the bidding of their director, laughed and cheered. Then, before the youth had well time to recover, Dionysodorus took him in hand, and said: Yes, Cleinias; and when the grammar-master dictated to you, were they the wise boys or the unlearned who learned the dictation?

The wise, replied Cleinias.

Then after all the wise are the learners and not the unlearned; and your last answer to Euthydemus was wrong.

Then followed another peal of laughter and shouting, which came from the admirers of the two heroes, who were ravished with their wisdom, while the rest of us were silent and amazed. Euthydemus perceiving this determined to persevere with the youth; and in order to heighten the effect went on asking another similar question, which might be compared to the double turn of an expert dancer. Do those, said he, who learn, learn what they know, or what they do not know?

Dionysodorus said to me in a whisper: That, Socrates, is just another of the same sort.

Good heavens, I said; and your last question was so good!

Like all our other questions, Socrates, he replied,—inevitable.

I see the reason, I said, why you are in such reputation among your disciples.

Meanwhile Cleinias had answered Euthydemus that those who learned, learn what they do not know; and he put him through a series of questions as before.

Don't you know letters?

He assented.

All letters?

Yes.

But when the teacher dictates to you, does he not dictate letters?

He admitted that.

Then if you know all letters, he dictates that which you know?

He admitted that also.

Then, said the other, you do not learn that which he dictates; but he only who does not know letters learns?

Nay, said Cleinias; but I do learn.

Then, said he, you learn what you know, if you know all the letters?

He admitted that.

Then, he said, you were wrong in your answer.

The word was hardly out of his mouth when Dionysodorus took up the argument, like a ball which he caught, and had another throw at the youth. Cleinias, he said, Euthydemus is deceiving you. For tell me now, is not learning acquiring knowledge of that which one learns?

Cleinias assented.

And knowing is having knowledge at the time?

He agreed.

And not knowing is not having knowledge at the time?

He admitted that.

And are those who acquire those who have or have not a thing?

Those who have not.

And have you not admitted that those who do not know are of the number of those who have not?

He nodded assent.

Then those who learn are of the class of those who acquire, and not of those who have?

He agreed.

Then, Cleinias, he said, those who do not know learn, and not those who know.

Euthydemus was proceeding to give the youth a third fall, but I knew that he was in deep water, and therefore, as I wanted to give him a rest, and also in order that he might not get out of heart, I said to him consolingly: You must not be surprised, Cleinias, at the singularity of their mode of speech: This I say because you may not understand what they are doing with you; they are only initiating you after the manner of the Corybantes [13] in the mysteries [14]; and this answers to

---

[13] The Corybantes (kŏr-y-băn'tēz) were priests of a Phrygian goddess Cybele (sȳb'e-le), whose worship was introduced into Greece among the lower ranks of people. Her festivals were celebrated with wild music and dancing, in the frenzy of which the worshippers wounded themselves and one another.

[14] Secret religious ceremonies, employed in the worship of certain gods and goddesses (one of them Cybele) in which only those who had been initiated could take part.

the enthronement, which, if you have ever been initiated, is, as you will know, accompanied by dancing and sport ; and now they are just prancing and dancing about you, and will next proceed to initiate you; and at this stage you must imagine yourself to have gone through the first part of the sophistical ritual, which, as Prodicus says, begins with initiation into the correct use of terms. The two strange gentlemen wanted to explain to you, as you do not know, that the word " to learn " has two meanings, and is used, first, in the sense of acquiring knowledge of some matter of which you previously have no knowledge, and also, when you have the knowledge, in the sense of reviewing this same matter done or spoken by the light of this knowledge; this last is generally called " knowing " rather than " learning " ; but the word " learning " is also used, and you did not see that the word is used of two opposite sorts of men, of those who know, and of those who do not know, as they explained. There was a similar trick in the second question, when they asked you whether men learn what they know or what they do not know. These parts of learning are not serious, and therefore I say that these gentlemen are not serious, but only in fun with you. And if a man had all that sort of knowledge that ever was, he would not be at all the wiser; he would only be able to play with men, tripping them up and oversetting them with distinctions of words. He would be like a person who pulls away a stool from some one when he is about to sit down, and then laughs and claps his hands at the sight of his friend sprawling on the ground. And you must regard all that has passed hitherto as merely play. But now I am certain that they will proceed to business, and keep their promise (I will show them how); for they promised to give me a sample of the hortatory philosophy, but I suppose that they wanted to have a game of play with you first. And now, Euthydemus and Dionysodorus, I said, I think that we have had enough of this. Will you let me see you exhibiting to the young man, and showing him how he is to apply himself to the study of virtue and wisdom? And I will first show you what I conceive to be the nature of the task, and what I desire to hear ; and if I do this in a very inartistic and ridiculous manner, do not laugh at me, for I only venture to improvise before you because I am eager to hear your wisdom :

278

and I must therefore ask you to keep your countenances, and your disciples also. And now, O son of Axiochus, let me put a question to you: Do not all men desire happiness? And yet, perhaps, this is one of those ridiculous questions which I am afraid to ask, and which ought not to be asked by a sensible man: for what human being is there who does not desire happiness?

There is no one, said Cleinias, who does not.

279 Well, then, I said, since we all of us desire happiness, how can we be happy?—that is the next question. Shall we not be happy if we have many good things? And this perhaps, is even a more simple question than the first, for there can be no doubt of the answer.

He assented.

And what things do we esteem good? No solemn sage is required to tell us this, which may be easily answered; for every one will say that wealth is a good.

Certainly, he said.

And are not health and beauty goods, and other personal gifts?

He agreed.

Now, can there be any doubt that good birth, and power, and honors in one's own land, are goods?

He assented.

And what other goods are there? I said. What do you say of justice, temperance, courage: do you not verily and indeed think, Cleinias, that we shall be more right in ranking them as goods than in not ranking them as goods? For a dispute might possibly arise about this. What then do you say?

They are goods, said Cleinias.

Very well, I said; and in what company shall we find a place for wisdom—among the goods or not?

Among the goods.

And now, I said, think whether we have left out any considerable goods.

I do not think that we have, said Cleinias.

Upon recollection, I said, indeed I am afraid that we have left out the greatest of them all.

What is that? he asked.

Fortune, Cleinias, I replied; which all, even the most foolish, admit to be the greatest of goods.

True, he said.

On second thoughts, I added, how narrowly, O son of Axiochus, have you and I escaped making a laughing-stock of ourselves to the strangers.

Why do you say that?

Why, because we have already spoken of fortune, and are but repeating ourselves.

What do you mean?

I mean that there is something ridiculous in putting fortune again forward, and saying the same thing twice over.

He asked what was the meaning of this, and I replied: Surely wisdom is good fortune; even a child may know that.

The simple-minded youth was amazed; and, observing this, I said to him: Do you not know, Cleinias, that flute-players are most fortunate and successful in performing on the flute?

He assented.

And are not the scribes most fortunate in writing and reading letters?

Certainly.

Amid the dangers of the sea, again, are any more fortunate on the whole than wise pilots?

None, certainly.

And if you were engaged in war, in whose company would you rather take the risk—in company with a wise general, or with a foolish one?

With a wise one.

And if you were ill, whom would you rather have as a companion in a dangerous illness—a wise physician, or an ignorant one?

A wise one.

You think, I said, that to act with a wise man is more fortunate than to act with an ignorant one?

He assented.

Then wisdom always makes men fortunate: for by wisdom no man would ever err, and therefore he must act rightly and succeed, or his wisdom would be wisdom no longer. At last we somehow contrived to agree in a general conclusion, that he who had wisdom had no longer need of fortune. I then recalled to his mind the previous state of the question. You remember, I said, our making the admission that we should be happy and fortunate if many good things were present with us?

He assented.

And should we be happy by reason of the presence of good things, if they profited us not, or if they profited us?

If they profited us, he said.

And would they profit us, if we only had them and did not use them? For example, if we had a great deal of food and did not eat, or a great deal of drink and did not drink, should we be profited?

Certainly not, he said.

Or would an artisan, who had all the implements necessary for his work, and did not use them, be any better for the possession of all that he ought to possess? For example, would a carpenter be any the better for having all his tools and plenty of wood, if he never worked?

Certainly no, he said.

And if a person had wealth, and all the goods of which we were just now speaking, and did not use them; would he be happy because he possessed them?

No indeed, Socrates.

Then, I said, a man who would be happy must not only have the good things, but he must also use them; there is no advantage in merely having them.

True.

Well, Cleinias, but if you have the use as well as the possession of good things, is that sufficient to confer happiness?

Yes, in my opinion.

And may a person use them either rightly or wrongly?

He must use them rightly.

That is quite true, I said. And the wrong use of a thing is far worse than the non-use; for the one is an evil, and the other is neither a good nor an evil. You admit that?

He assented.

Now in the working and use of wood, is not that which gives the right use simply the knowledge of the carpenter?

Nothing else, he said.

And surely, in the manufacture of vessels, knowledge is that which gives the right way of making them?

He agreed.

And in the use of the goods of which we spoke at first,—

wealth and health and beauty,—is not knowledge that which directs us to the right use of them, and guides our practice about them?

Knowledge, he replied.

Then in every possession and every use of a thing, knowledge is that which gives a man not only good fortune but success?

He assented.

And tell me, I said, O tell me, what do possessions profit a man, if he have neither sense nor wisdom? Would a man be better off, having and doing many things without wisdom, or a few things with wisdom? Look at the matter thus: if he did fewer things would he not make fewer mistakes? if he made fewer mistakes would he not have fewer misfortunes? and if he had fewer misfortunes would he not be less miserable?

Certainly, he said.

And who would do least—a poor man or a rich man?

A poor man.

A weak man or a strong man?

A weak man.

A noble man or a mean man?

A mean man.

And a coward would do less than a courageous and temperate man?

Yes.

And an indolent man less than an active man?

He assented.

And a slow man less than a quick; and one who had dull perceptions of seeing and hearing less than one who had keen ones?

All this was mutually allowed by us.

Then, I said, Cleinias, the sum of the matter appears to be that the goods of which we spoke before are not to be regarded as goods in themselves, but the degree of good and evil in them depends on whether they are or are not under the guidance of knowledge: under the guidance of ignorance, they are greater evils than their opposites, inasmuch as they are more able to minister to the evil principle which rules them; and when under the guidance of wisdom and virtue, they are greater goods: but in themselves they are nothing?

That, he said, appears to be certain.

What then, I said, is the result of all this? Is not this the result—that other things are indifferent, and that wisdom is the only good, and ignorance the only evil?

He assented.

Let us consider this further point, I said: Seeing that all men desire happiness, and happiness, as has been shown, is gained by a use, and a right use, of the things of life, and the right use of them, and good fortune in the use of them, is given by knowledge, the inference is that every man ought by all means to try and make himself as wise as he can?

282

Yes, he said.

And the desire to obtain this treasure, which is far more precious than money, from a father or a guardian or a friend or a suitor, whether citizen or stranger—the eager desire and prayer to them that they would impart wisdom to you, is not at all dishonorable, Cleinias; nor is any one to be blamed for doing any honorable service or ministration to any man, whether a lover or not, if his aim is wisdom. Do you agree to that, I said.

Yes, he said, I quite agree, and think that you are right.

Yes, I said, Cleinias, if only wisdom can be taught, and does not come to man spontaneously; for that is a point which has still to be considered, and is not yet agreed upon by you and me.

But I think, Socrates, that wisdom can be taught, he said.

Best of men, I said, I am delighted to hear you say that; and I am also grateful to you for having saved me from a long and tiresome speculation as to whether wisdom can be taught or not. But now, as you think that wisdom can be taught, and that wisdom only can make a man happy and fortunate, will you not acknowledge that all of us ought to love Wisdom, and that you in particular should be of this mind and try to love her?

Certainly, Socrates, he said; and I will do my best.

I was pleased at hearing this; and I turned to Dionysodorus and Euthydemus and said: That is an example, clumsy and tedious I admit, of the sort of exhortations which I desire you to offer; and I hope that one of you will set forth what I have been saying in a more artistic style: at any rate take up the inquiry where I left off, and next show the youth whether he should have all knowledge; or whether there is one sort of knowledge only which will make him good and happy, and what that is. For, as I was saying at first, the improvement of this young man in virtue and wisdom is a matter which we have very much at heart.

Thus I spoke, Crito, and was all attention to what was coming. I wanted to see how they would approach the question, and where they would start in their exhortation to the young man that he should practice wisdom and virtue. Dionysodorus the elder spoke first. Everybody's eyes were directed toward him, perceiving that something wonderful might shortly be expected. And certainly they were not far wrong; for the man, Crito, began a remarkable discourse well worth hearing, and wonderfully persuasive as an exhortation to virtue.

283

Tell me, he said, Socrates and the rest of you who say that you want this young man to become wise, are you in jest or in real earnest?

(I was led by this to imagine that they fancied us to have been jesting when we asked them to converse with the youth, and that this made them jest and play, and being under this impression, I was the more decided in saying that we were in profound earnest.) Dionysodorus said.

Reflect, Socrates; you may have to deny your words.

I have reflected, I said; and I shall never deny my words.

Well, said he, and so you say that you wish Cleinias to become wise?

Undoubtedly.

And he is not wise yet?

At least his modesty will not allow him to say that he is.

You wish him, he said, to become wise and not to be ignorant?

That we do.

You wish him to be what he is not, and no longer to be what he is.

I was thrown into consternation at this.

Taking advantage of my consternation he added: You wish him no longer to be what he is, which can only mean that you wish him to perish. Pretty lovers and friends they must be who want their favorite not to be, or to perish!

When Ctesippus heard this he got very angry (as a lover might) and said: Strangers of Thurii—if politeness would allow me I should say, You be hanged. What can make you tell such a lie about me and the others, which I hardly like to repeat, as that I wish Cleinias to perish?

Euthydemus replied: And do you think, Ctesippus, that it is possible to tell a lie?

Yes, said Ctesippus; I should be mad to deny that.

284 And in telling a lie, do you tell the thing of which you speak or not?

You tell the thing of which you speak.

And he who tells, tells that thing which he tells, and no other?

Yes, said Ctesippus.

And that is a distinct thing apart from other things?

Certainly.

And he who says that thing says that which is?

Yes.

And he who says that which is, says the truth. And therefore Dionysodorus, if he says that which is, says the truth of you and no lie.

Yes, Euthydemus, said Ctesippus; but in saying this, he says what is not.

Euthydemus answered: And that which is not is not.

True.

And that which is not is nowhere?

Nowhere.

And can any one do anything about that which has no existence, or do to Cleinias that which is not and is nowhere?

I think not, said Ctesippus.

Well, but do rhetoricians, when they speak in the assembly do nothing?

Nay, he said, they do something.

And doing is making?

Yes.

And speaking is doing and making?

He agreed.

Then no one says that which is not, for in saying that, he would be doing nothing; and you have already acknowledged that no one can do what is not. And therefore, upon your own showing, no one says what is false; but if Dionysodorus says anything, he says what is true and what is.

Yes, Euthydemus, said Ctesippus; but he speaks of things in a certain way and manner, and not as they really are.

Why, Ctesippus, said Dionysodorus, do you mean to say that any one speaks of things as they are?

Yes, he said,—all gentlemen and truth-speaking persons.

And are not good things good, and evil things evil?

He assented.

And you say that gentlemen speak of things as they are?

Yes.

Then the good speak evil of evil things, if they speak of them as they are?

Yes, indeed, he said; and they speak evil of evil men. And if I may give you a piece of advice, you had better take care that they don't speak evil of you, since I can tell you that the good speak evil of the evil.

And do they speak great things of the great, rejoined Euthydemus, and warm things of the warm?

Yes, indeed, said Ctesippus; and they speak coldly of the insipid and cold dialectician.

You are abusive, Ctesippus, you are abusive!

Indeed, I am not, Dionysodorus, he replied; for I love you and am giving you friendly advice, and, if I could, would persuade you not to make so uncivil a speech to me as that I desire my beloved, whom I value above all men, to perish.

285

I saw that they were getting exasperated with one another, so I made a joke with him and said: O Ctesippus, I think that we must allow the strangers to use language in their own way, and not quarrel with them about words, but be thankful for what they give us. If they know how to destroy men in such a way as to make good and sensible men out of bad and foolish ones—whether this is a discovery of their own, or whether they have learned from some one else, this new sort of death and destruction, which enables them to get rid of a bad man and put a good one in his place—if they know this (and they do know this—at any rate they said just now that this was the secret of their newly-discovered art)—let them, in their phraseology, destroy the youth and make him wise, and all of us with him. But if you young men do not like to trust yourselves with them, then let the experiment be made on the body of an old man. I will be the Carian[15] on whom they shall operate. And here I offer my old person to Dionysodorus; he may put me into the pot, like Medea[16] the Colchian, kill me, pickle me, eat me, if he will make me good.

Ctesippus said: And I, Socrates, am ready to commit myself to the stranger; they may skin me alive, if they please (and I am pretty well skinned by them already), if only my skin is made at last, not like that of Marsyas,[17] into a leathern bottle, but into a piece of virtue. And here is Dionysodorus fancying that I am angry with him, when I am really not angry at all; I do but contradict him when he seems to me to be in the wrong: and you must not confound abuse and contradiction, O illustrious Dionysodorus; for they are quite different things.

Contradiction! said Dionysodorus; why, there never was such a thing.

Certainly there is, he replied; there can be no question of that. Do you, Dionysodorus, maintain that there is not?

You will never prove to me, he said, that you have heard any one contradicting any one else.

Indeed, he said: then now you may hear Ctesippus contradicting Dionysodorus. Are you prepared to make that good?

Certainly, he said.

Well, then, are not words expressive of things?

Yes.

Of their existence or of their non existence?

Of their existence. For, as you may remember, Ctesippus, we just now proved that no man could affirm a negative; for no one could affirm that which is not.

And what does that signify, said Ctesippus; you and I may contradict all the same for that.

[15] Caria (kā'ri-a): a district of Asia Minor whose inhabitants the Greeks regarded as despicable and stupid. Many of the Greek slaves were Carians. "In later times the Carians hired themselves out as mercenaries; as such they were used in forlorn hopes, so as to spare the lives of citizen-soldiers; whence the proverb,—to make the risk not with one's own person but with a Carian." L. and S.

[16] Medea (mē-dē'a) the Colchian: a mythical princess and sorceress of Colchis (kŏl'kĭs) in Asia, said to have the power to make the old young by means of a magic liquid which she prepared.

[17] Marsyas (mär'sy̆-as): a minor divinity who found the flute discarded by the goddess Athene and who became so skilful with it that he challenged Apollo, patron god of the lyre, to a contest. The Muses decided in favor of Apollo, who then flayed Marsyas alive.

But can we contradict one another, said Dionysodorus, when both of us are describing the same thing? Then we must surely be speaking the same thing?

He admitted that.

Or when neither of us is speaking of the same thing? For then neither of us says a word about the thing at all?

He granted that also.

Bnt when I describe something and you describe another thing, or I say something and you say nothing, is there any contradiction? How can he who speaks contradict him who speaks not?

Here Ctesippus was silent; and I in my astonishment said: What do you mean, Dionysodorus? I have often heard, and have been amazed, to hear this thesis of yours, which is maintained and employed by the disciples of Protagoras,[18] and others before them, and which to me appears to be quite wonderful and suicidal, as well as destructive, and I think that I am most likely to hear the truth of this from you. The dictum is that there is no such thing as falsehood; a man must either say what is true or say nothing. Is not that your position?

He assented.

But if he cannot speak falsely, may he not think falsely?

No, he cannot, he said.

Then there is no such thing as false opinion?

No, he said.

Then there is no such thing as ignorance, or men who are ignorant; for is not ignorance, if there be such a thing, a mistake of facts?

Certainly, he said.

And that is impossible?

Impossible, he replied.

Are you saying this as a paradox, Dionysodorus; or do you seriously maintain that no man is ignorant?

Do you refute me? he said.

But how can I refute you, if, as you say, falsehood is impossible?

Very true, said Euthydemus.

Neither did I tell you just now to refute me, said Dionysodorus; for how can I tell you to do that which is not?

[18] Protagoras (prŏ-tăg'o-ras): a celebrated Sophist. See the dialogue Protagoras.

O Euthydemus, I said, I have but a dull conception of these subtleties and excellent devices of wisdom; I am afraid that I hardly understand them, and you must forgive me therefore if I ask a very stupid question: if there be no falsehood or false opinion or ignorance, there can be no such thing as erroneous action, for a man cannot fail of acting as he is acting—that is what you mean?

287

Yes, he replied.

And now, I said, I will ask my stupid question: If there is no such thing as error in deed, word, or thought, then what, in the name of goodness, do you come hither to teach? And were you not just now saying that you could teach virtue best of all men, to any one who could learn?

And are you such an old fool, Socrates, rejoined Dionysodorus, that you bring up now what I said at first—and if I had said anything last year, I suppose that you would bring that up—but are nonplussed at the words I have just uttered?

Why, I said, they are not easy to answer; for they are the words of wise men: and indeed I have a great difficulty in knowing what you mean in that last expression of yours, "That I am nonplussed at them." What do you mean by that, Dionysodorus? You must mean that I have no refutation of them. Tell me if the words have any other sense.

No, he said; the sense or meaning of them is that there is a difficulty in answering them; and I wish that you would answer.

What, before you, Dionysodorus? I said.

Answer, said he.

And is that fair?

Yes, quite fair, he said.

Upon what principle? I said. I can only suppose that you are a very wise man, who comes to us in the character of a great logician, and who knows when to answer and when not to answer—and now you won't open your mouth at all, because you know that you ought not.

You prate, he said, instead of answering. But if, my good sir, you admit that I am wise, answer as I tell you.

I suppose that I must obey, for you are master. Put the question.

Are the things which have sense alive or lifeless?

They are alive.

And do you know of any word which is alive?

I cannot say that I do.

Then why did you ask me what sense my words had?

Why, because I was stupid and made a mistake. And yet, perhaps, I was right after all in saying that words have a sense; what do you say, wise man? If I was not in error, and you do not refute me, all your wisdom will be nonplussed; but if I did fall into error, then again you are wrong in saying that there is no error,—and this remark was made by you not quite a year ago. I am inclined to think, however, Dionysodorus and Euthydemus, that this argument is not very likely to advance: even your skill in the subtleties of logic, which is really amazing, has not found out the way of throwing another and not falling yourself. 288-302

Ctesippus said: Men of Chios, Thurii, or however and whatever you call yourselves, I wonder at you, for you seem to have no objection to talking nonsense.

Fearing that there would be high words, I endeavored to soothe Ctesippus, and said to him: To you, Ctesippus, I must repeat what I said before to Cleinias—that you don't understand the peculiarity of these philosophers. They are not serious, but, like the Egyptian wizard, Proteus,[19] they take different forms and deceive us by their enchantments; and let us, like Menelaus, refuse to let them go until they show us their real form and character. When they are in earnest their full beauty will appear: let us then beg and entreat and beseech them to shine forth. And I think that I had better show them once more the form in which I pray to behold them.

[Socrates gives another example of his method, but the conversation again returns to the level of the two sophists. Several pages of this quibbling are omitted. Their last masterpiece was a proof that all things which have life are animals, that the gods have life and so are animals, that the gods are your gods, and so you may sell them as you do other animals.]

---

[19] Proteus (prō′teŭs): a minor sea divinity who lived on an island off the coast of Egypt. He possessed prophetic power but was reluctant to exercise the gift and, to avoid doing so, would assume all kinds of shapes. If the one consulting him caught and held him fast through all these changes he returned to his own form and told the truth. Menelaus, the legendary king of Sparta, in this way once forced Proteus to prophesy.

303 At this I was quite struck dumb, Crito, and lay prostrate. Ctesippus came to the rescue.

Bravo, Heracles,[20] brave words, said he.

Bravo Heracles, or is Heracles a bravo? said Dionysodorus.

Poseidon,[21] said Ctesippus, what awful distinctions. I will have no more of them ; the pair are invincible.

Then, my dear Crito, there was universal applause of the speakers and their words, and what with laughing and clapping of hands and rejoicings the two men were quite overpowered ; for hitherto only their partisans had cheered at each successive hit, but now the whole company shouted with delight until the columns of the Lyceum returned the sound, seeming almost to sympathize in their joy. To such a pitch was I affected myself, that I made a speech, in which I acknowledged that I had never seen the like of their wisdom ; I was their devoted servant, and fell to praising and admiring of them. What marvellous dexterity of wit, I said, enabled you to acquire this great perfection in such a short time? There is much, indeed, to admire in your words, Euthydemus and Dionysodorus, but there is nothing that I admire more than your magnanimous disregard of any opinion,—whether of the many, or of the grave and reverend seigniors,—which is not the opinion of those who are like-minded with you. And I do verily believe that there are few who are like you, and would approve of your arguments ; the majority of mankind are so ignorant of their value, that they would be more ashamed of employing them in the refutation of others than of being refuted by them. I must further express my approval of your kind and public-spirited denial of all differences, whether of good and evil, white or black, or any other; the result of which is that, as you say, every mouth is stopped, not excepting your own, which graciously follows the example of others ; and thus all ground of offense is taken away. But what appears to me to be more than all is, that this art and invention of yours is so admirably contrived, that in a very short time it can be imparted to any one. I observe that

---

[20] Heracles (hĕr'a-klēz) or Hercules (hēr'kū-lēz) : one of the oldest and most famous heroes in Greek mythology ; by his gigantic strength he accomplished many wonderful labors.

[21] Poseidon (pō-sī'don): god of the sea, and of flowing waters, corresponding to the Roman Neptune.

Ctesippus learned to imitate you in no time. Now this quickness of attainment is an excellent thing; but at the same time I would advise you not to have any more public entertainments; there is a danger that men may undervalue an art which they have so easy an opportunity of learning; the exhibition would be best of all, if the discussion were confined to your two selves; but if there must be an audience, let him only be present who is willing to pay a handsome fee, —you should be careful of this,—and if you are wise, you will also bid your disciples discourse with no man but you and themselves. For only what is rare is valuable; and water, which, as Pindar [22] says, is the best of all things, is also the cheapest. And now I have only to request that you will receive Cleinias and me among your pupils.

304

Such was the discussion, Crito; and after a few more words had passed between us we went away. I hope that you will come to them with me, since they say that they are able to teach any one who will give them money, however old or stupid. And one thing which they said I must repeat for your especial benefit,—that not even the business of making money need hinder any man from taking in their wisdom with ease.

Cri. Truly, Socrates, though I am curious and ready to learn, yet I fear that I am not like-minded with Euthydemus, but one of the other sort, who, as you were saying, would rather be refuted by such arguments than use them in refutation of others. And though I may appear ridiculous in venturing to advise you, I think that you may as well hear what was said to me by a man of very considerable pretensions—he was a professor of legal oratory—who came away from you while I was walking up and down. "Crito," said he to me, "are you attending to these wise men?" "No, indeed," I said to him; "I could not get within hearing of them, there was such a crowd." "You would have heard something worth hearing if you had." "What was that?" I said. "You would have heard the greatest masters of the art of rhetoric discoursing." "And what did you think of them?" I said. "What did I think of them," he said; "what any one would think of them who heard them talking nonsense, and making much ado about nothing." That was the expression which he used. "Surely," I said, "philosophy is a charming thing." "Charming!" he

---

[22] Pindar (pĭn'dar, 522-450 B.C.): greatest of Greek lyric poets.

said; "what simplicity! philosophy is nought; and I think that if you had been present you would have been ashamed of your friend—his conduct was so very strange in placing himself at the mercy of men who care not what they say, and fasten upon every word. And these, as I was telling you, are supposed to be the most eminent professors of their time. But the truth is, Crito, that the study and the men themselves are both equally mean and ridiculous." Now his censure of the pursuit, Socrates, whether coming from him or from others, appears to me to be undeserved; but as to the impropriety of holding a public discussion with such men, I confess that I thought he was in the right about that.

Soc. O Crito, they are marvellous men; but what was I going to say? What manner of man was he who came up to you and censured philosophy; was he an orator who himself practises in the courts, or an instructor of orators, who makes the speeches with which they do battle?

Cri. He was certainly not an orator, and I doubt whether he had ever been into court; but they say that he knows the business, and is a clever man, and composes wonderful speeches.

Soc. Now I understand, Crito; he is one of an amphibious class, whom I was on the point of mentioning—one of those whom Prodicus describes as on the border-ground between philosophers and statesmen—they think that they are the wisest of all men, and that they are generally esteemed the wisest; nothing but the rivalry of the philosophers stands in their way; and they are of the opinion that if they can prove the philosophers to be good for nothing, no one will dispute their title to the palm of wisdom, for that they are really the wisest, although they are apt to be mauled by Euthydemus and his friend, when they get hold of them in conversation. This opinion which they entertain of their own wisdom is very natural; for they have a certain amount of philosophy, and a certain amount of political wisdom; there is reason in what they say, for they argue that they have just enough of both, while they keep out of the way of all risks and conflicts and reap the fruits of their wisdom.

Cri. What do you say of them, Socrates? There is certainly something specious in that notion of theirs.

Soc. Yes, Crito, there is more speciousness than truth; they cannot be made to understand the nature of intermediates. For all persons or things, which are intermediate between two other things, and participant of them—if one of these two things is good and the other evil, are better than the one and worse than the other; but if they are in a mean between two good things which do not tend to the same end, they fall short of either of their component elements in the attainment of their ends. Only in the case when the two component elements which do not tend to the same end are evil is the participant better than either. Now if philosophy and political action are both good, but tend to different ends, and they perticipate in both, and are in a mean between them, then they are talking nonsense, for they are worse than either; or, if the one be good and the other evil, they are better than the one and worse than the other; only on the supposition that they are both evil could there be any truth in what they say. I do not think that they will admit that their two pursuits are either wholly or partly evil; but the truth is, that these philosopher-politicians who aim at both fall short of both in the attainment of their respective ends, and are really third, although they would like to stand first. There is no need, however, to be angry at this ambition of theirs—they may be forgiven that; for every man ought to be loved who says and manfully pursues and works out anything which is at all like wisdom: at the same time we shall do well to see them as they really are.

Cri. I have often told you, Socrates, that I am in a constant difficulty about my two sons. What am I to do with them? There is no hurry about the younger one, who is only a child; but the other, Critobulus, is getting on, and needs some one who will improve him. I cannot help thinking, when I hear you talk, that there is a sort of madness in many of our anxieties about our children: in the first place, about marrying a wife of good family to be the mother of them, and then about heaping up money for them—and yet taking no care about their education. But then again, when I contemplate any of those who pretend to educate others, I am amazed. They all seem to me to be such outrageous beings, if I am to confess the truth: so that I do not know how I can advise the youth to study philosophy.

Soc. Dear Crito, do you not know that in every profession

the inferior sort are numerous and good for nothing, and the good are few and beyond all price: for example, are not gymnastic and rhetoric and money-making and the art of the general, noble arts?

Cri. Certainly they are, in my judgment.

Soc. Well, and do you not see that in each of these arts the many are ridiculous performers?

Cri. Yes, indeed, that is very true.

Soc. And will you on this account shun all these pursuits yourself and refuse to allow them to your son?

Cri. That would not be reasonable, Socrates.

Soc. Do you then be reasonable, Crito, and do not mind whether the teachers of philosophy are good or bad, but think only of Philosophy herself. Try and examine her well and truly, and if she be evil seek to turn away all men from her, and not your sons only; but if she be what I believe that she is, then follow her and serve her, you and your house, as the saying is, and be of good cheer.

PROTAGORAS

INTRODUCTION

The Euthydemus shows Socrates in contrast with the baser sort of sophists; the Protagoras shows him in contrast with the higher sort.*

The points of contrast between the philosopher and the Sophists are, however, by no means so clear in the latter dialogue. A fundamental difficulty in the interpretation of this dialogue lies in the fact that one can not always be sure what Plato's own opinion is about the views expressed by the different speakers. Protagoras and his fellow Sophists are made to speak effectively, sometimes nobly. Socrates is sometimes deeply in earnest, sometimes deeply ironical. To decide just what Plato himself believes on every question discussed is therefore difficult and sometimes impossible.

The dialogue is in fact deeply dramatic. The Sophists here portrayed are not men of straw labelled with opinions which are to be destroyed in the conclusion. These men have dramatic if not also historic vitality. They are exhibited as scholars and gentlemen, whose views are at any rate worth serious attention. (Consider for example the views of Protagoras on the treatment of animals, on the capacity of man for improvement as compared with the lower animals, and on the influence of civilized as compared with savage life upon the individual.) The main contentions of Protagoras, that virtue can be taught, and that there are

* See General Introduction, pages xviii, xx, and xxvii.

many distinct virtues, are also in an important sense true. It may even seem to some that Protagoras appears to advantage in comparison with Socrates. The views set forth by Socrates are strange, paradoxical, and to many will seem false. That virtue can not be taught, that the virtues are one and that virtue is the knowledge of the pleasures and pains involved in action, are all statements which are likely to meet with strong denial. Careful study will serve to clear up some of the difficulties. That virtue can not be taught means with Socrates that virtue can not be brought to a man but must be born in him. That all the virtues are one means with him, that all particular forms or manifestations of virtue, such as those we call courage, temperance, etc., spring from a common principle, and are in fact one in idea. The common principle to which all the virtues are reduced is knowledge. Virtue can therefore be taught,—not indeed brought to one from without but awakened in one by proper influences. The view that virtue is knowledge of the total pleasure and pain involved in action has been most severely criticized. Plato modified this view in his later dialogues. He continued to hold, however, that the purest virtue leads to the greatest happiness in this and the future life.

Taking the dialogue as a whole, one may see that Plato means to show the Sophists at their best and then to show that Socrates was superior to them not simply with their own weapons, but in a far higher sense. The Sophists have views which often appear excellent, but which are self-contradictory and for which in any case they can give no deep and real reason. Socrates wishes to judge upon the questions in issue from the stand-point of absolute truth as revealed by philosophy. The contrast between the method of the Sophists and that of Socrates is as significant as that between the doctrines. They put their trust in rhetoric,—in the forms of discourse which charm and persuade. Socrates chooses the less attractive method of cross-examination, with the purpose of revealing the contradictions involved in the fine speeches of his antagonists, and with the purpose of arriving at positive results which are not self-contradictory.

While the Protagoras is a brilliant example of the sort of dispute which, without doubt, frequently took place between Socrates and the Sophists, it can not be regarded as Plato's most successful presentation of his own point of view. For the most complete victory of the philosopher over the Sophist, in regard to the whole theory of life, one must look to the Republic.

PROTAGORAS

PERSONS OF THE DIALOGUE.[1]

SOCRATES, *who is the narrator of the Dialogue to his* COMPANION.
HIPPOCRATES.
ALCIBIADES.
CRITIAS.
PROTAGORAS,
HIPPIAS,
PRODICUS,
} *Sophists.*
CALLIAS, *a wealthy Athenian.*

SCENE:—The House of Callias.

Com. Where do you come from, Socrates? And yet I need hardly ask the question, as I know that you have been in chase of the fair Alcibiades. I saw him the day before yesterday; and he had got a beard like a man,—and he is a man, as I may tell you in your ear. But I thought that he was still very charming.

Steph. 309

---

[1] Hippocrates (hĭp-pŏk′ra-tēz): comparatively unknown; not mentioned elsewhere by Plato.

Alcibiades (ăl″sĭ-bī′a-dēz): a beautiful and wealthy Athenian of great ability, who spent himself in reckless dissipation. He was in youth an intimate friend of Socrates, who saw his talent and sought, though without success, to win him from vice to virtue. See Symposium, 212 and following; Apology, note 34.

Protagoras (prō-tăg′o-ras): a celebrated Sophist from Abdera (ăb-dē′ra, a city of Thrace on the Ægean) celebrated especially for his skill as a rhetorician. He was the first philosopher who received pay for teaching. He was very popular and received as much as 100 minæ ($1,600 to $1,800) from a pupil. He was more serious in his instruction than most of the other Sophists.

Hippias (hĭp′pĭ-as) of Elis (a city of Greece about one hundred and thirty miles west of Athens), was noted for his remarkable memory and general learning. He was boastful and superficial. Two dialogues, attributed to Plato, bear his name.

Prodicus (prŏd′ĭ-cus) of Ceos (sē′os, an island in the Ægean), was a grammarian, rhetorician, and orator. The expression "wiser than Prodicus" became a proverb.

Callias (kăl′lĭ-as). See Apology, note 9.

Critias (krĭt′ĭ-as): an accomplished Athenian; in youth, a disciple of Socrates, later the chief of the Thirty Tyrants. See Apology, note 34.

Soc. What of his beard? Are you not of Homer's opinion, who says that—

"Youth is most charming when the beard first appears?"

And that is now the charm of Alcibiades.

Com. Well, and how do matters proceed? Have you been visiting him, and was he gracious to you?

Soc. Yes, I thought that he was very gracious; and especially to-day, for I have just come from him, and he has been helping me in an argument. But shall I tell you a strange thing? Although he was present, I never attended to him, and several times he quite passed out of my mind.

Com. What is the meaning of this? Has anything happened between you and him? For surely you cannot have discovered a fairer love[2] than he is; certainly not in this city of Athens.

Soc. Yes, much fairer.

Com. What do you mean—a citizen or a foreigner?

Soc. A foreigner.

Com. Of what country?

Soc. Of Abdera.

Com. And is this stranger really in your opinion fairer than the son of Cleinias?[3]

Soc. And is not the wiser always the fairer, sweet friend?

Com. But have you really met, Socrates, with some wise one?

Soc. Yes; I would say rather, with the wisest of all living men, if you are willing to accord that title to Protagoras.

Com. What! Do you mean to say that Protagoras is in Athens?

Soc. Yes; he has been here two days.

Com. And do you just come from an interview with him?

Soc. Yes; and I have heard and said many things.

Com. Then, if you have no engagement, suppose that you sit down and tell me what passed, and my attendant shall give up his place to you.

Soc. To be sure; and I shall be grateful to you for listening.

Com. Thank you, too, for telling us.

---

[2] See Phædrus, note 9.   [3] Son of Cleinias (klī'nĭ-as): Alcibiades.

Soc. That is thank you twice over. Listen then :—

Last night, or rather very early this morning, Hippocrates, the son of Apollodorus and the brother of Phason,[4] gave a tremendous thump with his staff at my door; some one opened to him, and he came rushing in and bawled out: Socrates, are you awake or asleep?

I knew his voice, and said : Hippocrates, is that you? and do you bring any news?

Good news, he said ; nothing but good.

Very good, I said ; but what news? and why have you come here at this unearthly hour?

He drew nearer to me and said : Protagoras is come.

Yes, I said ; he came two days ago ; have you only just heard of his arrival?

Yes, indeed, he said ; I heard yesterday evening.

At the same time he felt for the truckle-bed, and sat down at my feet, and then he said : I heard yesterday quite late in the evening, on my return from Œnoe[5] whither I had gone in pursuit of my runaway slave Satyrus[6]—as I was going to have told you if some other matter had not come in the way; on my return, when we had done supper and were about to retire to rest, my brother said to me : Protagoras is come. And I was going to you at once, if I had not considered that the night was far spent. But when sleep relaxed her hold on me after my toil, I got up and came hither direct.

I, who knew the very courageous madness of the man, said: What is the matter? has Protagoras robbed you of anything?

He replied, laughing : Yes, indeed he has, Socrates, of the wisdom which he keeps to himself.

But, surely, I said, if you give him money, and make friends with him, he will make you as wise as he is himself.

Would to heaven, he replied, that he would! He might take all that I have, and all that my friends have, if he would. And that is why I have come to you now, in order that you may speak to him on my behalf; for I am young, and also I have never seen nor heard him (when he visited Athens before I was but a child); and all men praise him, Socrates, as being the most accomplished of speakers. There is no

311

---
[4] Apollodorus (à-pŏl'lō-dō'rus) ; Phason (fā'son) : neither one mentioned in other dialogues of Plato.
[5] Œnöe (ĕn-ō'e) : a deme of Attica. See Apology, note 36.
[6] Satyrus (săt'y̆-rus).

reason why we should not go to him at once, and then we shall find him at home. He lodges, as I hear, with Callias, the son of Hipponicus.[7] Let us start.

I replied: Not yet, my good friend; the hour is too early. But let us rise and take a turn in the court and wait there until daybreak, and when the day breaks, then we will go; for Protagoras is generally at home, and we shall be sure to find him; never fear.

Upon this we got up and walked about in the court, and I thought that I would make trial of the strength of his resolution. So I examined him and put questions to him. Tell me, Hippocrates, I said, as you are going to Protagoras, and will be paying your money to him, what is he to whom you are going? and what will he make of you? If you were going to Hippocrates, the Coan, the Asclepiad,[8] and were about to give him your money, and some one said to you: As being what, do you give money to your namesake Hippocrates, O Hippocrates? what would you answer?

I should say, he replied, that I give money to him as a physician.

And what will he make of you?

A physician, he said.

And if you went to Polycleitus[9] the Argive, or Phidias[10] the Athenian, and intended to give them money, and some one were to ask you: As being what, do you give this money to Polycleitus and Phidias? what would you answer?

I should answer, as being statuaries.

And what will they make of you?

A statuary, of course.

Well now, I said, you and I are going to Protagoras, and we are ready to pay him money for you. If our own means

---

[7] Hipponicus (hĭp′pŏ·nī′cus).

[8] Hippocrates (hĭp-pŏk′ra-tēz, 460–377 B.C.): a famous Greek physician, born in Cos, an island of the Ægean. He belonged to the race of the Asclepiadæ (ăs′klē-pī′a dē) so called because supposed to be descendants of Asclepius (ăs-klē′pĭ-us) or Æsculapius (ĕs′kū-lā′pĭ-us), god of medicine. This family were an order of priests who regarded the knowledge of medicine as a secret which they handed down from father to son.

[9] Polycleitus (pŏl′ў-klī′tus, 5th century B.C.): a noted Greek sculptor who contributed much to the development of Greek art; a native of Argos, a city of Greece about sixty miles southwest of Athens.

[10] Phidias (fĭd′i-as 490?–432? B.C.): the greatest sculptor and statuary of Greece. His works were the glory of Greece, and have never been surpassed.

are sufficient, and we can gain him with these, we shall be too glad; but if not, then we are to spend your friends' money as well. Now suppose, that while we are in this intense state of excitement, some one were to say to us: Tell me, Socrates, and you Hippocrates, as being what, are you going to pay money to Protagoras? how should we answer him? I know that Phidias is a sculptor, and Homer is a poet; but what appellation is given to Protagoras? how is he designated?

They call him a Sophist, Socrates, he replied.

Then we are going to pay our money to him in the character of a Sophist?

Certainly.

But suppose a person were to ask this further question:

And how about yourself? what will Protagoras make you if you go to see him?

He answered, with a blush upon his face (for the day 312 was just beginning to dawn, so that I could see him): Unless this differs in some way from the former instances, I suppose that he will make a Sophist of me.

And are you not in sober earnest ashamed, I said, at having to appear before the Hellenes[11] in the character of a Sophist?

Indeed, Socrates, if I am to confess the truth, I am.

But why do you assume, Hippocrates, that the instruction of Protagoras is of this nature? and why may you not learn of him in the same way that you learned the arts of the grammarian, or musician, or trainer,[12] not with the view of making any of them a profession, but only as a part of education, and because a private gentleman and freeman ought to know them?

Just so, he said; and that, in my opinion, is a far truer account of the teaching of Protagoras.

I said: I wonder whether you know what you are doing?

And what am I doing?

You are going to commit your soul to the care of a man whom you call a Sophist. And yet I hardly think that you

---

[11] Hellenes (hĕl-lē′nēz): In very ancient times the name Hellas (hĕl′las) was applied to a small district in northern Greece and the name Hellenes to the people of that district. In the course of time the application of these terms was gradually extended until in Plato's day all Greek people were called Hellenes and all countries inhabited by them were included under the name Hellas.
[12] Teacher of gymnastics.

know what a Sophist is, and if not, then you do not even know whether you are committing your soul to good or evil.

I certainly think that I do know, he replied.

Then tell me, what do you imagine that he is?

I take him to be one who is wise and knowing, he replied, as his name implies.[13]

And might you not, I said, affirm this of the painter and the carpenter also; are not they, too, wise and knowing? But suppose a person were to ask us: In what are the painters wise? We should answer: In what relates to the making of likenessess, and similarly of other things. And if he were further to ask: What is the wisdom of the Sophist, and what is the manufacture over which he presides? how should we answer him?

How should we answer him, Socrates? What other answer could there be but that he presides over the art which makes men eloquent?

Yes, I replied, that is very likely a true, but not a sufficient answer; for a further question is involved: About what does the Sophist make a man eloquent? The player on the lyre may be supposed to make a man eloquent about that which he makes him understand, that is about playing the lyre. Is not that true?

Yes.

Then about what does the Sophist make him eloquent? must not he make him eloquent in that which he understands?

Yes, that may be assumed.

And what is that which the Sophist knows and makes his disciple know?

Indeed, he said, that I cannot tell.

Then I proceeded to say: Well, but are you aware of the danger which you are incurring? If you were going to commit the body to some one, and there was a risk of your getting good or harm from him, would you not carefully consider and ask the opinion of your friends and kindred, and deliberate many days as to whether you should give him the care of your body? But when the soul is in question, which you hold to be of far more value than the body, and upon the well or ill-being of which depends your all,—about this you never consulted either with your father or with your

[13] The term Sophist is derived from the Greek word *sophos*, wise.

brother or with any one of us who are your companions. But no sooner does this foreigner appear, than you instantly commit your soul to his keeping. In the evening, as you say, you hear of him, and in the morning you go to him, never deliberating, or taking the opinion of any one as to whether you ought to intrust yourself to him or not; you have quite made up your mind that you will be a pupil of Protagoras, and are prepared to expend all the property of yourself and of your friends in carrying out at any price this determination, although, as you admit, you do not know him, and have never spoken with him: and you call him a Sophist, but are manifestly ignorant of what a Sophist is; and yet you are going to commit yourself to his keeping.

When he heard me say this he replied: That I suppose, Socrates, is the conclusion which I must draw from your words.

I proceeded: Is not a Sophist, Hippocrates, one who deals wholesale or retail in the food of the soul? To me that appears to be the sort of man.

And what, Socrates, is the food of the soul?

Surely, I said, knowledge is the food of the soul; and we must take care, my friend, that the Sophist does not deceive us when he praises what he sells, like the dealers wholesale or retail who sell the food of the body; for they praise indiscriminately all their goods, without knowing what are really beneficial or hurtful: neither do their customers know, with the exception of any trainer or physician who may happen to buy of them. In like manner those who carry about the wares of knowledge, and make the round of the cities, and sell or retail them to any customer who is in want of them, praise them all alike; and I should not wonder, O my friend, if many of them were really ignorant of their effect upon the soul; and their customers equally ignorant, unless he who buys of them happens to be a physician of the soul. If therefore you have understanding of what is good and evil, you may safely buy knowledge of Protagoras or of any one; but if not, then, O my friend, pause, and do not hazard your dearest interests at a game of chance. For there is 314 far greater peril in buying knowledge than in buying meat and drink: the one you purchase of the wholesale or retail dealer, and carry them away in other vessels, and before you receive them into the body as food, you may deposit them at home and call in any experienced friend who knows what is good to be eaten or drunken, and what not, and how much and when; and hence the danger of purchasing them is not so great. But when you buy the wares of knowledge you cannot carry them away in another vessel; they have been sold to you, and you must take them into the soul and go your way, either greatly harmed or greatly benefited by the lesson: and therefore we should think about this and take counsel with our elders; for we are still young—too young to determine such a matter. And now let us go, as we were intending, and hear Protagoras; and when we have heard what he has to say, we may take counsel of others; for not only is Protagoras at the house of Callias, but there is Hippias of Elis, and, if I am not mistaken, Prodicus of Ceos, and several other wise men.

To this we agreed, and proceeded on our way until we reached the vestibule of the house; and there we stopped in order to finish a dispute which had arisen as we were going along; and we stood talking in the vestibule until we had finished and come to an understanding. And I think that the door-keeper, who was a eunuch, and who was probably annoyed at the great inroad of the Sophists, must have heard us talking. At any rate, when we knocked at the door, and he opened and saw us, he grumbled: They are Sophists— he is not at home; and instantly gave the door a hearty bang with both his hands. Again we knocked, and he answered without opening: Did you not hear me say that he was not at home, fellows? But, my friend, I said, we are not Sophists, and we are not come to see Callias; fear not, for we want to see Protagoras; and I must request you to announce us. At last, after a good deal of difficulty, the man was persuaded to open the door.

When we entered, we found Protagoras taking a walk in the portico; [14] and next to him, on one side, were walking Callias the son of Hipponicus, and Paralus [15] the son of Pericles, who,

---

[14] The better Athenian houses were built around an inner open court surrounded by a kind of portico.

[15] Paralus (păr'a-lus); Pericles (pĕr'ĭ-klēz); Charmides (kăr'mĭ-dēz); Glaucon (glạu'kon); Xanthippus (zăn-tĭp'pus); Philippides (fĭ-lĭp'pi-dēz); Philomelus (fĭl'o-mē'lus); Antimœrus (ăn'tĭ-mē'rus); Mende (mĕn'de). These Greeks, who are all doubtless historical personages, are of no importance in this dialogue except to show the class of persons whom the Sophists gathered about them. Most of them are known to have belonged to wealthy aristocratic families.

by the mother's side, is his half-brother, and Charmides the
son of Glaucon. On the other side of him were Xanthippus
the other son of Pericles, Philippides the son of Philomelus; also Antimœrus of Mende, who of all the dis- 315
ciples of Protagoras is the most famous, and intends to make
sophistry his profession. A train of listeners followed him, of
whom the greater part appeared to be foreigners, who accompanied Protagoras out of the various cities through which
he journeyed. Now he, like Orpheus,[16] attracted them by his
voice, and they followed the attraction. I should mention
also that there were some Athenians in the company. Nothing delighted me more than the precision of their movements:
they never got into his way at all, but when he and those who
were with him turned back, then the band of listeners divided
into two parts on either side; he was always in front, and
they wheeled round and took their places behind him in perfect order.

After him, as Homer says,[17] "I lifted up my eyes and saw"
Hippias the Elean sitting in the opposite portico on a chair
of state, and around him were seated on benches Eryximachus[18]
the son of Acumenus, and Phædrus[19] the Myrrhinusian, and
Andron[20] the son of Androtion, and there were strangers
whom he had brought with him from his native city of Elis,
and some others: they appeared to be asking Hippias certain
physical and astronomical questions, and he, *ex cathedrâ*,[21]
was determining their several questions to them and discoursing of them.

Also, "my eyes beheld Tantalus"; for Prodicus the Caen
was at Athens: he had been put into a room which, in the
days of Hipponicus, was a storehouse; but as the house was
full, Callias had cleared this out and made the room into a

[16] The mythical musician and poet, celebrated especially for his lyre playing, which so enchanted even the trees and rocks that they followed him.
[17] By this and the following quotation from Homer's Odyssey, Socrates
wittily represents himself as like Odysseus, wandering through the lower
world, and seeing one after another, the celebrated personages there.
[18] Eryximachus (ĕr'y̆x-ĭm'a-kus) and Acumenus (à-kū'mē-nus) were both
learned physicians. Both are mentioned in Phædrus, 268, and the former in
Symposium, 176, and following.
[19] See the dialogue Phædrus, note 1; he is a speaker in the Symposium.
Myrrhinus (my̆r'rĭ-nus): a deme of Attica.
[20] Andron (ăn'dron); Androtion (ăn-drŏ'shĭ-on).
[21] Ex cathedra (kăth'e-drà): Literally, from the chair; figuratively, with
authcrity. Probably both meanings were intended here.

guest-chamber. Now Prodicus was still in bed, wrapped up in sheepskins and bedclothes, of which there seemed to be a great heap; and there were sitting by him on the couches near, Pausanias of the deme of Cerameis,[22] and with Pausanias was a youth quite young, who is certainly remarkable for his good looks, and, if I am not mistaken, is also of a fair and gentle nature. I think that I heard him called Agathon,[23] and my suspicion is that he is the beloved of Pausanias. There was this youth and also there were the two Adeimantuses,[24] one the son of Cepis, and the other of Leucolophides, and some others. I was very anxious to hear what Prodicus was saying, for he seemed to me to be an extraordinarily wise and divine man; but I was not able to get into the inner circle, and his fine deep voice made an echo in the room which rendered his words inaudible.

316

No sooner had we entered than there followed us Alcibiades the beautiful, as you say, and I believe you; and also Critias the son of Callæschrus.[25]

On entering we stopped a little, in order to look about us, and then walked up to Protagoras, and I said: Protagoras, my friend Hippocrates and I have come to see you.

Do you wish, he said, to speak with me alone, or in the presence of others?

That is as you please, I said: you shall determine when you have heard the object of our visit.

And what is that? he said.

I must explain, I said, that my friend Hippocrates is a native Athenian; he is the son of Apollodorus, and of a great and prosperous house, and he is himself in natural ability quite a match for those of his own age. I believe that he aspires to political eminence; and this he thinks that conversation with you is most likely to procure for him: now it is for you to decide whether you would wish to speak to him of these matters alone or in company.

Thank you, Socrates, for your consideration of me. For certainly a stranger finding his way into great cities, and persuading the flower of the youth in them to leave the company

---

[22] Pausanias (paw-sā'nĭ-us): speaker in Symposium. Cerameis (sĕr'a-mĭs).
[23] See Symposium, note 1.
[24] Adeimantus (ăd'ĭ-măn'tus); Cepis (sē'pis); Leucolophides (lū'ko-lŏf'ĭ-dēz).
[25] Callæschrus (kăl-lĕs'krus).

of their other kinsmen or acquaintance, and live with him, under the idea that they will be improved by his conversation, ought to be very cautious; great jealousies are occasioned by his proceedings, and he is the subject of many enmities and conspiracies. I maintain the art of the Sophist to be of ancient date; but that in ancient times the professors of the art, fearing this odium, veiled and disguised themselver under various names: some under that of poets, as Homer, Hesiod, and Simonides [26]; some as hierophants [27] and prophets, as Orpheus and Musæus; [28] and some, as I observe, even under the name of gymnastic masters, like Iccus [29] of Tarentum, or the more recently celebrated Herodicus, now of Selymbria and formerly of Megara, [30] who is a first-rate Sophist. Your own Agathocles [31] pretended to be a musician, but was really an eminent Sophist; also Pythocleides [32] the Cean; and there were many others; and all of them, as I was saying, adopted these arts as veils or disguises because they were afraid of the envy of the multitude. But that is not my way, for I do not believe that they effected their purpose, which was to deceive the government, who were not blinded by them; and as to the people, they have no understanding, and only repeat what their rulers are pleased to tell them. Now to run away, and to be caught in running away, is the very height of folly, and also greatly increases the exasperation of mankind; for they regard him who runs away as a rogue, in addition to any other objections which they have to him; and therefore I take an entirely opposite course, and acknowledge myself to be a Sophist and instructor of mankind; such an open ac-

317

---

[26] For Homer and Hesiod see Apology, notes 39 and 53. Simonides (si-mŏn'ĭ-dēz, 556-467 B.C.), of Ceos: a celebrated Greek lyric poet.
[27] Priests who taught to initiates the mysteries and duties of certain secret religious ceremonies.
[28] See Apology, notes 51 and 52. Orpheus was said to have taught the doctrine of immortality and to have been the first to use divination and rites for expiation from sin. To Musæus was attributed a collection of oracles, hymns, and chants of dedication and purification.
[29] Iccus [(ĭk'kus) of Tarentum (tă-rĕn'tum), a Greek town in southern Italy]: a philosopher and celebrated gymnast. He won the prize in the national games. He taught that gymnastic training produced temperance.
[30] Herodicus (he-rŏd'ĭ-kus): a Thracian physician, one of the first to insist upon the importance of exercise for health. Selymbria (se-lўm'brĭ-a): a town of Thrace on the Propontis. Megara (mĕg'a-ra): a city of Greece about twenty miles west of Athens.
[31] Agathocles (a-găth'o-klēz).
[32] Pythocleides (pȳth'o-klī'dēz).

knowledgment appears to me to be a better sort of caution than concealment. Nor do I neglect other precautions, and therefore I hope, as I may say, by the favor of Heaven that no harm will come of the acknowledgment that I am a Sophist. And I have been now many years in the profession—for all my years when added up are many—and there is no one here present of whom I might not be the father. Wherefore I should much prefer conversing with you, if you do not object, in the presence of the company.

As I suspected that he would like to have a little display and glory in the presence of Prodicus and Hippias, and would gladly show us to them in the light of his admirers, I said: But why should we not summon Prodicus and Hippias and their friends to hear us?

Very good, he said.

Suppose, said Callias, that we hold a council in which you may sit and discuss. This was determined, and great delight was felt at the prospect of hearing wise men talk; we ourselves all took the chairs and benches, and arranged them by Hippias, where the other benches had been already placed. Meanwhile Callias and Alcibiades got up Prodicus and brought in him and his companions.

When we were all seated, Protagoras said: Now that the company are assembled, Socrates, tell me about the young man of whom you were just now speaking.

318   I replied: I will begin again at the same point, Protagoras, and tell you once more the purport of my visit: this is my friend Hippocrates, who is desirous of making your acquaintance; he wants to know what will happen to him if he associates with you. That is all I have to say.

Protagoras answered: Young man, if you associate with me, on the very first day you will return home a better man than you came, and better on the second day than on the first, and better every day than you were on the day before.

When I heard this, I said: Protagoras, I do not at all wonder at hearing you say this; even at your age, and with all your wisdom, if any one were to teach you what you did not know before, you would become better no doubt: but please to answer in a different way; I will explain how by an example. Let me suppose that Hippocrates, instead of desiring your acquaintance, wished to become acquainted with the young man Zeuxippus of Heraclea,[33] who has newly come to Athens, and he were to go to him as he has gone to you, and were to hear him say, as he has heard you say, that every day he would grow and become better if he associated with him: and then suppose that he were to ask him, "In what would he be better, and in what would he grow?" Zeuxippus would answer, "In painting." And suppose that he went to Orthagoras the Theban,[34] and heard him say the same, and asked him, "In what would he become better day by day?" he would reply, "In flute-playing." Now I want you to make the same sort of answer to this young man and to me, who am asking questions on his account. When you say that on the first day on which he associates with you he will return home a better man, and on every day will grow in like manner—in what, Protagoras, will he be better? and about what?

When Protagoras heard me say this, he replied: You ask questions fairly, and I like to answer a question which is fairly put. If Hippocrates comes to me he will not experience the sort of drudgery with which other Sophists are in the habit of insulting their pupils; who, when they have just escaped from the arts, are taken and driven back into them by these teachers, and made to learn calculation, and astronomy, and geometry, and music (he gave a look at Hippias as he said this); but if he comes to me, he will learn that which he comes to learn. And this is prudence in affairs private as well as public; he will learn to order his own house in the best manner, and he will be best able to speak and act in the affairs of the State.

Do I understand you, I said; and is your meaning that you teach the art of politics, and that you promise to make men good citizens? 318

That, Socrates, is exactly the profession which I make.

Then, I said, you do indeed possess a noble art, if there is no mistake about this; for I will freely confess to you, Protagoras, that I have a doubt whether this art is capable of being taught, and yet I know not how to disbelieve your assertion. And I

---

[33] Zeuxippus (zūks-ĭp′pus) or Zeuxis (zūks′ĭs) (——400 B.C.): a celebrated Greek painter, a native of Heraclea (hĕr′a-klē′a), a town in southern Italy.

[34] Orthagoras (ôr-thăg′o-ras); Thebes (thēbz): a city of Greece in Bœotia, about thirty-five miles northwest of Athens. The Thebans were celebrated flute players.

ought to tell you why I am of opinion that this art cannot be taught or communicated by man to man. I say that the Athenians are an understanding people, as indeed they are esteemed by the other Hellenes. Now I observe that when we are met together in the Assembly,[35] and the matter in hand relates to building, the builders are summoned as advisers; when the question is one of ship-building, then the ship-builders; and the like of other arts which they think capable of being taught and learned. And if some person offers to give them advice who is not supposed by them to have any skill in the art, even though he be good-looking, and rich, and noble, they don't listen to him, but laugh at him, and hoot him, until either he is clamored down and retires of himself; or if he persists, he is dragged away or put out by the constables at the command of the prytanes.[36] This is their way of behaving about the arts which have professors. When, however, the question is an affair of state, then everybody is free to have a say—carpenter, tinker, cobbler, sailor, passenger; rich and poor, high and low—any one who likes gets up, and no one reproaches him, as in the former case, with not having learned, and having no teacher, and yet giving advice; evidently because they are under the impression that this sort of knowledge cannot be taught. And not only is this true of the state, but of individuals; the best and wisest of our citizens are unable to impart their political wisdom to others: as, for example,

320 Pericles,[37] the father of these young men, who gave them excellent instruction in all that could be learned from masters, in his own department of politics taught them nothing; nor did he give them teachers, but they were allowed to wander at their own free-will, in a sort of hope that they would light upon virtue of their own accord. Or take another example: There was Cleinias, the younger brother of our friend Alcibiades, of whom this very same Pericles was the guardian; and he being in fact under the apprehension that Cleinias would be corrupted by Alcibiades, took him

---

[35] At Athens, the formal assembly of all the citizens which exercised certain legislative and judiciary functions, and had, with the senate, power of decision in all matters affecting the supreme interests of the State. See Apology, note 29.

[36] Presidents, or those who presided over the senate and assembly at Athens. See Apology, note 29.

[37] Pericles (495-429 B.C.): the greatest of Athenian statesmen, distinguished also as an orator and great general.

away, and placed him in the house of Ariphron to be educated, but before six months had elapsed, Ariphron sent him back, not knowing what to do with him. And I could mention numberless other instances of persons who were good themselves, and never yet made any one else good, whether friend or stranger. Now I, Protagoras, when I reflect on all this, am inclined to think that virtue cannot be taught. But then again, when I listen to your words, I am disposed to waver; and I believe that there must be something in what you say, because I know that you have great experience, and learning, and invention. And I wish that you would, if possible, show me a little more clearly that virtue can be taught. Will you be so good?

That I will, Socrates, and gladly. But what would you like? Shall I, as an elder, speak to you as younger men in an apologue or myth, or shall I argue the question?

To this several of the company answered that he should choose for himself.

Well, then, he said, I think that the myth will be more interesting.

Once upon a time there were gods only, and no mortal creatures. But when the time came that these also should be created, the gods fashioned them out of earth and fire and various mixtures of both elements in the inward parts of the earth; and when they were about to bring them into the light of day, they ordered Prometheus and Epimetheus[38] to equip them, and to distribute to them severally their proper qualities. Epimetheus said to Prometheus: "Let me distribute, and do you inspect." This was agreed, and Epimetheus made the distribution. There were some to whom he gave strength without swiftness, or again swiftness without strength; some he armed, and others he left unarmed; and devised for the latter some other means of preservation, making some large, and having their size as a protection, and others small, whose nature was to fly in the air or burrow in the ground; this was to be their way of escape. Thus did he compensate them with the view of preventing any race from

---

[38] Prometheus (prō-mē'thŭs), Epimetheus (ĕp'ĭ-mē'thŭs) : ancient divinities and brothers. The characters of the two are indicated by their names. Prometheus signifies forethought. Epimetheus, afterthought. See Longfellow's Masque of Pandora; Shelley's Prometheus Unbound; Mrs. Browning's Prometheus Bound.

becoming extinct. And when he had provided against their destruction by one another, he contrived also a means of protecting them against the seasons of heaven; clothing them with close hair and thick skins sufficient to defend them against the winter cold and summer heat, and for a natural bed of their own when they wanted to rest; also he furnished them with hoofs and hair and hard and callous skins under their feet. Then he gave them varieties of food,—to some herbs of the soil, to others fruits of trees, and to others roots, and to some again he gave other animals as food. And some he made to have few young ones, while those who were their prey were very prolific; and in this way the race was preserved. Thus did Epimetheus, who, not being very wise, forgot that he had distributed among the brute animals all the qualities that he had to give,—and when he came to man, who was still unprovided, he was terribly perplexed. Now while he was in this perplexity, Prometheus came to inspect the distribution, and he found that the other animals were suitably furnished, but that man alone was naked and shoeless, and had neither bed nor arms of defense. The appointed hour was approaching in which man was to go forth into the light of day; and Prometheus, not knowing how he could devise his salvation, stole the mechanical arts of Hephæstus[39] and Athene,[40] and fire with them (they could neither have been acquired nor used without fire), and gave them to man. Thus man had the wisdom necessary to the support of life, but political wisdom he had not; for that was in the keeping of Zeus, and the power of Prometheus did not extend to entering into the castle of heaven, in which Zeus[41] dwelt, who moreover had terrible sentinels; but he did enter by stealth into the common workshop of Athene and Hephæstus, in which they used to pursue their favorite arts, and took away Hephæstus' art of working by fire, and also the art of Athene, and gave them to man. And in this way man was supplied with the means of life. But Prometheus is said to have been after-

[39] Hephæstus (he-fĕs′tus): the god of fire and of the arts in which fire is used, corresponding to the Roman Vulcan.

[40] Athene (å-thē′ne): one of the chief divinities of Grecian mythology, often called the goddess of wisdom, corresponding to the Roman Minerva. To her was attributed the invention of many arts, especially those proper to women, like spinning and weaving.

[41] Zeus (zųs): the chief divinity of Grecian mythology, corresponding to the Roman Jupiter.

wards prosecuted for theft, owing to the blunder of Epimetheus.

Now man, having a share of the divine attributes, was at first the only one of the animals who had any gods, because he alone was of their kindred; and he would raise altars and images of them. He was not long in inventing language and names; and he also constructed houses and clothes and shoes and beds, and drew sustenance from the earth. Thus provided, mankind at first lived dispersed, and there were no cities. But the consequence was that they were destroyed by the wild beasts, for they were utterly weak in comparison of them, and their art was only sufficient to provide them with the means of life, and would not enable them to carry on war against the animals: food they had, but not as yet any art of government, of which the art of war is a part. After awhile the desire of self-preservation gathered them into cities; but when they were gathered together, having no art of government, they evil intreated one another, and were again in process of dispersion and destruction. Zeus feared that the race would be exterminated, and so he sent Hermes [42] to them, bearing reverence and justice to be the ordering principles of cities and the bonds of friendship and conciliation. Hermes asked Zeus how he should impart justice and reverence among men: should he distribute them as the arts are distributed; that is to say to a favored few only,—for one skilled individual has enough of medicine, or of any other art, for many unskilled ones? Shall this be the manner in which I distribute justice and reverence among men, or shall I give them to all? To all, said Zeus; I should like them all to have a share; for cities cannot exist, if a few only share in the virtues, as in the arts. And further, make a law by my order, that he who has no part in reverence and justice shall be put to death as a plague of the State.

And this is the reason, Socrates, why the Athenians and mankind in general, when the question relates to carpentering or any other mechanical art, allow but a few to share in their deliberations: and when any one else interferes, then, as you say, they object, if he be not of the favored few, and that, as I say, is very natural. But when they come to deliberate

---

[42] Hermes (hēr'mēz): messenger of the gods, corresponding to the Roman Mercury.

about political virtue, which proceeds only by way of justice and wisdom, they are patient enough of any man who speaks of them, as is also natural, because they think that every man ought to share in this sort of virtue, and that states could not exist if this were otherwise. I have explained to you, Socrates, the reason of this phenomenon.

323

And that you may not suppose yourself to be deceived in thinking that all men regard every man as having a share of justice and every other political virtue, let me give you a further proof, which is this. In other cases, as you are aware, if a man says that he is a good flute-player, or skilful in any other art in which he has no skill, people either laugh at him or are angry with him, and his relations think that he is mad and go and admonish him; but when honesty is in question, or some other political virtue, even if they know that he is dishonest, yet, if the man comes publicly forward and tells the truth about his dishonesty, in this case they deem that to be madness which in the other case was held by them to be good sense. They say that men ought to profess honesty whether they are honest or not, and that a man is mad who does not make such a profession. Their notion is, that a man must have some degree of honesty; and that if he has none at all he ought not to be in the world.

I have been showing that they are right in admitting every man as a counsellor about this sort of virtue, as they are of opinion that every man is a partaker of it. And I will now endeavor further to show that they regard this virtue, not as given by nature, or growing spontaneously, but as capable of being learned and acquired by study. For injustice is punished, whereas no one would instruct, or rebuke, or be angry at those whose calamities they suppose to come to them either by nature or chance; they do not try to alter them, they do but pity them. Who would be so foolish as to chastise or instruct the ugly, or the diminutive, or the feeble? And for this reason; they know, I imagine, that this sort of good and evil comes to them by nature and chance; whereas if a man is wanting in those good qualities which come to men from study and exercise and teaching, and has only the contrary evil qualities, men are angry with him, and punish him and reprove him. And one of those evil qualities is impiety and injustice, and they may be described generally as the opposite of political virtue. When this is the case, any man will be angry with another, and reprimand him,—clearly under the impression that by study and learning the virtue in which he is deficient may be acquired. For if you will think, Socrates, of the effect which punishment has on evil-doers, you will see at once that in the opinion of mankind virtue may be acquired; for no one punishes the evil-doer under the notion, or for the reason, that he has done wrong, —only the unreasonable fury of a beast acts in that way. But he who desires to inflict rational punishment does not retaliate for a past wrong, for that which is done cannot be undone, but he has regard to the future, and is desirous that the man who is punished, and he who sees him punished, may be deterred from doing wrong again. And he implies that virtue is capable of being taught; as he undoubtedly punishes for the sake of prevention. This is the notion of all who retaliate upon others either privately or publicly. And the Athenians, too, like other men, retaliate on those whom they regard as evil-doers; and this argues them to be of the number of those who think that virtue may be acquired and taught. Thus far, Socrates, I have shown you clearly enough, if I am not mistaken, that your countrymen are right in admitting the tinker and the cobbler to advise about politics, and also that they deem virtue to be capable of being taught and acquired.

There yet remains one difficulty which has been raised by you about the sons of good men. What is the reason why good men teach their sons the knowledge which is gained from teachers, and make them wise in that, but do nothing towards improving them in the virtues which distinguish themselves? And here, Socrates, I will leave the apologue and take up the argument. Please to consider: Is there or is there not some one quality in which all the citizens must be partakers, if there is to be a city at all? In the answer to this question is contained the only solution of your difficulty; there is no other. For if there be any such quality, and this quality or unity is not the art of the carpenter, or the smith, or the potter, but justice and temperance and holiness, and, in a word, manly virtue—if this is the quality of which all men must be partakers, and which is the very condition of their learning or doing anything else, and if he who is wanting in this, whether he be a child only or a grown-up man or woman, must be taught and punished, until by punishment he becomes better, and he who rebels against instruction and punishment is either exiled or condemned to death under the idea that he is incurable—if, I say, this be true, and nevertheless good men have their sons taught other things and not this, do consider how extraordinary would be their conduct. For we have shown that they think virtue capable of being taught and inculcated both in private and public; and yet, notwithstanding this, they teach their sons lesser matters, ignorance of which does not involve the punishment of death : but those things, the ignorance of which may cause death and exile to those who have no knowledge or training—aye, and confiscation as well as death, and, in a word, may be the ruin of families—those things, I say, they are supposed not to teach them, not to take the utmost care that they should learn. That is not likely, Socrates.

Education and admonition commence in the first years of childhood, and last to the very end of life. Mother and nurse and father and tutor are quarreling about the improvement of the child as soon as ever he is able to understand them : he cannot say or do anything without their setting forth to him that this is just and that is unjust ; this is honorable, that is dishonorable ; this is holy, that is unholy ; do this and abstain from that. And if he obeys, well and good; if not, he is straightened by threats and blows, like a piece of warped wood. At a later stage they send him to teachers, and enjoin them to see to his manners even more than to his reading and music ;[43] and the teachers do as they are desired. And when the boy has learned his letters and is beginning to understand what is written, as before he understood only what was spoken, they put into his hands the works of great poets, which he reads at school ; in these are contained many admonitions, and many tales, and praises, and encomia of ancient famous men, which he is required to learn by heart, in order that he may imitate or emulate them and desire to become like them. Then, again, the teachers of the lyre take similar care that their young disciple is temperate and gets into no mischief; and when they have taught him the use of the lyre, they introduce him to the poems of other excellent poets, who are the

[43] See Republic II., 376, and note 17.

lyric poets; and these they set to music, and make their harmonies and rhythms quite familiar to the children, in order that they may learn to be more gentle, and harmonious, and rhythmical, and so more fitted for speech and action; for the life of man in every part has need of harmony and rhythm. Then they send them to the master of gymnastic,[44] in order that their bodies may better minister to the virtuous mind, and that the weakness of their bodies may not force them to play the coward in war or on any other occasion. This is what is done by those who have the means, and those who have the means are the rich: their children begin education soonest and leave off latest. When they have done with masters, the State again compels them to learn the laws, and live after the pattern which they furnish, and not after their own fancies; and just as in learning to write, the writing-master first draws lines with a stylus for the use of the young beginner, and gives him the tablet and makes him follow the lines, so the city draws the laws, which were the invention of good lawgivers who were of old time; these are given to the young man, in order to guide him in his conduct whether as ruler or ruled; and he who transgresses them is to be corrected, or, in other words, called to account, which is a term used not only in your country, but also in many others. Now when there is all this care about virtue private and public, why, Socrates, do you still wonder and doubt whether virtue can be taught? Cease to wonder, for the opposite would be far more surprising.

But why then do the sons of good fathers often turn out ill? Let me explain that,—which is far from being wonderful, if, as I have been saying, the very existence of the State implies that virtue is not any man's private possession. If this be true —and nothing can be truer—then I will ask you to imagine, as an illustration, some other pursuit or branch of knowledge which may be assumed equally to be the condition of the existence of a State. Suppose that there could be no State unless we were all flute-players, as far as each had the capacity, and everybody was freely teaching everybody the art, both in private and public, and reproving the bad player as freely and openly as every man now teaches justice and the laws, not concealing them as he would conceal the other arts, but imparting them—for all of us have a mutual interest in the justice and

327

[44] See Republic III., 403, and following.

virtue of one another, and this is the reason why every one is ready to teach justice and the laws; suppose, I say, that there were the same readiness and liberality among us in teaching one another flute-playing, do you imagine, Socrates, that the sons of good flute-players would be more likely to be good than the sons of bad ones? I think not. Would not their sons grow up to be distinguished or undistinguished according to their own natural capacities as flute-players, and the son of a good player would often turn out to be a bad one, and the son of a bad player to be a good one, and all flute-players would be good enough in comparison of those who were ignorant and unacquainted with the art of flute-playing? In like manner I would have you consider that he who appears to you to be the worst of those who have been brought up in laws and humanities, would appear to be a just man and a master of justice if he were to be compared with men who had no education, or courts of justice, or laws, or any restraints upon them which compelled them to practice virtue—with the savages, for example, whom the poet Pherecrates [45] exhibited on the stage at the last year's Lenæan festival.[46] If you were living among men such as the man-haters in his Chorus,[47] you would be only too glad to meet with Eurybates and Phrynondas,[48] and you would sorrowfully desire the rascality of this part of the world. And you, Socrates, are discontented, and why? Because all men are teachers of virtue, each one according to his ability, and you say that there is no teacher. You might as well ask, Who teaches Greek? For of that too there will not be any teachers found. Or you might ask, Who is to teach the sons of our artisans this same art which they have learned of their fathers? He and his fellow-workmen have taught them to the best of their ability,—but who will carry them further

328

---

[45] Pherecrates (fe-rĕk′ra-tēz, 5th century B.C.): an Athenian writer of comedy.

[46] The Lenæa (le-nē′a) or Feast of Vats, was one of a series of religious festivals celebrated in Athens in honor of Dionysus, god of wine. After a public banquet the citizens went to the theatre, where tragedies and comedies were presented.

[47] The chorus was originally a number of persons who sang and danced at religious festivals. The drama was developed out of the chorus of the festivals in honor of Dionysus. Even after actors were introduced the chorus was retained as an important element of the drama, though its place became gradually limited and subordinate.

[48] Eurybates (ū-rȳb′a-tēz) and Phrynondas (frī-nŏn′das): "Notorious villains."—Jowett.

in their arts? And you would certainly have a difficulty, Socrates, in finding a teacher of them; but there would be no difficulty in finding a teacher of those who are wholly ignorant. And this is true of virtue or of anything; and if a man is better able than we are to promote virtue ever so little, that is as much as we can expect. A teacher of this sort I believe myself to be, and above all other men to have the knowledge which makes a man noble and good; and I give my pupils their money's-worth, and even more, as they themselves confess. And therefore I have introduced the following mode of payment: When a man has been my pupil, if he likes he pays my price, but there is no compulsion; and if he does not like, he has only to go into a temple and take an oath of the value of the instructions, and he pays no more than he declares to be their value.

Such is my apologue, Socrates, and such is the argument by which I endeavor to show that virtue may be taught, and that this is the opinion of the Athenians. And I have also attempted to show that you are not to wonder at good fathers having bad sons, or at good sons having bad fathers, as may be seen in the sons of Polycleitus, who are of the same age as our friends Paralus and Xanthippus, and who are very inferior to their father; and this is true of many other artists. But I ought not to say the same as yet of Paralus and Xanthippus themselves, for they are young and there is still hope of them.

Protagoras ended, and in my ear —

"So charming left his voice, that I the while
Thought him still speaking; still stood fixed to hear."

At length when I saw that he had really finished, I gradually recovered consciousness, and looking at Hippocrates, I said to him: O son of Apollodorus, how deeply grateful I am to you for having brought me hither; I would not have missed the speech of Protagoras for a great deal. For I used to imagine that no human care could make men good; but I know better now. Yet I have still one very small difficulty which I am sure that Protagoras will easily explain, as he has already explained so much. For if a man were to go and consult Pericles or any of our great speakers about these matters, he might perhaps hear as fine a discourse; but then if any one has a question to ask of any of them, like books, they can

329-
334

neither answer nor ask; and if any one challenges the least particular of their speech, they go ringing on in a long harangue, like brazen pots, which when they are struck continue to sound unless some one puts his hand upon them; whereas our friend Protagoras can not only make a good speech, as he has already shown, but when he is asked a question he can answer briefly; and when he asks he will wait and hear the answer; and this is a very rare gift. Now I, Protagoras, have a little question that I want to ask of you, and if you will only answer me that, I shall be quite satisfied. You were saying that virtue can be taught; that I will take upon your authority, and there is no one to whom I am more ready to trust. But I marvel at one thing about which I should like to have my mind set at rest. You were speaking of Zeus sending justice and reverence to men; and several times while you were speaking, justice and temperance and holiness, and all these qualities, were described by you as if together they made up virtue. Now I want you to tell me truly whether virtue is one whole, of which justice and temperance and holiness are parts; or whether all these are only the names of one and the same thing: that is the doubt which still lingers in my mind.

[Protagoras replies that the qualities which Socrates mentions are not different names for one and the same thing, but are parts of a whole, just as the features are parts of a face, each entirely different from all the others and having its own function. Socrates proceeds by a cross-examination of Protagoras to test the truth of this theory. First he shows that if the parts of virtue are unlike, if, for example, justice is not of the nature of holiness, nor holiness of the nature of justice, then justice is unholy. Protagoras cannot agree to this. He admits that justice bears a resemblance to holiness, but denies that they are identical. He prefers to say simply that they are different. The most unlike things, he claims, can be shown to be alike from some point of view.

Socrates continues his questioning and draws Protagoras into making statements which contradict his own theory that the virtues are many and unlike. Protagoras asserts at one time that folly is opposed to wisdom, and at another time that folly is opposed to temperance; but he has also been led to affirm that everything has one opposite and only one. It becomes clear that he must renounce one of these statements or admit that wisdom and temperance are the same.

Having obtained the reluctant consent of Protagoras to this and reminding him that justice and holiness have been shown to be nearly the same, Socrates begins a third attack which Protagoras foresees must lead him to the admission that temperance and justice are one and the same. To evade this conclusion, Protagoras takes refuge in a long speech, which sounds well but is not much to the point.]

When he had given this answer, the company cheered him. And I said: Protagoras, I have a wretched memory, and when any one makes a long speech to me I never remember what he is talking about. As then, if I had been deaf, and you were going to converse with me, you would have had to raise your voice; so now, having such a bad memory, I will ask you to cut your answers shorter, if you would take me with you.

What do you mean? he said: how am I to shorten my answers? shall I make them too short?

Certainly not, I said.

But short enough? he said.

Yes, I said.

Shall I answer what appears to me to be short enough, or what appears to you to be short enough?

I have heard, I said, that you can speak and teach others to speak about the same things at such length that words never seemed to fail, or with such brevity that no one could use fewer of them. Please therefore, if you talk with me, to adopt the latter or more compendious method. 335

Socrates, he replied, many a battle of words have I fought, and if I had followed the method of disputation which my adversaries desired, as you want me to do, I should have been no better than another, and the name of Protagoras would have been nowhere.

I saw that he was not satisfied with his previous answers, and that he would not play the part of answerer any more if he could help; and I considered that there was no call upon me to continue the conversation; so I said: Protagoras, I don't wish to force the conversation upon you if you had rather not, but when you are willing to argue with me in such a way that I can follow you, then I will argue with you. Now you, as is said of you by others and as you say of yourself, are able to have discussions in shorter forms of speech as well as in longer, for you are a master of wisdom; but I cannot manage these long speeches: I only wish that I could. You, on the other hand, who are capable of either, ought to speak shorter as I beg you, and then we might converse. But I see that you are disinclined, and as I have an engagement which will prevent my staying to hear you at length (for I have to be in another place), I will depart; although I should have liked to have heard you.

Thus I spoke, and was rising from my seat, when Callias seized me by the hand, and in his left hand caught hold of this old cloak of mine. He said: We cannot let you go, Socrates, for if you leave us there will be an end of our discussions: I must therefore beg you to remain, as there is nothing in the world that I should like better than to hear you and Protagoras discourse. Do not deny the company this pleasure.

Now I had got up, and was in the act of departure. Son of Hipponicus, I replied, I have always admired, and do now heartily applaud and love your philosophical spirit, and I would gladly comply with your request, if I could. But the truth is that I cannot. And what you ask is as great an impossibility to me, as if you bade me run a race with Crison of Himera [49] when in his prime, or with some one of the long or day course runners.[50] To that I should reply, that I humbly make the same request to my own legs; and they can't comply. And therefore if you want to see Crison and me in the same stadium,[51] you must bid him slacken his speed to mine, for I cannot run quickly, and he can run slowly. And in like manner if you want to hear me and Protagoras discoursing, you must ask him to shorten his answers, and keep to the point, as he did at first; if not, how can there be any discussion? For discussion is one thing, and

---

[49] Crison (krī'son); Himera (hĭm'e-ra): a Greek city on the north coast of Sicily.

[50] It is interesting to note in this connection that in the revived Olympian Games which took place at Athens in the summer of 1896, while American, German, and other foreign athletes won most of the prizes, a Greek peasant won the long race from Marathon to Athens, a distance of over twenty miles.

[51] Stadium (stā'dĭ-ŭm): Greek name for the foot-race course.

making an oration is quite another, according to my way of thinking.

But you see, Socrates, said Callias, that Protagoras may fairly claim to speak in his own way, just as you claim to speak in yours.

Here Alcibiades interposed, and said: That, Callias, is not a fair statement of the case. For our friend Socrates admits that he cannot make a speech—in this he yields the palm to Protagoras; but I should be greatly surprised if he yielded to any living man in the power of holding and apprehending an argument. Now if Protagoras will make a similar admission, and confess that he is inferior to Socrates in argumentative skill, that is enough for Socrates; but if he claims a superiority in argument as well, let him ask and answer—not, when a question is asked, having recourse to shifts and evasions, and instead of answering, making a speech at such length that most of his hearers forget the question at issue (not that Socrates is likely to forget—I will be bound for that, although he may pretend in fun that he has a bad memory). And Socrates appears to me to be more in the right than Protagoras; that is my opinion, and every man ought to say what he thinks.

When Alcibiades had done speaking, some one—Critias, I believe—went on to say: O Prodicus and Hippias, Callias appears to me to be a partisan of Protagoras. And this led Alcibiades, who loves opposition, to take the other side. But we should not be partisans either of Socrates or Protagoras; let us rather unite in entreating both of them not to break up the discussion.

Prodicus added: That, Critias, seems to me to be well said, for those who are present at such discussions ought to be impartial hearers of both the speakers; remembering, however, that impartiality is not the same as equality, for both sides should be impartially heard, and yet an equal meed should not be assigned to both of them; but to the wiser a higher meed should be given, and a lower to the less wise. And I as well as Critias would beg you, Protagoras and Socrates, to grant our request, which is, that you will argue with one another and not wrangle; for friends argue with friends out of good-will, but only adversaries and enemies wrangle. And then our meeting will be delightful; for in this way you, who are the speakers, will be most likely to win esteem, and not praise only, among us who are your audience; for esteem is a sincere conviction of the hearers' souls, but praise is often an insincere expression of men uttering words contrary to their conviction. And thus we who are the hearers will be gratified and not pleased; for gratification is of the mind when receiving wisdom and knowledge, but pleasure is of the body when eating or experiencing some other bodily delight. Thus spoke Prodicus, and many of the company applauded his words.

Hippias the sage spoke next. He said: All of you who are here present I reckon to be kinsmen and friends and fellow-citizens, by nature and not by law; for by nature like is akin to like, whereas law is the tyrant of mankind, and often compels us to do many things which are against nature. How great would be the disgrace then, if we, who know the nature of things, and are the wisest of the Hellenes, and as such are met together in this city, which is the metropolis of wisdom, and in the greatest and most glorious house of this city, should have nothing to show worthy of this height of dignity, but should only quarrel with one another like the meanest of mankind. I do pray and advise you, Protagoras, and you, Socrates, to agree upon a compromise. Let us be your peacemakers. And do not you, Socrates, aim at this precise and extreme brevity in discourse, if Protagoras objects, but loosen and let go the reins of speech, that your words may be grander and become you better. Neither do you, Protagoras, go forth on the gale with every sail set out of sight of land into an ocean of words, but let there be a mean observed by both of you. Do as I say. And let me also suggest and suppose further, that you choose an arbiter or overseer or president; he will keep watch over your words and reduce them to their proper length.

338-
347

This proposal was received by the company with universal approval; and Callias said that he would not let me off, and that I was to choose an arbiter. But I said that to choose an umpire of discourse would be unseemly; for if the person chosen was inferior, then the inferior or worse ought not to preside over the better; or if he was equal, neither would that be well; for he who is our equal will do as we do, and what will be the use of choosing him? And if you say "Let us have a better then," to that I answer that you cannot have any one who is wiser than Protagoras. And if you choose another who is not really better, and whom you only say is better, to put another over him as though he were an inferior person would be an unworthy reflection on him; not that, as far as I am concerned, any reflection is of much consequence to me. Let me tell you then what I will do in order that the conversation and discussion may go on as you desire. If Protagoras is not disposed to answer, let him ask and I will answer; and I will endeavor to show at the same time how, as I maintain, he ought to answer: and when I have answered as many questions as he likes to ask, let him in like manner answer; and if he seems to be not very ready at answering the exact questions, you and I will unite in entreating him, as you entreated me, not to spoil the discussion. And this will require no special arbiter: you shall all of you be arbiters.

This was generally approved, and Protagoras, though very much against his will, was obliged to agree that he would ask questions; and when he had put a sufficient number of them, that he would answer in his turn those which he was asked in short replies.

[Protagoras proposes to base his questions on a certain passage from the poet Simonides, relating to virtue. The ensuing discussion which forms a long digression, some scholars claim to be a satire on the hypercritical methods of interpretation employed by the Sophists. In the course of the discussion however, Socrates gives expression to his doctrine that knowledge is virtue, as follows:] **339-347**

Simonides was not so ignorant as to say that he praised those who did no evil voluntarily, as though there were some who did evil voluntarily. For no wise man, as I believe, will allow that any human being errs voluntarily, or voluntarily does evil and dishonorable actions; but they are very well aware that all who do evil and dishonorable things do them against their will.

[The doctrine that a man cannot knowingly do wrong is fundamental with Socrates and is brought out more fully later in the dialogue. At present he employs it to interpret the poem under discussion. His explanation of the poem is long and elaborate. When he had finished,]

Hippias said: I think, Socrates, that you have given a very good explanation of this poem; but I have also an excellent interpretation of my own which I will expound to you, if you will allow me.

Nay, Hippias, said Alcibiades; not now, but another time. At present we must abide by the compact which was made between Socrates and Protagoras, to the effect that as long as Protagoras is willing to ask, Socrates should answer; or that if he would rather answer, then that Socrates should ask.

I said: I wish Protagoras either to ask or answer as he is inclined; but I would rather have done with poems and odes, if you do not object, and come back to the question about which I was asking you at first, Protagoras, and by your help make an end of that. The talk about the poet seems to me like a commonplace entertainment to which a vulgar company have recourse; who, because they are not able to converse or amuse one another, while they are drinking, with the sound of their own voices and conversation by reason of their stupidity, raise the price of flute-girls in the market, hiring for a great sum the voice of a flute instead of their own breath, to be the medium of intercourse among them: but where the company are real gentlemen and men of education, you will see no flute-girls, nor dancing-girls, nor harp-girls; and they have no nonsense or games, but are contented with one another's conversation, of which their own voices are the medium, and which they carry on by turns and in an orderly manner, even though they are very liberal in their potations. And a company like this of ours, and men such as we profess to be, do not require the help of another's voice, or of the poets whom you cannot interrogate about the meaning of what they are saying; people who cite them declaring, some that the poet has one meaning, and others that he has another; and there arises a dispute which can never be put to the proof. This sort of entertainment they decline, and prefer to talk with one another, and try one another's mettle in conversation. And these are the sort of models which I desire that you and I should imitate. Leaving the poets, and keeping to ourselves, let us try the mettle of one another and of the truth in conversation. And if you have a mind to ask I am ready to answer; or if you would rather, do you answer, and give me the opportunity of taking up and completing our unfinished argument.

I made these and some similar observations; but Protagoras would not distinctly say which he would do. Thereupon Alcibiades turned to Callias, and said: Do you think, Callias, that Protagoras is fair in refusing to say whether he will or will not answer? for I certainly think that he is unfair; he ought either to proceed with the argument, or distinctly to refuse to proceed, that we may know his intention; and then Socrates will be able to discourse with some one else, and the rest of the company will be free to talk with one another.

I think that Protagoras was really made ashamed by these words of Alcibiades, and when the prayers of Callias and the company were superadded, he was at last induced to argue, and said that I might ask and he would answer.

So I said: Do not imagine, Protagoras, that I have any other interest in asking questions of you but that of clearing up my own difficulties. For I think that Homer was very right in saying that "When two go together one sees before the other," for all men who have a companion are readier in deed, word, or thought; but if a man "sees a thing when he is alone," he goes about straightway seeking until he finds some one to whom he may show his discoveries, and who may confirm him in them. And I would rather hold discourse with you than with any one, because I think that no man has a better understanding of most things which a good man may be expected to understand, and in particular of virtue. For who is there, but you?—who not only claim to be a good man and a gentleman, for many are this, and yet have not the power of making others good. Whereas you are not only good yourself, but also the cause of goodness in others. Moreover such confidence have you in yourself, that although other Sophists conceal their profession, you proclaim in the face of Hellas that you are a Sophist or teacher of virtue and education, and are the first who demanded pay in return. How then can I do otherwise than invite you to the examination of these subjects, and ask questions and take advice of you? Indeed, I must.

[Socrates now returns to the original question—whether the virtues are one or many—and wishes Protagoras to state his opinion again. Protagoras answers that the virtues are not one but many, and that while four of the virtues, justice, temperance, holiness, and wisdom, are to some extent similar, the fifth, courage, is very different from the rest. For, he claims, a man may be remarkable for his courage, but utterly lacking in justice, temperance, wisdom, and holiness.

Socrates proceeds in the following way to prove that courage is one with the other virtues. First, the courageous man is the confident man, as Protagoras himself allows. What gives confidence to a man, for example, to a horseman or a soldier? Clearly in every case, the confidence of a man comes from his knowledge of his profession. When a man is confident about matters of which he is ignorant, we call him mad. His is not true courage. When Protagoras concedes that confidence or courage is always derived from knowledge, he contradicts his previous assertion that a man may be ignorant and still courageous. To be consistent he must admit that courage and wisdom are one. He evades the point by complaining that Socrates has unfairly attributed to his words meanings that he did not intend, and he tries to show how he would make a distinction between courage and confidence.

Socrates abruptly changes his point of attack. Some men, he says, live well, and others ill. Those who live pleasantly, live well, and those who live in pain, live ill. Protagoras agrees. Now Socrates wishes to know whether pleasure is the only good and pain the only evil. Protagoras hesitates to make such an assumption without qualification. He would rather say with most men, that some pleasant things are good and some painful things evil. He wishes, however, to inquire into the truth of the matter, and Socrates, who is to lead the discussion, begins by asking the nature of knowledge (This seems to be a digression, but only for the moment):]

Now the rest of the world are of opinion that knowledge is a principle not of strength, or of rule, or of command; their notion is that a man may have knowledge, and yet that the knowledge which is in him may be overmastered by anger, or pleasure, or pain, or love, or perhaps fear,—just as if knowledge were a slave, and might be dragged about anyhow. Now is that your view ? or do you think that knowledge is a noble and commanding thing, which cannot be overcome, and will not allow a man, if he only knows the difference of good and evil, to do anything which is contrary to knowledge, but that wisdom will have strength to help him ?

[Protagoras holds the latter view, for he believes that wisdom and knowledge are the highest of human things. He is not inclined to trouble himself about the opinion of the common people. Socrates, however, has a purpose in showing how it is that mankind in general have come to have a wrong opinion of knowledge. The error, he claims, arises from a mistaken notion of pleasure and pain, good and evil. That it is impossible for a man who has knowledge of good and evil, to do evil, will be clear when we understand the true relations of pleasure, pain, good and evil. The common saying that men are overcome by pleasure implies that pleasures are sometimes evil. Now, are the pleasures of eating and drinking, for example, by which men are said to be overcome, evil simply because they are pleasant? No one would claim this. All will agree that they are evil solely on account of their evil consequences—because they produce disease, pain, poverty and the like, in the future. Moreover, disease with its accompanying ills, deprives men of many pleasures greater than those of eating and drinking. So in all cases when we say men are overcome by pleasure, we mean that they are overcome by a lesser pleasure. In a similar way, painful things are sometimes spoken of as good. Burning, cutting and starving, as employed by the physician, though they occasion the greatest immediate suffering, are good because they bring afterwards health, power, and wealth. Since even pain is good when it takes away greater pain or brings pleasure, and since pleasure is evil only when it ends in pain or deprives us of greater pleasure, we are justified in saying that pleasure is good and pain evil. Thus it becomes clear how it is impossible for a man knowingly to do evil, for every man wishes to be happy and to have as much pleasure and as little pain in life a possible.]

If you weigh pleasures against pleasures, you of course take the more and greater; or if you weigh pains against pains, you take the fewer and the less ; or if pleasures against pains, then you choose that course of action in which the painful is exceeded by the pleasant, whether the distant by the near or the near by the distant; and you avoid that course of action in which the pleasant is exceeded by the painful.

[When we make the many choices in life whereby we endeavor to attain a sum of pleasures greater than the sum of pains, what is to be our guide to right choice? In the physical world, objects appear greater when near and smaller when remote, and we need some standard of measurement in order to judge truly of their size. We have seen that the same is true in the case of pleasures and pains. Distance affects their apparent size. We are in danger of being deceived by appearance, and our only salvation lies in an ability to measure pleasures and pains and judge rightly of their true size and relation.]

Is not the power of appearance that deceiving art which makes us wander up and down and take the things at one time of which we repent at another, both in our actions and in our choice of things great and small? But the art of measurement is that which would do away with the effect of appearances, and, showing the truth, would fain teach the soul at last to find rest in the truth, and would thus save our life.

[Since this sort of measuring is clearly one kind of knowledge, we see that knowledge is the mighty and ruling principle in human life. Ignorance must then be the origin of all evil, for no one will knowingly pursue a course of evil which leads to pain when he knows the path of good to pleasure. Hippias, Prodicus, and Protagoras agree with this conclusion.

Socrates now returns to re-examine the virtue of courage in the light of what has just been said about knowledge. Fear is defined as expectation of evil. A man will not voluntarily pursue what he fears, for no one will voluntarily pursue what he thinks to be evil. Ignorance causes a man to judge that to be evil which is not evil. The cowardly man is he who through ignorance fears that which is really not evil. For example, the coward refuses to go to war because he forms a wrong estimate of what is good, honorable, and pleasurable.

The courageous man goes to war, because he knows it will bring future honor and good; and for these he is willing to bear the present pain. Thus we see courage is knowledge and cowardice is ignorance. The five virtues which Protagoras at first held to be different in nature are proven to be one —wisdom.[52] Protagoras is reluctant to assent.

Socrates closes the narration of the dialogue as follows:]

My only object, I said, in continuing the discussion, has been the desire to ascertain the relations of virtue and the essential nature of virtue; for if this were clear, I am very sure that the other controversy which has been carried on at great length by both of us—you affirming and I denying that virtue can be taught—would also have become clear. The result of our discussion appears to me to be singular. For if the argument has a human voice, that voice would be heard laughing at us and saying: Protagoras and Socrates, you are strange beings; there are you who were saying that virtue cannot be taught, contradicting yourself now in the attempt to show that all things are knowledge, including justice, and temperance, and courage—which tends to show that virtue can certainly be taught; for if virtue were other than knowledge, as Protagoras attempted to show, then clearly virtue cannot be taught; but if virtue is entirely knowledge, as you, Socrates, are seeking to show, then I cannot but suppose that virtue is capable of being taught. Protagoras, on the other hand, who started by saying that it might be taught, is now eager to show that it is anything rather than knowledge; and if this is true, it must be quite incapable of being taught. Now I, Protagoras, perceiving this terrible confusion of ideas, have a great desire that they should be cleared up. And I should like to carry on the discussion until we ascertain what virtue is, and whether capable of being taught or not, lest haply Epimetheus should trip us up and deceive us in the argument, as he forgot to provide for us in the story; and I prefer

[52] " He (Socrates) defines all the particular virtues in such a way as to make them consist in knowledge of some kind, the difference between them being determined by the difference of their objects. He is pious who knows what is right toward God; he is just who knows what is right toward men; he is brave who knows how to treat dangers properly; he is prudent and wise who knows how to use what is good and noble, and how to avoid what is evil. In a word, all virtues are referred to wisdom or knowledge, which are one and the same."—Zeller's Socrates, Chap. VII.

your Prometheus to your Epimetheus: of him I make use whenever I am busy about these questions in Promethean care of my own life. And if you have no objection, as I said at first, I should like to have your help in the inquiry.

Protagoras replied: Socrates, I am not of a base nature, and I am the last man in the world to be envious. I cannot but applaud your enthusiasm in the conduct of an argument. As I have often said, I admire you above all men whom I know, certainly above all men of your age; and I believe that you will become very eminent in philosophy. Let us come back to the subject at some future time; at present we had better turn to something else.

By all means, I said, if that is your wish; for I too ought long since to have kept the engagement of which I spoke before, and only tarried because I could not refuse the request of the noble Callias. This finished the conversation, and we went our way.

THE SYMPOSIUM

INTRODUCTION

THE subject of the Symposium is love. Five set speeches are made upon this theme besides that of Alcibiades, which, though professedly about Socrates, is also really about love. Phædrus dwells especially upon love as an incentive to courageous deeds. Pausanias distinguishes between the heavenly and the earthly love. Eryximachus, the physician, seeks to show a common principle in the love of the body and the love of the mind. Aristophanes, the writer of comedy, under the guise of an extravagant myth, suggests that man cannot live in isolation, that love is the necessary mediator between men, and that the love of the world is a type of the higher love. Agathon, as becomes the master of tragedy, makes a noble poem in eloquent praise of love the divine. The earthly love is repeatedly discussed in these speeches with a frankness which seems to our ears very gross. Each of the speeches, however, makes some contribution to the theme, which Plato considers of value. Socrates pretends to have been instructed as to the sober truth about love by a wise woman, Diotima. In a word, he believes that love is a principle which ranges all the way from animal desire to the hunger and thirst after wisdom, and that in the highest as well as in the lowest form of love, the soul longs to beget the likeness of itself in others. True love is not love of the beautiful for itself or for oneself alone, but it is love of the " birth in beauty " in others. In such fashion does Plato realize the idea of love for God and for man.

But the Symposium is not simply a series of arguments. It is perhaps more evidently than any other of Plato's writings, a dramatic portrayal of the theme and of the varied views of men about the theme. The five speeches preceding that of Socrates are doubtless to be regarded as dramatic in this sense. Besides this, many incidents of the story illustrate the theme. In a variety of ways it is suggested that Socrates is so wholly a lover of truth that the things of this world are nothing to him. He stands in the snow without feeling it. He conducts himself in battle without fear. He drinks and is not made drunk. He is assailed with temptation to vice, but is not really tempted. Above all he passes at times (two instances are mentioned in the dialogue) into an ecstatic state where the search of his soul after truth makes him for hours completely oblivious to all earthly things. The best illustration of the nature and power of true love is given in the speech of Alcibiades.[1] Here is shown in the most perfect way that strong and genuine love of wisdom and holiness is, inevitably, also strong and genuine desire and power to allure others toward wisdom and holiness.

A word of warning should be given. As Jowett says, "if it be true that there are more things in the Symposium than any commentator has dreamed of, it is also true that many things have been imagined which are not really to be found there." Do not pigeon-hole the Symposium after one reading. It is "full of divine and golden images," with which a life-time is not too long to make full acquaintance.

[1] See General Introduction, page xxx.

THE SYMPOSIUM

PERSONS OF THE DIALOGUE.[1]

APOLLODORUS, who repeats to his
COMPANION *the dialogue which
he had heard from Aristodemus,
and had already once narrated
to Glaucon.*
PHÆDRUS.

PAUSANIAS.
ERYXIMACHUS.
ARISTOPHANES.
AGATHON.
SOCRATES.
ALCIBIADES.

A TROOP OF REVELERS.

SCENE:—The House of Agathon.

I BELIEVE that I am prepared with an answer. For the day before yesterday I was coming from my own home at Phalerum[2] to the city, and one of my acquaintance, who had caught a sight of the back of me at a distance, in merry mood commanded me to halt: Apollodorus, he cried, O thou man of Phalerum, halt! So I did as I was bid; and then he said, I was looking for you, Apollodorus, only just now, that I might hear about the discourses in praise of love, which were delivered by Socrates, Alcibiades, and others, at Agathon's supper. Phœnix the son of Philip told another person, who told me of them, and he said that you knew; but he was himself very indistinct, and I wish

Steph.
172

---

[1] Apollodorus (à-pŏl'lo-dō'rus): friend and disciple of Socrates, and present at his death. See Phædo, 59 and 117.
Phædrus: see the dialogue Phædrus.
Pausanias: see Protagoras, 315 and note 22.
Eryximachus: a physician. See Protagoras, 315 and note 18; Phædrus, 268.
Aristophanes: comic poet. See Apology, note 5.
Agathon (ăg'a-thon, —-400 B.C.); an Athenian tragic poet, called the "fair Agathon" on account of his extreme beauty. See Protagoras, 315.
Alcibiades: see Protagoras, note 1.
[2] Phalerum (fă-lē'rum): one of the harbors of Athens.

that you would give me an account of them. Who but you should be the reporter of the words of your friend? And first tell me, he said, were you present at this meeting?

Your informant, Glaucon, I said, must have been very indistinct indeed, if you imagine that the occasion was recent, or that I could have been present.

Why, yes, he replied, that was my impression.

But how is that possible? I said. For Agathon has not been in Athens for many years (are you aware of that?), and my acquaintance with Socrates, of whose every action and word I now make a daily study, is not as yet of three years' standing. I used to be running about the world, thinking that I was doing something, and would have done anything rather than be a philosopher: I was almost as miserable as you are now.

173

Well, he said, cease from jesting, and tell me when the meeting occurred.

In our boyhood, I replied, when Agathon won the prize with his first tragedy,[3] on the day after that on which he and his chorus offered the sacrifice of victory.

That is a long while ago, he said; and who told you—did Socrates?

No indeed, I replied, but the same person who told Phœnix; he was a little fellow, who never wore any shoes, Aristodemus, of the deme of Cydathenæum.[4] He had been at this feast; and I think that there was no one in those days who was a more devoted admirer of Socrates. Moreover, I asked Socrates about the truth of some parts of his narrative, and he confirmed them. Then, said Glaucon, let us have the tale over again; is not the road to Athens made for conversation? And so we walked, and talked of the discourses on love; and therefore, as I said at first, I am prepared with an answer, and will have another rehearsal, if you like. For I love to speak or to hear others speak of philosophy; there is

---

[3] The Greek drama had its origin in one of the chief religious festivals of the people—the Dionysia (dī'o-nȳ'sĭ-a). It was originally a chorus, sung in honor of the god Dionysus (dī'o-nȳ'sus). Later, actors were introduced, but the chorus was retained. The drama became an important part of the festival. Three days were given to the public presentation of new dramas. The State offered prizes to the contesting authors. The first prize was a crown, publicly presented. This was the highest distinction that could be conferred on a dramatic author at Athens.

[4] Aristodemus (ȧ-rĭs'to-dē'mus). Cydathenæum (sĭd-ath-e-nē'um).

the greatest pleasure in that, to say nothing of the profit. But when I hear any other discourses, especially those of you rich men and traders, they are irksome to me; and I pity you who are my companions, because you always think that you are hard at work when really you are idling. And I dare say that you pity me in return, whom you regard as an unfortunate wight, which I perhaps am. But I certainly know of you what you only think of me—there is the difference.

Companion. I see, Apollodorus, that you are just the same,—always speaking evil of yourself, and of others; and I do believe that you pity all mankind, beginning with yourself and including everybody else with the exception of Socrates, true in this to your old name, which, however deserved, I know not how you acquired, of Apollodorus the madman; for your humor is always to be out of humor with yourself and with everybody except Socrates.

Apollodorus. Yes, friend, and I am proved to be mad, and out of my wits, because I have these notions of myself and you; no other evidence is required.

Com. I have no wish to dispute about that, Apollodorus; but let me renew my request that you would repeat the tale of love.

Apoll. Well, the tale of love was on this wise: But perhaps I had better begin at the beginning, and endeavor to repeat to you the words as Aristodemus gave them. 174

He said that he met Socrates fresh from the bath and sandaled; and as the sight of the sandals was unusual, he asked him whither he was going that he was so fine.

To a banquet at Agathon's, he replied, whom I refused yesterday, fearing the crowd that there would be at his sacrifice, but promising that I would come to-day instead; and I have put on my finery because he is a fine creature. What say you to going with me unbidden?

Yes, I replied, I will go with you, if you like.

Follow then, he said, and let us demolish the proverb that—

" To the feasts of lesser men the good unbidden go; "

instead of which our proverb will run that—

" To the feasts of the good unbidden go the good;"

and this alteration may be supported by the authority of Homer, who not only demolishes but literally outrages this proverb. For after picturing Agamemnon [5] as the most valiant of men, he makes Menelaus, who is but a soft-hearted warrior, come of his own accord to the sacrificial feast of Agamemnon, the worse to the better.

I am afraid, Socrates, said Aristodemus, that I shall rather be the inferior person, who, like Menelaus in Homer,—

"To the feasts of the wise unbidden goes."

But I shall say that I was bidden of you, and then you will have to make the excuse.

"Two going together,"

he replied, in Homeric fashion, may invent an excuse by the way.

This was the style of their conversation as they went along; and a comical thing happened—Socrates stayed behind in a fit of abstraction, and desired Aristodemus, who was waiting, to go on before him. When he reached the house of Agathon he found the doors wide open, and a servant coming out met him, and led him at once into the banqueting-hall in which the guests were reclining, for the banquet was about to begin. Welcome, Aristodemus, said Agathon; you are just in time to sup with us; if you come on any other errand put that off, and make one of us, as I was looking for you yesterday and meant to have asked you, if I could have found you. But what have you done with Socrates?

I turned round and saw that Socrates was missing, and I had to explain that he had been with me a moment before, and that I came by his invitation.

You were quite right in coming, said Agathon; and where is he himself?

175 He was behind me just now, as I entered, he said, and I cannot think what has become of him.

Go and look for him, boy, said Agathon, and bring him in; do you, Aristodemus, meanwhile take the place by Eryximachus.

Then he said that the attendant assisted him to wash, and that he lay down, and presently another servant came in and said that our friend Socrates had retired into the portico of the neighboring house. "There he is fixed, and when I call to him," said the servant, "he will not stir."

How strange, said Agathon; then you must call him again, and keep calling him.

[5] See Apology, note 21.

Let him alone, said my informant; he has just a habit of stopping anywhere and losing himself without any reason; don't disturb him, as I believe he will soon appear.

Well, if you say that, I will not interfere with him, said Agathon. My domestics, who on these occasions become my masters, shall entertain us as their guests. "Put on the table whatever you like," he said to the servants, "as usual when there is no one to give you orders, which I never do. Imagine that you are our hosts, and that I and the company are your guests; and treat us well, and then we shall commend you." After this they supped; and during the meal Agathon several times expressed a wish to send for Socrates, but Aristodemus would not allow him; and when the feast was half over—for the fit, as usual, was not of long duration—Socrates entered. Agathon, who was reclining alone at the end of the table, begged that he would take the place next to him; that I may touch the sage, he said, and get some of that wisdom which came into your mind in the portico. For I am certain that you would not have left until you had found what you were seeking.

How I wish, said Socrates, taking his place as he was desired, that wisdom could be infused through the medium of touch, out of the full into the empty man, like the water which the wool sucks out of the full vessel into an empty one; in that case how much I should prize sitting by you! For you would have filled me full of gifts of wisdom, plenteous and fair, in comparison of which my own is of a very mean and questionable sort, no better than a dream; but yours is bright and only beginning, and was manifested forth in all the splendor of youth the day before yesterday, in the presence of more than thirty thousand Hellenes.[6]

You are insolent, said Agathon; and you and I will have to settle hereafter who bears off the palm of wisdom, and of this Dionysus[7] shall be the judge; but at present you are better occupied with the banquet.

Socrates took his place on the couch; and when the meal was ended, and the libations offered, and after a hymn had been sung to the God, and there had been the usual ceremonies,—as they were about to commence drinking, Pausanias reminded them that they had had a bout yesterday, from which

---
[6] Greeks. See Protagoras, note 11.
[7] The god whose festival the city was then celebrating.

he and most of them were still suffering, and they ought to be allowed to recover, and not go on drinking to-day. He would therefore ask, How the drinking could be made easiest?

I entirely agree, said Aristophanes, that we should, by all means, get off the drinking, having been myself one of those who were yesterday drowned in drink.

I think that you are right, said Eryximachus the son of Acumenus; but I should like to hear one other person speak. What are the inclinations of our host?

I am not able to drink, said Agathon.

Then, said Eryximachus, the weak heads like myself, Aristodemus, Phædrus, and others who never can drink, are fortunate in finding that the stronger ones are not in a drinking mood. (I do not include Socrates, who is an exceptional being, and able either to drink or to abstain.) Well, then, as the company seem indisposed to drink much, I may be forgiven for saying, as a physician, that drinking is a bad practice, which I never, if I can help, follow, and certainly do not recommend to another, least of all to any one who still feels the effects of yesterday's carouse.

I always follow what you advise, and especially what you prescribe as a physician, rejoined Phædrus the Myrrhinusian, and the rest of the company, if they are wise, will do the same.

All agreed that drinking was not to be the order of the day. Then, said Eryximachus, as you are all agreed that drinking is to be voluntary, and that there is to be no compulsion, I move, in the next place, that the flute-girl, who has just made her appearance, be told to go away; she may play to herself, or, if she has a mind, to the women who are within. But on this day let us have conversation instead; and, if you will allow me, I will tell you what sort of conversation. This proposal having been accepted, Eryximachus proceeded as follows:—

I will begin, he said, after the manner of Melanippe in Euripides[8],—

"Not mine the word"

which I am about to speak, but that of Phædrus. For he is in the habit of complaining that, whereas other gods have

---

[8] Euripides (ū-rĭp'ĭ-dēz, 480-406 B.C.): a celebrated Athenian tragic poet. Melanippe (mĕl'a-nĭp'pe): a character in a lost play by him.

poems and hymns made in their honor by the poets, who are so many, the great and glorious god, Love, has not a single panegyrist or encomiast. Many Sophists also, as for example the excellent Prodicus,[9] have descanted in prose on the virtues of Heracles[10] and other heroes; and, what is still more extraordinary, I have met with a philosophical work in which the utility of salt has been made the theme of an eloquent discourse; and many other like things have had a like honor bestowed upon them. And only to think that there should have been an eager interest created about them, and yet that to this day, as Phædrus well and truly says, no one has ever dared worthily to hymn Love's praises. This mighty deity has been neglected wholly! Now I want to offer Phædrus a contribution to his feast; nor do I see how the present company can, at this moment, do anything better than honor the god Love. And if you agree to this, there will be no lack of conversation; for I mean to propose that each of us in turn shall make a discourse in honor of Love. Let us have the best which he can make; and Phædrus, who is sitting first on the left hand, and is the father of the thought, shall begin.

No one will oppose that, Eryximachus, said Socrates; I certainly cannot refuse to speak on the only subject of which I profess to have any knowledge, and Agathon and Pausanias will surely assent; and there can be no doubt of Aristophanes, who is always in the company of Dionysus[11] and Aphrodite[12]; nor will any one disagree of those whom I see around me. The proposal, as I am aware, may seem hard upon us whose place is last; but that does not matter if we hear some good speeches first. Let Phædrus begin the praise of Love, and good luck to him. All the company expressed their assent, and desired him to do as Socrates bade him.

178-188

["Phædrus began by affirming that Love is a mighty god, and wonderful among gods and men, but especially won-

---

[9] See Protagoras, note 1.
[10] See Euthydemus, note 20.
[11] God of wine—the Roman Bacchus.
[12] Aphrodite (ăf'rō-dī'te): goddess of love and beauty, corresponding to the Roman Venus.

derful in his birth." He is the oldest of the gods and without parentage. As Hesiod says:

> "First Chaos came, and then broad-bosomed Earth,
> The everlasting seat of all that is,
> And Love."

Parmenides [13] agrees with Hesiod. Love is not only the oldest but also the most beneficent of the gods. The greatest blessing to any youth is to love and be loved. Love implants in the youth the sense of honor. The veriest coward becomes an inspired hero when the god breathes love into his soul. An army of lovers, though a mere handful, would overcome the world. For love a man will surrender his life as Alcestis [14] did for her husband, and as Achilles [15] did to avenge the death of his friend.]

Now Achilles was quite aware, for he had been told by his mother, that he might avoid death and return home, and live to a good old age, if he abstained from slaying Hector. Nevertheless he gave his life to revenge his friend, and dared to die, not only on his behalf, but after his death. Wherefore the gods honored him even above Alcestis, and sent him to the Islands of the Blest. These are my reasons for affirming that Love is the eldest and noblest and mightiest of the gods, and the chiefest author and giver of happiness and virtue, in life and after death.

This, or something like this, was the speech of Phædrus; and some other speeches followed which Aristodemus did not remember; the next which he repeated was that of Pausanias.

[Pausanias said that the speech of Phædrus had assumed that there was only one love, whereas there are really two—one a heavenly, the other a common. Pausanias characterized these two kinds of love as follows:]

Evil is the vulgar lover who loves the body rather than the soul, and who is inconstant because he is a lover of the incon-

---

[13] Parmenides (păr-měn'ĭ-dēz, 520?— B.C.): a Greek philosopher and poet.
[14] Alcestis (ăl-sěs'tĭs): the beautiful young wife of Admetus (ăd-mē'tus), a mythical king of Thessaly. She sacrificed her own life to save that of her husband when the Fates decreed that he could live only on condition that some one die in his stead.
[15] See Apology, note 21.

stant; and therefore when the bloom of youth which he was desiring is over, he takes wings and flies away, in spite of all his words and promises; whereas the love of the noble mind, which is in union with the unchangeable, is everlasting.
. . . This is that love which is the love of the heavenly goddess, and is heavenly, and of great price to individuals and cities, making the lover and the beloved alike eager in the work of their own improvement. But all other loves are the offspring of the common or vulgar goddess. To you, Phædrus, I offer this my encomium of love, which is as good as I could make on the sudden.

When Pāusănĭăs căme tŏ ă păuse (this is the balanced way in which I have been taught by the wise to speak), Aristodemus said that the turn of Aristophanes was next, but that either he had eaten too much, or from some other cause he had the hiccough, and was obliged to change with Eryximachus the physician, who was reclining on the couch below him. Eryximachus, he said, you ought either to stop my hiccough, or to speak in my turn until I am better.

I will do both, said Eryximachus: I will speak in your turn, and do you speak in mine; and while I am speaking let me recommend you to hold your breath, and if this fails, then to gargle with a little water; and if the hiccough still continues, tickle your nose with something and sneeze; and if you sneeze once or twice, even the most violent hiccough is sure to go. In the mean time I will take your turn, and you shall take mine. I will do as you prescribe, said Aristophanes, and now get on.

[Eryximachus constructed a myth whose purpose was to show that love is the principle of unity and health in body and soul and in all nature. He concluded as follows:]

And that love, especially, which is concerned with the good, and which is perfected in company with temperance and justice, whether among gods or men, has the greatest power, and is the source of all our happiness and harmony and friendship with the gods which are above us, and with one another. I dare say that I have omitted several things which might be said in praise of Love, but this was not intentional, and you, Aristophanes, may now supply the omission or take some other line of commendation; as I perceive that you are cured of the hiccough.

189-193 Yes, said Aristophanes, who followed, the hiccough is gone; not, however, until I applied the sneezing; and I wonder whether the principle of order in the human frame requires this sort of noises and ticklings, for I no sooner applied the sneezing than I was cured.

Eryximachus said: Take care, friend Aristophanes, you are beginning with a joke, and I shall have to watch if you talk nonsense; and the interruption will be occasioned by your own fault.

You are very right, said Aristophanes, laughing, and I will retract what I said; and do you please not to watch me, as I fear that in what I am going to say, instead of making others laugh, which is to the manner born of our muse and would be all the better, I shall only be laughed at by them.

[Aristophanes related another myth in which he represented that the principle of all human activity is desire to complete our deficiencies and attain wholeness and unity of life. He concluded as follows:]

And I believe that if all of us obtained our love, and each one had his particular beloved, thus returning to his original nature, then our race would be happy. And if this would be best of all, that which would be best under present circumstances would be the nearest approach to such a union; and that will be the attainment of a congenial love. Therefore we shall do well to praise the god Love, who is the author of this gift, and who is also our greatest benefactor, leading us in this life back to our own nature, and giving us high hopes for the future, that if we are pious, he will restore us to our original state, and heal us and make us happy and blessed. This, Eryximachus, is my discourse of love, which, although different from yours, I must beg you to leave unassailed by the shafts of your ridicule, in order that each may have his turn; each, or rather either, for Agathon and Socrates are the only ones left.

Indeed, I am not going to attack you, said Eryximachus, for I thought your speech charming, and did I not know that Agathon and Socrates are masters in the art of love, I should be really afraid that they would have nothing to say, after all the world of things which have been said already. But, for all that, I am not without hopes.

Socrates said: You did your part well, Eryximachus; **194** but if you were as I am now, or rather as I shall be when Agathon has spoken, you would, indeed, be in a great strait.

You want to cast a spell over me, Socrates, said Agathon, in the hope that I may be disconcerted, thinking of the anticipation which the theatre has of my fine speech.

I should be strangely forgetful, Agathon, replied Socrates, of the courage and magnanimity which you showed when your own compositions were about to be exhibited, coming upon the stage with the actors and facing the whole theatre altogether undismayed, if I thought that your nerves could be fluttered at a small party of friends.

Do you think, Socrates, said Agathon, that my head is so full of the theatre as not to know how much more formidable to a man of sense a few good judges are than many fools?

Nay, replied Socrates, I should be very wrong in attributing to you, Agathon, that or any other want of refinement. And I am quite aware that if you happened to meet with any one whom you thought wise, you would care for his opinion much more than for that of the many. But then we, having been a part of the foolish many in the theatre, cannot be regarded as the select wise; though I know that if you chanced to light upon a really wise man, you would be ashamed of disgracing yourself before him,—would you not?

Yes, said Agathon.

But you would not be ashamed of disgracing yourself before the many?

Here Phædrus interrupted them, saying: Don't answer him, my dear Agathon; for if he can only get a partner with whom he can talk, especially a good-looking one, he will no longer care about the completion of our plan. Now I love to hear him talk; but just at present I must not forget the encomium on Love which I ought to receive from him and every one. When you and he have paid the tribute to the God, then you may talk.

Very good, Phædrus, said Agathon; I see no reason why I should not proceed with my speech, as I shall have other opportunities of conversing with Socrates. Let me say first how I ought to speak, and then speak.

The previous speakers, instead of praising the god Love, or unfolding his nature, appear to have congratulated mankind on the benefits which he confers upon them. But I would rather praise the God first, and then speak of his gifts; this is always the right way of praising everything. May I express unblamed then, that of all the blessed gods he is the blessedest and the best? And also the fairest, which I prove in this way: for, in the first place, Phædrus, he is the youngest, and of his youth he is himself the witness, fleeing out of the way of age, which is swift enough surely, swifter than most of us like: yet he cannot be overtaken by him; he is not a bird of that feather; youth and love live and move together,—like to like, as the proverb says. There are many things which Phædrus said about Love in which I agree with him; but I cannot agree that he is older than Iapetus [16] and Kronos [17]—that is not the truth; as I maintain, he is the youngest of the gods, and youthful ever. The ancient things of which Hesiod and Parmenides speak, if they were done at all, were done of necessity and not of love; had love been in those days, there would have been no chaining or mutilation of the gods, or other violence, but peace and sweetness, as there is now in heaven, since the rule of Love began. Love is young and also tender; he ought to have a poet like Homer to describe his tenderness, as Homer says of Ate,[18] that she is a goddess and tender:—

> " Her feet are tender, for she sets her steps,
> Not on the ground but on the heads of men: "

which is an excellent proof of her tenderness, because she walks not upon the hard but upon the soft. Let us adduce a similar proof of the tenderness of Love; for he walks not upon the earth, nor yet upon the skulls of men, which are hard enough, but in the hearts and souls of men: in them he walks and dwells and has his home. Not in every soul without ex-

---

[16] Iapetus (i-ăp'e-tus): an ancient Greek divinity, son of Uranus (Heaven), and Gæa (Earth). The Greeks regarded him as the ancestor of the human race.
[17] Kronos (krō'nos): brother of Iapetus, and father of Zeus.
[18] Ate (ā'tē): the goddess of infatuation; also the avenger of unrighteousness.

ception, for where there is hardness he departs, where there is softness there he dwells; and clinging always with his feet and in all manner of ways in the softest of soft places, how can he be other than the softest of all things? And he is the youngest as well as the tenderest, and also he is of flexile form; for without flexure he could not enfold all things, or wind his way into and out of every soul of man without being discovered, if he were hard. And a proof of his flexibility and symmetry of form is his grace, which is universally admitted to be in an especial manner the attribute of Love; ungrace and love are always at war with one another. The fairness of his complexion is revealed by his habitation among the flowers, for he dwells not amid unflowering or fading beauties, whether of body or soul or aught else, but in the place of flowers and scents, there he dwells and abides. Enough of his beauty,—of which, however, there is more to tell. But I must now speak of his virtue: his greatest glory is that he can neither do nor suffer wrong from any god or any man; for he suffers not by force if he suffers, for force comes not near him, neither does he act by force. For all serve him of their own free-will, and where there is love as well as obedience, there, as the laws which are the lords of the city say, is justice. And not only is he just but exceedingly temperate, for Temperance is the acknowledged ruler of the pleasures and desires, and no pleasure ever masters Love; he is their master and they are his servants; and if he conquers them he must be temperate indeed. As to courage, even the God of War is no match for him; he is the captive and Love is the lord, for love, the love of Aphrodite, masters him, as the tale runs; and the master is stronger than the servant. And if he conquers the bravest of all he must be himself the bravest. Of his courage and justice and temperance I have spoken; but I have yet to speak of his wisdom, and I must try to do my best, according to the measure of my ability. For in the first place he is a poet (and here, like Eryximachus, I magnify my art), and he is also the source of poesy in others, which he could not be if he were not himself a poet. And at the touch of him every one becomes a poet, even though he had no music in him before; this also is a proof that Love is a good poet and accomplished in all the musical arts; for no one can give to another that which he has not himself, or teach that of which he has

196

no knowledge. Who will deny that the creation of the animals is his doing? Are they not all the works of his wisdom, born and begotten of him? And as to the artists, do we not know that he only of them whom love inspires has the light of fame?—he whom love touches not walks in darkness. The arts of medicine and archery and divination were discovered by Apollo,[19] under the guidance of love and desire, so that he too is a disciple of Love. Also the melody of the Muses,[20] the metallurgy of Hephæstus,[21] the weaving of Athene,[22] the empire of Zeus[23] over gods and men, are all due to Love, who was the inventor of them. Love set in order the empire of the gods,—the love of beauty, as is evident, for of deformity there is no love. And formerly, as I was saying, dreadful deeds were done among the gods, because of the rule of necessity; but now since the birth of Love, and from the love of the beautiful, has sprung every good in heaven and earth. Therefore, Phædrus, I say of Love that he is the fairest and best in himself, and the cause of what is fairest and best in all other things. And I have a mind to say of him in verse that he is the god who—

"Gives peace on earth and calms the stormy deep,
Who stills the waves and bids the sufferer sleep."

He makes men to be of one mind at a banquet such as this, fulfilling them with affection and emptying them of disaffection. In sacrifices, banquets, dances, he is our lord,—supplying kindness and banishing unkindness, giving friendship and forgiving enmity, the joy of the good, the wonder of the wise, the amazement of the gods; desired by those who have no part in him, and precious to those who have the better part in him; parent of delicacy, luxury, desire, fondness, softness, grace; careful of the good, uncareful of the evil. In every word, work, wish, fear,—pilot, helper, defender, saviour; glory of gods and men, leader best and brightest: in whose footsteps let every man follow, chanting a hymn and joining

---

[19] One of the greatest and most beneficent of the Greek gods, commonly called the god of light.
[20] See Euthydemus, note 12.
[21] See Protagoras, note 39.
[22] See Protagoras, note 40.
[23] See Protagoras, note 41.

in that fair strain with which Love charms the souls of gods and men. Such is the discourse, Phædrus, half playful, yet having a certain measure of seriousness, which, according to my ability, I dedicate to the God.

When Agathon had done speaking, Aristodemus said that there was a general cheer; the fair youth was thought to have spoken in a manner worthy of himself, and of the God. And Socrates, looking at Eryximachus, said: Tell me, son of Acumenus, was I not a prophet? Did I not anticipate that Agathon would make a wonderful oration, and that I should be in a strait?

I think, said Eryximachus, that you were right in the first anticipation, but not in the second.

Why, my dear friend, said Socrates, must not I or any one be in a strait who has to speak after such a rich and varied discourse as that? I am especially struck with the beauty of the concluding words—who could listen to them without amazement? When I reflected on the immeasurable inferiority of my own powers, I was ready to run away for shame, if there had been any escape. For I was reminded of Gorgias,[24] and at the end of his speech I fancied that Agathon was shaking at me the Gorginian or Gorgonian head of the great master of rhetoric, which was simply to turn me and my speech into stone, as Homer says, and strike me dumb. And then I perceived how foolish I had been in consenting to take my turn with you in praising love, and saying that I too was a master of the art, when I really had no idea of the meaning of the word "praise," which appears to be another name for glorification, whether true or false; in which sense of the term I am unable to praise anything. For I in my simplicity imagined that the topics of praise should be true; this was to be the foundation, and that out of them the speaker was to choose the best and arrange them in the best order. And I felt quite proud, and thought that I could speak as well as another, as I knew the nature of true praise. Whereas I see now that the intention was to attribute to Love every species of greatness and glory, whether really belonging to him or not, without regard

---

[24] See Apology, note 7. Socrates here makes a play on the names Gorgias and Gorgon. The Gorgon was a legendary monster with hair of hissing snakes, and whose aspect was so terrible it turned all beholders to stone. The Greeks carved the Gorgon's head on their armor, and on walls and gates, in the belief that it would terrify and paralyze an enemy.

to truth or falsehood—that was no matter; for the original proposal seems to have been not that you should praise, but only that you should appear to praise him. And you attribute to Love every imaginable form of praise, and say that "he is all this," "the cause of all this" in order that you may exhibit him as the fairest and best of all; and this of course imposes on the unwary, but not on those who know him: and a noble and solemn hymn of praise have you rehearsed. But as I misunderstood the nature of the praise when I said that I would take my turn, I must beg to be absolved from the promise which (as Euripides would say) was a promise of the lips and not of the mind. Farewell then to such a strain: for that is not my way of praising; no, indeed, I cannot attain to that. But if you like to hear the truth about love, I am ready to speak in my own manner, though I will not make myself ridiculous by entering into any rivalry with you. Say then, Phædrus, whether you would like to have the truth about love, spoken in any words and in any order which may happen to come into my mind at the time. Will that be agreeable to you?

199-202

Aristodemus said that Pæhdrus and the company bid him take his own course.

[After his usual manner, Socrates avoided a long set speech in the outset. He pretended that he had once met a very wise woman by the name of Diotima[25] who had taught him the nature of love. She led Socrates to the view that love is not as the former speakers had declared, beautiful or good or wise or divine. Love is child of the god Plenty and of Poverty. Love is a mediator between the divine and human.]

"Love is a great spirit, and like all that is spiritual he is intermediate between the divine and the mortal." "And what is the nature of this spiritual power?" I said. "This is the power," she said, "which interprets and conveys to the gods the prayers and sacrifices of men, and to men the commands and rewards of the gods; and this power spans the chasm which divides them, and in this all is bound together, and through this the arts of the prophet and the

203

---

[25] Diotima (dī'o-tī'ma): spoken of below (211) as the stranger of Mantineia (măn'tĭ-nī'a).

priest, their sacrifices and mysteries and charms, and all prophecy and incantation, find their way. For God mingles not with man; and through this power all the intercourse and speech of God with man, whether awake or asleep, is carried on. The wisdom which understands this is spiritual; all other wisdom, such as that of arts or handicrafts, is mean and vulgar."

[Love is not wise or good or beautiful, but is in passionate search for wisdom, goodness and beauty.]

"The truth of the matter is just this: No god is a philosopher or seeker after wisdom, for he is wise already; nor does any one else who is wise seek after wisdom. Neither do the ignorant seek after wisdom. For herein is the evil of ignorance, that he who is neither good nor wise is nevertheless satisfied: he feels no want, and has therefore no desire." "But who then, Diotima," I said, "are the lovers of wisdom, if they are neither the wise nor the foolish?" "A child may answer that question," she replied; "they are those who, like Love, are in a mean between the two. For wisdom is a most beautiful thing, and love is of the beautiful; and therefore Love is also a philosopher or lover of wisdom, and being a lover of wisdom is in a mean between the wise and the ignorant. And this again is a quality which Love inherits from his parents; for his father is wealthy and wise, and his mother poor and foolish. Such, my dear Socrates, is the nature of the spirit Love. The error in your conception of him was very natural, and as I imagine from what you say, has arisen out of a confusion of love and the beloved—this made you think that love was all beautiful. For the beloved is the truly beautiful, delicate, and perfect and blessed; but the principle of love is of another nature, and is such as I have described."

[204-209]

[But love is not love of the beautiful and good only. Love is essentially love of "birth in beauty." "To the mortal creature, generation is a sort of eternity and immortality," and all true love is essentially love of immortality. Some beget earthly children, but some are more creative in their souls than in their bodies. "Such creators are poets and all artists who are deserving the name inventor. But the greatest and fairest sort of wisdom by far is that which is concerned with the ordering of states and families, and which is called temperance and justice." He who in youth has the seed of these implanted in him desires to implant them in others. "When he finds a fair and noble and well-nurtured soul . . . he is full of fair speech about virtue and the nature and pursuits of a good man; and he tries to educate him; . . . and they are bound together by a far nearer tie and have a closer friendship than those who beget mortal children, for the children who are their common offspring are fairer and more immortal."]

"These are the lesser mysteries of love, into which even you, Socrates, may enter; to the greater and more hidden ones which are the crown of these, and to which, if you pursue them in a right spirit, they will lead, I know not whether you will be able to attain. But I will do my utmost to inform you, and do you follow if you can. For he who would proceed rightly in this matter should begin in youth to turn to beautiful forms; and first, if his instructor guide him rightly, he should learn to love one such form only—out of that he should create fair thoughts; and soon he will himself perceive that the beauty of one form is truly related to the beauty of another; and then if beauty in general is his pursuit, how foolish would he be not to recognize that the beauty in every form is one and the same! And when he perceives this he will abate his violent love of the one, which he will despise and deem a small thing, and will become a lover of all beautiful forms; this will lead him on to consider that the beauty of the mind is more honorable than the beauty of the outward form. So that if a virtuous soul have but a little comeliness, he will be content to love and tend him, and will search out and bring to the birth thoughts which may improve the young, until his beloved is compelled to contemplate and see the beauty of institutions and laws, and understand that all is of one kindred, and that personal beauty is only a trifle; and after laws and institutions he will lead him on to the sciences, that he may see their beauty, being not like a servant in love with the beauty of one youth or man or institution, himself a slave mean and calculating, but looking at the abundance of beauty and drawing towards the sea of beauty, and creating and beholding many fair and noble thoughts and notions in boundless love of wisdom ; until at length he grows and waxes strong, and at last the vision is revealed to him of a single science, which is the science of beauty everywhere. To this I will proceed; please to give me your very best attention.

"For he who has been instructed thus far in the things of love, and who has learned to see the beautiful in due order and succession, when he comes toward the end will suddenly perceive a nature of wondrous beauty—and this, Socrates, is that final cause of all our former toils, which in the first place is everlasting—not growing and decaying, or waxing and waning ; in the next place not fair in one point of view and foul in another, or at one time or in one relation or at one place fair, at another time or in another relation or at another place foul, as if fair to some and foul to others, or in the likeness of a face or hands or any other part of the bodily frame, or in any form of speech or knowledge, nor existing in any other being ; as for example, an animal, whether in earth or heaven, but beauty only, absolute, separate, simple, and everlasting, which without diminution and without increase, or any change, is imparted to the ever-growing and perishing beauties of all other things. He who under the influence of true love rising upward from these begins to see that beauty, is not far from the end. And the true order of going or being led by another to the things of love, is to use the beauties of earth as steps along which he mounts upwards for the sake of that other beauty, going from one to two, and from two to all fair forms, and from fair forms to fair actions, and from fair actions to fair notions, until from fair notions he arrives at the notion of absolute beauty, and at last knows what the essence of beauty is. This, my dear Socrates," said the stranger of Mantineia, "is that life above all others which man should live, in the contemplation of beauty absolute ; a beauty which if you once beheld, you would see not to be after the measure of gold, and garments, and fair boys and youths, which when you now behold you are in fond amazement, and you and many a one are content to live seeing only and conversing with them without meat or drink, if that were possible—you only want to be with them and to look at them.

But what if man had eyes to see the true beauty—the divine beauty, I mean, pure and clear and unalloyed, not clogged with the pollutions of mortality, and all the colors and vanities of human life—thither looking, and holding converse with the true beauty divine and simple, and bringing into being and educating true creations of virtue and not idols only? Do you not see that in that communion only, beholding beauty with the eye of the mind, he will be enabled to bring forth, not images of beauty, but realities; for he has hold not of an image but of a reality, and bringing forth and educating true virtue to become the friend of God and be immortal, if mortal man may. Would that be an ignoble life?"

Such, Phædrus—and I speak not only to you, but to all men—were the words of Diotima; and I am persuaded of their truth. And being persuaded of them, I try to persuade others, that in the attainment of this end human nature will not easily find a better helper than Love. And therefore, also, I say that every man ought to honor him as I myself honor him, and walk in his ways, and exhort others to do the same, even as I praise the power and spirit of love according to the measure of my ability now and ever.

The words which I have spoken, you, Phædrus, may call an encomium of love, or anything else which you please.

When Socrates had done speaking, the company applauded, and Aristophanes was beginning to say something in answer to the allusion which Socrates had made to his own speech, when suddenly there was a great knocking at the door of the house, as of revelers, and the sound of a flute-girl was heard. Agathon told the attendants to go and see who were the intruders. "If they are friends of ours," he said, "invite them in, but if not say that the drinking is over." A little while afterwards they heard the voice of Alcibiades resounding in the court; he was in a great state of intoxication, and kept roaring and shouting "Where is Agathon? Lead me to Agathon," and at length, supported by the flute-girl and some of his companions, he found his way to them. "Hail, friends!" he said, appearing at the door crowned with a massive garland of ivy and wall-flowers, and having his head flowing with ribbons. "Will you have a very drunken man as a companion of your revels? Or shall I crown Agathon, as was my intention in coming, and go my way? For I was unable to come yesterday, and therefore I come to-day, carrying on my head these ribbons, that taking them from my own head, I may crown the head of this fairest and wisest of men, as I may be allowed to call him. Will you laugh at me because I am drunk? Yet I know very well that I am speaking the truth, although you may laugh. But first tell me whether I shall come in on the understanding that I am drunk. Will you drink with me or not?"

The company were vociferous in begging that he would take his place among them, and Agathon specially invited him. Thereupon he was led in by the people who were with him; and as he was being led he took the crown and ribbons from his head, intending to crown Agathon, and had them before his eyes; this prevented him from seeing Socrates, who made way for him, and Alcibiades took the vacant place between Agathon and Socrates, and in taking the place he embraced Agathon and crowned him. Take off his sandals, said Agathon, and let him make a third on the same couch.

By all means; but who makes the third partner in our revels? said Alcibiades, turning round and starting up as he caught sight of Socrates. By Heracles, he said, what is this? here is Socrates always lying in wait for me, and always, as his way is, coming out at all sorts of unsuspected places: and now, what have you to say for yourself, and why are you lying here, where I perceive that you have contrived to find a place, not by a professor or lover of jokes, like Aristophanes, but by the fairest of the company?

Socrates turned to Agathon and said: I must ask you to protect me, Agathon; for this passion of his has grown quite a serious matter. Since I became his admirer I have never been allowed to speak to any other fair one, or so much as to look at them. If I do he goes wild with envy and jealousy, and not only abuses me but can hardly keep his hands off me, and at this moment he may do me some harm. Please to see to this, and either reconcile me to him, or, if he attempts violence, protect me, as I am in bodily fear of his mad and passionate attempts.

There can never be reconciliation between you and me, said Alcibiades; but for the present I will defer your chastisement. And I must beg you, Agathon, to give me back some of the ribbons that I may crown the marvelous head of this universal despot,—I would not have him complain of me for crowning you, and neglecting him, who in conversation is the conqueror of all mankind; and this not once only, as you were the day before yesterday, but always. Then taking some of the ribbons, he crowned Socrates, and again reclined. When he had lain down again, he said: You seem, my friends, to be sober, which is a thing not to be endured; you must drink,—for that was the agreement which I made with you,—and I elect myself master of the feast until you are well drunk. Let us have a large goblet, Agathon, or rather, he said, addressing the attendant, bring me that wine-cooler. The wine-cooler was a vessel holding more than two quarts which caught his eye,—this he filled and emptied, and bid the attendant fill it again for Socrates. Observe, my friends, said Alcibiades, that my ingenious device will have no effect on Socrates, for he can drink any quantity of wine and not be at all nearer being drunk. Socrates drank the cup which the attendant filled for him.

Eryximachus said: What is this, Alcibiades? Are we to have neither conversation nor singing over our cups; but simply to drink as if we were thirsty?

Alcibiades replied: Hail, worthy son of a most wise and worthy sire!

The same to you, said Eryximachus; but what shall we do?

That I leave to you, said Alcibiades.

"The wise physician skilled our wounds to heal."

shall prescribe and we will obey. What do you want?

Well, Eryximachus said: Before you appeared a resolution was agreed to by us that each one in turn should speak a discourse in praise of love, and as good a one as he could: this was passed round from left to right; and as all of us have spoken, and you have not spoken but have well drunken, you ought to speak, and then impose upon Socrates any task which you please, and he on his right hand neighbor, and so on.

That is good, Eryximachus, said Alcibiades; and yet the comparison of a drunken man's speech with those of sober men is hardly fair; and I should like to know, sweet friend, whether you really believe what Socrates was just now saying; for I can assure you that the very reverse is the fact, and that if I praise any one but himself in his presence, whether God or man, he will hardly keep his hands off me.

For shame, said Socrates.

By Poseidon,[26] said Alcibiades, there is no use in your denying this, for no creature will I praise in your presence.

Well then take your own course, said Eryximachus, and if you like praise Socrates.

What do you think, Eryximachus? said Alcibiades; shall I attack him and inflict the punishment in your presence?

What are you about? said Socrates; are you going to raise a laugh at me? Is that the meaning of your praise?

I am going to speak the truth, if you will permit me.

I not only permit you but exhort you to speak the truth.

Then I will begin at once, said Alcibiades, and if I say anything that is not true, you may interrupt me if you will, and say that I speak falsely, though my intention is to speak the truth. But you must not wonder if I speak anyhow as things come into my mind; for the fluent and orderly enumeration of all your wonderful qualities is not a task the accomplishment of which is easy to a man in my condition.

I shall praise Socrates in a figure which will appear to him to be a caricature, and yet I do not mean to laugh at him, but only to speak the truth. I say then, that he is exactly like the masks of Silenus,[27] which may be seen sitting in the statuaries' shops, having pipes and flutes in their mouths; and they are made to open in the middle, and there are images of gods inside them. I say also that he is like Marsyas[28] the satyr.[29] You will not deny, Socrates, that your face is like that of a satyr.[30] Aye, and there is a resemblance in other points too. For example, you are a bully,—that I am in a

215

---

[26] See Euthydemus, note 21.

[27] Silenus (si-lē'nus): the childhood instructor and constant companion of Bacchus, god of wine. He is mentioned with others as the inventor of the flute, which he often plays. He was a jovial fat old man, fond of wine and music, and generally intoxicated; but he was also regarded as an inspired prophet, and a sage who despised the gifts of fortune. "Figures of Silenus were used as caskets for precious pieces of sculpture." (L. and S.)

[28] See Euthydemus, note 17.

[29] The satyrs were a class of minor divinities—the companions of Bacchus—dwelling in the forest, and fond of sleep, wine, and music. They are represented with bristling hair, blunt, up-turned nose, pointed ears, small horns, and dressed in the skins of animals.

[30] Though of robust constitution, Socrates is said to have had a remarkably ugly face, with flat nose, thick lips, and prominent eyes.

position to prove by the evidence of witnesses, if you will not confess. And are you not a flute-player? That you are, and a far more wonderful performer than Marsyas. For he indeed with instruments charmed the souls of men by the power of his breath, as the performers of his music do still; for the melodies of Olympus [31] are derived from the teaching of Marsyas, and these, whether they are played by a great master or by a miserable flute-girl, have a power which no others have; they alone possess the soul and reveal the wants of those who have need of gods and mysteries,[32] because they are inspired. But you produce the same effect with the voice only, and do not require the flute: that is the difference between you and him. When we hear any other speaker, even a very good one, his words produce absolutely no effect upon us in comparison, whereas the very fragments of you and your words, even at second-hand, and however imperfectly repeated, amaze and possess the souls of every man, woman, and child who comes within hearing of them. And if I were not afraid that you would think me drunk, I would have sworn as well as spoken to the influence which they have always had and still have over me. For my heart leaps within me more than that of any Corybantian reveler,[33] and my eyes rain tears when I hear them. And I observe that many others are affected in the same way. I have heard Pericles[34] and other great orators, but though I thought that they spoke well, I never had any similar feeling; my soul was not stirred by them, nor was I angry at the thought of my own slavish state. But this Marsyas has often brought me to such a pass, that I have felt as if I could hardly endure the life which I am leading (this,

216

---

[31] Olympus (ō-lȳm′pus): a mythical poet and musician, a pupil of Marsyas, whose art of flute-playing he perfected.

[32] Secret religious ceremonies of ancient origin employed in the worship of certain gods and goddesses. Only those who had been initiated could take part in these rites, which consisted of purifications, sacrifices, processions, songs, dances, and dramatic spectacles. On account of the secrecy maintained, there is much doubt concerning the nature and purpose of the mystic rites. The dramatic spectacles were probably scenic representations of mythical legends about the god worshipped. Passages in the Greek poets seem to indicate that the mysteries were intended to encourage belief in a future life, and in reward or punishment there, as merited by the life on earth. Certain of the rites were supposed to be a means of purification from sin, and reconciliation with the gods.

[33] Those who took part in the wild and furious rites in honor of the goddess Cybele. See Euthydemus, note 13.

[34] See Protagoras, note 37.

Socrates, you admit); and I am conscious that if I did not shut my ears against him, and fly from the voice of the siren,[35] he would detain me until I grew old sitting at his feet. For he makes me confess that I ought not to live as I do, neglecting the wants of my own soul, and busying myself with the concerns of the Athenians; therefore I hold my ears and tear myself away from him. And he is the only person who ever made me ashamed, which you might think not to be in my nature, and there is no one else who does the same. For I know that I cannot answer him or say that I ought not to do as he bids, but when I leave his presence the love of popularity gets the better of me. And therefore I run away and fly from him, and when I see him I am ashamed of what I have confessed to him. And many a time I wish that he were dead, and yet I know that I should be much more sorry than glad, if he were to die: so that I am at my wit's end.

And this is what I and many others have suffered from the flute-playing of this satyr. Yet hear me once more while I show you how exact the image is, and how marvelous his power. For I am sure that none of you know him; but I know him and will describe him, as I have begun. See you how fond he is of the fair? He is always with them and is always being smitten by them, and then again he knows nothing and is ignorant of all things—that is the appearance which he puts on. Is he not like a Silenus in this? Yes, surely: that is, his outer mask, which is the carved head of the Silenus; but when he is opened, what temperance there is, as I may say to you, O my companions in drink, residing within. Know you that beauty and wealth and honor, at which the many wonder, are of no account with him, and are utterly despised by him: he regards not at all the persons who are gifted with them; mankind are nothing to him; all his life is spent in mocking and flouting at them. But when I opened him, and looked within at his serious purpose, I saw in him 217-219 divine and golden images of such fascinating beauty that I was ready to do in a moment whatever Socrates commanded (they may have escaped the observation of others, but I saw them). . . .

[35] The sirens were maidens living on an island in the Mediterranean Sea. By their sweet singing they charmed all who sailed by, and allured them to destruction. Whoever heard them, and drew near, never saw wife or home again.

[Alcibiades next gives a long account of how he tried to entice Socrates into vice, but without success.]

All this, as I should explain, happened before he and I went on the expedition to Potidæa; there we messed together, and I had the opportunity of observing his extraordinary power of sustaining fatigue and going without food when our supplies were intercepted at any place, as will happen with an army. In the faculty of endurance he was superior not only to me but to everybody; there was no one to be compared to him. Yet at a festival he was the only person who had any real powers of enjoyment, and though not willing to drink, he could if compelled beat us all at that, and the most wonderful thing of all was that no human being had ever seen Socrates drunk; and that, if I am not mistaken, will soon be tested. His endurance of cold was also surprising. There was a severe frost, for the winter in that region was really tremendous, and everybody else either remained indoors, or if they went out had on no end of clothing, and were well shod, and had their feet swathed in felts and fleeces: in the midst of this, Socrates, with his bare feet on the ice, and in his ordinary dress, marched better than any of the other soldiers who had their shoes on, and they looked daggers at him because he seemed to despise them.

I have told you one tale, and now I must tell you another, which is worth hearing, of the doings and sufferings of this enduring man while he was on the expedition. One morning he was thinking about something which he could not resolve; and he would not give up, but continued thinking from early dawn until noon—there he stood fixed in thought; and at noon attention was drawn to him, and the rumor ran through the wondering crowd that Socrates had been standing and thinking about something ever since the break of day. At last, in the evening after supper, some Ionians[36] out of curiosity (I should explain that this was not in winter but in summer), brought out their mats and slept in the open air that they might watch him and see whether he would stand all night. There he stood all night as well as all day and the following morning; and with the return of light he offered up a prayer

---

[36] Ionians: Greeks from Ionia (i-ō'nĭ-a), a region on the west coast of Asia Minor.

to the sun, and went his way. I will also tell, if you please—
and indeed I am bound to tell—of his courage in battle; for
who but he saved my life? Now this was the engagement in
which I received the prize of valor: for I was wounded and
he would not leave me, but he rescued me and my arms; and
he ought to have received the prize of valor which the generals
wanted to confer on me partly on account of my rank, and I
told them so (this Socrates will not impeach or deny), but he
was more eager than the generals that I and not he should have
the prize. There was another occasion on which he was very
noticeable; this was in the flight of the army after the
battle of Delium, and I had a better opportunity of seeing him than at Potidæa[37] as I was myself on horseback, and
therefore comparatively out of danger. He and Laches were
retreating as the troops were in flight, and I met them and told
them not to be discouraged, and promised to remain with
them; and there you might see him, Aristophanes, as you
describe, just as he is in the streets of Athens, stalking like a
pelican, and rolling his eyes, calmly contemplating enemies as
well as friends, and making very intelligible to anybody, even
from a distance, that whoever attacks him will be likely to
meet with a stout resistance; and in this way he and his companions escaped—for these are the sort of persons who are
never touched in war; they only pursue those who are running away headlong. I particularly observed how superior he
was to Laches[38] in presence of mind. Many are the wonders
of Socrates which I might narrate in his praise; most of his
ways might perhaps be paralleled in others, but the most
astonishing thing of all is his absolute unlikeness to any human
being that is or ever has been. You may imagine Brasidas[39]
and others to have been like Achilles[40]; or you may imagine
Nestor[41] and Antenor[42] to have been like Pericles; and the
same may be said of other famous men; but of this strange

221

---

[37] See Apology, note 22.
[38] Laches (lā′kēz): an Athenian general. A dialogue of Plato bears his name.
[39] Brasidas (brăs′ĭ-das): a distinguished Spartan general in the Peloponnesian War. He was long honored by annual sacrifices and games.
[40] See Apology, note 21.
[41] Nestor (nĕs′tor): a legendary Greek hero, distinguished for wisdom,
justice, and eloquence. He rendered great service to the Greeks during
the Trojan War, by his prudent and persuasive counsels.
[42] Antenor (ăn-tē′nor): a Trojan prince, who took part in the Trojan War.

being you will never be able to find any likeness however remote, either among men who now are or who ever have been, except that which I have already suggested of Silenus and the satyrs; and this is an allegory not only of himself, but also of his words. For, although I forgot to mention this before, his words are ridiculous when you first hear them; he clothes himself in language that is as the skin of the wanton satyr—for his talk is of pack-asses and smiths and cobblers and curriers, and he is always repeating the same things in the same words, so that an ignorant man who did not know him might feel disposed to laugh at him; but he who pierces the mask and sees what is within will find that they are the only words which have a meaning in them, and also the most divine, abounding in fair examples of virtue, and of the largest discourse, or rather extending to the whole duty of a good and honorable man. . . .

222-223

Agathon arose in order that he might take his place on the couch by Socrates, when suddenly a band of revelers entered, and spoiled the order of the banquet. Some one who was going out having left the door open, they had found their way in, and made themselves at home; great confusion ensued, and every one was compelled to drink large quantities of wine. Aristodemus said that Eryximachus, Phædrus, and others went away—he himself fell asleep, and as the nights were long took a good rest: he was awakened towards daybreak by a crowing of cocks, and when he awoke, the others were either asleep, or had gone away; there remained awake only Socrates, Aristophanes, and Agathon, who were drinking out of a large goblet which they passed round, and Socrates was discoursing to them. Aristodemus did not hear the beginning of the discourse, and he was only half awake, but the chief thing which he remembered, was Socrates insisting to the other two that the genius of comedy was the same as that of tragedy, and that the writer of tragedy ought to be a writer of comedy also. To this they were compelled to assent, being sleepy, and not quite understanding his meaning. And first of all Aristophanes dropped, and then, when the day was already dawning, Agathon. Socrates, when he had put them to sleep, rose to depart, Aristodemus, as his manner was, following him. At the Lyceum he took a bath and passed the day as usual; and when evening came he retired to rest at his own home.

PHÆDRUS

INTRODUCTION

THIS dialogue apparently has two subjects: rhetoric or the art of discourse, and love. The two subjects are introduced by the reading of a rhetorical discourse by Lysias on love. Socrates follows this by another rhetorical discourse on love. He then declares himself conscience-stricken for having discoursed upon the most sacred subject in an artificial way. He will redeem himself by setting forth the true nature of love.

Love is, he says, in reality, a divine mania or ecstasy like that which moves the poet and prophet, or like that which purges the soul of sin. The love ecstasy may be of a baser sort leading the soul toward earthly pleasure which corrupts, or of a purer sort leading the soul into communion with God and to the winning of other souls to the divine life.

The criticism which Socrates makes upon his own first discourse and that of Lysias leads to a further discussion of rhetoric. The professors of rhetoric, Socrates holds, do not at all understand the true nature of the art of discourse. That art requires a knowledge of the truth, and a knowledge of the souls to be spoken to, not only as to their general character, but also as to their individual peculiarities.

Let us now consider more closely the connection between Plato's two subjects, love and discourse. Plato believed in the reality of absolute truth; that absolute truth lies ready to be born in every soul; that the truth may be brought to birth in the soul by pure reflection (dialectic); and that the chief end of man is in this way to find the truth for himself and then induce others to do likewise. Since these things are so, I must not regard the truth and must not regard other souls with indifferent contemplation. I must love the truth with my whole soul, heart, strength and mind; otherwise I shall never by any process find it. I must in the truest sense love my neighbor as myself, for I must seek to bring about in my neighbor the same "birth of beauty" which has come to myself.

Now if I am in this sense a lover of truth and a lover of men, what sort of discourse shall I employ in speaking to men? Shall I go to those whom I passionately long to see born in the beauty of holiness, with a fine-feathered oration like that of Lysias? Shall I go to those whom I see wandering blind and helpless for lack of insight into the truth, with quibbling disputations which show only that I have skill to prove either side of any question? Shall I go to those who intend to teach others by speaking or writing, with sciences of how to do these things, whose elaborate and arbitrary learning is far from the real spirit of man and far from the spirit of truth?

If I do any of these things I am traitor to the truth and to the souls of men. But if I really love the truth, and love to see men born into the truth, I will come to them with the purest light I have. I will seek to know not only what souls need, but what this soul needs. I will not stand at a distance. I will not trust to writing. I will face the man. I will sit beside him. As Socrates did with Phædrus, I will first hear his say. I will let him praise Lysias, if Lysias is his present love. I will myself praise Lysias so far as I truly can. I will join in his enthusiasms so far as they are good,—and the enthusiasms of youth have always something of good. But when we are together, he and I, in close and joyful comradeship, I will ask him to walk with me. He has shown me the flash and smoke of Lysias' fireworks. Let us go into the clear where we can see the stars.

I believe that Plato says in this dialogue that the greatest thing in the world is such love as Socrates had for truth and for Phædrus, and that the highest expression of this love is in such free face-to-face talk as they had together that day on the banks of the Ilissus.

PHÆDRUS

PERSONS OF THE DIALOGUE.

SOCRATES.   PHÆDRUS.[1]

SCENE:—Under a plane-tree, by the banks of the Ilissus.[2]

Socrates. My dear Phædrus, whence come you, and whither are you going?   **Steph. 227**

Phædrus. I am come from Lysias[3] the son of Cephalus, and I am going to take a walk outside the wall, for I have been with him ever since the early dawn, which is a long while, and our common friend Acumenus[4] advises me to walk in the country; he says that this is far more refreshing than walking in the courts.

Soc. There he is right. Lysias then, I suppose, was in the city?

Phædr. Yes, he was with Epicrates,[5] at the house of Morychus,[6] that house which is near the temple of Olympian Zeus.[7]

Soc. And how did he entertain you? Can I be wrong in supposing that Lysias gave you a feast of discourse?

Phædr. You shall hear, if you have leisure to stay and listen.

[1] Phædrus (fē'drŭs): our knowledge of Phædrus is obtained principally from this dialogue.
[2] Ilissus (i-lĭs'sus): a small river flowing through the east side of Athens.
[3] Lysias (lĭs'ĭ-as); an Athenian orator. The father, Cephalus (cĕf'a-lus), was on intimate terms with Socrates, and his house was the scene of Plato's Republic. See Republic, I., note 1.
[4] The physician. See Protagoras, note 18.
[5] Epicrates (e-pĭk'ra-tēz): a politician.
[6] Morychus (mō'rĭ-kus): a tragic poet.
[7] Zeus, supreme ruler of the universe, was supposed to have his throne on the highest peak of Mt. Olympus, in Thessaly.

Soc. And would I not regard the conversation of you and Lysias as "a thing of higher import," as I may say in the words of Pindar,[8] "than any business?"

Phædr. Will you go on?

Soc. And will you go on with the narration?

Phædr. My tale, Socrates, is one of your sort, for the theme which occupied us was love,—after a fashion: Lysias imagined a fair youth who was being tempted, but not by a lover; and this was the point: he ingeniously proved that the non-lover should be accepted rather than the lover.[9]

Soc. O that is noble of him. And I wish that he would say a poor man rather than a rich, and an old man rather than a young one; he should meet the case of me, and all of us, and then his words would indeed be charming, and of public utility; and I am so eager to hear them that if you walk all the way to Megara, and when you have reached the wall come back, as Herodicus[10] recommends, without going in, I will not leave you.

Phædr. What do you mean, Socrates? How can you imagine that I, who am quite unpracticed, can remember or do justice to an elaborate work, which the greatest rhetorician of the day spent a long time in composing. Indeed, I cannot; I would give a great deal if I could.

Soc. I believe that I know Phædrus about as well as I know myself, and I am very sure that he heard the words of Lysias, not once only, but again and again he made him say them, and Lysias was very willing to gratify him; at last, when nothing else would satisfy him, he got hold of the book, and saw what he wanted,—this was his morning's occupation,— and then when he was tired with sitting, he went out to take a walk, not until, as I believe, he had simply learned by heart the entire discourse, which may not have been very long; and as he was going to take a walk outside the wall in order that he might practice, he saw a certain lover of discourse who had

---

[8] See Euthydemus, note 22.

[9] Owing in part to the ignorance and seclusion of women, close companionships between men were common in ancient Greece. Such relationships were in some cases entered into voluntarily, while in other cases the younger of the two was placed by parents or guardian in charge of the elder. The feeling between the two was sometimes slight, sometimes so intense as to be almost unintelligible to us. The influence of the relationship was sometimes highly beneficial and sometimes grossly corrupting.

[10] See Protagoras, note 30.

the same complaint as himself: he saw and rejoiced; now, thought he, "I shall have a partner in my revels." And he invited him to come with him. But when the lover of discourse asked to hear the tale, he gave himself airs and said, "No, I can't," as if he didn't like; although, if the hearer had refused, the end would have been that he would have made him listen whether he would or no. Therefore, Phædrus, as he will soon speak in any case, beg him to speak at once.

Phædr. As you don't seem very likely to let me off until I speak in some way, the best thing that I can do is to speak as I best may.

Soc. That is a very true observation of yours.

Phædr. I will do my best, for believe me, Socrates, I did not learn the very words; O no, but I have a general notion of what he said, and will repeat concisely, and in order, the several arguments by which the case of the non-lover was proved to be superior to that of the lover; let me begin at the beginning.

Soc. Yes, my friend; but you must first of all show what you have got in your left hand under your cloak, for that roll, as I suspect, is the actual discourse. Now, much as I love you, I would not have you suppose that I am going to have your memory exercised upon me, if you have Lysias himself here.

Phædr. Enough; I see that I have no hope of practicing upon you. But if I am to read, where would you please to sit? 229

Soc. Turn this way; let us go to the Ilissus, and sit down at some quiet spot.

Phædr. I am fortunate in not having my sandals, and as you never have any, I think that we may go along the brook and cool our feet in the water: this is the easiest way, and at midday and in the summer is far from being unpleasant.

Soc. Lead on, and look out for a place in which we can sit down.

Phædr. Do you see that tallest plane-tree in the distance?

Soc. Yes.

Phædr. There are shade and gentle breezes, and grass on which we may either sit or lie down.

Soc. Move on.

Phædr. I should like to know, Socrates, whether the place

is not somewhere here at which Boreas[11] is said to have carried off Orithyia from the banks of the Ilissus.

Soc. That is the tradition.

Phædr. And is this the exact spot? The little stream is delightfully clear and bright; I can fancy that there might be maidens playing near.

Soc. I believe that the spot is not exactly here, but about a quarter of a mile lower down, where you cross to the temple of Artemis,[12] and I think that there is some sort of altar of Boreas at the place.

Phædr. I don't recollect; but I wish that you would tell me whether you believe this tale.

Soc. The wise are doubtful, and if, like them, I also doubted, there would be nothing very strange in that. I might have a rational explanation that Orithyia was playing with Pharmacia,[13] when a northern gust carried her over the neighboring rocks: and this being the manner of her death, she was said to have been carried away by Boreas. There is a discrepancy, however, about the locality, as according to another version of the story she was taken from the Areopagus,[14] and not from this place. Now I quite acknowledge that these explanations are very nice, but he is not to be envied who has to give them; much labor and ingenuity will be required of him; and when he has once begun, he must go on and rehabilitate centaurs[15] and chimeras[16] dire. Gorgons[17] and winged steeds flow in apace, and numberless other inconceivable and impossible monstrosities and marvels of nature. And if he is skeptical about them, and would fain reduce them all to the rules of probability, this sort of crude philosophy will take up all his time. Now I have certainly not time for

---

[11] Boreas (bō'rē-as): mythological personification of the north wind, who lived in Thrace. He loved Orithyia (ôr'ĭ-thȳ'yȧ), daughter of the king of Athens, and carried her away from the banks of the Ilissus where she was playing games.

[12] Artemis (är'te-mĭs): one of the major Greek divinities, goddess of the moon, and of the chase, corresponding to the Roman Diana.

[13] Pharmacia (fär-mā'sĭ-a): the nymph of a spring near the Ilissus, and playmate of Orithyia.

[14] Areopagus (ăr'ē-ŏp'a-gus) or Mars Hill: a hill in Athens. See Acts xvii. 22.

[15] Centaur (sĕn'taur): a fabulous creature, half man and half horse.

[16] Chimera (kĭ-mē'rȧ): a fire-breathing monster with the head of a lion, the body of a goat, and the tail of a serpent.

[17] See Symposium, note 24.

this; shall I tell you why? I must first know myself, as the Delphian inscription [18] says; and I should be absurd indeed, if while I am still in ignorance of myself I were to be curious about that which is not my business. And therefore I say farewell to all this; the common opinion is enough for me. For, as I was saying, I want to know not about this, but about myself. Am I indeed a wonder more complicated and swollen with passion than the serpent Typho,[19] or a creature of a gentler and simpler sort, to whom Nature has given a diviner and lowlier destiny? But here let me ask you, friend: Is not this the plane-tree to which you were conducting us? 230

Phædr. Yes, this is the tree.

Soc. Yes, indeed, and a fair and shady resting-place, full of summer sounds and scents. There is the lofty and spreading plane-tree, and the agnus castus [20] high and clustering, in the fullest blossom and the greatest fragrance; and the stream which flows beneath the plane-tree is deliciously cold to the feet. Judging from the ornaments and images, this must be a spot sacred to Achelous [21] and the Nymphs [22]; moreover, there is a sweet breeze, and the grasshoppers chirrup; and the greatest charm of all is the grass like a pillow gently sloping to the head. My dear Phædrus, you have been an admirable guide.

Phædr. I always wonder at you, Socrates; for when you are in the country, you really are like a stranger who is being led about by a guide. Do you ever cross the border? I rather think that you never venture even outside the gates.

Soc. Very true, my good friend; and I hope that you will excuse me when you hear the reason, which is, that I am a lover of knowledge, and the men who dwell in the city are my teachers, and not the trees, or the country. Though I do, indeed, believe that you have found a spell with which to draw me out of the city into the country, as hungry cows are led by shaking before them a bait of leaves or fruit. For only hold

---

[18] The words "know thyself" were inscribed upon the temple of Apollo at Delphi.

[19] Typho (tỹ′fō): a fearful monster with one hundred dragon heads, eyes that shot fire, and many terrible voices. He tried to usurp the throne of Zeus, but failed.

[20] A willow-like tree.

[21] Achelous (ăk′ē-lō′us): god of the river Achelous, the largest in Greece.

[22] Goddesses of lower rank, dwelling in groves, forests, caves, beside springs and rivers, on hills and lonely islands.

up the bait of discourse, and you may lead me all round Attica, and over the wide world. And now having arrived, I intend to lie down, and do you choose any posture in which you can read best. Begin.

231-234 [Phædrus reads the speech [23] of Lysias about love. The lover, Lysias claims, should be avoided as an unreasonable, disagreeable, fickle, jealous person, who spoils the object of his affection by undue praise, selfishly deprives him of other friends and of many like advantages, and at last deserts him for another. Whereas the non-lover is a truly disinterested admirer, who desires at all times only the good of his friend. His affection is for the advantage of both, and for the injury of neither.

The speech is very pretentious in style, and although it contains a germ of truth, the author's purpose is evidently to make fine phrases, and not to arrive at a true conclusion about his subject. When he has finished reading, Phædrus appeals to Socrates thus:]

Now, Socrates, what do you think? Is not the discourse excellent, especially the language?

Soc. Yes indeed, admirable; the effect on me was ravishing. And this I owe to you, Phædrus, for I observed you while reading to be in an ecstasy, and thinking that you are more experienced in these matters than I am, I followed your example, and, like you, became inspired with a divine frenzy.

Phædr. Indeed, you are pleased to be merry.

Soc. Do you mean that I am not in earnest?

Phædr. Now, don't talk in that way, Socrates, but let me have your real opinion; I adjure you, by the god of friendship, to tell me whether you think that any Hellene [24] could have said more or spoken better on the same subject.

Soc. Well, but are you and I expected to praise the sentiments of the author, or only the clearness, and roundness, and **235** accuracy, and tournure of the language? As to the first I willingly submit to your better judgment, for I am unworthy to form an opinion, having only attended to the rhetorical manner; and I was doubting whether Lysias him-

---

[23] Probably not written by Lysias but invented by Plato.
[24] Greek.

self would be able to defend that; for I thought, though I speak under correction, that he repeated himself two or three times, either from want of words or from want of pains; and also, he appeared to me wantonly ambitious of showing how well he could say the same thing in two or three ways.

Phædr. Nonsense, Socrates; that was his exhaustive treatment of the subject; for he omitted nothing; this is the special merit of the speech, and I do not think that any one could have made a fuller or better.

Soc. I cannot go so far as that with you. Ancient sages, men and women, who have spoken and written of these things, would rise up in judgment against me, if I lightly assented to you.

Phædr. Who are they, and where did you hear anything better than this?

Soc. I am sure that I must have heard; I don't remember at this moment from whom; perhaps from Sappho [25] the fair, Anacreon [26] the wise; or, possibly, from a prose writer. What makes me say this? Why, because I perceive that my bosom is full, and that I could make another speech as good as that of Lysias and different. Now I am certain that this is not an invention of my own, for I am conscious that I know nothing, and therefore I can only infer that I have been filled through the ears, like a pitcher from the waters of another, though I have actually forgotten in my stupidity who was my informant.

Phædr. That is grand. But never mind where you heard the discourse or of whom; let that, if you will, be a mystery not to be divulged even at my earnest desire. But do as you say; promise to make another and better oration of equal length on the same subject, with other arguments; and I, like the nine Archons,[27] will promise to set up a golden image at Delphi [28] not only of myself, but of you, and as large as life.

Soc. You are a dear golden simpleton if you suppose me to mean that Lysias has altogether missed the mark, and that I can make a speech from which all his arguments are to be excluded. The worst of authors will say something that is to

---

[25] Sappho (săf'fō): a celebrated Greek lyric poetess living in the latter part of the seventh century B.C.
[26] Anacreon (ă-năk'rē-on, 550 (?) — B.C.): a famous Greek lyric poet.
[27] Archons (är'konz): the chief magistrates at Athens, nine in number.
[28] See Apology, note 12. It was customary to place there statues and other votive offerings in honor of the god.

the point. Who, for example, could speak on this thesis of yours without praising the discretion of the non-lover and blaming the folly of the lover? These are the commonplaces which must come in (for what else is there to be said?) and must be allowed and excused; the only merit is in the arrangement of them, for there can be none in the invention; but when you leave the commonplaces, then there may be some originality.

Phædr. I admit that there is reason in that, and I will be reasonable too, and will allow you to start with the premise that the lover is more disordered in his wits than the non-lover; and if you go on after that and make a longer and better speech than Lysias, and use other arguments, then I say again that a statue you shall have of beaten gold, and take your place by the colossal offering of the Cypselids at Olympia.[29]

Soc. Is not the lover serious, because only in fun I lay a finger upon his love? And so, Phædrus, you really imagine that I am going to improve upon his ingenuity?

Phædr. There I have you as you had me, and you must speak "as you best can," and no mistake. And don't . . . compel me to say to you as you said to me, "I know Socrates as well as I know myself, and he was wanting to speak, but he gave himself airs." Rather I would have you consider that from this place we stir not until you have unbosomed yourself of the speech; for here are we all alone, and I am stronger, remember, and younger than you; therefore perpend, and do not compel me to use violence.

Soc. But, my sweet Phædrus, how can I ever compete with Lysias in an extempore speech? He is a master in his art and I am an untaught man.

Phædr. You see how matters stand; and therefore let there be no more pretences; for, indeed, I know the word that is irresistible.

Soc. Then don't say it.

---

[29] Olympia (ŏ-lĭm'pĭ-a): a small plain in Elis near the south-western coast of Greece, about 110 miles from Athens. Here was a grove sacred to Zeus, adorned with many temples, altars, statues, and votive offerings. Of the offerings of the Cypselids, who were descendants of Cypselus (sў̆p'sē-lus 655-625 B.C.), a tyrant of Corinth, Grote says: "Their offerings consecrated at Olympia excited great admiration, especially the gilt colossal statue of Zeus." [History of Greece, I., ch. 9.]

Phædr. Yes, but I will; and my word shall be an oath. "I say, or rather swear"—but what god will be the witness of my oath?—"I swear by this plane-tree, that unless you repeat the discourse here, in the face of the plane-tree, I will never tell you another; never let you have word of another!"

Soc. Villain! I am conquered; the poor lover of discourse has no more to say.

Phædr. Then why are you still at your tricks?

Soc. I am not going to play tricks now that you have taken the oath, for I cannot allow myself to be starved.

Phædr. Proceed.

Soc. Shall I tell you what I will do?

Phædr. What?

Soc. I will veil my face and gallop through the discourse as fast as I can, for if I see you, I shall feel ashamed and not know what to say.

237-241

Phædr. Only go on and you may do as you please.

[After an invocation to the Muses, Socrates begins his speech, which he addresses to an imaginary youth, by inquiring into the nature and power of love. He says that in every person there are two principles, a better and a worse, which are in conflict with each other. The better one, reason, if allowed to rule, leads to temperance. The worse, desire, when victorious, leads to excess. Excess has many forms and many names, and among them is found love.]

And now, dear Phædrus, I shall pause for an instant to ask whether you do not think me, as I appear to myself, inspired?

Phædr. Yes, Socrates, you seem to have a very unusual flow of words.

Soc. Listen to me, then, in silence; for surely the place is holy; so that you must not wonder, if, as I proceed, I appear to be in a divine fury, for already I am getting into dithyrambics.[30]

Phædr. That is quite true.

---

[30] The dithyramb was a kind of poetry of a lofty but often inflated style. The term was used metaphorically, as here, of any bombastic language. (L. and S.)

Soc. And that I attribute to you. But hear what follows, and perhaps the fit may be averted ; all is in their hands above. And now I will go on talking to my youth. Listen :—

[Socrates proceeds in much the same strain as Lysias, to set forth all the disadvantages and harm that result to a youth from his association with a lover. His speech is a parody on that of Lysias. He shows that he can surpass the rhetoricians in their own art. At the same time he develops still further the germ of truth presented by Lysias, that there is an unworthy and spurious form of love which should be rejected. He concludes his censure of the lover thus :]

Consider this, fair youth, and know that in the friendship of the lover there is no real kindness : he has an appetite and wants to feed upon you.

"As wolves love lambs so lovers love their loves."

But, as I said before, I am speaking in verse, and therefore I had better make an end ; that is enough.

Phædr. I thought that you were only half-way and were going to make a similar speech about all the advantages of accepting the non-lover. Why don't you go on?

Soc. Does not your simplicity observe that I have got out of dithyrambics into epics; and if my censure was in verse, what will my praise be? Don't you see that I am already overtaken by the Nymphs to whom you have mischievously exposed me? And therefore I will only add that the non-lover has all the advantages in which the lover is charged with being deficient. And now I will say no more; there has been enough said of both of them. Leaving the tale to its fate, I will cross the river and make the best of my way home, lest a worse thing be inflicted upon me by you.

242

Phædr. Not yet, Socrates; not until the heat of the day has passed ; don't you see that the hour is noon, and the sun is standing over our heads ? Let us rather stay and talk over what has been said, and then return in the cool.

Soc. Your love of discourse, Phædrus, is superhuman, simply marvelous, and I do not believe that there is any one of your contemporaries who in one way or another has either made or been the cause of others making an equal number of speeches. I would except Simmias [31] the Theban, but all the rest are far behind you. And now I do verily believe that you have been the cause of another.

Phædr. That is good news. But what do you mean?

Soc. I mean to say that as I was about to cross the stream the usual sign was given to me; that is the sign which never bids but always forbids me to do what I am going to do [32]; and I thought that I heard a voice saying in my ear that I had been guilty of impiety, and that I must not go away until I had made an atonement. Now I am a diviner, though not a very good one, but I have enough religion for my own needs, as you might say of a bad writer—his writing is good enough for him. And, O my friend, how singularly prophetic is the soul! For at the time I had a sort of misgiving, and, like Ibycus,[33] "I was troubled," and I suspected that I might be receiving honor from men at the expense of sinning against the gods. Now I am aware of the error.

Phædr. What error?

Soc. That was a dreadful speech which you brought with you, and you made me utter one as bad.

Phædr. How was that?

Soc. Foolish, I say, and in a degree impious; and what can be more dreadful than this?

Phædr. Nothing, if the speech was really such as you describe.

Soc. Well, and is not Eros [34] the son of Aphrodite [35] a mighty god?

Phædr. That is the language of mankind about him.

Soc. But that was not the language of Lysias' speech any more than of that other speech uttered through my lips when under the influence of your enchantments, and which I may call yours and not mine. For Love, if he be a god or divine, cannot be evil. Yet this was the error of both our speeches. There was also a solemnity about them which was truly charming; they had no truth or honesty in them, and yet they pretended to be something, hoping to succeed in

243

---

[31] See Phædo, note 1.
[32] See Apology, 31 and 40.
[33] Ibycus (īb'y̆-cus): a Greek lyric poet who wrote about 530 B.C.
[34] Eros (ē'ros): the god of love. See Symposium, note 16.
[35] See Symposium, note 12.

deceiving the manikins of earth and be famous among them. And therefore I must have a purgation. And now I bethink me of an ancient purgation of mythological error which was devised, not by Homer [36] for he never had the wit to discover why he was blind, but by Stesichorus,[37] who was a philosopher and knew the reason why; and, therefore, when he lost his eyes, for that was the penalty which was inflicted upon him for reviling the lovely Helen, he purged himself. And the purgation was a recantation, which began with the words:—

"That was a lie of mine when I said that thou never embarkedst on the swift ships, or wentest to the walls of Troy."

And when he had completed his poem, which is called "the recantation," immediately his sight returned to him. Now I will be wiser than either Stesichorus or Homer, in that I am going to make a recantation before I lose mine; and this I will attempt, not as before, veiled and ashamed, but with forehead bold and bare.

Phædr. There is nothing which I should like better to hear.

Soc. Only think, my good Phædrus, what an utter want of delicacy was shown in the two discourses; I mean, in my own and in the one which you recited out of the book. Would not any one who was himself of a noble and gentle nature, and who loved or ever had loved a nature like his own, when he heard us speaking of the petty causes of lovers' jealousies, and of their exceeding animosities, and the injuries which they do to their beloved, have imagined that our ideas of love were taken from some haunt of sailors to which good manners were unknown—he would certainly never have admitted the justice of our censure?

Phædr. Certainly not.

Soc. Therefore, because I blush at the thought of this person, and also because I am afraid of the god Love, I desire to wash down that gall and vinegar with a wholesome draught; and I would counsel Lysias not to delay, but to write another

---

[36] See Apology, note 39. According to tradition Homer was a wandering minstrel, poor and blind.

[37] Stesichorus (stē-sĭk'o-rus, 632–552 B.C.): a celebrated Greek poet of Sicily. There is a fable of his being miraculously struck blind after writing an attack upon Helen (see Apology, note 21), and recovering his sight after he composed a recantation.

discourse, which shall prove other things being equal that the lover ought to be accepted rather than the non-lover.

Phædr. Be assured that he shall. You shall speak the praises of the lover, and Lysias shall be made to write them in another discourse. I will compel him to do this.

Soc. You will be true to your nature in that, and therefore I believe you.

Phædr. Speak, and fear not.

Soc. But where is the fair youth whom I was addressing, and who ought to listen, in order that he may not be misled by one side before he has heard the other?

Phædr. He is close at hand, and always at your service.

[The second discourse of Socrates is a serious attempt on his part to make clear what he regards as the truth about love in its highest form. He begins—" That was a lie in which I said that the beloved ought to accept the non-lover and reject the lover, because the one is sane and the other mad. For that might have been truly said if madness were simply an evil; but there is also a madness which is the special gift of heaven and the source of the chiefest blessings among men." This divine madness is of four kinds—the gift of prophecy, religious ecstasy in which the soul is purified from sin, poetical inspiration, and lastly the madness of love.] 244-245

I might tell of many other noble deeds which have sprung from inspired madness. And therefore, let no one frighten or flutter us by saying that temperate love is preferable to mad love, but let him further show, if he would carry off the palm, that love is not sent by the gods for any good to lover or beloved. And we, on our part, will prove in answer to him that the madness of love is the greatest of Heaven's blessings, and the proof shall be one which the wise will receive, and the witling disbelieve. And, first of all, let us inquire what is the truth about the affections and actions of the soul, divine as well as human. And thus we begin our proof :—

[The soul is immortal because it is the source of all motion both in itself and in all other things.]

Her form is a theme of divine and large discourse; human language may, however, speak of this briefly, and in a figure.

246 Let our figure be of a composite nature,—a pair of winged horses and a charioteer. Now the winged horses and the charioteer of the gods are all of them noble, and of noble breed, while ours are mixed; and we have a charioteer who drives them in a pair, and one of them is noble and of noble origin, and the other is ignoble and of ignoble origin; and, as might be expected, there is a great deal of trouble in managing them. I will endeavor to explain to you in what way the mortal differs from the immortal creature. The soul or animate being has the care of the inanimate, and traverses the whole heaven in divers forms appearing; when perfect and fully winged she soars upward, and is the ruler of the universe; while the imperfect soul loses her feathers, and drooping in her flight at last settles on the solid ground,—there, finding a home, she receives an earthly frame which appears to be self-moved, but is really moved by her power; and this composition of soul and body is called a living and mortal creature. For no such union can be reasonably believed, or at all proved to be other than mortal; although fancy may imagine a god whom, not having seen nor surely known, we invent—such a one, an immortal creature having a body, and having also a soul which have been united in all time. Let that, however, be as God wills, and be spoken of acceptably to him. But the reason why the soul loses her feathers should be explained, and is as follows:—

The wing is intended to soar aloft and carry that which gravitates downwards into the upper region, which is the dwelling of the gods; and this is that element of the body which is most akin to the divine. Now the divine is beauty, wisdom, goodness, and the like; and by these the wing of the soul is nourished, and grows apace; but when fed upon evil and foulness, and the like, wastes and falls away. Zeus,

247 the mighty lord holding the reins of a winged chariot, leads the way in heaven, ordering all and caring for all; and there follows him the heavenly array of gods and demi-gods, divided into eleven bands; for only Hestia[38] is

---

[38] Hestia (hĕs'tĭ-a): goddess of the hearth, corresponding to the Roman Vesta.

left at home in the house of heaven; but the rest of the twelve greater deities march in their appointed order. And they see in the interior of heaven many blessed sights; and there are ways to and fro, along which the happy gods are passing, each one fulfilling his own work; and any one may follow who pleases, for jealousy has no place in the heavenly choir. This is within the heaven. But when they go to feast and festival, then they move right up the steep ascent, and mount the top of the dome of heaven. Now the chariots of the gods, self-balanced, upward glide in obedience to the rein; but the others have a difficulty, for the steed who has evil in him, if he has not been properly trained by the charioteer, gravitates and inclines and sinks towards the earth: and this is the hour of agony and extremest conflict of the soul. For the immortal souls, when they are at the end of their course, go out and stand upon the back of heaven, and the revolution of the spheres carries them round, and they behold the world beyond. Now of the heaven which is above the heavens, no earthly poet has sung or ever will sing in a worthy manner. But I must tell, for I am bound to speak truly when speaking of the truth. The colorless and formless and intangible essence is visible to the mind, which is the only lord of the soul. Circling around this in the region above the heavens is the place of true knowledge. And as the divine intelligence, and that of every other soul which is rightly nourished, is fed upon mind and pure knowledge, such an intelligent soul is glad at once more beholding being; and feeding on the sight of truth is replenished, until the revolution of the worlds brings her round again to the same place. During the revolution she beholds justice, temperance, and knowledge absolute, not in the form of generation or of relation, which men call existence, but knowledge absolute in existence absolute; and beholding other existences in like manner, and feeding upon them, she passes down into the interior of the heavens and returns home, and there the charioteer putting up his horses at the stall, gives them ambrosia to eat and nectar to drink.

This is the life of the gods; but of other souls, that which follows God best and is likest to him lifts the head of the charioteer into the outer world and is carried round in the revolution, troubled indeed by the steeds, and beholding true being, but hardly; another rises and falls, and sees, and again fails to see by reason of the unruliness of the steeds. The rest of the souls are also longing after the upper world and they all follow, but not being strong enough they sink into the gulf as they are carried round, plunging, treading on one another, striving to be first; and there is confusion and the extremity of effort, and many of them are lamed or have their wings broken through the ill driving of the charioteers; and all of them after a fruitless toil go away without being initiated into the mysteries of being, and are nursed with the food of opinion. The reason of their great desire to behold the plain of truth is that the food which is suited to the highest part of the soul comes out of that meadow; and the wing on which the soul soars is nourished with this. And there is a law of the goddess Retribution, that the soul which attains any vision of truth in company with the god is preserved from harm until the next period, and he who always attains is always unharmed. But when she is unable to follow, and fails to behold the vision of truth, and through some ill-hap sinks beneath the double load of forgetfulness and vice, and her feathers fall from her and she drops to earth, then the law ordains that this soul shall in the first generation pass, not into that of any other animal, but only of man; and the soul which has seen most of truth shall come to the birth as a philosopher or artist, or musician or lover; that which has seen truth in the second degree shall be a righteous king or warrior or lord; the soul which is of the third class shall be a politician or economist or trader; the fourth shall be a lover of gymnastic toils or a physician; the fifth a prophet or hierophant [39]; to the sixth a poet or imitator will be appropriate; to the seventh the life of an artisan or husbandman; to the eighth that of a Sophist or demagogue; to the ninth that of a tyrant; all these are states of probation, in which he who lives righteously improves, and he who lives unrighteously deteriorates his lot.

Ten thousand years must elapse before the soul can return to the place from whence she came, for she cannot grow her wings in less; only the soul of a philosopher, guileless and true, or the soul of a lover, who is not without philosophy, may acquire wings in the third recurring period of

[39] See Protagoras, note 27.

a thousand years: and if they choose this life three times in succession, then they have their wings given them, and go away at the end of three thousand years. But the others receive judgment when they have completed their first life, and after the judgment they go, some of them to the houses of correction which are under the earth, and are punished; others to some place in heaven whither they are lightly borne by justice, and there they live in a manner worthy of the life which they led here when in the form of men. And at the end of the first thousand years the good souls and also the evil souls both come to cast lots and choose their second life, and they may take any that they like. And then the soul of the man may pass into the life of a beast, or from the beast again into the man. But the soul of him who has never seen the truth will not pass into the human form, for man ought to have intelligence of universals, proceeding from many particulars of sense to one conception of reason; and this is the recollection of those things which our soul once saw when in company with God—when looking down from above on that which we now call being and upwards towards the true being. And therefore the mind of the philosopher alone has wings; and this is just, for he is always, according to the measure of his abilities, clinging in recollection to those things in which God abides, and in beholding which He is what he is. And he who employs aright these memories is ever being initiated into perfect mysteries and alone becomes truly perfect. But, as he forgets earthly interests and is rapt in the divine, the vulgar deem him mad, and rebuke him; they do not see that he is inspired.

Thus far I have been speaking of the fourth and last kind of madness, which is imputed to him who, when he sees the beauty of earth, is transported with the recollection of the true beauty; he would like to fly away, but he cannot; he is like a bird fluttering and looking upward and careless of the world below; and he is therefore esteemed mad. And I have shown that this is of all inspirations the noblest and best, and comes of the best, and that he who has part or lot in this madness is called a lover of the beautiful. For, as has been already said, every soul of man has in the way of nature beheld 250 true being; this was the condition of her passing into the form of man. But all men do not easily recall the things of the other world; they may have seen them for a short time only, or they may have been unfortunate when they fell to earth, and may have lost the memory of the holy things which they saw there, through some evil and corrupting association. Few there are who retain the remembrance of them sufficiently; and they, when they behold any image of that other world, are rapt in amazement; but they are ignorant of what this means, because they have no clear perceptions. For there is no light in the earthly copies of justice or temperance or any of the higher qualities which are precious to souls: they are seen but through a glass dimly; and there are few who, going to the images, behold in them the realities, and they only with difficulty. They might have seen beauty shining in brightness, when, with the happy band following in the train of Zeus, as we philosophers did, or with other gods as others did, they saw a vision and were initiated into most blessed mysteries, which we celebrated in our state of innocence; and having no feeling of evils as yet to come; beholding apparitions innocent and simple and calm and happy as in a mystery; shining in pure light, pure ourselves and not yet enshrined in that living tomb which we carry about, now that we are imprisoned in the body, as in an oyster-shell. Let me linger thus long over the memory of scenes which have passed away.

But of beauty, I repeat again that we saw her there shining in company with the celestial forms; and coming to earth we find her here too, shining in clearness through the clearest aperture of sense. For sight is the keenest of our bodily senses; though not by that is wisdom seen, for her loveliness would have been transporting if there had been a visible image of her, and this is true of the loveliness of the other ideas as well. But beauty only has this portion, that she is at once the loveliest and also the most apparent. Now he who has not been lately initiated, or who has become corrupted, is not easily carried out of this world to the sight of absolute beauty in the other; he looks only at that which has the name of beauty in this world, and instead of being awed at the sight of her, like a brutish beast he rushes on to enjoy. . . .

251- 254 But he whose initiation is recent, and who has been the spectator of many glories in the other world, is amazed when he sees any one having a godlike face or form, which is the expression or imitation of divine beauty; and at first a shudder runs through him, and some "misgiving" of a former world steals over him; then looking upon the face of his beloved as of a god he reverences him, and if he were not afraid of being thought a downright madman, he would sacrifice to his beloved as to the image of a god.

[When the lover beholds the divine beauty of his beloved he receives the effluence of that beauty into his own soul, and by it the nobler and diviner part of his nature is nourished. He is filled with joy, because the wing of his soul thus begins to grow, and he is happy only when in the presence of his beloved. When the beloved is absent, and the holy effluence is withdrawn, this growth of the soul's wing ceases, and the lover is filled with pain and unrest. He is constrained to flee to his beloved as to a physician.]

And this state, my dear imaginary youth, is by men called love, and among the gods has a name which you, in your simplicity, may be inclined to mock ; there are two lines in honor of love in the Homeric Apocrypha [40] in which the name occurs. One of them is rather outrageous, and is not quite metrical ; they are as follow :—

> " Mortals call him Eros (love),
> But the immortals call him Pteros (fluttering dove)
> Because fluttering of wings is a necessity to him."

You may believe this or not as you like. At any rate the loves of lovers and their causes are such as I have described.

[Now the character of the lover depends upon the god whom he followed in the upper world, and this same character the lover tries to cultivate in the object of his love. The followers of every god]

seek a love who is to be like their god, and when they have found him, they themselves imitate their god, and persuade their love to do the same, and bring him into harmony with the form and ways of the god as far as they can ; for they have no feelings of envy or mean enmity towards their beloved,

---

[40] Writings falsely attributed to Homer.

but they do their utmost to create in him the greatest likeness of themselves and the god whom they honor. And the desire of the lover, if effected, and the initiation of which I speak into the mysteries of true love, is thus fair and blissful to the beloved when he is chosen by the lover who is driven mad by love. . . .

255-256 And so the beloved who, like a god, has received every true and loyal service from his lover, not in pretense but in reality, being also himself of a nature friendly to his admirer, if in former days he has blushed to own his passion and turned away his lover, because his youthful companions or others slanderously told him that he would be disgraced, now as years advance, at the appointed age and time is led to receive him into communion. For fate, which has ordained that there shall be no friendship among the evil, has also ordained that there shall ever be friendship among the good. And when he has received him into communion and intimacy, then the beloved is amazed at the good-will of the lover; he recognizes that the inspired friend is worth all other friendship or kinships, which have nothing of friendship in them in comparison. . . . After this their happiness depends upon their self-control; if the better elements of the mind which lead to order and philosophy prevail, then they pass their life in this world in happiness and harmony—masters of themselves and orderly—enslaving the vicious and emancipating the virtuous elements; and when the end comes, being light and ready to fly away, they conquer in one of the three heavenly or truly Olympian victories [41]; nor can human discipline or divine inspiration confer any greater blessing on man than this.

[If, however, they abandon philosophy and lead the lower life of ambition, they lose the fairest reward which might have been theirs; and still their destiny is not an unhappy one.]

For those who have once begun the heavenward pilgrimage may not go down again to darkness and the journey beneath the earth, but they live in light always; happy companions in their pilgrimage, and when the time comes at which they receive their wings they have the same plumage because of their love.

[41] Compare 249.

Thus great are the heavenly blessings which the friendship of a lover will confer on you, my youth. Whereas the attachment of the non-lover which is just a vulgar compound of temperance and niggardly earthly ways and motives, will breed meanness—praised by the vulgar as virtue in your inmost soul; will send you bowling round the earth during a period of nine thousand years, and leave you a fool in the world below.[42]

₂₅₇₋₂₅₈

And thus, dear Eros, I have made and paid my recantation, as well as I could and as fairly as I could; the poetical figures I was compelled to use, because Phædrus would have them. And now forgive the past and accept the present, and be gracious and merciful to me, and do not deprive me of sight or take from me the art of love, but grant that I may be yet more esteemed in the eyes of the fair. And if Phædrus or I myself said anything objectionable in our first speeches, blame Lysias, who is the father of the brat, and let us have no more of his progeny; bid him study philosophy, like his brother Polemarchus; and then his lover Phædrus will no longer halt between two, but dedicate himself wholly to love and philosophical discourses.

Phædr. I say with you, Socrates, may this come true if this be for my good. But why did you make this discourse of yours so much finer than the other? I wonder at that. And I begin to be afraid that I shall lose conceit of Lysias, even if he be willing to make another as long as yours, which I doubt. For one of our politicians lately took to abusing him on this very account; he would insist on calling him a speech-writer. So that a feeling of pride may probably induce him to give up writing.

Soc. That is an amusing notion; but I think that you are a little mistaken in your friend if you imagine that he is frightened at every noise; and, possibly, you think that his assailant was in earnest?

Phædr. I thought, Socrates, that he was. And you are aware that the most powerful and considerable men among our statesmen are ashamed of writing speeches and leaving them in a written form because they are afraid of posterity, and do not like to be called Sophists.

---

[42] Compare 249.

[Socrates replies that it is only a case of sour grapes with the assailants of Lysias. As a matter of fact there is nothing of which the great politicians are so fond as of writing speeches. They seek to display their own wisdom and attain immortality by the authorship of laws. A king or an orator who does attain immortality through his laws is looked upon by posterity as a god, and such he considers himself. Since the politicians are really great rhetoricians, in reproaching Lysias they would be casting a slur on their own favorite pursuit.]

Soc. Any one may see that there is no disgrace in the fact of writing?

Phædr. Certainly not.

Soc. There may however be a disgrace in writing, not well, but badly?

Phædr. That is true.

Soc. And what is well and what is badly,—need we ask Lysias, or any other poet or orator, who ever wrote or will write either a political or any other work, in metre or out of metre, poet or prose writer, to teach us this?

Phædr. Need we? What motive has a man to live if not for the pleasures of discourse? Surely he would not live for the sake of bodily pleasures, which almost always have previous pain as a condition of them, and therefore are rightly called slavish.

Soc. There is time yet. And I can fancy that the grasshoppers who are still chirruping in the sun over our heads are talking to one another and looking at us. What would they say if they saw that we also, like the many, are not talking but slumbering at midday, lulled by their voices, too indolent to think? They would have a right to laugh at us, and might imagine that we are slaves coming to our place of resort, who like sheep lie asleep at noon about the fountain. But if they see us discoursing, and like Odysseus sailing by their siren voices,[43] they may perhaps, out of respect, give us of the gifts which they receive of the gods and give to men.

[43] See Symposium, note 35. When the Greek hero Odysseus passed the island of the Sirens on his way home from the Trojan War, he had the ears of his companions stopped with wax and himself bound to the mast, so that they all sailed by in safety.

Phædr. What gifts do you mean? I never heard of any.

Soc. A lover of music like yourself ought surely to have heard the story of the grasshoppers, who are said to have been human beings in an age before the Muses. And when the Muses came and song appeared they were ravished with delight; and singing always, never thought of eating and drinking, until at last they forgot and died. And now they live again in the grasshoppers; and this is the return which the Muses make to them,—they hunger no more, neither thirst any more, but are always singing from the moment that they are born, and never eating or drinking; and when they die they go and inform the Muses in heaven who honors them on earth. They win the love of Terpsichore [44] for the dancers by their report of them; of Erato [45] for the lovers, and of the other Muses for those who do them honor, according to the several ways of honoring them: of Calliope [46] the eldest Muse, and of her who is next to her [47] for the votaries of philosophy; for these are the Muses who are chiefly concerned with heaven and the ideas, divine as well as human, and they have the sweetest utterance. For many reasons, then, we ought always to talk and not to sleep at midday.

Phædr. Let us talk.

Soc. Shall we discuss the rules of writing and speech as we were proposing?

Phædr. Very good.

260-265

[The first rule of good speaking, Socrates claims, is that the speaker must have knowledge—he must know the truth of the matter about which he is going to speak. This seems doubtful at first, for rhetoric does not deal with truth but only with the opinions of men. The art of rhetoric, whether employed in public or private, in regard to matters great or small, good or bad, is "a universal art of enchanting the mind by arguments." It makes the good appear evil, the just unjust, the like unlike, or *vice versa*, just as the speaker pleases. Nevertheless, though knowledge of the truth alone will not give one the art of persuasion, neither can that art be

---

[44] Terpsichore (terp-sĭk′o-re): the Muse who presided over choral song and dancing.
[45] Erato (ĕr′a-tō): the Muse who presided over love-poetry.
[46] Calliope (kăl-lī′o-pe): the Muse of Epic poetry and eloquence.
[47] Jowett says this refers to Urania (ū-rā′ni-a), the Muse of Astronomy.

separated from such knowledge. Even when the object of the speaker is to deceive his hearers, he must depart from the truth very gradually indeed or he will be detected. He must present to his audience something which very nearly resembles the truth, for error slips in through resemblances. Now in order to know what resembles the truth, the deceiver must know the truth itself. This knowledge of the truth also enables him to detect a deception employed against himself. "Then he who would be a master of the art must know the real nature of everything; or he will never know either how to contrive or how to escape the gradual departure from truth into the opposite of truth which is effected by the help of resemblances."

Socrates proposes that they use the speech of Lysias and his own about love as illustrations of the art of rhetoric. Lysias is first criticised for not beginning with a definition of his subject. Love is a term as to whose meaning we are not all agreed, and it should be defined by a speaker in the opening of his discourse. Socrates began with a definition of love, but Lysias began with what should have been the end of his speech. Socrates' speeches are also superior to that of Lysias in respect to arrangement. Lysias seems to have written things down just as they came into his head without any regard to arrangement. "Every discourse," says Socrates, "ought to be a living creature, having its own body and head and feet; there ought to be a middle, beginning, and end, which are in a manner agreeable to one another, and to the whole." Such a vital connection does not exist between the parts of Lysias' discourse. Although the myth which Socrates related was only the creation of fancy, it "involved two principles which would be charming if they could be fixed by art."]

Phædr. What are they?

Soc. First, the comprehension of scattered particulars in one idea: the speaker defines his several notions in order that he may make his meaning clear, as in our definition of love, which whether true or false certainly gave clearness and consistency to the discourse.

Phædr. What is the other principle, Socrates?

Soc. Secondly, there is the faculty of division according to the natural ideas or members, not breaking any part as a bad carver might. But, as the body may be divided into a left side and into a right side, having parts right and left, so in the two discourses there was assumed, first of all, the general idea of unreason, and then one of the two proceeded to divide the parts of the left side and did not desist until he found in them an evil or left-handed love which the speaker justly reviled; and the other leading us to the right portion in which madness lay, found another love, having the same name, but yet divine, which he held up before us and applauded as the author of the greatest benefits.

Phædr. That is most true.

Soc. I am a great lover of these processes of division and generalization; they help me to speak and think. And if I find any man who is able to see unity and plurality in nature, him I follow, and walk in his steps as if he were a god. And those who have this art, I have hitherto been in the habit of calling dialecticians; but God knows whether the name is right or not. And I should like to know what name you would give to your or Lysias' disciples, and whether this may not be that famous art of rhetoric which Thrasymachus [48] and others practice? Skillful speakers they are, and impart their skill to any who will consent to worship them as kings and to bring them gifts.

Phædr. Yes, they are royal men; but their art is not the same with the art of those whom you call, and rightly, in my opinion, dialecticians.

[The rhetorician does not employ the "processes of division and generalization" which Socrates praises in the art of the dialectician. Instead of this, he relies upon a great array of technical devices which are given imposing names and the rules for which fill many books on rhetoric. It is true that rhetoric has very great power in public meetings. The orator, however, does not acquire his power by a study of rules, as the rhetoricians seem to think. Rules are only the preliminaries of an art, and should not be confused with the art itself.]

Soc. Suppose a person to come to your friend Eryximachus, or to his father Acumenus,[49] and to say to him: "I know how

---

[48] See Rep., I., note 1.   [49] See Protagoras, note 18.

to apply drugs which shall have either a heating or a cooling effect, and I can give a vomit and also a purge, and all that sort of thing; and knowing all this, as I do, I claim to be a physician and a teacher of physic"—what do you suppose that they would say?

Phædr. They would be sure to ask him whether he knew "to whom" he would give them, and "when," and "how much."

Soc. And suppose that he were to reply: "No; I know nothing of that; I expect those whom I have taught all this to do that of themselves."

Phædr. They would reply that he is a madman or a pedant who fancies that he is a physician, because he has read something in a book, or has stumbled on a few drugs, although he has no real understanding of the art of medicine.

Soc. And suppose a person were to come to Sophocles or Euripides [50] and say that he knows how to make a long speech about a small matter, and a short speech about a great matter, and also a sorrowful speech, or a terrible, or threatening speech, or any other kind of speech, and in teaching this fancies that he is teaching the art of tragedy?

Phædr. They too would surely laugh at him if he fancies that tragedy is anything but the arranging of these elements in a manner suitable to one another and to the whole.

Soc. But I do not suppose that they would be rude to him or revile him. Would they not treat him as a musician would treat a man who thinks that he is a harmonist because he knows how to pitch the highest and lowest note; happening to meet such a one he would not say to him savagely, "Fool, you are mad!" O, no; he would rather say to him in a gentle and musical tone of voice: "My good friend, he who would be a harmonist must certainly know this, and yet he may understand nothing of harmony if he has not got beyond your stage of knowledge, for you only know the preliminaries of harmony and not harmonies."

Phædr. Very true.

269 *Soc.* And would not Sophocles say to the display of the would-be tragedian, that this was not tragedy but the preliminaries of tragedy, and would not Acumenus say to

---

[50] Sophocles (sŏf'o-klēz, 495-405 B.C.), Euripides (û-rĭp'ĭ-dēz, 480-406 B.C.): great Athenian writers of tragedy.

the would-be doctor that this was not medicine but the preliminaries of medicine?

Phædr. Very true.

Soc. And if Adrastus[51] the mellifluous or Pericles[52] heard of these wonderful arts, brachylogies and eikonologies[53] and all the hard names which we have been endeavoring to draw into the light of day, what would they say? Instead of losing temper and applying uncomplimentary epithets, as you and I have been doing to the authors of such an imaginary art, their superior wisdom would rather censure us, as well as them. Have a little patience, Phædrus and Socrates, they would say, and don't be angry with those who from some want of dialectical skill are unable to define the nature of rhetoric, and consequently suppose that they have found the art in the preliminary conditions of the art, and when they have taught these to others, fancy that they have been teaching the whole art of rhetoric; but as to persuasion in detail and unity of composition, that they regard as an easy thing with which their disciples may supply themselves.

Phædr. I quite admit, Socrates, that the art of rhetoric which these men teach and of which they write is such as you describe—in that I agree with you. But I still want to know where and how the true art of rhetoric and persuasion is to be acquired.

Soc. The perfection of oratory is, or rather must be, like the perfection of all things, partly given by nature; but this is assisted by art, and if you have the natural power you will be famous as a rhetorician, if you only add knowledge and practice, and in either you may fall short. But the art, as far as there is an art, of rhetoric does not lie in the direction of Tisias[54] or Thrasymachus.

Phædr. But in what direction then?

Soc. I should conceive that Pericles was the most accomplished of rhetoricians.

Phædr. What of that?

Soc. All the higher arts require much discussion and lofty contemplation of nature; this is the source of sublimity and

---

[51] Adrastus (à-drăs'tus).
[52] See Protagoras, note 37.
[53] Brachylogies: brevity in speech or writing. Eikonology: figurative speaking.
[54] Tisias (tĭs'ĭ-as): a rhetorician.

perfect comprehensive power. And this, as I conceive, was the quality which, in addition to his natural gifts, Pericles acquired from his happening to know Anaxagoras.[55] He was imbued with the higher philosophy, and attained the knowledge of mind and matter, which was the favorite theme of Anaxagoras, and hence he drew what was applicable to his art.

Phædr. Explain.

Soc. Rhetoric is like medicine.

Phædr. How is that?

Soc. Why, because medicine has to define the nature of the body and rhetoric of the soul—if you would proceed, not empirically but scientifically, in the one case to impart health and strength by giving medicine and food, in the other to implant the conviction which you require by the right use of words and principles.

Phædr. You are probably right in that.

[The physician must study the body in whole and part that he may understand its nature and know how it may be affected at different times and in different ways. Just so must the rhetorician study the soul that his efforts may be intelligent when he seeks to produce conviction in a soul.]

Soc. Then clearly, Thrasymachus or any one else who elaborates a system of rhetoric will give an exact description of the soul; which he will make to appear either as single and same, or, like the body, multiform. That is what we should call showing the nature of the soul.

Phædr. Exactly.

Soc. He will next proceed to speak of the instruments by which the soul acts or is affected in any way.

Phædr. True.

Soc. Thirdly, having arranged men and speeches, and their modes and affections in different classes, and fitted them into one another he will point out the connection between them— he will show why one is naturally persuaded by a particular form of argument, and another not.

---

[55] Anaxagoras (ăn-ăks-ăg'o-ras 500 (?)-420 B.C.) :a Greek philosopher; a friend of Pericles; banished from Athens 434 B.C. on charge of atheism. He attempted to explain nature partly by blindly working material causes, and partly by the occasional intervention of mind. See Phædo, 97, summary.

Phædr. That will certainly be a very good way.

Soc. Yes, that is the true and only way in which any subject can be set forth or treated by rules of art, whether in speaking or writing. But the writers of the present day, at whose feet you have sat, improperly conceal all this about the soul which they know quite well. Nor, until they adopt our method of reading and writing, can we admit that they write by rules of art.

Phædr. What is our method?

Soc. I cannot give you the exact details; but I should like to tell you generally, as far as I can, how a man ought to proceed according to the rules of art.

Phædr. Let me hear.

Soc. Oratory is the art of enchanting the soul, and therefore he who would be an orator has to learn the differences of human souls—they are so many and of such a nature, and from them come the differences between man and man—he will then proceed to divide speeches into their different classes. Such and such persons, he will say, are affected by this or that kind of speech in this or that way, and he will tell you why; he must have a theoretical notion of them first, and then he must see them in action, and be able to follow them with all his senses about him, or he will never get beyond the precepts of his masters. But when he is able to say what persons are persuaded by what arguments, and recognize the individual about whom he used to theorize as actually present to him, and say to himself, "This is he and this is the sort of man who ought to have that argument applied to him in order to convince him of this;" when he has attained the knowledge of all this, and knows also when he should speak and when he should abstain from speaking, and when he should make use of pithy sayings, pathetic appeals, aggravated effects, and all the other figures of speech; when, I say, he knows the times and seasons of all these things, then, and not till then, he is perfect and a consummate master of his art; but if he fail in any of these points, whether in speaking or teaching or writing them, and says that he speaks by rules of art, he who denies this has the better of him. Well, the teacher will say, is this, Phædrus and Socrates, your account of the art of rhetoric, or am I to look for another?

Phædr. He must take this, Socrates, for there is no possibility of another, and yet the creation of such an art is not easy.

[Now some say that this is a long rough road to the art of rhetoric, and that there is a shorter and easier one which ought to be followed. Their argument is like this: Where goodness or justice is the question at issue, the rhetorician has no need of truth. In the law courts, for example, men care nothing about truth, but only about conviction. Now conviction is based on probability, and facts ought to be withheld. It is the business of either party to invent lies which the other cannot refute. Therefore the orator should say good-by to truth and give his whole attention to probability.]

These and others like them are the precepts of the doctors of the art. Am I not right, Phædrus?

Phædr. Certainly.

Soc. I cannot help feeling that this is a wonderfully mysterious art which Tisias has discovered, or whoever the gentleman was, or whatever his name or country may have been, who was the discoverer. Shall we say a word to him or not?

Phædr. What shall we say to him?

Soc. Let us tell him that, before he appeared, you and I were saying that probability was engendered in the minds of the many by the likeness of the truth, and were setting forth that he who knew the truth would always know how best to discover the resemblances of the truth. If he has anything further to say about the art of speaking we should like to hear him; but if not, we are satisfied with our own view, that unless a man estimates the various characters of his hearers and is able to divide existences into classes and to sum them up in single ideas, he will never be a skillful rhetorician even within the limits of human power. And this art he will not attain without a great deal of trouble, which a good man ought to undergo, not for the sake of speaking and acting before men, but in order that he may be able to say what is acceptable to God and in all things to act acceptably to him as far as in him lies; for there is a saying of wiser men than ourselves, that a man of sense should not try to please his fellow-servants (at least this should not be his principal object) but his good and noble masters, so that, if the way is

274

long and circuitous, marvel not at this; for, where the end is great, there the way may be permitted to be long, but not for lesser ends such as yours. Truly, the argument may say, Tisias, that if you do not mind going so far, rhetoric has a fair beginning in this.

Phædr. I think, Socrates, that this is admirable, if only practicable.

Soc. But even to fail in an honorable object is honorable.

Phædr. True.

Soc. I think that enough has been said of a true and false art of speaking.

Phædr. Certainly.

Soc. But there is something yet to be said of propriety and impropriety of writing.

Phædr. Yes.

Soc. Do you know how you can speak or act about rhetoric in a manner which will be acceptable to God?

Phædr. No, indeed. Do you?

Soc. I have heard a tradition of antiquity, whether true or not, antiquity only knows. If we had the truth ourselves, do you think that we should care much about the opinions of men?

Phædr. That is a question which needs no answer; but I wish that you would tell me what you say that you have heard.

Soc. At the Egyptian city of Naucratis,[56] there was a famous old god, whose name was Theuth [57]; the bird which is called the Ibis was sacred to him, and he was the inventor of many arts, such as arithmetic and calculation and geometry and astronomy and draughts and dice, but his great discovery was the use of letters. Now in those days Thamus[58] was the king of the whole of Upper Egypt, which is the district surrounding that great city which is called by the Hellenes Egyptian Thebes,[59] and they call the god himself Ammon. To him came Theuth and showed his inventions, desiring that the other Egyptians might be allowed to have the benefit of them; he went through them, and Thamus inquired about their sev-

---

[56] Naucratis (nau-krā'tis): a city in the Delta of Egypt, on a branch of the Nile.
[57] Theuth (thŭth).
[58] Thamus (thā'mus).
[59] Thebes (thēbz): the ancient capital of Upper Egypt.

eral uses, and praised some of them and censured others, as he approved or disapproved of them. There would be no use in repeating all that Thamus said to Theuth in praise or blame of the various arts. But when they came to letters, This, said Theuth, will make the Egyptians wiser and give them better memories; for this is the cure of forgetfulness and of folly. Thamus replied: O most ingenious Theuth, he who has the gift of invention is not always the best judge of the utility or inutility of his own inventions to the users of them. And in this instance a paternal love of your own child has led you to say what is not the fact; for this invention of yours will create forgetfulness in the learners' souls, because they will not use their memories; they will trust to the external written characters and not remember of themselves. You have found a specific, not for memory but for reminiscence, and you give your disciples only the pretence of wisdom; they will be hearers of many things and will have learned nothing; they will appear to be omniscient and will generally know nothing; they will be tiresome, having the reputation of knowledge without the reality.

Phædr. Yes, Socrates, you can easily invent tales of Egypt, or of any other country that you like.

Soc. There was a tradition in the temple of Dodona[60] that oaks first gave prophetic utterances. The men of that day, unlike in their simplicity to young philosophy, deemed that if they heard the truth even from " oak or rock," that was enough for them; whereas, you seem to think not of the truth but of the speaker, and of the country from which the truth comes.

Phædr. I acknowledge the justice of your rebuke; and I think that the Theban is right in his view about letters.

Soc. He would be a simple person, and quite without understanding of the oracles Thamus and Ammon, who should leave in writing or receive in writing any art under the idea that the written word would be intelligible or certain; or who deemed that writing was at all better than knowledge and recollection of the same matters.

Phædr. That is most true.

[60] Dodona (dṓ-dō'na): a city in Epirus (epī'rus), a country of ancient Greece. Dodona was the seat of a very ancient and celebrated oracle of the same name. Responses were said to be given in the rustling of leaves.

Soc. I cannot help feeling, Phædrus, that writing is unfortunately like painting; for the creations of the painter have the attitude of life, and yet if you ask them a question they preserve a solemn silence. And the same may be said of speeches. You would imagine that they had intelligence, but if you want to know anything and put a question to one of them, the speaker always gives one unvarying answer. And when they have been once written down they are tossed about anywhere among those who do and among those who do not understand them. And they have no reticences or proprieties towards different classes of persons; and, if they are unjustly assailed or abused, their parent is needed to protect his offspring, for they cannot protect or defend themselves.

Phædr. That again is most true.

Soc. May we not imagine another kind of writing or speaking far better than this is, and having far greater power, —which is one of the same family, but lawfully begotten? Let us see what his origin is.

276

Phædr. Who is he, and what do you mean about his origin?

Soc. I am speaking of an intelligent writing which is graven in the soul of him who has learned, and can defend itself, and knows when to speak and when to be silent.

Phædr. You mean the word of knowledge which has a living soul, and of which the written word is properly no more than an image?

Soc. Yes, of course that is what I mean. And I wish that you would let me ask you a question: Would a husbandman, who is a man of sense, take the seeds, which he values and which he wishes to be fruitful, and in sober earnest plant them during the heat of summer, in some garden of Adonis,[61] that he may rejoice when he sees them in eight days appearing in beauty (at least he does that, if at all, only as the show of a festival); but those about which he is in earnest he sows in fit-

---

[61] Adonis (á-dō'nis): a beautiful youth greatly beloved by Aphrodite. Her grief was so great at his death that he was allowed to return to earth and spend half of every year with her. His coming was attended by the springing up of grass and flowers, and the singing of birds, and was symbolical of the return of vegetation in spring after six months of hiding in the ground. The Greek women celebrated yearly a festival in honor of Adonis, and for this occasion cresses and other such quick-growing herbs were grown in pots. (L. and S.)

ting soil, and practices husbandry, and is satisfied if in eight months they arrive at perfection?

Phædr. Yes, Socrates, that will be his way when he is in earnest; he will do the other, as you say, only as an amusement.

Soc. And can we suppose that he who knows the just and good and honorable has less understanding in reference to his own seeds than the husbandman?

Phædr. Certainly not.

Soc. Then he will not seriously incline to write them in water with pen and ink, or in dumb characters which have not a word to say for themselves and cannot adequately express the truth?

Phædr. No, that is not likely.

Soc. No, that is not likely,—in the garden of letters he will plant them only as an amusement, or he will write them down as memorials against the forgetfulness of old age, to be treasured by him and his equals when they, like him, have one foot in the grave; and he will rejoice in beholding their tender growth; and they will be his pastime while others are watering the garden of their souls with banqueting and the like.

Phædr. A pastime, Socrates, as noble as the other is ignoble, when a man is able to pass time merrily in the representation of justice and the like.

Soc. True, Phædrus. But nobler far is the serious pursuit of the dialectician, who finds a congenial soul, and then with knowledge engrafts and sows words which are able to help themselves and him who planted them, and are not unfruitful, but have in them seeds which may bear fruit in other natures, nurtured in other ways,—making the seed everlasting and the possessors happy to the utmost extent of human happiness.

Phædr. Yes, indeed, that is far nobler.

Soc. And now, Phaedrus, having agreed upon the premises we may decide about the conclusion.

Phædr. About what conclusion?

Soc. About Lysias, whom we censured, and his art of writing, and his discourses, and the rhetorical skill or want of skill which was shown in them; for he brought us to this point. And I think that we are now pretty well informed about the nature of art and its opposite.

Phædr. Yes, I think with you; but I wish that you would repeat what was said.

Soc. Until a man knows the truth of the several particulars of which he is writing or speaking, and is able to define them as they are, and having defined them again to divide them until they can be no longer divided, and until in like manner he is able to discern the nature of the soul and discover the different modes of discourse which are adapted to different natures, and to arrange and dispose them in such a way that the simple form of speech may be addressed to the simpler nature, and the complex and composite to the complex nature —until he has accomplished all this, he will be unable to handle arguments according to rules of art, as far as their nature allows them to be subjected to art, either for the purpose of teaching or persuading; that is the view which is implied in the whole preceding argument.

Phædr. Yes, that was our view, certainly.

Soc. Secondly, as to the justice of the censure which was passed on speaking or writing discourses—did not our previous argument show—

Phædr. Show what?

Soc. That whether Lysias or any other writer that ever was or will be, whether private man or statesman, writes a political treatise in his capacity of legislator, and fancies that there is a great certainty and clearness in his performance, the fact of his writing as he does is only a disgrace to him, whatever men may say. For entire ignorance about the nature of justice and injustice, and good and evil, and the inability to distinguish the dream from the reality, cannot in truth be otherwise than disgraceful to him, even though he have the applause of the whole world.

Phædr. Certainly.

Soc. But he who thinks that in the written word there is necessarily much which is not serious, and that neither poetry nor prose, spoken or written, are of any great value—if, like the compositions of the rhapsodes,[62] they are only recited in order to be believed, and not with any view to criticism or instruction; and who thinks that even the best of them are but a reminiscence of what we know, and that only

---

[62] A class of wandering minstrels, who earned their living by reciting the poems of Homer and other epics.

in principles of justice and goodness and nobility taught and communicated orally and written in the soul, which is the true way of writing, is there clearness and perfection and seriousness; and that such principles are like legitimate offspring; being, in the first place, that which the man finds in his own bosom; secondly, the brethren and descendants and relations of this which has been duly implanted in the souls of others; and who cares for them and no others—this is the right sort of man; and you and I, Phædrus, would pray that we may become like him.

Phædr. That is most assuredly my desire and prayer.

Soc. And now the play is played out; and of rhetoric enough. Go and tell Lysias that to the fountain and school of the Nymphs we went down, and were bidden by them to convey a message to him and to other composers of speeches —to Homer and other writers of poems, whether set to music or not. And to Solon[63] and the writers of political documents, which they term laws, we are to say that if their compositions are based on knowledge of the truth, and they can defend or prove them, when they are put to the test, by spoken arguments, which leave their writings poor in comparison of them, then they are not only poets, orators, legislators, but worthy of a higher name.

Phædr. What name is that?

Soc. Wise, I may not call them; for that is a great name which belongs to God only,—lovers of wisdom or philosophers is their modest and befitting title.

Phædr. Very good.

Soc. And he who cannot rise above his own compilations and compositions, which he has been long patching and piecing, adding some and taking away some, may be justly called poet or speech-maker or law-maker.

Phædr. Certainly.

Soc. Now go and tell this to your companion.

Phædr. But there is also a friend of yours who ought not to be forgotten.

Soc. Who is that?

Phædr. Isocrates[64] the fair.

---

[63] Solon (638-558 B.C.): a celebrated Athenian statesman and law-giver.
[64] Isocrates (i-sŏk′ra-tēz, 436-338 B.C.): a Greek orator and teacher of rhetoric. He came under the influence of Socrates, but never belonged to the circle of his most intimate friends and disciples.

Soc. What of him?

Phædr. What message shall we send to him?

Soc. Isocrates is still young, Phædrus; but I am willing to risk a prophecy concerning him.

Phædr. What would you prophesy?

Soc. I think that he has a genius which soars above the orations of Lysias, and he has a character of a finer mould. My impression of him is that he will marvelously improve as he grows older, and that all former rhetoricians will be as children in comparison of him. And I believe that he will not be satisfied with this, but that some divine impulse will lead him to things higher still. For there is an element of philosophy in his nature. This is the message which comes from the gods dwelling in this place, and which I will myself deliver to Isocrates, who is my delight; and do you give the other to Lysias, who is yours.

Phædr. I will; and now as the heat is abated let us depart.

Soc. Should we not offer up a prayer first of all to the local deities?

Phædr. By all means.

Soc. Beloved Pan,[65] and all ye other gods who haunt this place, give me beauty in the inward soul; and may the outward and inward man be at one. May I reckon the wise to be the wealthy, and may I have such a quantity of gold as none but the temperate can carry. Anything more? That, prayer, I think, is enough for me.

Phædr. Ask the same for me, for friends should have all things in common.

Soc. Let us go.

---

[65] Pan: god of woods and fields, of flocks and shepherds; he dwelt in caves or forests, and wandered over mountains and valleys.

THE REPUBLIC

INTRODUCTION

I. THE subject of the Republic is given in the dialogue as justice. Justice, as here used, may be described quite generally as the right conduct of individual and social life. The conduct of life is held to be determined by the nature of the world in which we live and by the nature of man.

II. We are said to live in two worlds. One of these is the world which is eternal, unchangeable, absolutely good, absolutely beautiful, absolutely one, in all ways absolutely perfect. It is called the world of being, world of essence, the real world, the one, the good, the absolute, and other such names. The soul is said to belong by its highest nature to the eternal world, and by pure reflection it may know the real world as it is. This is the only true knowledge, the only true guide for the conduct of individual and social life. While we are on earth we are, through our bodies, in connection with the world of imperfect things. The knowledge which we have of this world through our bodily senses is not true knowledge, and the life of the individual or state is corrupted in so far as it is guided by such pseudo-knowledge. For a further discussion of this point see General Introduction, p. xxiv. For the several grades of knowledge, from total ignorance to pure science, see especially V., 476, to VII., 521.

III. The Nature of Man: The life of man is said to have three principles, (a) the appetitive principle which impels him toward the satisfaction of bodily desires; (b) the spirited principle which impels him to fight; and (c) the rational principle which tends to control all his actions in accordance with the absolute truth.

The virtues which the soul should possess are accordingly as follows: (1) Courage: "He is deemed courageous who, having the element of passion working within him, preserves in the midst of pain and pleasure the notion of danger which reason requires." (2) Wisdom: "He is wise who has in him that little part which rules and gives orders, that part being suffered to have a knowledge of what is for the interest of each and all of the three parts." (3) Temperance: "He is temperate who has these same elements in friendly harmony, in whom the one ruling principle of reason, and the two subject ones of spirit and desire, are equally agreed that reason ought to rule and do not rebel." (4) Justice: Justice is the perfect harmony of the other three virtues. "The just man does not permit the several elements within him to interfere with one another or any of them to do the work of the others; but he sets in order his own inner life and is his own master and at peace with himself; and when he has bound together the three principles within him which may be compared to the middle, higher, and lower divisions of the scale and the intermediate intervals,—when he has bound together all these and is no longer many, but has become one entirely temperate and perfectly adjusted nature," then he will truly distinguish justice and injustice, and will act accordingly. In a word, Justice is health—the harmonious organic unity of all the elements of man's life in accordance with the absolute truth.

IV. The Nature of the State: The true nature of the State corresponds to the nature of the individual man. There are three classes of persons in the State, the laborers, the soldiers, and the statesmen. The proper virtue for the statesmen is wisdom; for the soldiers courage; for all classes temperance. Where all classes have their proper virtues and occupations, the State has the virtue of justice, or perfect health. On III. and IV. see Book IV. especially 428 to close.

V. Education: Since the State as a whole and the lives of all the citizens can be rightly determined only by the absolute truth, and since the absolute truth or knowledge of the eternal world is attained only by the philosophers, the philosophers alone are fit to rule the State. A question of primary importance is therefore the selection and education of those who are to become the philosopher-statesmen. Very few, Plato holds, are fit by nature for this high office; for the necessary perfection of body and mind, especially the right mingling of gentleness with spirit, are rarely found in the same individual. When fit children are found, they should be given the education proper for a guardian, to whatever class their parents belong.

The elementary education of these children should consist of music and gymnastics. With Plato, music includes poetry, and, in a wider sense, all the arts. (See Republic, II., Note 17.) The essential thing about the elementary education is that all things therein shall be determined by the philosopher in accordance with the absolute truth. The greater part of the literature and other art of Greece is condemned by Plato, because its beauty is not a beauty which is in harmony with the absolute good.

At a later stage (20 years), the youth who is preparing to be a philosopher-statesman should study the pure abstract sciences of arithmetic, plane geometry, solid geometry, astronomy, and musical harmony. Only after this preparation, and at the age of thirty, is he fit to begin the study of pure philosophy or dialectic. After pursuing this subject for five years, he enters active public life for fifteen years. After the age of fifty he returns to the study of philosophy for the remainder of his life, with occasional re-entrance into active life as emergencies may require. A State governed by such men in accordance with absolute truth is, according to Plato, ideally good, and every citizen therein will be better and happier than under any other conditions; for every citizen will be doing, in obedience to the wise rulers, what he is best fitted to do for himself and for others, and will be receiving from all others that which is his due. See II., 374 to end of III., VI., VII., and X., 595 to 608.

VI. The decline of the State: The State will be preserved as it should be only as long as it is wholly guided by the absolute truth, through the philosophers. If men whose highest principle is love of honor, succeed those whose highest principle is obedience to the truth, the next generation will likely put love of money in place of love of honor, the next will put love of pleasure in place of money, and presently all virtue and health will give place to the wildest license, and so at last, to general ruin of State and of the people.

The several forms of government (to each of which there corresponds a certain kind of man) are named and described as follows: (1.) Aristocracy: Literally, government by the best. With Plato, this meant government by the philosophers. (2.) Timocracy: Literally, government by honor. With Plato, this meant government by those whose highest principle is soldierly ambition, and who are ignorant of and indifferent to true wisdom. (3.) Oligarchy: Literally, government by the few. With Plato, this meant government by those whose highest virtues are those involved in the acquisition of wealth, and who are indifferent to true wisdom and to soldierly honor. (4.) Democracy: Literally, government by the common people. With Plato, this meant government by the mob whose highest desire is license regardless of true wisdom, honor, or the virtues that lead to wealth. (5.) Tyranny: Literally, government by one absolute ruler. With

Plato, this meant government by one man who has absolute power over his subjects, and who uses this power solely for his own lowest self-interest, without regard to wisdom or honor, and without regard to the material prosperity or the desires of his people. See VIII. and IX.

VII. Virtue and happiness: As already stated, virtue is health, the harmonious organic unity of all the elements of man's life in accordance with absolute truth. Every breach of virtue is a breach of health. Vice is disease. Vice can appear to be more pleasurable than virtue only for a little time. The wages of sin are always quickly misery and ruin. The virtuous soul, on the contrary, is completely fortified against real harm or unhappiness. It is at one with itself and at one with God. It has the joy which springs from perfect health, and it has that joy not only in this life but in that which is to come. See IV., 445, IX., 576 to 581 and X., 608 to close.

NOTE.—Most of the first book of the Republic is given up to an argument between Socrates, Thrasymachus, and others, in which no conclusions satisfactory to any one are reached. Here, as in other dialogues, Socrates sometimes appears to be as sophistical as his opponents. This part of the Republic is probably to be regarded as a dramatic portrayal of the way in which the Sophists dealt with questions. The serious consideration of justice in the individual and State begins with the second book.

THE REPUBLIC

BOOK I

PERSONS OF THE DIALOGUE.[1]

SOCRATES, *who is the narrator.*
GLAUCON.
ADEIMANTUS.
POLEMARCHUS.
CEPHALUS.
THRASYMACHUS.
CLEITOPHON.

And others who are mute auditors.

The scene is laid in the house of Cephalus at the Piræus; and the whole discourse is narrated the day after it actually took place to Timæus, Hermocrates, Critias,[2] and a nameless person, who all reappear in the Timæus.

I WENT down to the Piræus[3] yesterday with Glaucon the son of Ariston, that I might offer up a prayer to the goddess; and also because I wanted to see in what manner they would

---

[1] Glaucon (glạu′kon): brother of Plato. He is said to have written a number of dialogues, but none are extant.
Adeimantus (ăd′i-măn′tus): brother of Plato; mentioned in Apology, 34; little is known of him beyond the representation in this dialogue.
Polemarchus (pŏl′e-măr′kus): son of Cephalus, and brother of Lysias, the orator. The brothers owned a shield factory and amassed great wealth, on account of which they were seized by the Thirty Tyrants. Lysias escaped, but Polemarchus was forced, without trial, to drink the hemlock.
Cephalus (sĕf′a-lus): a resident alien from Syracuse. "We are to think of Cephalus, not as the Athenian aristocrat, but, rather as the cultivated manufacturer or merchant prince, residing, no doubt, in a good house, but in a commercial or industrial quarter. He accepted, we are told, the burdens of an Athenian citizen, and lived for thirty years, unharming and unharmed, under the popular government."—*Bosanquet.*
Thrasymachus (thra-sy̆m′a-kus): a native of Chalcedon (kăl-sē′don), a Greek city on the Bosphorus. He was a Sophist, and a famous teacher of rhetoric. He is mentioned in the Phædrus.
Cleitophon (klī′to-fon): son of Aristonymus (ăr′ĭs-tŏn′y-mus); not mentioned elsewhere by Plato.

[2] Timæus (ti-mē′us). Hermocrates (her-mŏk′ra-tēz). Critias (krĭt′i-as).

[3] Piræus (pī-rē′us): the most important of the harbors of Athens, situated about five miles southwest of Athens, and connected with that city by the Long Walls. Many foreigners resided there.

celebrate the festival of Bendis,[4] which was a new thing. I was delighted with the procession of the inhabitants; this, however, was equalled or even exceeded in beauty by that of the Thracians. When we had finished our prayers and the spectacle was over, we turned in the direction of the city; and at that instant, Polemarchus the son of Cephalus, who had caught sight of us at a distance as we were departing homewards, told his servant to run and bid us wait for him. The servant took hold of me by the cloak behind, and said: Polemarchus desires you to wait.

Steph. 327

I turned round, and asked him where his master was.

He is coming, said the youth, if you will only wait.

Certainly we will, said Glaucon; and in a few minutes Polemarchus appeared, and with him Adeimantus, Glaucon's brother, Niceratus the son of Nicias,[5] and several others who had been at the procession.

Polemarchus said to me: I perceive, Socrates, that you and your companion are already on your way to the city.

That is a good guess, I said.

But do you see, he said, how many we are?

I do.

And are you stronger than all these? for if not, you will have to remain where you are.

May there not be yet another possibility, I said, that we may persuade you to let us go?

But can you persuade us, if we refuse to listen to you? he said.

No indeed, replied Glaucon.

Then we are not going to listen; of that you may be assured.

Adeimantus added: Has no one told you that there is to be an equestrian torch-race in the evening in honor of the goddess?

328

Indeed, that is a novelty, I replied. Will the horsemen carry torches and pass them to one another during the race?

---

[4] Bendis (bĕn′dĭs): a Thracian goddess, sometimes identified with the Greek Artemis, goddess of the moon and the chase. The worship of Bendis was introduced into this part of Greece by Thracian aliens, residing at the Piræus. The public festival, the Bendideia (bĕn′dĭ-dī′a), instituted in honor of Bendis, was celebrated for the first time upon the occasion to which Socrates here refers.

[5] Niceratus (nĭ-sĕr′a-tus). Nicias (nĭsh′ĭ-as).

Yes, he said; and there will also be a festival at night which is well worth seeing. If we rise from supper in good time we shall see this, and we shall find youths enough there with whom we may discourse. Stay then, and do not be perverse.

Glaucon said: I suppose that we must stay.

Well, as you please, I replied.

Accordingly we went with Polemarchus to his house; and there we found his brothers Lysias[6] and Euthydemus,[7] and with them Thrasymachus the Chalcedonian, Charmantides the Pæanian,[8] and Cleitophon the son of Aristonymus. There too was their father Cephalus, whom I had not seen for a long time, and I thought him very much aged. He was seated on a cushioned chair, and had a garland on his head, for he had been holding a sacrifice[9] in the court; and we sat down by him on other chairs, which were arranged in a circle around him. He welcomed me eagerly, and then he said:—

You don't come to see me, Socrates, as often as you ought. For if I were able to go to you I would not ask you to come to me. But at my age I can hardly get to the city, and therefore you ought to come oftener to the Piræus. For, indeed, I find that at my time of life, as the pleasures and delights of the body fade away, the love of discourse grows upon me. I only wish therefore that you would come oftener, and be with your young friends here, and make yourself altogether at home with us.

I replied: There is nothing which I like better, Cephalus, than conversing with aged men like yourself; for I regard them as travellers who have gone a journey which I too may have to go, and of whom I ought to inquire, whether the way is smooth and easy, or rugged and difficult. And this is a question which I should like to ask of you who have arrived at that time which the poets call the "threshold of old age,"—Is life harder towards the end, or what report do you give of it?

I will tell you, Socrates, he said, what my own feeling is. Old men flock together; they are birds of a feather, as the

[6] See Phædrus, note 3.
[7] Euthydemus, not the one for whom the dialogue Euthydemus is named.
[8] Charmantides (kar-măn'tĭ-dēz). Pæania (pē-ā'nĭ-a): a deme of Attica.
[9] Probably an act of private worship. It was customary among the Greeks for one who took part in sacrifice to wear a wreath.

proverb says; and at our meetings the tale of my acquaintance commonly is—I cannot eat, I cannot drink; the pleasures of youth and love are fled away: there was a good time once, but that is gone, and now life is no longer life. Some of them lament over the slights which are put upon them by their relations, and then they tell you plaintively of how many evils old age is the cause. But I do not believe, Socrates, that the blame is where they say; for if old age were the cause, I too being old, and every other old man, would have felt the same. This, however, is not my own experience, nor that of others whom I have known. How well I remember the aged poet Sophocles,[10] when in answer to the question, How does love suit with age, Sophocles,—are you still the man you were? Peace, he replied; most gladly have I escaped that, and I feel as if I had escaped from a mad and furious master. That saying of his has often come into my mind since, and seems to me still as good as at the time when I heard him. For certainly old age has a great sense of calm and freedom; when the passions relax their hold, then, as Sophocles says, you have escaped from the control not of one master only, but of many. And of these regrets, as well as of the complaint about relations, Socrates, the cause is to be sought, not in men's ages, but in their characters and tempers; for he who is of a calm and happy nature will hardly feel the pressure of age, but he who is of an opposite disposition will find youth and age equally a burden.

I was delighted at his words, and wanting to draw him out I went on to say: Yes, Cephalus; but I suspect that people in general do not believe you when you say this; they think that old age sits lightly upon you, not because of your happy disposition, but because you are rich, and wealth is well known to be a great comforter.

That is true, he replied; they do not believe me: and there is something in what they say; not, however, so much as they imagine. I might answer them as Themistocles[11] answered the Seriphian[12] who was abusing him and saying that he was famous, not for his own merits but because

---

[10] See Phædrus, note 50.
[11] Themistocles (the-mĭs′tọ-klēz, 514 ?—B.C.): a great Athenian statesman.
[12] Seriphos (se-rī′fos): a small island in the Ægean Sea, colonized by Greeks.

he was an Athenian: "If you had been an Athenian and I a Seriphian, neither of us would have been famous." And to those who are not rich and are impatient of old age, the same reply may be made; for neither can a good poor man lightly bear age, nor can a bad rich man ever be at peace with himself.

May I ask, Cephalus, whether you inherited or acquired the greater part of your wealth?

How much did I acquire, Socrates? he replied,—is that your question? Well, the property which Cephalus, my grandfather, originally inherited was nearly of the same value as my own is at present; this he doubled and trebled, but my father Lysanias reduced below the original amount; and I, who am neither a spender of money like the one, nor a gainer of money like the other, shall be satisfied if I leave my sons a little more than I received.

That was why I asked you the question, I said, because I saw that you were not fond of money, which is a characteristic rather of those who have inherited their fortunes than of those who have acquired them; for the latter have a second or extraordinary love of money as a creation of their own, resembling the affection of authors for their own poems, or of parents for their children, besides that other love of money for the sake of use and enjoyment which is common to them and all men. And hence they are very bad company, for they talk about nothing but the praises of wealth.

That is true, he said.

Yes, that is very true, I said; but may I ask you one more question? which is this—What do you consider to be the greatest blessing which you have reaped from wealth?

Not one, he said, of which I could easily convince others. For let me tell you, Socrates, that when a man thinks himself to be near death he has fears and cares which never entered into his mind before; the tales of a life below and the punishment which is exacted there of deeds done here were a laughing matter to him once, but now he is haunted with the thought that they may be true: either because of the feebleness of age, or from the nearness of the prospect, he seems to have a clearer view of the other world; suspicions and alarms crowd upon him, and he begins to reckon up in his own mind what wrongs he has done to others. And when he finds that the sum of his transgressions is great, he will many a time like a child, start up in his sleep for fear, and he is filled with dark forebodings. But he who is conscious of no sin has in age a sweet hope which, as Pindar [13] charmingly says, is a kind nurse to him.

"Hope," as he says, "cherishes the soul of him who lives in holiness and righteousness, and is the nurse of his age and the companion of his journey—hope, which is mightiest to sway the eager soul of man."

That is an expression of his which wonderfully delights me. And this is the great blessing of riches, I do not say to every man, but to a good man, that he has had no occasion to deceive another, either intentionally or unintentionally; and when he departs to the other world he is not in any apprehension about offerings due to the gods or debts which he owes to men. Now the possession of wealth has a great deal to do with this; and therefore I say that, setting one thing against another, this, in my opinion, is to a man of sense the greatest of the many advantages which wealth has to give.

That is excellent, Cephalus, I replied; but then is justice no more than this—to speak the truth and pay your debts? And are there not exceptions even to this? If I have received arms from a friend when in his right mind, and he asks for them when he is not in his right mind, ought I to give them back to him? No one would say that I ought, any more than they would say that I ought always to speak the truth to one who is in that condition.

You are quite right, he replied.

But then, I said, speaking the truth and paying your debts is not a correct definition of justice.

And yet, said Polemarchus, that is the definition which has the authority of Simonides.[14]

I fear, said Cephalus, that I must look to the sacrifices; and therefore I now take leave of this argument, which I bequeath to you and Polemarchus.

Is not Polemarchus your heir? I said.

To be sure, he answered, and went away laughing to the sacrifices.

---

[13] See Euthydemus, note 22.
[14] See Protagoras, note 26. The authority of the greater poets was revered almost as we revere that of the Bible.

[Socrates and Polemarchus enter into a discussion of the definition of justice. They examine the view mentioned above that justice consists in speaking the truth and paying one's debts. They finally agree that this definition is unsatisfactory and cannot be the true one.]

Several times in the middle of our discourse Thrasymachus had made an attempt to get the argument into his own hands by interrupting us, and had been put down by the rest of the company, who wanted to hear the end. But when I had done speaking and there was a pause, he could no longer hold his peace; and, gathering himself up, he came at us like a wild beast seeking to devour us, and Polemarchus and I quaked with fear.

What folly has possessed you, Socrates? he said, with a roar. Why do you drop down at one another's feet in this silly way? I say that if you want to know what justice really is, you should answer and not ask, and you shouldn't pride yourself in refuting others, but have your own answer; for there is many a one who can ask and cannot answer. And don't tell me that justice is duty or advantage or profit or gain or interest, for that sort of watery stuff won't do for me; I must and will have a precise answer.

I was panic-stricken at these words, and trembled at the very look of him; and I verily believe that if I had not caught his eye first, I should have been deprived of utterance: but now, when I saw his fury rising, I had the presence of mind to keep my eye upon him, and this enabled me to reply to him.

Thrasymachus, I said, with a quiver, have mercy on us. Our error, if we were guilty of any error, was certainly unintentional; and therefore you, in your wisdom, should have pity upon us, and not be angry with us. If we were seeking for gold, you would not imagine that we were pretending only, or dropping down, as you say, out of foolish complaisance, at one another's feet. Do not imagine, then, that we are pretending to seek for justice, which is a treasure far more precious than gold.

How characteristic of Socrates! he replied, with a bitter laugh; that's your ironical way! Did I not foresee—did I not tell you all that he would refuse to answer, and try

337

irony or any other shift in order that he might avoid answering?

You are a philosopher, Thrasymachus, I replied, and well know that if you ask what numbers make up twelve, taking care to prohibit the person whom you ask from answering twice six, or three times four, or six times two, or four times three, "for this sort of nonsense won't do for me," then obviously, if that is your way of putting the question to him, neither he nor any one can answer. And suppose he were to say, "Thrasymachus, what do you mean? And if the true answer to the question is one of these numbers which you interdict, am I to say some other number which is not the right one?—is that your meaning?" How would you answer him?

Yes, said he; but how remarkably parallel the two cases are!

Very likely they are, I replied; but even if they are not, and only appear to be parallel to the person who is asked, can he to whom the question is put avoid saying what he thinks, even though you and I join in forbidding him?

Well, then, I suppose you are going to make one of the interdicted answers?

I dare say that I may, notwithstanding the danger, if upon reflection I approve of any of them.

But what if I give you a new and better answer, he said, than any of these? What do you deserve to have done to you?

Done to me! I can but suffer the penalty of ignorance; and the penalty is to learn from the wise—and that is what I deserve to have done to me.

What, and no payment! that's a pleasant notion!

I will pay when I have the money, I replied.

But you have, Socrates, said Glaucon; and you, Thrasymachus, need be under no anxiety about money, for we will all make a contribution for Socrates.

Yes, he replied, and I know what will happen; Socrates will do as he always does—not answer, but take and pull the argument to pieces.

Why, my good friend, I said, how can any one answer who knows, and says that he knows, just nothing; and who, even if he had some faint notions of his own, is told by a man of authority not to utter them? The natural thing is, that the speaker should be one who knows, like yourself; and I must earnestly request that you will kindly answer for the edification of the company and of myself.

Glaucon and the rest of the company joined in my request, and Thrasymachus, as any one might see, was really eager to speak; for he thought that he had an excellent answer, and would distinguish himself. But at first he affected to insist on my answering; at length he consented to begin. Behold, he said, the wisdom of Socrates; he refuses to teach himself, and goes about learning of others, to whom he never even says Thank you.

That I learn of others, I replied, is quite true; but that I am ungrateful I wholly deny. Money I have none, and therefore I pay in praise, which is all I have; and how ready I am to praise any one who speaks well you will very soon find out when you answer, for I expect that you will answer well.

Listen, then, he said; I proclaim that might is right, justice the interest of the stronger. But why don't you praise me?

Let me first understand you, I replied.

[Socrates now puts a series of questions to Thrasymachus, and in answering Thrasymachus is led to admit statements which contradict his own definition of justice. When he finds himself cornered in the argument, he tries to escape by means of a long speech upon the advantages of injustice, as follows:]

You fancy that the shepherd or neatherd fattens or tends the sheep or oxen with a view to their own good and not to the good of himself or his master; and you further imagine that the rulers of States, who are true rulers, never think of their subjects as sheep, and that they are not studying their own advantage day and night. O, no; and so entirely astray are you in the very rudiments of justice and injustice as not even to know that justice and the just are in reality another's good; that is to say, the interest of the ruler and stronger, and the loss of the subject and servant; whereas the reverse holds in the case of injustice; for the unjust is lord over the truly simple and just: he is the stronger, and his subjects do what is for his benefit, and minister to his happiness, which is very far from being their own. Consider further, most foolish Socrates, that the just is always a loser in comparison with the unjust. First of all in their private dealings: wherever the unjust is the partner of the just the conclusion of the affair always is that the unjust man has more and the just less. Next, in their dealings with the State: when there is an income-tax, the just man will pay more and the unjust less on the same amount of income ; and when there is anything to be received the one gains nothing and the other much. Observe also that when they come into office, there is the just man neglecting his affairs and perhaps suffering other losses, but he will not compensate himself out of the public purse because he is just ; moreover he is hated by his friends and relations for refusing to serve them in unlawful ways. Now all this is reversed in the case of the unjust man. I am speaking of injustice on a large scale in which the advantage of the unjust is most apparent, and my meaning will be most clearly seen in that highest form of injustice the perpetrator of which is the happiest of men, as the sufferers or those who refuse to do injustice are the most miserable—I mean tyranny, which by fraud and force takes away the property of others, not retail but wholesale ; comprehending in one, things sacred as well as profane, private and public ; for any one of which acts of wrong, if he were detected perpetrating them singly, he would be punished and incur great dishonor ; for they who are guilty of any of these crimes in single instances are called robbers of temples and man-stealers and burglars and swindlers and thieves. But when a man has taken away the money of the citizens and made slaves of them, then, instead of these dishonorable names, he is called happy and blessed, not only by the citizens but by all who hear of his having achieved the consummation of injustice. For injustice is censured because the censurers are afraid of suffering, and not from any fear which they have of doing injustice. And thus, as I have shown, Socrates, injustice, when on a sufficient scale, has more strength and freedom and mastery than justice ; and, as I said at first, justice is the interest of the stronger, whereas injustice is a man's own profit and interest.

Thrasymachus, when he had thus spoken, having, like a bath-man, deluged our ears with his words, had a mind to go away. But the company would not allow this, and they compelled him to remain and defend his position; and I myself added my own humble request that he would not leave us. Thrasymachus, I said to him, excellent man, how suggestive are your words! And are you going away before you have fairly taught or learned whether they are true or not? Is the attempt to determine the way of man's life such a small matter in your eyes—the attempt to determine the way in which life may be passed by one of us to the greatest advantage?

My reason is that I do not agree with you, he replied.

I should rather think, Thrasymachus, that you have no feeling about us, I said; you don't seem to care whether we live better or worse from not knowing what you say you know. Prithee, friend, be obliging and impart your wisdom to us; any benefit which is conferred on a large party such as this is will not be unrewarded. For my own part I frankly admit that I am not convinced, and that I do not believe injustice to be more gainful than justice, even if uncontrolled and allowed to have free play. For, granting that there may be an unjust man who is able to commit injustice either by fraud or force, still this does not convince me of the superior advantage of injustice, and there may be others who are in the same predicament as myself. Perhaps we may be wrong; if so, you should convince us that we are mistaken in preferring justice to injustice.

345-354

[In the discussion which follows, Thrasymachus again finds himself caught in the net of Socrates' questions and his argument refuted. But they arrive at no conclusion satisfactory to Socrates for they have not yet defined justice. At the close of the discussion Thrasymachus says:]

Let this, Socrates, be your entertainment at the Bendidea.

And for this I am indebted to you, I said, now that you have grown gentle toward me, and have left off scolding. Nevertheless, I have not been well entertained; but that was my own fault and not yours. I may liken myself to an epicure who snatches a taste of every dish which is successively brought to table before he has fairly enjoyed the one before; and this has been the case with me. For before I discovered the nature of justice, I left that and proceeded to inquire whether justice was virtue and wisdom or evil and folly; and then arose a further question about the comparative advantages of justice and injustice, and I could not refrain from passing on to that. And the result of all is that I know nothing at all. For I know not what justice is, and therefore I am not likely to know whether it is or is not a virtue, nor can I say whether the just is happy or unhappy.

BOOK II

WITH these words I was thinking that I had made an end of the discussion ; but the end, in truth, proved to be only a beginning. For Glaucon, who is at all times the boldest of men, was dissatisfied at Thrasymachus' retirement ; he wanted to have the battle out. So he said to me : Socrates, do you wish really to persuade us, or only to seem to have persuaded us, that to be just is always better than to be unjust?   357

I should wish really to persuade you, I replied, if I could.

Then you certainly have not succeeded. And will you tell me, he said, how you would arrange goods ; is there not one class of goods which are desirable in themselves, and independently of their results, as, for example, mere innocent pleasures and enjoyments, upon which nothing follows?

I think that there is such a class, I replied.

What would you say to a second class of goods which are desirable not only in themselves, but also for their results, such as knowledge, sight, health?

To that likewise I assent.

Thirdly, would you recognize a class of goods troublesome in themselves, yet profitable to us ; such, for example, as gymnastic exercises, or the healing and treatment of disease, and the business of money-making, which no one would choose for their own sakes, but only for the sake of some reward or result of them?

There is, I said, this third class also. But why do you ask?

Because I want to know in which of the three classes you would place justice?

In the highest and noblest class, I replied, of goods, which he who is to be happy desires for their own sakes as well as for their results.   358

Then the many are of another mind ; they think that justice is of the troublesome class of goods, which are to be pursued for the sake of rewards and reputation, but in themselves are rather to be avoided.

I know, I said, that this is their doctrine, and this was also the sentiment of Thrasymachus, when originally he blamed justice and praised injustice; but I appear not to understand him.

I wish, he said, that you would hear me as well as him, and then I shall see whether you and I agree. For Thrasymachus seems to me to have been charmed by your voice, like a snake, sooner than he ought to have been; and I am not yet satisfied with the account which has been given of the nature of justice and injustice. Leaving the rewards and results of them, I want to know what they, either of them, are in themselves, and what power they have in the soul. If you please, then, I will revive the argument of Thrasymachus. And first I will speak of the nature and origin of justice according to the common view of them. Secondly, I will show that all men who practice justice do so against their will, and not as a good, but as a necessity. And thirdly, I will maintain that there is reason in this, for in their view, the life of the unjust is better far than the life of the just. That is only what they say, Socrates, for I myself am not of their opinion. But still I acknowledge that I am perplexed when I hear the voices of Thrasymachus and myriads of others dinning in my ears; and, on the other hand, I have never yet heard the thesis that justice is better than injustice maintained in a satisfactory way. If I could hear the praises of justice and injustice considered in themselves, then I should be satisfied, and you are the person from whom I expect to hear this; and therefore I will praise the unjust life to the utmost of my power, and the manner in which I speak will indicate also the manner in which I desire to hear you praising justice and censuring injustice. Will you say whether you approve of this?

Indeed I do; nor can I imagine any theme about which a man of sense would oftener wish to converse.

I am delighted, he replied, to hear you say that, and shall begin by speaking of the nature and origin of justice.

They say that to do injustice is, by nature, good; to suffer injustice, evil; but that the evil is greater than the good. And when men have done and suffered and had experience of both, not being able to avoid the one and obtain the other, they think that they had better agree with one another to have neither, and thence arise laws and covenants among them; and that which is ordained by law they term lawful and just. This, as they affirm, is the origin and nature of justice, arising out of a mean or compromise between the best of all, which is to do and not to suffer injustice, and the worst of all, which is to suffer without the power of retaliation ; and justice, being in a mean between the two, is tolerated not as a good, but as the lesser evil, and honored by reason of the inability of men to do injustice. For no man who is worthy to be called a man would submit to such an agreement if he were able to resist ; he would be mad if he did. This, Socrates, is the received account of the nature and origin of justice.

Now that justice is only the inability to do injustice will best appear if we imagine something of this kind : suppose we give both the just and the unjust entire liberty to do what they will, and let us attend and see whither desire will lead them ; then we shall detect the just man in the very act ; the just and unjust will be found going the same way,—following their interest, which all natures conceive to be their good, and are only diverted into the path of justice by the force of law. The liberty which we are supposing may be most conveniently given to them in the form of such a power as is said to have been possessed by Gyges,[1] the ancestor of Crœsus,[2] the Lydian. For Gyges, according to the tradition, was a shepherd and servant of the king of Lydia, and, while he was in the field, there was a storm and earthquake, which made an opening in the earth at the place where he was feeding his flock. He was amazed at the sight, and descended into the opening, where, among other marvels, he beheld a hollow brazen horse having doors, at which he, stooping and looking in, saw a dead body, of stature, as appeared to him, more than human, and having nothing on but a gold ring ; this he took from the finger of the dead, and reascended out of the opening. Now the shepherds met together, according to custom, that they might send their monthly report concerning the flock to the king ; and into their assembly he came having the ring on his finger, and as he was sitting among them he chanced to turn the collet of the ring towards the inner side of the hand, when instantly he became invisible, and the others began to speak of him as if he were no longer there. He

[1] Gyges (gī'jĕz).
[2] Crœsus (6th century B C.) : a king of Lydia in Asia Minor, whose wealth became proverbial in all languages.

was astonished at this, and again touching the ring he turned the collet outward and reappeared; thereupon he made trials of the ring, and always with the same result; when he turned the collet inwards he became invisible, when outwards he reappeared. Perceiving this, he immediately contrived to be chosen messenger to the court, where he no sooner arrived than he seduced the queen, and with her help conspired against the king and slew him, and took the kingdom. Suppose now that there were two such magic rings, and the just put on one of them and the unjust the other; no man is of such adamantine temper that he would stand fast in justice,—that is what they think. No man would dare to be honest when he could safely take what he liked out of the market, or go into houses and lie with any one at his pleasure, or kill or release from prison whom he would, and in all respects be like a god among men. Then the actions of the just would be as the actions of the unjust; just or unjust would arrive at last at the same goal. And this is surely a great proof that a man is just, not willingly or because he thinks that justice is any good to him individually, but of necessity, for wherever any one thinks that he can safely be unjust, there he is unjust. For all men believe in their hearts that injustice is far more profitable to the individual than justice, and he who takes this line of argument will say that they are right. For if you could imagine any one having such a power, and never doing any wrong or touching what was another's, he would be thought by the lookers on to be a most wretched idiot, although they would praise him to one another's faces, and keep up appearances with one another from a fear that they too might be sufferers of injustice. Enough of this.

Now, if we are to form a real judgment of the life of the just and unjust, we must isolate them; there is no other way; and how is the isolation to be effected? I answer: Let the unjust man be entirely unjust, and the just man entirely just; nothing is to be taken away from either of them, and both are to be perfected for the fulfillment of their respective parts. First, let the unjust be like other distinguished masters of crafts; like the skillful pilot or physician, who knows his own powers and attempts only what is within their limits, and who, if he fails at any point, is able to recover himself. So let the unjust make his unjust attempts in the right way, and keep in the dark if he means to be great in his injustice (he who is detected is nobody) : for the highest reach of injustice is, to be deemed just when you are not. Therefore, I say that to the perfectly unjust man we must attribute the most perfect injustice; there is to be no deduction, and we must allow him, while doing the most unjust acts, to have won for himself the greatest reputation for justice. If he has taken a false step he must be able to retrieve himself, being one who can speak with effect, if any of his deeds come to light, and force his way where force is required, and having gifts of courage and strength, and command of money and friends. And at his side let us place the just man in his nobleness and simplicity, being, as Æschylus[3] says, and not seeming. There must be no seeming, for if he seem to be just he will be honored and rewarded, and then we shall not know whether he is just for the sake of justice or for the sake of honors and rewards; therefore, let him be clothed in justice only, and have no other covering; and he must be imagined in a state of life very different from that of the last. Let him be the best of men, and be esteemed to be the worst; then let us see whether his virtue is proof against infamy and its consequences. And let him continue thus to the hour of death; being just, let him seem to be unjust. Then when both have reached the uttermost extreme, the one of justice and the other of injustice, let judgment be given which of them is the happier of the two.[4]

Heavens! my dear Glaucon, I said, how energetically you polish them up for the decision, first one and then the other, as if they were two statues.

I do my best, he said. And now that we know what they are like there is no difficulty in tracing out the sort of life which awaits either of them. But as you may think the description of this a little too coarse, I will ask you to fancy, Socrates, that the words which follow are not mine. Let me put them into the mouths of the eulogists of injustice. They will tell you that in the case described the just man will be scourged, racked, bound—will have his eyes burnt out; and, at last, after suffering every kind of evil, he will be impaled. This will teach him

---

[3] Æschylus (ĕs'kў-lus, 525-456 B.C.): earliest of the three great tragic poets of Greece.
[4] "There is a just man that perisheth in his righteousness, and there is a wicked man that prolongeth his life in wickedness."—Eccl. vii. 15.

that he ought to seem only, and not to be, just; and that the words of Æschylus may be more truly spoken of the unjust than of the just. For the unjust, as they will say, is pursuing a reality; at any rate, he does not live with a view to appearances, he wants to be really unjust, and not to seem only:—

> "His mind is like a deep and fertile soil
> Out of which his prudent counsels spring."

In the first place, he is thought just, and therefore bears rule; he can marry whom he will, and give in marriage to whom he will; also he can trade and deal where he likes, and always to his own advantage, because he has no misgivings about injustice; and in every contest, whether public or private, he gets the better of his antagonists; and has gains, and is rich, and out of his gains he can benefit his friends, and harm his enemies; moreover, he can offer sacrifices, and dedicate gifts to the gods abundantly and magnificently, and can honor the gods and any man whom he wants to honor in far better style than the just, which is a very good reason why he should be dearer to the gods than the just. Thus they make to appear, Socrates, that the life of the unjust is so ordered both by gods and men as to be more blessed than the life of the just.

I was going to say something in answer to Glaucon, when Adeimantus his brother interposed: Socrates, he said, you don't suppose that there is nothing more to be urged?

Why, what else is there? I answered.

The strongest point of all has not been even mentioned, he replied.

Well, then, according to the proverb, "Let brother help brother;" and if he fails in any part do you assist him; although I must confess that Glaucon has already said quite enough to lay me in the dust, and take from me the power of helping justice.

Nonsense, he replied; I want you to hear the converse of Glaucon's argument, which is equally required in order to bring out what I believe to be his meaning; I mean the argument of those who praise justice and censure injustice, with a view to their consequences only. Parents and tutors are always telling their sons and their wards that they are to be just; but why? not for the sake of justice, but for the sake of character and reputation; in the hope of obtaining some of those offices and marriages and other advantages which Glaucon was enumerating as accruing to the unjust from a fair reputation. More, however, is made of appearances by this class than by the others; for they throw in the good opinion of the gods, and will tell you of a shower of benefits which the heavens, as they say, rain upon the pious; and this accords with the testimony of the noble Hesiod and Homer, the first of whom says, that for the just the gods make—

"The oaks to bear acorns at their summit, and bees in the middle;
And the sheep are bowed down with the weight of their own fleeces,"

and many other blessings of a like kind are provided for them. And Homer has a very similar strain; for he speaks of one whose fame is—

" As the fame of some blameless king who, like a god,
Maintains justice; to whom the black earth brings forth
Wheat and barley, whose trees are bowed with fruit,
And his sheep never fail to bear, and the sea gives him fish."

Still grander are the gifts of Heaven which Musæus [5] and his son [5] offer the just; they take them down into the world below where they have the saints feasting on couches with crowns on their heads, and passing their whole time in drinking; their idea seems to be that an immortality of drunkenness is the highest meed of virtue. Some extend their rewards to the third and fourth generation; the posterity, as they say, of the faithful and just shall survive them. This is the style in which they praise justice. But about the wicked there is another strain; they bury them in a slough, and make them carry water in a sieve [b]; that is their portion in the world below, and even while living they bring them to infamy, and inflict upon them the punishments which Glaucon described as the portion of the just, who are reputed unjust; nothing else does their invention supply. Such is their manner of praising the one and censuring the other.

[b] See Apology, note 52; Protagoras, note 28. Son, Eumolpus (ū-mŏl'-pus).
[a] As a punishment for killing their husbands, the Danaïdes (da-nā'ī-dēz), daughters of Danaüs (dā'na-us), were compelled, in Tartarus, to draw water forever in sieves.

Again, Socrates, let me mention another way of speaking about justice and injustice, which is not confined to the poets, but is also found in prose writers. The universal voice of mankind is saying that justice and virtue are honorable, but grievous and toilsome; and that the pleasures of vice and injustice are easy of attainment, and are only censured by law and opinion. They say also that honesty is generally less profitable than dishonesty; and they are quite ready to call wicked men happy, and to honor them both in public and private when they are rich or have other sources of power, while they despise and neglect those who may be weak and poor, even though acknowledging that these are better than the others. But the most extraordinary of all their sayings is about virtue and the gods: they say that the gods apportion calamity and evil to many good men, and good and happiness to the evil. And mendicant prophets go to rich men's doors and persuade them that they have a power committed to them of making an atonement for their sins or those of their fathers by sacrifices or charms, with rejoicings and games; and they promise to harm an enemy, whether just or unjust, at a small charge; with magic arts and incantations binding the will of Heaven to do their work. And the poets are the authorities to whom they appeal, some of them dispensing indulgences out of them, as when the poet sings,—

"Vice may be easily found, and many are they who follow after her; the way is smooth and not long. But before virtue the gods have set toil,"

and a path which they describe as tedious and steep. Others, again, cite Homer as a witness that the gods may be influenced by men, as he also says,—

"The gods, too, may be moved by prayers; and men pray to them and turn away their wrath by sacrifices and entreaties, and by libations and the odor of fat, when they have sinned and transgressed."

And they produce a host of books written by Musæus and Orpheus, who are children of the Moon and the Muses [7]—that is what they say—according to which they perform their ritual,

---

[7] Musæus was the son of Selene (se-lē'ne), goddess of the Moon. Orpheus was the son of the Muse Calliope and of Apollo, who as god of song and poetry was called the leader of the Muses.

and persuade not only individuals, but whole cities, that expiations and atonements for sin may be made by sacrifices and amusements which fill a vacant hour, and are equally at the service of the living and the dead; the latter they call mysteries,[8] and they redeem us from the pains of hell, but if we neglect them no one knows what awaits us.[9]

He proceeded: And now when the young hear all this said about virtue and vice, and the manner in which gods and men regard them, how are they likely to be affected, my dear Socrates; those of them, I mean, who are quickwitted, and, like bees on the wing, light on everything which they hear, and thence gather inferences as to the character and way of life which are best for them? Probably the youth will say to himself in the words of Pindar—

"Can I by justice or by crooked ways of deceit ascend a loftier tower, which shall be a house of defense to me all my days?"

For what men say is that, if I am really just without being thought just, this is no good, but evident pain and loss. But if, though unjust, I acquire the character of justice, a heavenly life is to be mine. Since then, as philosophers say, appearance is master of truth and lord of bliss, to appearance I must wholly devote myself. Around and about me I will draw the simple garb of virtue, but behind I will trail the subtle and crafty fox,

---

[8] See Symposium, note 32.
[9] On true and false worship, compare: "Now, God is the measure of all things in a sense far higher than any man could be, as the common saying affirms. And he who would be dear to God must, as far as is possible, be like him, and such as he is. Wherefore the temperate man is the friend of God, for he is like him; and the intemperate man is unlike him, and different from him, and unjust. And the same holds of other things, and this is the conclusion, which is also the noblest and truest of all sayings: That for the good man to offer sacrifices to the gods, and hold converse with them by means of prayers and offerings, and every kind of service, is the noblest and best of all things, and also the most conducive to a happy life, and very fit and meet. But with the bad man, the opposite of this holds; for the bad man has an impious soul, whereas the good is pure; and from one who is polluted, neither a good man nor God is right in receiving gifts. And, therefore, the unholy waste their much service upon the gods, which, when offered by any holy man, is always accepted of them."—Plato, Laws IV., 716.

Compare the attitude of the Old Testament prophets toward ritualism: "To what purpose is the multitude of your sacrifices unto me? saith the Lord: I am full of the burnt offerings of rams, and the fat of fed beasts; and I delight not in the blood of bullocks, or of lambs, or of he-goats.

"When ye come to appear before me, who hath required this at your hands, to tread my courts?

"Bring no more vain oblations; incense is an abomination unto me; the

as Archilochus,[10] first of sages, counsels. But I hear some one exclaiming that wickedness is not easily concealed; to which I answer that nothing great is easy. Nevertheless, this is the road to happiness; and the way by which we must go, following in the steps of the argument; and as to concealment, that may be secured by the coöperation of societies and political clubs. And there are professors of rhetoric who teach the philosophy of persuading courts and assemblies; and so, partly by persuasion and partly by force, I shall make unlawful gains and not be punished. Still I hear a voice saying that the gods cannot be deceived, neither can they be compelled. But what if there are no gods? or, suppose that the gods have no care about human things—in either case the result is the same, that we need not trouble ourselves with concealment. And even if there are gods, and they have a care of us, yet we know about them only from the traditions and genealogies of the poets; and these are the very persons who say that they may be influenced by prayers and offerings. Let us be consistent then, and

new moons and sabbaths, the calling of assemblies, I cannot away with; it is iniquity, even the solemn meeting.

"Your new moons and your appointed feasts my soul hateth; they are a trouble to me; I am weary to bear them.

"And when ye spread forth your hands, I will hide mine eyes from you: yea, when ye make many prayers, I will not hear: your hands are full of blood.

"Wash you, make you clean; put away the evil of your doing from before mine eyes; cease to do evil.

"Learn to do well."—Isaiah i. 11-17.

"I hate, I despise your feast days, and I will not smell in your solemn assemblies.

"Though ye offer me burnt offerings and your meat offerings, I will not accept them: neither will I regard the peace offerings of your fat beasts.

"Take thou away from me the noise of thy songs; for I will not hear the melody of thy viols.

"But let judgment run down as waters, and righteousness as a mighty stream."—Amos v. 21-24.

"Will the Lord be pleased with thousands of rams, or with ten thousands of rivers of oil? shall I give my first-born for my transgression, the fruit of my body for the sin of my soul?"—Micah vi. 7.

"To what purpose cometh there to me incense from Sheba, and the sweet cane from a far country? your burnt offerings are not acceptable nor your sacrifices sweet unto me."—Jeremiah vi. 20.

"The sacrifice of the wicked is an abomination to the Lord: but the prayer of the upright is his delight."—Proverbs xv. 8.

"For thou desirest not sacrifice; else would I give it: thou delightest not in burnt offering.

"The sacrifices of God are a broken spirit: a broken and a contrite heart, O God, thou wilt not despise."—Psalms vi. 16, 17.

[10] Archilochus (är-kĭl′o-kus, 714?-676 B.C.): Greek lyric poet, noted especially for his satire.

either believe both or neither. And if we believe them, why then we had better be unjust, and offer of the fruits of injustice ; for if we are just we shall indeed escape the vengeance of heaven, but we shall lose the gains of injustice ; whereas, if we are unjust, we shall keep the gains, and by our sinning and praying, and praying and sinning, the gods will be propitiated, and we shall be forgiven. "But there is a world below in which either we or our children will suffer for our deeds." Yes, my friend, will be the reply, but there are mysteries and atoning deities, and these have great power. That is what mighty cities declare ; and the children of the gods, who are their poets and prophets, affirm the same.

366

On what principle, then, shall we choose justice rather than the worst injustice ? when, if we only unite the latter with a deceitful regard to appearances, we shall fare to our mind both with gods and men, here as well as hereafter, as say the most numerous and the highest authorities. Knowing all this, Socrates, how can any one who has any advantage of mind or person or rank or wealth, be willing to honor, or indeed refrain from laughing at the praises of justice ? For even if there should be any one who is able to disprove my words, and who is satisfied that justice is best, still he is not angry with the unjust ; he is very ready to forgive them, knowing as he also does that men are not just of their own free will ; unless, peradventure, there be some one whom the divinity within him has inspired with a hatred of injustice, or who abstains because he has found knowledge—but no other man. He only blames injustice who, owing to cowardice or age or some weakness, is incapable of being unjust. And this is proved by the fact that those who are incapable, when they have the power, and in as far as they have the power, are the first to be unjust.

Now all this simply arises out of the circumstance which you may remember, Socrates, that my brother and I both mentioned to you at the beginning of the argument. We told you how astonished we were to find that of all the professing panegyrists of justice—beginning with the heroes of old, of whom any memorial has been preserved to us, and ending with the men of our own time—no one has ever blamed injustice or praised justice except with a view to the glories, honors, and benefits which flow from them. No one has ever adequately described either in verse or prose the true essential nature of either of these immanent in the soul, and invisible to any human or divine eye; or shown that of all the things of a man's soul which he has within him, justice is the greatest good, and injustice the greatest evil. Had this been the universal strain, had you sought to persuade us of this from our youth upwards, we should not have been on the watch to keep one another from doing wrong, but every one would have been his own watchman, because afraid, if he did wrong, of having the greatest evil dwelling with him. I dare say that Thrasymachus and others would seriously hold the language which I have been only repeating, and more of the same sort about justice and injustice, grossly, as I conceive, perverting their true nature. But I am speaking with all my might, as I must confess, only because I want to hear you speak on the opposite side; and I would ask you to show not only the superiority of justice over injustice, but what they do to the possessors of them that makes the one to be a good and the other an evil to him.[11] And please, as Glaucon said, to exclude reputation; for unless you clothe the just in the garb of injustice, and the unjust in that of justice, we shall say that you do not praise justice, but the appearance of justice; we shall think that you are only exhorting us to keep injustice dark, and that you really agree with Thrasymachus in thinking that justice is another's good and the interest of the stronger, and that injustice is a man's own profit and interest, though injurious to the weaker. Now as you have admitted that justice is one of that highest class of goods which are desired as well for their results as, in a far greater degree, for their own sakes—just as sight or knowledge or health, or any other real and natural and not merely conventional goods, are desired for their own sakes—I would ask you to direct your praises to that one point only: I mean to the essential good of justice and evil of injustice. Let others praise the rewards and appearances of justice; that is a manner of arguing which, as coming from them, I am ready to tolerate, but from you who have spent your whole life in thinking of this, unless I hear the contrary from your own lips, I expect something better. And therefore, I say, not only prove to us that

---

[11] "The labour of the righteous tendeth to life; the fruit of the wicked to sin."—Proverbs x. 16.

justice is better than injustice, but show what they either of them do to the possessors of them, which makes the one to be good and the other an evil, whether seen or unseen by gods and men.

I had always admired the genius of Glaucon and Adeimantus, but when I heard this I was quite charmed, and said: That was not a bad beginning of the Elegiacs [12] in which the admirer of Glaucon addressed you as your father's sons after you had distinguished yourselves at the battle of Megara [13].—

368

"Sons of Ariston, divine offspring of a glorious hero."

The epithet is very appropriate, for there is something truly divine in being able to argue as you have done for the superiority of injustice, and remaining uninfluenced by your own arguments. And I do believe that you are not influenced; this I infer from your general character, for had I judged only from your speeches I should have mistrusted you. But now, trusting you, I have all the greater mistrust of myself. For I am in a strait between two; on the one hand I feel my own inability to maintain the cause of justice—your unwillingness to accept the answer which I made to Thrasymachus about the superiority of justice over injustice proves to me that I am unequal to the task; and yet on the other hand I cannot refuse to help, for I fear that there may be a sin when justice is evil spoken of in standing by and failing to offer help or succor while breath or speech remain to me. And therefore I must give such help as I can. Glaucon and the rest entreated me by all means not to let the question drop, but to proceed in the investigation. They wanted to arrive at the truth, first, about the nature of justice and injustice, and secondly, about their relative advantages. I told them, what I really thought, that the search would be no easy one, and would require very good eyes. Seeing then, I said, we are no great wits, I think that we had better adopt a method which might be recommended to those who are short-sighted, and are bidden by some one to read small letters a long way off; one

---

[12] Refers merely to the metre, not the subject of the poem from which the quotation is made.

[13] It is uncertain which of the many battles fought at Megara is here referred to.

of the party recollects that he has seen the very same letters elsewhere written larger and on a larger scale—if they were the same and we could read the larger letters first, and then proceed to the lesser—that would be thought a rare piece of good fortune.

Very true, said Adeimantus, but how does this apply to our present inquiry?

I will tell you, I replied; justice, which is the subject of our inquiry, is, as you know, sometimes spoken of as a virtue of an individual, and sometimes as the virtue of a State.

True, he replied.

And is not a State larger than an individual?

It is.

Then in the larger the quantity of justice will be larger and more easily discernible. I propose therefore that we inquire into the nature of justice and injustice as appearing in the State first, and secondly in the individual, proceeding from the greater to the lesser and comparing them.

That, he said, is an excellent proposal.

And suppose we imagine the State as in a process of creation, and then we shall see the justice and injustice of the State in process of creation also.

Very likely.

When the State is completed there may be a hope that the object of our search will be more easily discovered.

Yes, more easily.

And shall we make the attempt? I said; although I cannot promise you as an inducement that the task will be a light one. Reflect therefore.

I have reflected, said Adeimantus, and am anxious that you should proceed.

A State, I said, arises, as I conceive, out of the needs of mankind; no one is self-sufficing, but all of us have many wants. Can any other origin of a State be imagined?

None, he replied.

Then, as we have many wants, and many persons are needed to supply them, one takes a helper for one purpose and another for another; and when these helpers and partners are gathered together in one habitation, the body of inhabitants is termed a State.

True, he said.

And they exchange with one another, and one gives, and another receives, under the idea that the exchange will be for their good.

Very true.

Then, I said, let us begin and create a State ; and yet the true creator is necessity, who is the mother of our invention.

True, he replied.

Now the first and greatest of necessities is food, which is the condition of life and existence.

Certainly.

The second is a dwelling, and the third clothing and that sort of thing.

True.

And now let us see how our city will be able to supply this great demand. We may suppose that one man is a husbandman, another a builder, some one else a weaver : shall we add to them a shoemaker, or perhaps some other purveyor to our bodily wants ?

Quite right.

The barest notion of a State must include four or five men.

Clearly.

And how then will they proceed ? Will each give the result of his labors to all ?—the husbandman, for example, producing, for four, and laboring in the production of food for himself and others four times as long and as much as he needs to labor ; or shall he leave others and not be at the trouble of producing for them, but produce a fourth for himself in a fourth of the time, and in the remaining three fourths of his time be employed in making a house or a coat or a pair of shoes ? 370

Adeimantus thought that the former would be the better way.

I dare say that you are right, I replied, for I am reminded as you speak that we are not all alike ; there are diversities of natures among us which are adapted to different occupations.

Very true.

And will you have a work better done when the workman has many occupations, or when he has only one ?

When he has only one.

Further, there can be no doubt that a work is spoilt when not done at the right time ?

No doubt of that.

For business is not disposed to wait until the doer of the business is at leisure; but the doer must be at command, and make the business his first object.

He must.

Thus then all things are produced more plentifully and easily and of a better quality when one man does one thing which is natural to him and is done at the right time, and leaves other things.

Undoubtedly.

Then more than four citizens will be required, for the husbandman will not make his own plough or mattock, or other implements of agriculture, if they are to be good for anything. Neither will the builder make his tools—and he, too, needs many; and the same may be said of the weaver and shoemaker.

True.

Then carpenters, and smiths, and other artisans, will be sharers in our little State, which is already beginning to grow.

True.

Yet even if we add neatherds, shepherds, and other herdsmen, in order that our husbandmen may have oxen to plough with, and builders as well as husbandmen have the use of beasts of burden for their carrying, and weavers and curriers of their fleeces and skins,—still our State will not be very large.

That is true; yet neither will that be a very small State which contains all these.

Further, I said, to place the city on a spot where no imports are required is well nigh impossible.

Impossible.

Then there must be another class of citizens who will bring the required supply from another city?

There must.

371 But if the trader goes empty-handed, taking nothing which those who are to supply the need want, he will come back empty-handed.

That is certain.

And therefore what they produce at home must be not only enough for themselves, but such both in quantity and quality as to accommodate those from whom their wants are supplied.

That is true.

Then more husbandmen and more artisans will be required?

They will.

Not to mention the importers and exporters, who are called merchants.

Yes.

Then we shall want merchants?

We shall.

And if merchandise is to be carried over the sea, skillful sailors will be needed, and in considerable numbers?

Yes, in considerable numbers.

Then, again, within the city, how will they exchange their productions? and this, as you may remember, was the object of our society.

The way will be, that they will buy and sell.

Then they will need a market-place, and a money-token for purposes of exchange.

Certainly.

Suppose now that a husbandman, or possibly an artisan, brings some production to market, and he comes at a time when there is no one to exchange with him,—is he to leave his work and sit idle in the market-place?

Not at all; he will find people there who, seeing this want, take upon themselves the duty of sale. In well-ordered States they are commonly those who are the weakest in bodily strength, and therefore unable to do anything else; for all they have to do is to be in the market, and take money of those who desire to buy goods, and in exchange for goods to give money to those who desire to sell.

This want, then, will introduce retailers into our State. Is not "retailer" the term which is applied to those who sit in the market-place buying and selling, while those who wander from one city to another are called merchants?

Yes, he said.

And there is another class of servants, who are intellectually hardly on the level of companionship; still they have plenty of bodily strength for labor, which accordingly they sell, and are called, if I do not mistake, hirelings, hire being the name which is given to the price of their labor.

True.

Then hirelings will help to make our population.

And now, Adeimantus, is our State matured and perfected?

Surely.

Where, then, is justice, and where is injustice, and in which part of the State are they to be found?

372 Probably in the relations of these citizens with one another. I cannot imagine any other place in which they are more likely to be found.

I dare say that you are right in that suggestion, I said; still, we had better consider the matter further, and not shrink from the task.

First, then, let us consider what will be their way of life, now that we have thus established them. Will they not produce corn, and wine, and clothes, and shoes, and build houses for themselves? And when they are housed, they will work in summer commonly stripped and barefoot, but in winter substantially clothed and shod. They will feed on barley and wheat, baking the wheat and kneading the flour, making noble puddings and loaves; these they will serve up on a mat of reeds or clean leaves, themselves reclining the while upon beds of yew or myrtle boughs. And they and their children will feast, drinking of the wine which they have made, wearing garlands on their heads, and having the praises of the gods on their lips, living in sweet society, and having a care that their families do not exceed their means; for they will have an eye to poverty or war.

But, said Glaucon, interposing, you have not given them a relish to their meal.

True, I replied, I had forgotten that; of course they will have a relish,—salt, and olives, and cheese, and onions, and cabbages or other country herbs which are fit for boiling; and we shall give them a dessert of figs, and pulse, and beans, and myrtle-berries, and beech-nuts, which they will roast at the fire, drinking in moderation. And with such a diet they may be expected to live in peace to a good old age, and bequeath a similar life to their children after them.

Yes, Socrates, he said, and if you were making a city of pigs, how else would you feed the beasts?

But what would you have, Glaucon? I replied.

Why, he said, you should give them the properties of life.

People who are to be comfortable are accustomed to lie on sofas, and dine off tables, and they should have dainties and dessert in the modern fashion.

Yes, said I, now I understand; the question which you would have me consider is, not only how a State, but how a luxurious State is to be created; and possibly there is no harm in this, for in such a State we shall be more likely to see how justice and injustice grow up. I am certainly of opinion that the true State, and that which may be said to be a healthy constitution, is the one which I have described. But if you would like to see the inflamed constitution, there is no objection to this. For I suppose that many will be dissatisfied with the simpler way of life. They will be for adding sofas, and tables, and other furniture; also dainties, and perfumes, and incense, and courtesans, and cakes, not of one sort only, but in profusion and variety; our imagination must not be limited to the necessaries of which I was at first speaking, such as houses, and clothes, and shoes; but the art of the painter and embroiderer will have to be set in motion, and gold and ivory and other materials of art will be required.

373

True, he said.

Then we must enlarge our borders; for the original healthy State is too small. Now will the city have to fill and swell with a multitude of callings which go beyond what is required by any natural want; such as the whole tribe of hunters and actors [14] of which one large class have to do with figures and colors, another are musicians; there will be poets and their attendant train of rhapsodists,[15] players, dancers, contractors; also makers of divers kinds of utensils, not forgetting women's ornaments. And we shall want more servants. Will not tutors be also in request, and nurses wet and dry, tirewomen and barbers, as well as confectioners and cooks; and swineherds, too, who were not needed and therefore not included in the former edition of our State, but needed in this? They

---

[14] Bosanquet in his Companion to Plato's Republic, has the following note: "'Hunters' and 'imitators.' (1) The predatory classes, including lawyers, political orators, and professional teachers (Sophists); and (2) those who practice the arts of deception, again including the Sophist, together with the sculptor, painter, musician, poet, and here apparently those who have to do with women's toilet."

[15] See Phædrus, note 62.

must not be forgotten : and there will be hosts of animals, if people are to eat them.

Certainly.

And living in this way we shall have much greater need of physicians than before?

Much greater.

And the country which was enough to support the original inhabitants will be too small now, and not enough?

Quite true.

Then a slice of our neighbor's land will be wanted by us for pasture and tillage, and they will want a slice of ours, if, like ourselves, they exceed the limit of necessity, and give themselves up to the unlimited accumulation of wealth?

That, Socrates, will be unavoidable.

And then we shall go to war, Glaucon,—that will be the next thing.

So we shall, he replied.

Then, without determining as yet whether war does good or harm, thus much we may affirm, that now we have discovered war to be derived from causes which are also the causes of almost all the evils in States, private as well as public.

Undoubtedly.

Then our State must once more enlarge ; and this time the enlargement will be nothing short of a whole army, which will have to go out and fight with the invaders for all that we have, as well as for the precious souls whom we were describing above.

Why? he said; are they not capable of defending themselves?

No, I said; not if you and all of us were right in the principle which was acknowledged at the first creation of the State: that principle was, as you will remember, that one man could not practice many arts.

Very true, he said.

But is not war an art?

Certainly.

And an art requiring as much attention as shoemaking ?

Quite true.

And the shoemaker was not allowed to be a husbandman, or a weaver, or a builder—in order that we might have our shoes well made : but to him and to every other worker one work was assigned by us for which he was fitted by nature, and he was to continue working all his life long at that and at no other, and not to let opportunities slip, and then he would become a good workman. And is there any more important work than to be a good soldier? But is war an art so easily acquired that a man may be a warrior who is also a husbandman, or shoemaker, or other artisan; although no one in the world would be a good dice or draught [16] player who merely took up the game as a recreation, and had not from his earliest years devoted himself to this and nothing else? The mere handling of tools will not make a man a skilled workman, or master of defense, nor be of any use to him who knows not the nature of each, and has never bestowed any attention upon them. How then will he who takes up a shield or other implement of war all in a day become a good fighter, whether with heavy-armed or any other kind of troops?

Yes, he said, the tools which would teach their own use would be of rare value.

And the greater the business of the guardian is, I said, the more time, and art, and skill will be needed by him?

That is what I should suppose, he replied.

Will he not also require natural gifts?

Certainly.

We shall have to select natures which are suited to their task of guarding the city?

That will be our duty.

And anything but an easy duty, I said; but still we must endeavor to do our best as far as we can?

We must.

The dog is a watcher, I said, and the guardian is also a watcher; and regarding them in this point of view only, is not the noble youth very like a well-bred dog?

375

How do you mean?

I mean that both of them ought to be quick to observe, and swift to overtake the enemy; and strong too, if, when they have caught him, they have to fight with him.

All these qualities, he replied, will certainly be required.

Well, and your guardian must be brave if he is to fight well?

Certainly.

And is he likely to be brave who has no spirit, whether

---

[16] Draughts: a game similar to our checkers.

horse or dog or any other animal? Did you never observe how the presence of spirit makes the soul of any creature absolutely fearless and invincible?

Yes; I have observed that.

Then now we have a clear idea of both the bodily qualities which are required in the guardian.

True.

And also of the mental ones; his soul is to be full of spirit?

Yes.

But then, Glaucon, those spirited natures are apt to be furious with one another, and with everybody else.

That is a difficulty, he replied.

Whereas, I said, they ought to be gentle to their friends, and dangerous to their enemies; or, instead of their enemies destroying them, they will destroy themselves.

True, he said.

What is to be done then, I said? how shall we find a gentle nature which has also a great spirit, for they seem to be inconsistent with one another?

True.

And yet he will not be a good guardian who is wanting in either of these two qualities; and, as the combination of them appears to be impossible, this is equivalent to saying that to be a good guardian is also impossible.

I am afraid that is true, he replied.

Here feeling perplexed, I began to think over what preceded. My friend, I said, we deserve to be in a puzzle; for if we had only kept the simile before us, the perplexity in which we are entangled would never have arisen.

What do you mean? he said.

I mean to say that there are natures gifted with those opposite qualities, the combination of which we are denying.

And where do you find them?

Many animals, I replied, furnish examples of them; our friend the dog is a very good one: you know that well-bred dogs are perfectly gentle to their familiars and acquaintances, and the reverse to strangers.

I know that.

Then there is nothing impossible or out of the order of nature in our finding a guardian who has a similar combination of qualities?

Certainly not.

Would you not say that he should combine with the spirited nature the qualities of a philosopher?

I do not apprehend your meaning.

The trait of which I am speaking, I replied, may be also seen in the dog, and is very remarkable in an animal. 376

What trait?

Why a dog, whenever he sees a stranger, is angry; when an acquaintance, he welcomes him, although the one has never done him any harm, nor the other any good. Did this never strike you as curious?

I never before made the observation myself, though I quite recognize the truth of your remark.

And surely this instinct of the dog is very charming,—your dog is a true philosopher.

Why?

Why, because he distinguishes the face of a friend and of an enemy only by the criterion of knowing and not knowing. And must not the creature be fond of learning who determines what is friendly and what is unfriendly by the test of knowledge and ignorance?

Most assuredly.

And is not the love of learning the love of wisdom, which is philosophy?

They are the same, he replied.

And may we not say confidently of man also, that he who is likely to be gentle to his friends and acquaintances, must by nature be a lover of wisdom and knowledge?

That we may safely affirm.

Then he who is to be a really good and noble guardian of the State will require to unite in himself philosophy and spirit and swiftness and strength?

Undoubtedly.

Then we have found the desired natures; and now that we have found them, how are they to be reared and educated? Is this an inquiry which may be fairly expected to throw light on the greater inquiry which is our final end—How do justice and injustice grow up in States? for we do not want to admit anything which is superfluous, or leave out anything which is really to the point.

Adeimantus thought that the inquiry would be of use to us.

Then, I said, my dear friend, the task must not be given up, even if somewhat long.

Certainly not.

Come then, and like story-tellers, let us be at leisure, and our story shall be the education of our heroes.

By all means.

And what shall be their education? Can we find a better than the old-fashioned sort?—and this has two divisions, gymnastic for the body, and music [17] for the soul.

True.

Music is taught first, and gymnastic afterwards?

Certainly.

And when you speak of music, do you rank literature under music or not?

I do.

And literature may be either true or false?

Yes.

377-378 And the young are trained in both kinds, and in the false before the true?

I do not understand your meaning, he said.

You know, I said, that we begin by telling children stories, which, though not wholly destitute of truth, are in the main fictitious; and these stories are told them when they are not of an age to learn gymnastics.

Very true.

That was my meaning in saying that we must teach music before gymnastics.

---

[17] " Music to the ancients had a far wider significance than it has to us. It was opposed to gymnastic as 'mental' to 'bodily' training, and included equally reading and writing, mathematics, harmony, poetry, and music strictly speaking."—Jowett, 3d ed., v., p. 474.

" The word *music* is not to be judged according to the limited signification which it now bears. It comprehended from the beginning everything appertaining to the province of the Nine Muses—not merely learning the use of the lyre, or how to bear part in a chorus, but also the hearing, learning, and repeating of poetical compositions, as well as the practice of exact and elegant pronunciation. . . . As the range of ideas enlarged, so the word *music* and musical teacher acquired an expanded meaning, so as to comprehend matter of instruction at once ampler and more diversified. During the middle of the fifth century B.C. at Athens, there came thus to be found among the musical teachers, men of the most distinguished abilities and eminence; masters of all the learning and accomplishments of the age, teaching what was known of astronomy, geography, and physics, and capable of holding dialectical discussions with their pupils upon all the various problems then afloat among intellectual men."—Grote's History of Greece, III., chap. lxvii.

Quite right, he said.

You know also that the beginning is the chiefest part of any work, especially in a young and tender thing; for that is the time at which the character is formed and most readily receives the desired impression.

Quite true.

And shall we just carelessly allow children to hear any casual tales which may be framed by casual persons, and to receive into their minds notions which are the very opposite of those which are to be held by them when they are grown up?

We cannot allow that.

Then the first thing will be to have a censorship of the writers of fiction, and let the censors receive any tale of fiction which is good, and reject the bad; and we will desire mothers and nurses to tell their children the authorized ones only. Let them fashion the mind with these tales, and not the tender frame with the hands only. At the same time, most of those which are now in use will have to be discarded.

Of what tales are you speaking? he said.

You may find a model of the lesser in the greater, I said; for they are necessarily cast in the same mould, and there is the same spirit in both of them.

That may be very true, he replied; but I don't as yet know what you would term the greater.

Those, I said, which are narrated by Homer and Hesiod, and the rest of the poets, who have ever been the great story-tellers of mankind.

But which are the stories that you mean, he said; and what fault do you find with them?

A fault which is most serious, I said; the fault of telling a lie, and a bad lie.

But when is this fault committed?

Whenever an erroneous representation is made of the nature of gods and heroes,—like the drawing of a limner which has not the shadow of a likeness to the truth.

Yes, he said, that sort of thing is certainly very blamable; but what are the stories which you mean?

[Socrates gives examples of what he regards as objectionable mythology for the young. He condemns the tales in which the gods are represented as committing outrageous crimes or as quarreling and fighting among themselves, on the ground that they would lead the young man to believe that quarreling is honorable and holy, and that in committing the worst of crimes he is only following the example of the greatest among the gods. He says:]

Such tales must not be admitted into our State, whether they are supposed to have an allegorical meaning or not. For the young man cannot judge what is allegorical and what is literal, and anything that he receives into his mind at that age is apt to become indelible and unalterable; and therefore the tales which they first hear should be models of virtuous thoughts.

There you are right, he replied; that is quite essential: but, then, where are such models to be found? and what are the tales in which they are contained? when that question is asked, what will be our answer?

I said to him, You and I, Adeimantus, are not poets in what we are about just now, but founders of a State: now the founders of a State ought to know the general forms in which poets should cast their tales, and the limits which should be observed by them, but they are not bound themselves to make the tales.

That is true, he said; but what are these forms of theology [13] which you mean?

[The first rule to which Socrates would require all kinds of poetry to conform is, "God is always to be represented as he truly is." The question then arises, what is the nature of God? Adeimantus agrees with Socrates that God is truly good and therefore cannot be the cause of evil. Socrates continues:]

Then God, if he be good, is not the author of all things, as the many assert, but he is the cause of a few things only, and not of most things that occur to men; for few are the goods of human life, and many are the evils, and the good only is to be attributed to him: of the evil other causes have to be discovered.

---

[13] In this case theology means poetic representations of the gods.

That appears to me to be most true, he said.

Then we must not listen to Homer or any other poet who is guilty of the folly of saying that—

"At the threshold of Zeus lie two casks full of lots, one of good, the other of evil;"

and that he to whom Zeus gives a mixture of the two—

"Sometimes meets with good, at other times with evil fortune;"

but that he to whom is given the cup of unmingled ill,—

"Him wild hunger drives over the divine earth."

And again—

"Zeus, who is the dispenser of good and evil to us."

. . . Neither will we allow our young men to hear the words of Æschylus, when he says, that "God plants guilt among men when he desires utterly to destroy a house." 380-381

[Only that evil which comes as a just punishment to the wicked and by which they are benefited, may be attributed to God.]

But that God being good is the author of evil to any one, that is to be strenuously denied, and not allowed to be sung or said in any well-ordered commonwealth by old or young. Such a fiction is suicidal, ruinous, impious.

I agree with you, he replied, about this law, and am ready to give my assent.

Let this then be one of the rules of recitation and invention,—that God is not the author of evil, but of good only.

That will do, he said.

And what do you think of another principle? Shall I ask you whether God is a magician, that he should appear insidiously now in one shape, and now in another—sometimes himself changing and becoming different in form, sometimes deceiving us with the appearance of such transformations; or is he one and the same, immutably fixed in his own proper image?

[Adeimantus agrees that God cannot be changed by any external influence, and that he will not wish to change himself, for he is already perfect in virtue and beauty.]

Then, I said, my dear friend, let none of the poets tell us that

"The gods, in the disguise of strangers, prowl about cities, having diverse forms;"

and let no one slander Proteus [19] and Thetis,[20] neither let any one either in tragedy or any other kind of poetry, introduce Here disguised in the likeness of a priestess,—

"Asking an alms for the life-giving daughters of the river Inachus;" [21]

let us have no more lies of that sort. Neither must we have mothers under the influence of the poets scaring their children with abominable tales—

"Of certain gods who go about by night in the likeness, as is said, of strangers from every land;"

let them beware lest they blaspheme against the gods, and at the same time make cowards of their children.

That ought certainly to be prohibited, he said.

But still you may say that although God is himself unchangeable, he may take various forms in order to bewitch and deceive us.

Suppose that, he replied.

Well, but can you imagine that God will be willing to lie, whether in word or action, by making a false representation of himself?

382-383 I cannot say, he replied.

[Adeimantus is made to see that "the superhuman and divine is absolutely incapable of falsehood" and agrees with Socrates that "God is perfectly simple and true both in deed and word; he changes not; he deceives not, either by dream or waking vision, by sign or word."

The second rule then to which the poets must conform is that God is true.]

---

[19] See Euthydemus, note 19.
[20] Thetis (the′tĭs): a sea-nymph, who, like Proteus, had the power of assuming any form.
[21] Inachus (ĭn′-a-kus).

BOOK III

Such then, I said, are our principles of theology—some tales are to be told, and others are not to be told to our disciples from their youth upwards, if we mean them to honor the gods and their parents, and to value friendship with one another.

386-387

Yes; and I think that our principles are right, he said.

Well, I said, and if they are to be courageous, must they not learn, besides these, other lessons also, such as will have the effect of taking away the fear of death? Can any man be courageous who has the fear of death in him?

Certainly not, he said.

And can he be fearless of death, or will he choose death in battle rather than defeat and slavery, who believes in the reality and the terror of the world below?[1]

Impossible.

Then we must assume a control over this class of tales as well as over the others and beg the relators of them not simply to revile, but rather to commend the world below.

[We must destroy such passages as the one in Homer where he attributes to the shade of Achilles in Hades these words: "I would rather be a serf on the land of a poor and portionless man than rule over all the dead who have come to naught;" and such verses as "He feared lest the mansions grim and squalid which the gods abhor should be seen of mortals and immortals."]

And we must beg Homer and the other poets not to be angry if we strike out these and similar passages, not because they are unpoetical, or unattractive to the popular ear, but because the greater the charm of them as poetry, the less are they meet for the ears of boys and men who are to be sons of freedom, and are to fear slavery more than death.

Undoubtedly.

Also we shall have to reject all the terrible and appalling

[1] See Apology, note 23.

names which describe the world below—Cocytus and Styx,[2] ghosts under the earth, and sapless shades, and any other words of the same type, the very mention of which causes a shudder to pass through the inmost soul of him who hears them. I do not say that these tales may not have a use of some kind; but there is a danger that the nerves of our guardians may become affected by them.

[The youth must learn to endure calmly any misfortune which may befall, even the death of relative or friend.]

Reflect: our principle is that the good man will not consider death terrible to a good man.

Yes; that is our principle.

And therefore he will not sorrow for his departed friend as though he had suffered anything terrible?

He will not.

Such an one, as we further maintain, is enough for himself and his own happiness, and therefore is least in need of other men.

True, he said.

And for this reason the loss of a son or brother, or the deprivation of fortune, is to him of all men least terrible.

Assuredly.

And therefore he will be least likely to lament, and will bear with the greatest equanimity any misfortune of this sort which may befall him.

Yes, he will feel such a misfortune less than another.

Then we shall be right in getting rid of the lamentations of famous men, and making them over to women (and not even to women who are good for anything), or to men of a baser sort, that those who are being educated by us to be the defenders of their country may scorn to do the like.

388-391

We shall be very right.

Then we will once more entreat Homer and the other poets not to depict Achilles, who is the son of a goddess,[3] as first lying on his side, then on his back, and then on his face; then

---

[2] Cocytus (co-sȳ′tus): the River of Wailing. Styx (stȳx): the Hateful. Both according to myth, rivers of the world below.

[3] See Apology, note 21.

starting up again in a frenzy and in full sail upon the shores of the barren sea, nor again taking the dusky ashes in both his hands and pouring them over his head, or bewailing and sorrowing in the various modes which Homer has delineated. Nor should he describe Priam,[4] the kinsman of the gods,—

"Rolling in the dirt, calling each man loudly by his name."

[Still less should the gods themselves be introduced wailing over sorrows and woes.]

For if, my sweet Adeimantus, our youth seriously believe in such unworthy representations of the gods, instead of laughing at them as they ought, hardly will any of them deem that he himself, being but a man, can be dishonored by similar actions; neither will he rebuke any inclination that may arise in his mind to say and do the like. And instead of having any shame or self-control, he will be always whining and lamenting on slight occasions.

[Our guardians ought not to indulge in excessive laughter which almost always produces a violent reaction. We should therefore not suffer Homer to say in describing a feast of the gods,

"Inextinguishable laughter rose among the blessed gods."

Truth must be highly valued by the youth, for lying among the citizens is a practice destructive of the State.

The youth must be temperate. The chief elements of temperance are, in general, obedience to commanders and self-control in sensual pleasures. Therefore Socrates approves such words in Homer as

"The Greeks marched breathing prowess,
In silent awe of their leaders."

But he condemns the line

"Oh heavy with wine, who hast the eyes of a dog and the heart of a stag."

Nor should the poets' praises of eating and drinking and of lower forms of pleasure be repeated to the young. Instead,

[4] Priam, king of Troy, was said to be descended from Zeus.

they should hear of the endurance of famous men, for example:

> "He smote his breast and thus reproached his soul,
> Endure, my soul, thou hast endured worse."

The youth must not receive bribes or be lovers of money. So the poets must not be allowed to sing of

> "Gifts persuading gods, persuading reverend kings."

In short, all examples of ignoble action, of insolence, of cruelty, of crime, or of impiety on the part of the gods or the children of the gods, we must equally refuse to believe or allow to be repeated. Socrates says of the poets:]

We will not have them teaching our youth that the gods are the authors of evil, and that heroes are no better than men; for, as we were saying, these sentiments are neither pious nor true, being at variance with our demonstration that evil cannot come from God. Also they are likely to have a bad effect on those who hear them; for everybody will begin to excuse his own vices when he is convinced that similar wickednesses are always being perpetrated by the kindred of the gods,—

> "The relatives of Zeus, whose paternal altar is in the heavens and on the mount of Ida," [a]

and who have—

> "The blood of deity yet flowing in their veins."

And therefore let us put an end to such tales, lest they engender laxity of morals among the young.

[The poets must not be allowed to lie about men any more than about gods and demigods, or the shades below.]

Because, if I am not mistaken, we shall have to say that poets and story-tellers make the gravest misstatements about men when they say that many wicked men are happy, and good men miserable; and we shall forbid them to utter these things, and command them to sing and say the opposite.

---

[a] A mountain in Asia Minor, sacred to Zeus.

[Thus far Socrates has discussed the subject matter of poetry. He now turns to style. All poetry and mythology he claims to be a narration of events past, present, or to come. Narration may take one of three forms, simple narration, imitation, or a union of the two. We have simple narration where the poet speaks always in his own person and never leads us to suppose that he is any one else. We have imitation where the poet speaks in the person of another, as in tragedy and comedy. The poet here imitates the persons whose characters he assumes. We may have a combination of simple narration and imitation, as in the epic.

Socrates now asks this question, "Are the poets in narrating their stories to be allowed to imitate in whole or in part, or should all imitation be prohibited?" The answer to this question depends upon the answer to a second question, "Ought our guardians to be imitators?" Socrates thinks the latter question has already been answered. The rule has been laid down that one man can only do one thing well and not many. This is equally true of imitation; no man can imitate many things as well as he would imitate a single one. Still less can one person "play the serious part of life, and at the same time be an imitator and imitate [6] many other parts as well." Socrates continues:]

If then we would retain the notion with which we began, that our guardians are to be released from every other art, and to be the special artificers of freedom, and to minister to this and no other end, they ought not to practice or imitate anything else; and, if they imitate at all, they should imitate the characters which are suitable to their profession—the temperate, holy, free, courageous, and the like; but they should not depict or be able to imitate any kind of illiberality or other baseness, lest from imitation they should come to be what they imitate. Did you never observe how imitations, beginning in early youth, at last sink into the constitution and become a second nature of body, voice, and mind?

For this reason there is one sort of narration which may be used or spoken by a truly good man, and there is another sort

---

[6] Since the study of poetry involved the singing and reciting of it, the style had more effect on the student than in the simple reading to one's self.

which will be exclusively adapted to a man of another character and education.

And which are these two sorts? he asked.

Suppose, I answered, that a just and good man in the course of narration comes on some saying or action of another good man,—I should imagine that he will like to impersonate him, and will not be ashamed of this sort of imitation; he will be most ready to play the part of the good man when he is acting firmly and wisely; in a less degree when his steps falter, owing to sickness or love, or again from intoxication or any other mishap. But when he comes to a character which is unworthy of him, he will not make a study of that; he will disdain to wear the likeness of his inferiors, unless indeed during some brief interval when they may be doing any good; at other times he will be ashamed to play a part which he has never practiced, nor will he like to fashion and frame himself after the baser models; he feels that this would be beneath him, when carried beyond a pastime.

397 [The simplicity of that style of writing which is largely narration with no imitation or at least only the imitation of virtue, is best suited to the simplicity of the ideal state where one man plays but one part. Socrates continues:]

398-400 And therefore when any one of these clever multiform gentlemen, who can imitate anything, comes to our State, and proposes to exhibit himself and his poetry, we will fall down and worship him as a sweet and holy and wonderful being; but we must also inform him that there is no place for such as he is in our State,—the law will not allow them. And so when we have anointed him with myrrh, and set a garland of wool upon his head, we shall send him away to another city. For we mean to employ for our souls' health the rougher and severer poet and story-teller, who will imitate the style of the virtuous only, and will follow those models which we prescribed at first when we began to speak of the education of our soldiers.

[Having discussed both the subject matter and style of myth and poetry, Socrates turns next to song. The song or ode he says, has three parts, the words, the melody, and the rhythm.

"As for the words, there will be no difference between words that are and are not set to music; both will conform to the same laws, and these have been already determined by us."

Now the melody or harmony and the rhythm will depend upon the words. Harmony is first considered. As lamentations and strains of sorrow were forbidden, so harmonies which are expressive of sorrow must be banished. Likewise since the guardians must be temperate and not hear examples of drunkenness and indolence in poetry or song, drinking melodies must be banished. There are two kinds of harmony which Socrates would allow. He says:]

I want to have one warlike, which will sound the word or note which a brave man utters in the hour of danger and stern resolve, or when his cause is failing and he is going to wounds or death or is overtaken by some other evil, and at every such crisis meets fortune with calmness and endurance; and another which may be used by him in times of peace and freedom of action, when there is no pressure of necessity—expressive of entreaty or persuasion, of prayer to God, or instruction of man, or again, of willingness to listen to persuasion or entreaty and advice; and which represents him when he has accomplished his aim, not carried away by success, but acting moderately and wisely and acquiescing in the event. These two harmonies I ask you to leave; the strain of necessity and the strain of freedom, the strain of the unfortunate and the strain of the fortunate, the strain of courage, and the strain of temperance; these, I say, leave.

[As the harmonies which Socrates permits are very simple and do not require multiplicity of notes or a complex scale, there is no need for complex musical instruments. He would allow only the lyre and harp in the city and the shepherd's pipe in the country.

Rhythm is next considered. Here as everywhere the answer to the question what shall be permitted, must be determined by the end of education. "We ought not to have complex or manifold systems of metre, but rather to discover what rhythms are the expressions of a courageous and harmonious life; and the words should come first and the rhythms should be adapted to them." For, Socrates says:]

Our principle is that rhythm and harmony are regulated by the words, and not the words by them.

Certainly, he said, they should follow the words.

And the words and the character of the style should depend on the temper of the soul?

Yes.

And everything else on the words?

Yes.

Then good language and harmony and grace and rhythm depend on simplicity,—I mean the simplicity of a truly and nobly ordered mind, not that other simplicity which is only a euphemism for folly?

Very true, he replied.

And if our youth are to do their work in life, must they not make these their perpetual aim?

They must.

And all life is full of them, as well as every creative and constructive art; the art of painting, weaving and embroidery, and building, and the manufacture of vessels, as well as the frames of animals and of plants; in all of them there is grace or the absence of grace. And absence of grace and inharmonious movement and discord are nearly allied to ill words and ill nature, as grace and harmony are the sisters and images of goodness and virtue.

That is quite true, he said.

But is our superintendence to go no further, and are the poets only to be required by us to impress a good moral on their poems as the condition of writing poetry in our State? Or is the same control to be exercised over other artists, and are they also to be prohibited from exhibiting the opposite forms of vice and intemperance and meanness and indecency in sculpture and building and the other creative arts; and is he who does not conform to this rule of ours to be prohibited from practicing his art in our State, lest the taste of our citizens be corrupted by him? We would not have our guardians grow up amid images of moral deformity, as in some noxious pasture, and there browse and feed upon many a baneful herb and flower day by day, little by little, until they silently gather a festering mass of corruption in their own soul. Let our artists rather be those who are gifted to discern the true nature of beauty and grace; then will our youth dwell in a land of health, amid fair sights and sounds ; and beauty, the effluence of fair works, will meet the sense like a breeze, and insensibly draw the soul even in childhood into harmony with the beauty of reason.

There can be no nobler training than that, he replied.

Is not this, I said, the reason, Glaucon, why musical training is so powerful, because rhythm and harmony find their way into the secret places of the soul, on which they mightily fasten, bearing grace in their movements, and making the soul graceful of him who is rightly educated, or ungraceful if ill-educated ; and also because he who has received this true education of the inner being will most shrewdly perceive omissions or faults in art and nature, and with a true taste, while he praises and rejoices over, and receives into his soul the good, and becomes noble and good, he will justly blame and hate the bad, now in the days of his youth, even before he is able to know the reason of the thing ; and when reason comes he will recognize and salute her as a friend with whom his education has made him long familiar. *402-403*

Yes, he said, I quite agree with you in thinking that these are the reasons why there should be a musical education.

Just as in learning to read, I said, we want to know the various letters in all their recurring sizes and combinations ; not slighting them as unimportant whether they be large or small, but everywhere eager to make them out ; and are not supposed to be perfect in the art until we recognize them wherever they are found :

True—

Or, as we recognize the reflection of letters in the water, or in a mirror, only when we know the letters themselves ; the same art giving us the knowledge of both :

Exactly—

Even so, I have no hesitation in saying that neither we nor our guardians, whom we have to educate, can ever become musical until we know the essential forms of temperance, courage, liberality, magnificence, as well as the cognate and contrary forms, in all their combinations, and can recognize them and their images wherever they are found, not slighting them either in small things or great, but believing them all to be within the sphere of one art and study.

Most assuredly.

And when a beautiful soul harmonizes with a beautiful form, and the two are cast in one mould, that will be the fairest of sights to him who has the eye to contemplate the vision?

The fairest indeed.

And the fairest are also the loveliest?

That may be assumed.

And the man who has music in his soul will be most in love with the loveliest; but if they are inharmonious in soul he will not love them?

That is true, he replied, if the deformity be in the soul, but any merely personal defect he will be willing to regard with complacency.

. . . .

Thus much then is said of music which makes a fair ending, for what should be the end of music if not the love of beauty?

I agree, he said.

After music comes gymnastic,[7] in which our youth are next to be trained.

Certainly.

And gymnastic as well as music should receive careful attention in childhood, and continue through life. Now my belief is,—and this is a matter upon which I should like to have your opinion, but my own belief is,—not that the good body improves the soul, but that the good soul improves the body. What do you say?

Yes, I agree.

Then, if we have educated the mind, the minuter care of the body may properly be committed to the mind, and we need only indicate general principles for brevity's sake.

---

[7] "According to the scheme of studies in Book VII., the gymnastic training was to be pursued by itself from the age of seventeen or eighteen to twenty. This provision probably indicated the nature of the training in question, for these were the years in which a young Athenian discharged military or patrol duty within the borders of Attica as a foretaste of the full military service which was one great aspect of citizen life. Thus we are not here to think *merely* of 'gymnastics' with ropes and bars or of 'athletic sports,' but also of drill, riding, hunting, the practice of arms, and some limited share in actual campaigning."—Bosanquet, p. 110.

Bosanquet quotes Aristotle's Politics as criticising the current methods of gymnastic training. Some of the States he says gave a physical training fit rather for professional athletes than for future citizens. The Spartans trained men to be fierce, wild, and wolf-like, supposing mistakenly that this temper went with courage.

Very good.

That they must abstain from intoxication has been already remarked by us, for of all persons a guardian should be the last to get drunk and not know where in the world he is.

Yes, he said; that a guardian should require another to guard him is ridiculous indeed.

But next, what shall we say of their food; for the men are athletes in the great contest of all, are they not?

Yes, he said.

And will gymnastic exercises be a suitable training for them? 404

I cannot say.

I am afraid, I said, that such exercise is but a sleepy sort of thing, and rather perilous to health. Do you not observe that athletes sleep away their lives, and are liable to most dangerous illnesses if they depart, in ever so slight a degree, from their customary regimen?

Yes, I observe that.

Then, I said, a finer sort of training will be required for our warrior athletes, who are to be like wakeful dogs, and to see and hear with the utmost keenness; they will have to endure many changes of water and also of food, of summer heat and winter cold, and yet they must not be liable to break down in health.

That is quite my view, he said.

The really excellent gymnastic is twin sister of that simple music which we were just now describing.

How is that?

Why, I conceive that there is a gymnastic also which is simple and good; and that such ought to be the military gymnastic.

What do you mean?

My meaning may be learned from Homer; he, you know, feeds his heroes when they are campaigning on soldiers' fare; they have no fish, although they are on the shores of the Hellespont, and they are allowed nothing but roast meat—which only requires fire, and is therefore the most convenient diet for soldiers—and not boiled, as this would involve a carrying about of pots and pans.

True.

And I can hardly be mistaken in saying that sweet sauces

are not even mentioned by him. In this, however, he is not singular, as all professional athletes know that a man who is to be in good condition should take nothing of that sort.

[The effects of luxurious living upon the body may be likened to the effects of complex music upon the soul.]

There complexity engendered license, and here disease; whereas simplicity in music was the parent of temperance in the soul, and simplicity in gymnastic, of health in the body.

Most true, he said.

But when intemperance and diseases multiply in a State, halls of justice and medicine are always being opened; and the arts of the doctor and the lawyer begin to give themselves airs, finding how keen is the interest which the very freemen of a city take about them.

405-406

Most true.

And yet what greater proof can there be of a bad and disgraceful state of education than this, that not only the meaner classes and the artisans are in need of the high skill of physicians and judges, but also those who would tell us that they have had a liberal education? Is not this disgraceful, and a great sign of the want of education, that a man should have to go abroad for his law and physic because he has none of his own at home, and must therefore surrender himself into the hands of others?

Nothing, he said, can be more disgraceful.

Would you say that, I replied, when you consider that there is a further stage of the evil in which a man is not only a life-long litigant, passing his days always in the courts either as plaintiff or defendant, but is led by his bad taste even to pride himself on this; he is ready to fancy that he is a master in cunning; and he will take every crooked turn and wriggle into and out of every hole, bending like a withy and getting away, and all for what? in order that he may gain small points not worth mentioning, not knowing that so to order his life as to be able to do without a nodding judge is a far higher and nobler sort of thing. Is not that still more disgraceful?

Yes, he said, that is still more disgraceful.

Well, I said, and to require the help of medicine, not when a wound has to be cured, or on occasion of an epidemic, but just because, by their lives of indolence and luxury, men fill themselves like pools with waters and winds, compelling the ingenious sons of Asclepius [8] to give diseases the names of flatulence and catarrh; is not this, too, a disgrace?

[In the days of Asclepius and Homer, and before the time of Herodicus, most of the diseases which we now have did not exist and the practice of medicine was very simple. But the present system of medicine may be said to educate diseases.]

Herodicus, being a trainer, and himself of a sickly constitution, by a happy combination of training and doctoring, found out a way of torturing first and principally himself, and secondly the rest of the world.

How was that? he said.

By the invention of lingering death; for he had a mortal disease which he perpetually tended, and as recovery was out of the question, he passed his entire life as a valetudinarian; he could do nothing but attend upon himself, and he was in constant torment whenever he departed in anything from his usual regimen, and so dying hard, by the help of science he struggled on to old age.

What a noble reward of the physician's skill!

Yes, I said; such a reward as a man might fairly expect who knew not the wisdom of Asclepius, and did not consider that, if he failed to instruct his descendants in these arts, this arose not from ignorance or inexperience of such a department of medicine, but because he knew that in all well-ordered States every individual had an occupation to which he must attend, and therefore had no leisure to spend in continually being ill. This we remark in the case of the artisan, but, ludicrously enough, fail to apply the same rule to people of the richer sort.

How is that? he said.

I replied; when a carpenter is ill he asks the physician for a rough and ready remedy; an emetic or a purge or cautery or the knife,—these are his remedies. And if any one tells him that he must go through a course of dietetics, and swathe and swaddle his head, and all that sort of thing, he replies at once that he has no time to be ill, and that he sees no good in a life

---

[8] Physicians. See Protagoras, note 8.

which is spent in nursing his disease to the neglect of his ordinary calling; and therefore saying good-by to this sort of physician, he resumes his customary diet, and either gets well and lives and does his business, or, if his constitution fails, he dies and has done with it.

Yes, he said, and a man in his condition of life ought to use this summary art of medicine.

407-408 Has he not, I said, an occupation; and what profit would there be in his life if he were deprived of his occupation?

Very true, he said.

But the rich man, as we say, is a gentleman who has no work which he ought to do or die?

He is generally supposed to have nothing to do.

Then you never heard of the saying of Phocylides,[9] that as soon as a man has a livelihood he should practice virtue?

Nay, he said, I think that he need not wait for that.

I don't want to raise that question, I replied; I want rather to know whether the practice of virtue is obligatory on the rich, and ought to be a necessity of life to him; and if so, whether their dieting of disorders, which is an impediment to the application of the mind in carpentering and the mechanical arts, does not equally stand in the way of the maxim of Phocylides?

Of that, he replied, there can be no doubt; such excessive care of the body, when carried beyond the rules of gymnastic, is most inimical to the practice of virtue, and equally incompatible with the management of a house, an army, or an office of State.

Yes, and even more incompatible, I replied, with any kind of study or thought or self-reflection.

[Asclepius shows himself to have been a good statesman. He conserved the interests of the State in healing only those of healthy constitution and habits of life. He did not attempt to cure diseased constitutions because they were of no use to the State.]

All that, Socrates, he said, is excellent; but I should like to put a question to you. Ought there not to be good physi-

---

[9] Phocylides (fō-cў̄l'ĭ-dēz, 560- — B.C.): a Greek poet.

cians in a State, and are not the best those who have the greatest experience of constitutions good and bad, just as good judges are those who are acquainted with all sorts of moral natures?

Yes, I said, I quite agree about the necessity of having good judges and good physicians. But do you know whom I think good?

Will you inform me?

Yes, if I can. Let me however note that in the same question you join two things which are not the same.

How is that? he said.

Why, I said, you join physicians and judges. Now skillful physicians are those who, besides knowing their art, have from their youth upwards had the greatest experience of disease; they had better not be in robust health, and should have had all manner of diseases in their own persons. For the body, as I conceive, is not the instrument with which they cure the body; in that case we would not allow them ever to be sickly; but they cure the body with the mind, and the mind which is or has become sick can cure nothing.

That is very true, he said.

But with the judge the case is different; he governs mind by mind, and he cannot be allowed therefore to have been reared among vicious minds, and to have associated with them from youth upwards, in order that, having gone through the whole calendar of crime, he may infer the crimes of others like their diseases from the knowledge of himself; but the honorable mind which is to form a healthy judgment ought rather to have had no experience or contamination of evil habits when young. And this is the reason why in youth good men often appear to be simple, and are easily practiced upon by the evil, because they have no samples of evil in their own souls.

Yes, he said, that very often happens with them.

Therefore, I said, the judge should not be young; he should have learned to know evil, not from his own soul, but from late and long observation of the nature of evil in others: knowledge, and not his own experience, should be his guide.

Yes, he said, that is the ideal of a judge.

Yes, I replied, and he will be good too (and this answers your question); for he is good whose soul is good; now your cunning and suspicious character, who has committed many crimes, when he is among men who are like himself, is wonderful in his precautions against others, because he judges of them by himself: but when he gets into the company of men of virtue, who have the experience of age, he appears to be a fool again, owing to his unseasonable suspicion: he cannot recognize an honest man, because he has nothing in himself at all parallel to judge from; at the same time, as the bad are more numerous than the good, and he meets with them oftener, he thinks himself, and others think him, rather wise than foolish.

Most true, he said.

Then the good and wise judge whom we are seeking is not this man; the other is better suited to us; for vice cannot know virtue, but a virtuous nature, educated by time, will acquire a knowledge both of virtue and vice: the virtuous, and not the vicious man has wisdom; that is my view.

And mine also.

This is the sort of medicine, and this is the sort of law, which you will sanction. They will be healing arts to better natures in their souls and in their bodies; but the worse nature or constitution they will in the case of the body leave to die, and the diseased and incurable soul they will put to death themselves.

That is clearly best for them and for the State.

And thus our youth, having been educated only in that simple music which infuses temperance, will be reluctant to go to law.

That is evident.

And in the same way simple gymnastic will incline him to have as little as possible to do with medicine.

That I quite believe.

The very exercises and toils he will undertake in order to stimulate the spirited element of his nature, rather than with a view of increasing his strength; he will not, like common athletes, use exercise and regimen to develop his muscles.

Very right, he said.

Neither are the two arts of music and gymnastic really designed, the one for the training of the soul, the other for the training of the body.

But what is the real object?

I believe, I said, that the teachers of both have in view chiefly the improvement of the soul.

How is that? he asked.

Did you never observe, I said, the effect on the mind of exclusive devotion to gymnastic, or the opposite effect of an exclusive devotion to music?

In what is that shown? he said.

In producing a temper of hardness and ferocity, or again of softness and effeminacy, I replied.

Yes, he said, I am quite aware that your mere athlete becomes too much of a savage, and that the musician is melted and softened beyond what is good for him.

Moreover, I said, that fierce quality gives spirit, and, if educated rightly, will be valiant, but, if overstrained, is likely to become hard and brutal.

That I quite think.

The philosopher is the type of the gentler character. This, if too much relaxed, will turn to softness, but, if educated, will be gentle and modest.

True.

And our view is that the guardians ought to have both these qualities?

They ought.

They should be harmonized?

Beyond question.

And the harmonious soul is both temperate and valiant?

Yes.

And the inharmonious is cowardly and boorish?

Very true.

And, when a man allows music to play and pour over his soul through his ears, which are the funnel, those sweet and soft and melancholy airs of which we were just now speaking, and his whole life is passed in warbling and the delights of song; in the first stage of the process the passion or spirit which is in him is tempered like iron, and made useful, instead of brittle and useless. But, if he carries on the softening process, in the next stage he begins to melt and consume, until the passion of his soul is melted out of him, and what may be called the nerves of his soul are cut away, and he makes but a feeble warrior.

Very true.

If the element of spirit is naturally weak in him this is soon accomplished, but if he have a good deal, then the power of music weakening the spirit renders him excitable; he soon flames up, and is speedily extinguished; instead of having spirit he becomes irritable and violent and very discontented.

Exactly.

Thus in gymnastics also, if a man works hard and is a great feeder, and the reverse of a great student of music and philosophy, at first the high condition of his body fills him with pride and spirit, until he is twice the man that he was.

Certainly.

But if he do nothing else, and never cultivates the Muses, even that intelligence which there may be in him, having no taste of any sort of learning or inquiry or thought or music, becomes feeble and dull and blind, because never roused or sustained, and because the senses are not purged of their mists.

True, he said.

And he ends by becoming a hater of philosophy, uncultivated, never using the weapon of persuasion,—he is like a wild beast, all violence and fierceness, and knows no other way of dealing; and he lives in all ignorance and evil conditions, and has no sense of propriety and grace.

That is quite true, he said.

And as there are two principles of human nature, one the spirited and the other the philosophical, my belief is that God has given mankind two arts answering to them (and only indirectly to the soul and body), in order that these two principles may be duly attuned and harmonized with one another.

That I am disposed to believe.

And he who mingles music with gymnastic in the fairest proportions, and best attempers them to the soul, may be called the true musician and harmonist in a far higher sense than the tuner of the strings.

I dare say, Socrates.

And such a presiding genius will be always required in our State if the government is to last.

Yes, he will be absolutely necessary.

Such, then, are our principles of nurture and education. There would be no use in going into further details about their dances, their hunting or chasing with dogs, their gymnastic and equestrian contests; for these all follow the general principle, and there will be no longer any difficulty in discovering them.

I dare say that there will be no difficulty.

Very well, I said; and what is the next question? Must we not ask who are to be rulers and who subjects?

Certainly.

There can be no doubt that the elder sort must rule the younger.

Clearly.

And that the best of the elder sort must rule.

That is also clear.

Now, are not the best husbandmen those who are most devoted to husbandry?

Yes.

And as we must have the best guardians of our city, must they not be those who have most the character of guardians?

Yes.

And to this end they ought to be wise and efficient, and to have a special interest about the State?

True.

And a man will be most likely to care about that which he happens to love?

That may be truly inferred.

And he will be most likely to love that which he regards as having the same interests with himself, and anything the good or evil fortune of which he imagines to involve as a result his own good or evil fortune, and to be proportionably careless when he is less concerned?

Very true, he replied.

Then there must be a selection. Let us note among the guardians those who in their whole life show the greatest desire to do what is for the good of their country, and will not do what is against her interests.

Those are the right men.

They will have to be watched at every turn of their lives, in order that we may see whether they preserve this resolution, and never, under the influence either of force or enchantment, forget or let go their duty to the State.

I do not understand, he said, the meaning of the latter words.

I will explain them to you, I replied. A resolution may go out of a man's mind either with his will or against his will; with his will when he gets rid of a falsehood, against his will whenever he is deprived of a truth.

413

I understand, he said, the willing loss of a resolution; the meaning of the unwilling I have yet to learn.

Why, I said, do you not see that men are unwillingly deprived of good, and willingly of evil? Is not to have lost the truth an evil, and to have the truth a good? and you would allow that to conceive things as they are is to have the truth?

Yes, he replied; I agree with you in thinking that mankind are deprived of truth against their will.

And do they not experience this involuntary effect owing either to theft, or force, or enchantment?

Still, he replied, I do not understand you.

I fear that I must have been talking darkly, like the tragedians. All that I mean is that some men change and others forget; persuasion steals away the hearts of the one class, and time of the other; and this I call theft. Now you understand me?

Yes.

Those again who are forced, are those whom the violence of some pain or grief compels to change their opinion.

That, he said, I understand, and you are quite right.

And you would also acknowledge with me that those are enchanted who change their minds either under the softer influence of pleasure, or the sterner influence of fear?

Yes, he said; everything that deceives may be said to enchant.

Therefore, as I was just now saying, we must inquire who are the best guardians of their own conviction that the interest of the State is to be the rule of all their actions. We must watch them from their youth upwards, and propose deeds for them to perform in which they are most likely to forget or to be deceived, and he who remembers and is not deceived is to be selected, and he who fails in the trial is to be rejected. That will be the way.

Yes.

And there should also be toils and pains and conflicts prescribed for them, in which they will give further proof of the same qualities.

Very right, he replied.

And then, I said, we must try them with enchantments—that is the third sort of test—and see what will be their behavior; like those who take colts amid noises and cries to see if they are of a timid nature, so must we take our youth amid terrors of some kind, and again pass them into pleasures, and try them more thoroughly than gold is tried in the fire, in order to discover whether they are armed against all enchantments, and of a noble bearing always, good guardians of themselves and of the music which they have learned, and retain under all circumstances a rhythmical and harmonious nature, such as will be most serviceable to the man himself and to the State. And he who at every age, as boy and youth and in mature life, has come out of the trial victorious and pure, shall be appointed a ruler and guardian of the State; he shall be honored in life and death, and shall receive sepulture and other memorials of honor, the greatest that we have to give. And as he is chosen his opposite is rejected. I am inclined to think that this is the sort of way in which our rulers and guardians should be chosen. I speak generally, and not with any pretension to exactness. 414

And, speaking generally, I agree with you, he said.

And perhaps the word "guardian" in the fullest sense ought to be applied to this class only who are our warriors abroad and our peacemakers at home, and who save us from those who might have the will or the power to injure us. The young men whom we before called guardians may be more properly designated auxiliaries and allies of the principles of the rulers.

[Socrates suggests that the citizens be told an old Phœnician myth as part of their education. [10]]

They are to be informed that their youth was a dream, and the education and training which they received from us an appearance only; in reality during all that time they were in process of formation and nourishment in the womb of

[10] In this place, as also in Laws, II., 663, Socrates advises that the people should be taught as literal truth a myth, which is intended to convey a lesson. Here as elsewhere he justifies a certain kind of falsehood. Observe that the "Socratic method" in this case does not consist in asking questions but in the inculcation of truth by myth.

the earth, where they themselves and their arms and appurtenances were manufactured; and when they were completed, the earth, their mother, sent them up; and, their country being their mother and also their nurse, they are therefore bound to advise for her good, and to defend her against attacks, and her citizens they are to regard as children of the earth and their own brothers. . . . Citizens, we shall say to them in our tale, you are brothers, yet God has framed you differently. Some of you have the power of command, and these he has composed of gold, wherefore also they have the greatest honor; others of silver, to be auxiliaries; others again who are to be husbandmen and craftsmen he has made of brass and iron; and the species will generally be preserved in the children. But as you are of the same original family, a golden parent will sometimes have a silver son, or a silver parent a golden son. And God proclaims to the rulers, as a first principle, that before all they should watch over their offspring, and see what elements mingle in their nature; for if the son of a golden or silver parent has an admixture of brass and iron, then nature orders a transposition of ranks, and the eye of the ruler must not be pitiful towards his child because he has to descend in the scale and become a husbandman or artisan, just as there may be others sprung from the artisan class who are raised to honor, and become guardians and auxiliaries. For an oracle says that when a man of brass or iron guards the State, it will then be destroyed. Such is the tale; is there any possibility of making our citizens believe in it?

Not in the present generation, he replied; I do not see any way of accomplishing this; but their sons may be made to believe, and their sons' sons, and posterity after them.

I see the difficulty, I replied; yet even this amount of belief may make them care more for the city and for one another. Enough, however, of the fiction, which may now be borne on the wings of rumor, while we arm our earth-born heroes, and lead them forth under the command of their rulers. Let them look around and select a spot whence they can best prevent insurrection, if any prove refractory within, and also defend themselves against enemies, who like wolves may come down on the fold from without; there let them encamp, and when they have encamped, let them sacrifice and prepare their dwellings.

And what sort of dwellings are they to have?

Dwellings that will shield them against the cold of winter and the heat of summer.

I suppose that you mean houses, he replied.

Yes, I said; but they must be the houses of soldiers, and not of shop-keepers.

What is the difference? he said.

That I will endeavor to explain, I replied. To keep watch-dogs, who, from want of discipline or hunger, or some evil habit or other, would turn upon the sheep and worry them, and behave not like dogs but wolves, would be a foul and monstrous thing? 416

Truly monstrous, he said.

And, therefore, every care must be taken lest our auxiliaries, as they are stronger than our citizens, should prevail over them, and become savage tyrants instead of gentle allies to them?

Yes, care should be taken.

And would not education be the best preparation and safeguard of them?

But they are well-educated, he replied; that is a safeguard which they already have.

I cannot be so confident of that, my dear Glaucon, I said; I am much more certain that they ought to be, and that true education, whatever that may be, will greatly tend to civilize and humanize them in their relations to one another, and to those who are under their protection.

True, he replied.

And not only their education, but their habitations, and also their means of subsistence, should be such as will neither impair their virtue as guardians, nor tempt them to prey upon the other citizens. Any man of sense will say that.

He will.

Such is our conception of them; and now let us consider what way of life will correspond with this conception. In the first place, none of them should have any property beyond what is absolutely necessary; neither should they have a private house, with bars and bolts, closed against any one who has a mind to enter; their provisions should be only such as are required by trained warriors, who are men of temperance and courage; their agreement is to receive from the citizens a fixed rate of pay, enough to meet the expenses of the year and no more, and they will have common meals and live together, like soldiers in a camp. Gold and silver we will tell them that they have from God; the diviner metal is within them, and they have therefore no need of that earthly dross which passes under the name of gold, and ought not to pollute the divine by earthly admixture, for that commoner metal has been the source of many unholy deeds; but their own is undefiled. And they alone of all the citizens may not touch or handle silver or gold, or be under the same roof with them, or wear them, or drink from them. And this will be their salvation, and the salvation of the State. But should they ever acquire homes or lands or moneys of their own, they will become housekeepers and husbandmen instead of guardians, enemies and tyrants instead of allies of the other citizens; hating and being hated, plotting and being plotted against, they will pass through life in much greater terror of internal than of external enemies, and the hour of ruin, both to themselves and to the rest of the State, will be at hand. For all which reasons may we not say that these are to be the regulations of our guardians respecting houses and all other things, and that such shall be our laws?

Yes, said Glaucon.

BOOK IV

HERE Adeimantus interposed a question. He said: How would you answer, Socrates, if a person were to say that you make your citizens miserable, and all by their own doing; for they are the actual owners of the city, and yet they reap no advantage from this; whereas other men acquire lands, and build large and handsome houses, and have everything handsome about them; offering sacrifices to the gods on their own account, and practicing hospitality; and also, as you were saying only just now, they have gold and silver, and all that is usual among the favorites of fortune; while our poor citizens are no better than mercenaries who are fixed in the city and do nothing but mount guard?

Yes, I said; and you may add that they are only fed, and not paid, in addition to their food, like other men; and therefore they cannot make a journey of pleasure, they have no money to spend on a mistress or any other luxurious fancy, which, as the world goes, is thought to be happiness; and many other accusations of the same nature might be added.

But, said he, let us suppose all that included in the charge.

You mean to ask, I said, what is to be our answer?

Yes, he replied.

If we proceed along the path which we are already going, I said, my belief is that we shall find the answer. Even if our guardians were such as you describe, there would not be anything wonderful in their still being the happiest of men; but let that pass, for our object in the construction of the State is the greatest happiness of the whole, and not that of any one class; and in a State which is ordered with a view to the good of the whole, we think that we are most likely to find justice, and in the ill-ordered State injustice: and, having found them, we shall then be able to decide which of the two is the happier. At present we are constructing the happy State, not piecemeal, or with a view of making a few happy citizens, but as a whole; and by and by we will proceed to view the opposite kind of State. If we were painting a statue,[1] and some

---

[1] A peculiarity of ancient sculpture and architecture was the practice of painting all kinds of marble work. This is known from traces still present in many works of art and from passages in ancient writers.

one were to come and blame us for not putting the most beautiful colors on the most beautiful parts of the body—for the eyes, he would say, ought to be purple, but they are black—in that case we should seem to excuse ourselves fairly enough by saying to him, "Pray, sir, do not have the strange notion that we ought to beautify the eyes to such a degree that they are no longer eyes; but see whether, by giving this and the other features their due, we make the whole beautiful." And, I say again, in like manner do not compel us to assign to the guardians a sort of happiness which will make them anything but guardians; for we also should have no difficulty in clothing our husbandmen in fine linen, and setting crowns of gold on their heads, bidding them till the ground no more than they like. Neither is ignorance the reason why we do not allow our potters to repose on couches, and feast by the fireside, passing round the glittering bowl, while their wheel is conveniently at hand, and working at pottery as much as they like, and no more; or, why we do not make every class happy in this way—and then, as you imagine, the whole State would be happy. But do not suggest this; for, if we listen to you, the husbandman will be no longer a husbandman, the potter will cease to be a potter, and nobody will have any distinct character. Now this is not of much importance where the corruption of society, and pretension to be what you are not, extends only to cobblers; but when the guardians of the laws and of the government are only seemers and not real guardians, that, as you will observe, is the utter ruin of the State: for they alone are the authors of happiness and order in a State. If we are right in depicting our guardians as the saviours and not the destroyers of the State, and the author of the other picture is representing peasants at a festival, happy in a life of revelry, rather than fulfilling the duties of citizens, we mean different things, and he is speaking of something which is not a State. And therefore we must consider whether we appoint our guardians with a view to their greatest happiness, or whether this principle of happiness does not rather reside in the State as a whole; but if so, the guardians and auxiliaries, and all others equally with them, must be compelled or induced to do their own work in the best way and then the whole State growing up in a noble order, the several classes will only have to receive the proportion of happiness which nature assigns to them.

I think that you are quite right.

I wonder whether you will agree with another remark which occurs to me.

What may that be?

There seem to be two causes of the deterioration of the arts.

What are they?

Wealth, I said, and poverty.

How do they act?

The process is as follows: When a potter becomes rich he no longer takes the same pains with his art?

Certainly not.

He grows more and more indolent and careless?

Very true.

And the result is that he becomes a worse potter?

Yes; he greatly deteriorates.

But, on the other hand, if he has no money, and is unable to buy tools or instruments, he will not work equally well himself, nor will he teach his sons or apprentices to work equally well.

Certainly not.

Then workmen, and also their works, are apt to degenerate under the influence both of poverty and of wealth?

That is evident.

Here, then, is a discovery of new evils, I said, which the guardians will have to watch, or they will creep into the city unobserved.

What evils?

Wealth, I said, and poverty; for the one is the parent of luxury and indolence, and the other of meanness and viciousness, and both of discontent.[2]

422

That is very true, he replied; but still I should like to know, Socrates, how our city will be able to go to war, especially against an enemy who is rich and powerful, if deprived of the sinews of war.

There may possibly be a difficulty, I replied, in going to war with one such enemy; but there is no difficulty where there are two of them.

[2] " Give me neither poverty nor riches."—Proverbs xxx. 8.

How is that? he asked.

In the first place, I said, our side will be trained warriors fighting against a number of wealthy individuals.

That is true, he said.

And do you not suppose, Adeimantus, that a single boxer who was perfect in his art would easily be a match for two stout and well-to-do gentlemen who were not boxers?

Hardly, if they came upon him at once.

What, not, I said, if he were able to run away and then turn and strike at the one who first came up? And supposing he were to do this several times under the heat of a scorching sun, do not you think that he might overturn more than one stout personage?

Certainly, he said, there would be nothing wonderful in that.

And yet rich men are probably not so inferior to others in boxing as they are in military qualities.

That is very likely.

Then probably our athletes will be able to fight with three or four times their own number?

I believe that you are right, he said.

And suppose that, before engaging, our citizens send an embassy to one of the two cities, telling them the truth: Silver and gold we neither have nor are permitted to have; in that we are not like you; do you therefore come and help us in war, and take the spoils of the other city. Who, on hearing these words, would choose to fight the lean wiry dogs, rather than, with the dogs on their side, to fight fat and tender sheep?

Very true; but still there might be a danger to the poor State if the wealth of many States were to coalesce in one.

States! I said; why, what simplicity is this, that you should use the term "State" of any but our own State! Other States may indeed be spoken of more grandiloquently in the plural number, for they are many in one—a game of cities at which men play. Any ordinary city, however small, is in fact two cities, one the city of the poor, the other of the rich, at war with one another; and in either division there are many smaller ones, and you would make a great mistake if you treated them as single States; but if you deal with them as many, and give the money or means or persons of the one to the others, you will always have a great many friends, and not many enemies. And your State, while the wise order which has now been prescribed continues to prevail in her, will be the greatest of States, not in reputation or appearance only, but in deed and truth, though she number not more than a thousand defenders. A State which is her equal you will hardly find, either among Hellenes or barbarians,[3] though many that appear to be as great and many times greater.

That is most true, he said.

And this, I said, will be the best limit for our rulers to fix when they are considering the size of the State and the amount of territory which they are to include, and beyond which they will not go.

What limit?

I think, I said, that the State may increase to any size which is consistent with unity; that is the limit.

Yes, he said; that is excellent.

Here then, I said, is another order which will have to be conveyed to our guardians,—that our city is to be neither large nor small, but of such a size as is consistent with unity.

And surely, said he, this is not a very severe order which we impose upon them.

And this, said I, is lighter still of which we were speaking before,—I mean the duty of degrading the offspring of the guardians when inferior, and of elevating the offspring of the lower classes, when naturally superior, into the rank of guardians. The intention was, that, in the case of the citizens generally, we should put each individual man to that use for which nature designed him, and then every man would do his own business, and be one and not many, and the whole city would be one and not many.

Yes, he said; there will be even less difficulty in that.

These things, my good Adeimantus, are not, as might be supposed, a number of great principles, but trifling all of them, if care be taken, as the saying is, of the one great thing,—a thing, however, which I would rather call not great, but enough for our purpose.

What may that be? he asked.

Education, I said, and nurture. For if they are well edu-

[3] A term applied by the Greeks to all who were not Greeks.

cated, and grow into sensible men, they will easily see their way through all this as well as other matters which I do not mention; such, for example, as the possession of women and marriage and the procreation of children, which will all follow the general principle that friends have all things in common,[4] as the proverb says.

424

That will be excellent, he replied.

Also, I said, the State, if once started well, goes on with accumulating force like a wheel. For good nurture and education implant good constitutions, and these good constitutions having their roots in a good education improve more and more, and this improvement affects the breed in man as in other animals.

True, he said.

Then to sum up. This is the point to which, above all, the attention of our rulers should be directed,—that music and gymnastics be preserved in their original form, and no innovation made. They must do all they can to maintain this. And when any one says that mankind most regard—

"The song which is the newest that the singers have,"

they will be afraid that he may be praising, not new songs, but a new kind of song; and this ought not to be praised, nor is this to be regarded as the meaning of the poet; for any musical innovation is full of danger to the State, and ought to be prevented. This is what Damon[5] tells me, and I can quite believe him; he says that when modes of music change, the fundamental laws of the State always change with them.[6]

Yes, said Adeimantus; and you may add my suffrage to Damon's and your own.

Then, I said, our guardians must lay the foundations of the fortress in music?

Yes, he said; and license easily creeps in; there can be no doubt of that.

Yes, I replied, in a kind of play, and at first sight appears harmless.

[4] See Book V., 441-466.
[5] Damon: a distinguished musician of Athens, known also as a Sophist.
[6] The Greeks had originally three musical modes which differed in key. They believed that each of these had "its own peculiar emotional influence." See Grote, I., 644. Compare the saying: Let me make a people's songs and I care not who may make its laws.

Why, he said, and there is no harm; but the evil is, that little by little this spirit of license, finding a home, penetrates into manners and customs; thence, issuing with greater force, invades agreements between man and man, and from agreements proceeds to laws and constitutions, in utter recklessness, and ends by an overthrow of things in general, private as well as public.

Is all that true? I said.

That is my belief, he replied.

Then, as I was saying, our youth should be educated in a stricter rule from the first, for if education becomes lawless, and the youths themselves become lawless, they can never grow up into well-conducted and virtuous citizens. **425**

Very true, he said.

And the education must begin with their plays. The spirit of law must be imparted to them in music, and the spirit of order, instead of disorder, will attend them in all their actions, and make them grow, and if there be any part of the State which has fallen down, will raise that up again.

Very true, he said.

Thus educated, they will have no difficulty in rediscovering any lesser matters which have been neglected by their predecessors.

What do you mean?

I mean such things as these: when the young are to be silent before their elders; how they are to show respect to them by sitting down and rising up; what honor is due to parents; what garments or shoes are to be worn; what mode of wearing the hair is to be the pattern; and the fashions of the body, and manners in general. You would agree with me in that?

Yes.

You think, as I am disposed to think, that there would be small wisdom in legislating about them; for that is never done, nor are any precise verbal enactments about them likely to be lasting.

Impossible.

We may assume, Adeimantus, that the direction in which education starts a man will determine his future life. Does not like always invite like?

No question.

Ending, as you may say, at last in some one rare and grand result, which may be good, and may be the reverse of good.

That is not to be denied, he answered.

And for this reason, I said, I shall not attempt further to legislate about them.

Naturally enough, he replied.

Well, I said, and about the business of the agora,[7] or about bargains and contracts with artisans; about insult and injury, or the order in which causes are to be tried, and how judges are to be appointed; there may also be questions about impositions and exactions of market and harbor dues, and in general touching the administration of markets or towns or harbors and the like. But, O heavens! shall we condescend to legislate on any of these particulars?

I think, he said, that there is no need to impose them by law on good men; most of the necessary regulations they will find out soon enough for themselves.

Yes, I said, my friend, if God will only guard the laws that we have given them.

And without divine help, said Adeimantus, they will go on forever making and mending their laws and their lives in the hope of attaining perfection.

You would compare them, I said, to those invalids who, having no self-restraint, will not leave off their habits of intemperance?

Exactly.

Yes, I said; and how charming those people are! they are always doctoring and increasing and complicating their disorders, fancying they will be cured by some nostrum which somebody advises them to try,—never getting better, but rather growing worse.

That is often the case, he said, with invalids such as you describe.

Yes, I replied; they have a charming way of going on, and the charming thing is that they deem him their worst enemy who tells them the truth, which is simply that, unless they give up eating and drinking and lusting and sleeping, neither drug nor cautery nor spell nor amulet nor anything will be of any avail.

[7] See Apology, note 2.

Charming! he replied. I see nothing charming in going into a passion with a man who tells you what is good.

These gentlemen, I said, do not seem to be in your good graces?

No, indeed.

Nor would a State which acts like them stand high in your estimation. And are not ill-governed States like them, which begin by proclaiming to their citizens that no one, under penalty of death, shall alter the constitution of the State, while he who conforms to their politics and most sweetly serves them, who indulges them and fawns upon them and has a presentiment of their wishes, and is skillful in gratifying them, he is esteemed as their good man, and the wise and mighty one who is to be held in honor by them?

Yes, he said; the States are as bad as the men; and I am far from approving them.

But do you not admire, I said, the coolness and dexterity of these ready ministers of political corruption?

Yes, he said, that I do; but not of all of them, for there are some whom the applause of the multitude has deluded into the belief that they are really statesmen, and they are not much to be admired.

What do you mean? I said; you should have more feeling for them. When a man cannot measure, and a great many others who cannot measure declare that he is four cubits high, can he help believing them?

He cannot.

Well, then, do not be angry with them; for are they not as good as a play, trying their hand at legislation, and always fancying that by reforming they will make an end of the dishonesties and rascalities of mankind, not knowing that they are in reality cutting away the heads of a hydra?[8]

Yes, he said; that is a very just description of them.

I conceive, I said, that the true legislator will not trouble himself with enactments of this sort in an ill-ordered any more than in a well ordered State; for in the former they are useless, and in the latter there will be no difficulty in inventing them, and many of them will naturally flow out of our institutions.

---

[8] In Greek mythology, a monstrous water-serpent with many heads, each of which, if cut off, was succeeded by two others.

What, then, he said, is still remaining to us of the work of legislation?

Nothing to us, I replied; but to Apollo, the god of Delphi, there remains the ordering of the greatest and noblest and chiefest of all.

What is that? he said.

The institution of temples and sacrifices, and in general the service of gods, demigods, and heroes; also the ordering of the repositories of the dead, and the rites which have to be observed in order to propitiate the inhabitants of the world below. For these are matters of which we are ignorant, and as founders of a city we should be unwise in trusting to any interpreter but our ancestral deity. He is the god who sits in the centre, on the navel of the earth, and interprets them to all mankind.[9]

You are right, he said; we will do as you propose.

But where, amid all this, is justice? Son of Ariston, tell me where. Now that our city has been made habitable, light a candle and search, and get your brother and Polemarchus, and the rest of our friends, to help, and let us see whether we can discover the place of justice and injustice, and discern the difference between them, and find out which of them the man who would be happy should have as his portion, whether perceived or unperceived by gods and men.

Nonsense, said Glaucon; did you not promise to search yourself, saying that to desert justice in her need would be an impiety?

Very true, I said; and as you remind me, I will be as good as my word; but you must join.

That we will, he replied.

Well, then, I hope to make the discovery in this way. I mean to proceed by a method of residues, beginning with the assumption that our State, if rightly ordered, is perfect.

That is most certain.

And being perfect, our State is wise and valiant and temperate and just.

That is also clear.

---

[9] It was customary to consult the oracle of Apollo at Delphi (see Apology, note 12), about the founding of cities. "Delphi, or rather a round stone in the Delphic temple, was called navel, as marking the middle point of the earth." (L. and S.)

And of whatever is known, that which is unknown will be the residue; this is the next step.

Very good.

Suppose the number of terms to be four, and we were searching for one of them, that one might be known to us at first, and there would be no further trouble; or, if we knew the other three first, and could eliminate them, then the fourth would clearly be the remainder.

Very true, he said.

And is not this the method to be pursued about the virtues, which are also four in number?

Clearly.

First among the virtues found in the State wisdom comes into view, and in this I detect a certain peculiarity.

What is that?

The State that we have been describing is said to be wise as being good in counsel: that is true?

Yes.

And good counsel is clearly a kind of knowledge, for not by ignorance, but by knowledge, do men counsel well?

Clearly.

And the kinds of knowledge in a State are many and diverse?

Of course.

There is the knowledge of the carpenter; but is that the sort of knowledge which gives a city the title of wise and good in counsel?

Certainly not; that would only give a city the reputation of skill in carpentering.

Then a city is not to be called wise because possessed of knowledge which counsels for the best about wooden implements?

Certainly not.

Nor by reason of a knowledge which advises about brazen implements, I said, nor as possessing any other similar knowledge?

Not by reason of any of them, he said.

Nor by reason of agricultural knowledge; that would give the city the name of agriculture?

Yes, that is what I should suppose.

Well, I said, and is there any knowledge in our recently-founded State among any of the citizens which advises, not about any particular thing in the State, but about the whole State, and considers what may be regarded as the best policy, both internal and external?

There certainly is.

And what is this knowledge, and among whom found? I asked.

This is the knowledge of the guardians, he replied, and is found among those whom we were just now describing as perfect guardians.

And is there any name which the city derives from the possession of this sort of knowledge?

The name of good in counsel and truly wise.

And do you suppose that there will be as many of these true guardians as there are blacksmiths in a city?

No, he replied; the blacksmiths will be far more numerous.

Will they not be the smallest of all the classes who receive a name from the profession of some kind of knowledge?

Much the smallest.

And by reason of this smallest part or class of a State, which is the governing and presiding class, and of the knowledge which resides in them, the whole State, being in the order of nature, will be called wise; and nature appears to have ordained that this, which has the only knowledge worthy to be called knowledge, should be the smallest of all classes.

₄₂₉

Most true, he said.

Thus, then, I said, the nature and place in the State of one of the four virtues has somehow been discovered.

I am sure, he said, that the discovery is to my mind quite satisfactory.

Again, I said, there is no difficulty in seeing the nature of courage, and in what part that quality resides which gives the name of courageous to the State.

How do you mean?

Why, I said, every one who calls any State courageous or cowardly, will be thinking of that part which fights and goes to battle on the State's behalf.

No one, he replied, would ever think of any other.

The rest of the citizens may be courageous or may be

cowardly, but that, as I conceive, will not have the effect of making the city either one or the other.

Certainly not.

The city will be courageous in virtue of a portion of the city in which there resides a never-failing quality preservative of the opinion which the legislator inculcated about the right sort of fear; and this is what you term courage.

I should like to hear what you are saying once more, for I do not think that I perfectly understand you.

I mean, I said, that courage is a kind of preservation.

What kind of preservation?

The preservation, I said, of the opinion about the nature and manner of dangers which the law implants through education; and I mean by the word "never-failing," to intimate that in pleasure or in pain, or under the influence of desire or fear, a man preserves, and does not lose this opinion. Shall I give you an illustration of my meaning?

If you will.

You know, I said, that the dyers, when they want to dye wool for making the true sea-purple, begin by selecting their white color first; this they prepare and dress with no slight circumstance, in order that the white ground may take the purple hue in full perfection. The dyeing then proceeds; and whatever is dyed in this manner becomes a fast color, and no washing with lyes or without lyes can take away the bloom of the color. I dare say that you know how these, or indeed any colors, look when the ground has not been duly prepared?

Yes, he said; I know that they have a washed-out and ridiculous appearance.

Then now, I said, you will understand what our object was in selecting our soldiers, and educating them in music and gymnastic; we were contriving influences which would prepare them to take the dye of the laws in perfection, and the color of their opinions about dangers and every other opinion was to be indelibly fixed by their nurture and training, and not to be washed away by any such potent lyes as pleasure,—mightier agent far in washing the soul than any soda or lye; and sorrow, fear, and desire mightier solvents than any others. And this sort of universal preserving power of true opinion in conformity with law about real and false dangers, I call and maintain to be courage, unless you can suggest another view.

But I have no other to suggest, and I suppose that you mean to exclude mere uninstructed courage, such as that of a wild beast or of a slave,—this, in your judgment, is not courage in conformity with law, and ought to have another name.

That is as you say.

Then I may infer that this is courage?

Why, yes, said I, that you may infer, and if you add the word "political," you will not be far wrong: hereafter we may pursue that inquiry further, but at present we are seeking not for courage but justice, and with a view to this there is nothing more wanted.

You are right, he replied.

Two virtues remain to be discovered in the State,—first, temperance, and then justice, which is the great object of our search.

Very true.

Now, can we find justice without troubling ourselves about temperance?

I do not know how that can be accomplished, he said, nor do I desire that justice should be brought to light, and temperance lost sight of; and therefore I wish you would do me the favor of considering temperance first.

Certainly, I replied, I cannot be wrong in granting you a favor.

Then do as I ask, he said.

Yes, I replied, I will do as you ask, and next consider temperance; this, as far as I can see at present, has more of the nature of symphony and harmony than the preceding.

How is that? he asked.

Temperance, I replied, is, as I conceive, a sort of order and control of certain pleasures and desires; this is implied in the saying of a man being his own master; and there are other traces of the same notion.

No doubt, he said.

There is something ridiculous in the expression "master of himself;" for the master is also the slave and the slave the master; and in all these modes of speaking the same person is predicated.

431

Certainly.

But the real meaning of the expression, I believe, is that the human soul has a better principle, and has also a worse principle; and when the better principle controls the worse, then a man is said to be master of himself; and this is certainly a term of praise: but when, owing to evil education or association, the better principle, which is less, is overcome by the worse principle, which is greater, this is censured; and he who is in this case is called the slave of self and unprincipled.

Yes, he said, there is reason in that.

And now, I said, look at our newly-created State, and there you will find one of these two conditions realized; for the State, as you will acknowledge, may be justly called master of self, if the words temperance and self-mastery truly express the rule of the better over the worse.

Yes, he said, I have looked, and perceive the truth of what you say.

Moreover, I said, the pleasures and desires and pains, which are many and various, are found in children and women and servants, and in the lower classes of the free citizens.

Certainly, he said.

Whereas the simple and moderate desires which follow reason, and are under the guidance of mind and true opinion, are confined to a few, being those who are the best born and the best educated.

Very true, he said.

And these also, I said, as you may perceive, have a place in our State, but the meaner desires of the many are held down by the virtuous desires and wisdom of the few.

That I perceive, he said.

Then if there be any city which may be described as master of pleasures and desires, and master of self, ours may claim that designation?

Certainly, he replied.

And also that of temperate, and for the same reasons?

Yes, he said.

And if there be any State in which rulers and subjects will be agreed about the question who are to rule, that again will be our State?

No doubt at all of that.

And the citizens being thus agreed among themselves, in

which class will temperance be found,—in the rulers or in the subjects?

In both, as I should imagine, he replied.

Do you observe, I said, that we were pretty right in our anticipation that temperance was a sort of harmony?

Why do you say that?

Why, because temperance is unlike courage and wisdom, each of which resides in a portion of the State only, which the one makes wise and the other valiant; but that is not the way with temperance, which extends to the whole, and runs through the notes of the scale, and produces a harmony of the weaker and the stronger and the middle class, whether you suppose them to be stronger or weaker in wisdom or strength or numbers or wealth, or whatever else may be the measure of them. Most truly, then, do we describe temperance as the natural harmony of master and slaves, both in States and individuals, in which the subjects are as willing to obey as the governors are to rule.

432

I entirely agree with you.

And so, I said, three of the virtues have been discovered in our State, and this is the form in which they appear. There remains the last element of virtue in a State, which must be justice, if we only knew what that was.

That, he said, is obvious.

The time then has arrived, Glaucon, when, like huntsmen, we should surround the cover, and look sharp that justice does not slip away, and pass out of sight, and get lost; for there can be no doubt that we are in the right direction; only try and get a sight of her, and if you come within view first, let me know.

I wish that there were any chance of that, he said; but I believe that you will find in me a follower who has just eyes enough to see what you show him; that is as much as I am good for.

Offer up a prayer, I said, and follow.

I will follow, he said, but you must show me the way.

Here is no path, I said, and the wood is dark and perplexing, still we must push on.

Let us push on then.

Halloo! I said, I begin to perceive indications of a track, and I believe that the quarry will not escape.

That is good news, he said.
Truly, I said, we are very stupid.
Why so?
Why, my good sir, I said, when we first began, ages ago, there lay justice rolling at our feet, and we, fools that we were, failed to see her, like people who go about looking for what they have in their hands: And that was the way with us; we looked away into the far distance, and I suspect this to have been the reason why we missed her.

What do you mean?

I mean to say that we have already had her on our lips and in our ears, and failed to recognize her.

I get impatient at the length of your exordium.

Well, then, say whether I am right or not; you will remember the original principle of which we spoke at the foundation of the State, that every man, as we often insisted, should practice one thing only, that being the thing **433** to which his nature was most perfectly adapted; now justice is either this or a part of this.

Yes, that was often repeated by us.

Further, we affirmed that justice was doing one's own business, and not being a busybody; that was often said by us, and many others have said the same.

Yes, that was said by us.

Then this doing one's own business in a certain way may be assumed to be justice. Do you know why I say this?

I do not, and should like to be told.

Because I think that this alone remains in the State when the other virtues of temperance and courage and wisdom are abstracted; and this is the ultimate cause and condition of the existence of all of them, and while remaining in them is also their preservative; and we were saying that if the three were discovered by us, justice would be the fourth or remaining one.

That follows of necessity.

Still, I said, if a question should arise as to which of these four qualities contributed most by their presence to the excellence of the State, whether the agreement of rulers and subjects, or the preservation in the soldiers of the opinion which the law ordains about the true nature of dangers, or wisdom and watchfulness in the rulers would claim the palm, or whether this which I am about to mention, and which is found in children and women, bond and free, artisan, ruler, subject, is not the one which conduces most to the excellence of the State,—this quality, I mean, of every one doing his own work, and not being a busybody,—the question would not be easily determined.

Certainly, he replied, that would be difficult to determine.

Then the power of each individual in the State to do his own work appears to compete in the scale of political virtue with wisdom, temperance, and courage?

Yes, he said.

And the virtue which enters into this competition is justice?

Exactly.

Look at this in another light. Are not the rulers in a State those to whom you would entrust the office of determining causes?

Certainly.

And they will decide on the principle that individuals are neither to take what is another's nor to be deprived of what is their own; that will be the principle at which they will aim?

Yes; that will be their principle.

And that is a just principle?

Yes.

Then on this view also justice will be admitted to be the having and doing what is a man's own, and belongs to him?

That is true.

Think, now, and say whether you agree with me. Suppose a carpenter to be doing the business of a cobbler, or a cobbler of a carpenter; and suppose them to exchange implements or prerogatives, or the same person to be doing the work of both; do you think that any great harm would happen to the State?

434

Not at all, he said.

But when the cobbler leaves his last, and he or any other whom nature designed to be a trader, and whose heart is lifted up by wealth or strength or numbers, or any like advantage, attempts to force his way into the class of warriors, or a warrior into that of legislators and guardians, for which he is unfitted, or when one man is trader, legislator, and warrior all at once, then I think you will agree with me that this interchange of duties and implements and this meddling of one with another is the ruin of the State.

Most true.

Then, said I, as there are three distinct classes, any meddling of them with one another, or the change of one into another, is the greatest harm to the State, and may be most justly termed evil-doing?

Precisely.

And the greatest degree of evil-doing to one's own city you would characterize as injustice?

Certainly.

This then is injustice; and let us once more repeat the thesis in the opposite form. When the trader, the auxiliary, and the guardian do their own business, that is justice, and will make the city just.

I think that is true, he said.

Let us not, I said, be over-positive as yet; but if, on trial, this conception of justice be verified in the individual as well as in the State, then there will be no longer any room for doubt; but, if not, there must be another inquiry. At present, however, let us finish the old investigation, which we began, as you remember, under the impression that, if we could first examine justice on the larger scale, there would be less difficulty in recognizing her in the individual. That larger example appeared to be the State, and we made the best that we could, knowing well that in the good State justice would be found to exist. Let us now apply what we found there to the individual, and if they agree, well and good; or, if there be a difference in the individual, we will come back to the State and have another trial of the theory. The friction of the two when rubbed together may possibly strike a light in which justice will shine forth, and the vision which is then revealed we will fix in our souls.

That is the right way, he said; let us do as you say.

I proceeded to ask: When two things, a greater and less, are called by the same name, are they like or unlike in so far as they are called the same?

Like, he replied.

The just man then, in being just, and in reference to the mere principle of justice, will be like the just State?

He will.

And a State was thought by us to be just when the three classes in the State did their own business; and also thought to be temperate and valiant and wise by reason of certain other affections and qualities of these same classes?

True, he said.

And so of the individual; we shall be right in arguing that he has these same principles in his own soul, and may fairly receive the same appellations as possessing the affections which correspond to them?

Certainly, he said.

Once more then, O my friend, we have alighted upon an easy question—whether the soul has these three principles or not?

An easy question! Nay, rather, Socrates, the proverb holds that hard is the good.

Very true, I said; and I confess that the method which we are employing, in my judgment, seems to be altogether inadequate to the accurate solution of this question; for the true method is another and a longer one. Still we may arrive at a solution not below the level of the previous inquiry.

May we not be satisfied with that? he said: under the circumstances, I am quite content.

I too, I replied, shall be extremely well satisfied.

Then faint not in pursuing the speculation, he said.

Can I be wrong, I said, in acknowledging that in the individual there are the same principles and habits which there are in the State? for if they did not pass from one to the other, whence did they come? Take the quality of spirit or passion; there would be something ridiculous in thinking that this quality, which is characteristic of the Thracians, Scythians,[10] and in general of the northern nations, when found in States, does not originate in the individuals who compose them; and the same may be said of the love of knowledge, which is the special characteristic of our part of the world, or the love of money, which may, with equal truth, be attributed to the Phœnicians and Egyptians.[11]

Exactly, he said.

There is no difficulty in understanding this.

---

[10] The names Thracia (thrā′shĭ-a) and Scythia (Sȳ′thĭ-a) were applied to various regions at different periods. Here the reference is probably to regions on the west and north coasts of the Black Sea, whose inhabitants were semi-civilized, fierce, and war-like.

[11] The Phœnicians and Egyptians were the principal commercial peoples of antiquity with whom the Greeks were acquainted.

None whatever.

But the difficulty begins as soon as we raise the question whether these principles are three or one; whether, that is to say, we learn with one part of our nature, are angry with another, and with a third part desire the satisfaction of our natural appetites; or whether the whole soul comes into play in each sort of action—to determine that is the difficulty.

Yes, he said, that is the difficulty.

Then let us now try and determine whether they are the same or different.

[The same thing cannot at the same time, with the same part, act in contrary ways, about the same. If therefore we find in ourselves a principle which impels us to eat and drink and indulge in other passions, and another principle which at the same time restrains us from these indulgences, these two principles, the impelling and the restraining, must be distinct. The principle which impels us we may call the irrational or appetitive, and the principle which restrains we may call the rational. Socrates continues:]

Then let these be marked out as the two principles which there are existing in the soul.

And what shall we say of passion, or spirit? Is that a third, or akin to one of the preceding?

I should be inclined to say—akin to desire.

Well, I said, there is a story which I remember to have heard, and on which I rely. The story is that Leontius, the son of Aglaion,[12] was coming up from the Piræus, under the north wall on the outside, and observed some dead bodies lying on the ground by the executioner. He felt a longing desire to see them, and also a disgust and abhorrence of them; for a time he turned away and averted his eyes, and then, suddenly overcome by the impulse, forced them open, **440** and ran up, saying (to his eyes), Take your fill, ye wretches, of the fair sight.

I have heard the story myself, he said.

Now this seems to imply that anger differs from the desires, and is sometimes at war with them.

That is implied, he said.

---

[12] Leontius (lē-ŏn'shĭ-us). Aglaion (ăg-lī'yon).

And are there not many other cases in which we observe that, when a man's desires violently prevail over his reason, he reviles himself, and is angry at the violence within him, and that in this struggle, which is like the struggle of actions in a State, his spirit is on the side of his reason. But that the passionate or spirited element should side with the desires when reason decides that she is not to be opposed, this sort of thing, I believe, you will say that you never observed occurring in yourself, nor, as I think, in any one else?

Certainly not, he said.

Suppose, I said, that a man thinks he has done a wrong to another: the nobler he is the less able he is to get into a state of righteous indignation; his anger refuses to be excited at the hunger or cold or other suffering, which he deems that the injured person may justly inflict upon him?

True, he said.

But when he thinks that he is the sufferer of the wrong, then he boils and chafes, and is on the side of what he believes to be justice; and because he suffers hunger or cold or other pain he is only the more determined to persevere and conquer; he must do or die, and will not desist, until he hears the voice of the shepherd, that is, reason, bidding his dog bark no more.

That is a very good illustration, he replied; and in our State as we were saying, the auxiliaries were to be dogs, and to hear the voice of the rulers, who are their shepherds.

I perceive, I said, that you quite understand me; there is, however, a further point which I would wish you to consider.

What may that be?

You remember that passion or spirit appeared at first sight to be a sort of desire, but now we should say the contrary; for in the conflict of the soul spirit is arrayed on the side of the rational principle.

Most assuredly.

But a further question arises. Is spirit different from reason also, or only a sort of reason; in which case, instead of three principles in the soul, there will be only two, the rational and the concupiscent; or rather, as the State was composed of three classes, traders, auxiliaries, counsellors, so may there not be in the individual soul a third element which is passion or spirit, and which is the auxiliary of reason when not corrupted by education?

Yes, he said, there must be a third.

Yes, I replied, if passion, which has already been shown to be different from desire, turn out also to be different from reason.

But that is obvious, he said, and is proved in the case of young children, who are full of spirit almost as soon as they are born, whereas some of them never seem to attain to the use of reason, and a good many only late in life.

Excellent, I said, and the same thing is seen in brute animals, which is a further proof of the truth of what you are saying. And Homer, whose words we have already quoted, may be again summoned as a witness, where he says,—

"He smote his breast, and thus rebuked his soul;"

for in those lines Homer has clearly supposed the power which reasons about the better and worse to be different from the unreasoning principle which is the subject of the rebuke.

That is true, he said.

And now, after much tossing in the argument, we have reached land, and are fairly agreed that the principles which exist in the State, like those in the individual, are three in number, and the same with them.

Exactly.

And must we not infer that the individual is wise in the same way, and in virtue of the same quality which makes the State wise?

Certainly.

And the same quality which constitutes bravery in the State constitutes bravery in the individual, and the same is true of all the other virtues?

Assuredly.

And the individual will be acknowledged by us to be just in the same way that the State was just?

That will also follow of course.

And the justice of the State consisted, as we very well remember, in each of the three classes doing the work of that class?

We are not very likely to forget that, he said.

And we must also remember that the individual whose several principles do their own work will be just, and will do his own work?

Yes, he said, we must remember that.

And ought not the rational principle, which is wise, and has the care of the whole soul, to rule, and the passionate or spirited principle to be the subject and ally?

Certainly.

And, as you were saying, the harmonizing influence of music and gymnastic will bring them into accord, nerving and educating the reason with noble words and lessons, and softening and consoling and civilizing the wildness of passion with harmony and rhythm?

442

Quite true, he said.

And these two, thus nurtured and educated, and having learned truly to know their own functions, will set a rule over the concupiscent part of every man, which is the largest and most insatiable; over this they will set a guard, lest, waxing great with the fullness of bodily pleasures, as they are termed, and no longer confined to her own sphere, the concupiscent soul should attempt to enslave and rule those who are not her natural-born subjects, and overturn the whole life of man?

Very true, he said.

The two will be the defenders of the whole soul and the whole body against attacks from without; the one counseling, and the other fighting under the command of their leader, and courageously executing his counsels.

True.

And he is to be deemed courageous who, having the element of passion working in him, preserves, in the midst of pain and pleasure, the notion of danger which reason prescribes?

Right, he replied.

And he is wise who has in him that little part which rules and gives orders; that part being supposed to have a knowledge of what is for the interest of each and all of the three parts?

Assuredly.

And would you not say that he is temperate who has these same elements in friendly harmony, in whom the one ruling principle of reason, and the two subject ones of spirit and desire are equally agreed that reason ought to rule, and do not rebel?

Certainly, he said, that is the true account of temperance whether in the State or individual.

And surely, I said, a man will be just in the manner of which we have several times already spoken and no other?

That is very certain.

And is the edge of justice blunted in the individual, or is there any reason why our definition of justice should not apply equally to the individual and to the State?

None in my judgment, he said.

Because, I said, if any doubt is still lingering in our minds, a few commonplace instances will satisfy us of the truth of this.

What sort of instances do you mean?

Why, for example, I said, who would imagine that the just State, or the man who is trained in the principles of such a State, would be more likely than the unjust to make away with a deposit of gold or silver?

No one, as I should suppose, he replied.

Will such an one, I said, ever be guilty of sacrilege or theft, or treachery either to his friends or to his country?

That will be far from him.

Neither will he ever break faith where there have been oaths or agreements?

Impossible.

No one will be less likely to commit adultery, or to dishonor his father and mother, or to fail in his religious duties?

No one.

And the reason of this is that each part of him is doing his own business, whether in ruling or being ruled?

That is the truth.

Are you satisfied then that the quality which makes such men and such States is justice, or do you hope to discover some other?

Not I, indeed.

Then our dream has been realized; and as we were saying at the beginning of our work of construction, some divine power must have conducted us to a sort of first principle or form of justice—that suspicion of ours has been now verified?

Yes, certainly.

And the division of labor which required the carpenter and the shoemaker and the rest of the citizens to be doing each his own business, and not another's, was a kind of shadow of justice, and therefore of use?

Clearly.

And justice was the reality of which this was the semblance, dealing, however, not with the outward man, but with the inward, which is the true self and concernment of a man: for the just man does not permit the several elements within him to meddle with one another, or any of them to do the work of others, but he sets in order his own inner life, and is his own master, and at peace with himself; and when he has bound together the three principles within him, which may be compared to the middle, higher, and lower divisions of the scale, and the intermediate intervals—when he has bound together all these, and is no longer many, but has become one entirely temperate and perfectly adjusted nature, then he will begin to act, if he has to act, whether in a matter of property, or in the treatment of the body, or some affair of politics or private business; in all which cases he will think and call just and good action that which preserves and coöperates with this condition, and the knowledge which presides over this wisdom; and unjust action, that which at any time destroys this, and the opinion which presides over unjust action, ignorance.

444

That is the precise truth, Socrates.

Very good; and if we were to say that we had discovered the just man and the just State, and the place of justice in each of them, that would not be a very vain boast?

No, indeed.

May we be so bold then as to say this?

Let us be so bold, he replied.

And now, I said, injustice has to be considered.

That is evident.

Then, assuming the threefold division of the soul, must not injustice be a kind of quarrel between these three—a meddlesomeness, and interference, and rising up of a part of the soul against the whole soul, an assertion of unlawful authority, which is made by a rebellious subject against a true prince, of whom he is the natural vassal—that is the sort of thing; the confusion and error of these parts or elements is injustice and intemperance and cowardice and ignorance, and in general all vice?

Exactly so, he said.

And if the nature of justice and injustice be known, then the meaning of acting unjustly and being unjust, or, again, of acting justly, will also be perfectly clear?

What do you mean? he said.

Why, I said, they are like disease and health; being in the soul just what disease and health are in the body.

How is that? he said.

Why, I said, that which is healthy causes health, and that which is unhealthy causes disease.

Yes.

And just actions cause justice, and unjust actions cause injustice?

That is certain.

And the creation of health is the creation of a natural order and government of one another in the parts of the body; and the creation of disease is the creation of a state of things in which they are at variance with this natural order?

True.

And is not this equally true of the soul? Is not the creation of justice the creation of a natural order and government of one another in the parts of the soul, and the creation of injustice the opposite?

Exactly, he said.

Then virtue is the health and beauty and well-being of the soul, and vice is the disease and weakness and deformity of the soul?

True.

And good practices lead to virtue, and evil practices to vice?

Assuredly.

Still our old question of the comparative advantage of justice and injustice has not been answered: Which is the more profitable, to be just and do justly, and practice virtue, whether seen or unseen of gods and men, or to be unjust and do unjustly, if only unpunished and unimproved? 445

In my judgment, Socrates, the question has now become ridiculous. If, when the bodily constitution is gone, life is no longer endurable, though pampered with every sort of meats and drinks, and having all wealth and all power, shall we be told that life is worth having when the very essence of the vital principle is undermined and corrupted, even though a man be allowed to do whatever he pleases, if at the same time he is forbidden to escape from vice and injustice, or attain justice and virtue, seeing that we now know the true nature of each?

Yes, I said, that is ridiculous, as you say. Still, as we are near the spot at which we may see the truth with our own eyes, let us not faint by the way.

Certainly not, he replied.

Come hither then, I said, ascend the hill which overhangs the city, and see the various forms of vice.

I am following you, he replied: proceed.

I said, We seem to have reached a summit of speculation from which you may look down and see the single form of virtue, and the forms of vice innumerable; there being four special ones which are deserving of note.

What do you mean? he said.

I mean, I replied, that there appear to be as many forms of the soul as there are forms of the State.

How many?

There are five of the State, and five of the soul, I said.

What are they?

The first, I said, is that which we have been describing, and which may be said to have two names, monarchy and aristocracy,[18] according as rule is exercised by one or many.

True, he replied.

But I regard this as one form only; for whether the government is in the hands of one or many, if the governors have been trained in the manner which we have described, the fundamental laws of the State will not be subverted.

That is true, he replied.

---

[18] Monarchy: literally, government by one; according to Plato, by the best one.

Aristocracy: literally, government by the best; so in Plato, the best being the philosophers.

BOOK V

SUCH is the good and true State, and the good and true man is of the same pattern; and if this is right every other is wrong; and the error is one which affects not only the ordering of the State, but also the regulation of the individual soul. There are four forms of this evil.

449-466

What are they? he said.

I was proceeding to tell the order in which the four evil forms appeared to me to succeed one another, when Polemarchus began to whisper to his neighbor Adeimantus, who was sitting just beyond him on the further side. He put out his hand, and took him by the coat at the upper part, by the shoulder, and drew him towards him, leaning forward himself and saying something, of which I only caught the words, "Shall we let him off, or what?"

Certainly not, said Adeimantus, raising his voice.

What is that, I said, which you refuse to let off?

You, he said.

Still I asked for an explanation.

Why, he said, we think that you are lazy and mean to cheat us out of the best part of the story; and you have a notion that you will not be detected in passing lightly over an entire and very important division of the subject,—that which relates to women and children,—as if there could be no manner of doubt in this instance also that "friends will have all things in common."

[In what follows, Plato sets forth his view that property, wives, and children should be in common, and that men and women should have the same education. In the Laws he admits that communism is impracticable in this world, but says it is an ideal towards which we should strive. "The first and highest form of the State and of the government and of the law is that in which there prevails most widely the ancient saying, that 'Friends have all things in common.' Whether there is now, or ever will be, this communion of women and children and of property, in which the private and individual is altogether banished from life and things which are by nature private, such as eyes and ears and hands have become common, and in some way see and hear and act in common, and all men express praise and blame, and feel joy and sorrow, on the same occasions, and the laws unite the city to the utmost—whether all this is possible or not, I say that no man, acting upon any other principle, will ever constitute a State more exalted in virtue, or truer or better than this. Such a State, whether inhabited by gods or sons of gods, will make them blessed who dwell therein; and therefore to this we are to look for the pattern of the State, and to cling to this, and, as far as possible, to seek for one which is like this."—Laws, V., 739.]

The inquiry, I said, has yet to be made, whether such a community will be found possible—as among other animals so also among men—and if possible, in what way possible?

That, he said, is just the question which I was going to ask.

As to war, I said, there is no difficulty in seeing how that will be managed.

How will that be? he asked.

Why, of course, they will go on expeditions together; and will take with them any of their children who are strong enough, that, like the children of artisans in general, they may look on at the work, which they will have to do when they are grown up; and besides looking on they will be able to help and be of use in war, and to wait upon their fathers and mothers. Did you never observe in the arts how the potters' boys look on and help, long before they touch the wheel?

Certainly.

And shall potters be more careful than our guardians in educating their children and giving them the opportunity of seeing and practicing their duties?

That would be ridiculous, he said.

There is another thing; which is the effect on the parents, with whom, as with other animals, the presence of their cubs will be the greatest incentive to valor.

That is quite true, Socrates; and yet if they are defeated, which may often happen in war, how great the danger is! the children will be lost as well as their parents, and the State will never recover.

True, I said; but would you never allow them to run any risk?

I am far from saying that.

Well, but if they are ever to run a risk should they not run the risk when there is a chance of their improvement?

Clearly.

Whether the future soldiers do or do not see war in the days of their youth is a very important matter, for the sake of which some risk may fairly be incurred.

Yes, that is very important.

Then, in the first place, we must provide that the children should see war, and then contrive a way of safety for them; thus all will be well.

True.

Their parents may be supposed to have ordinary common sense and understanding of the risks of war; they will know what expeditions are safe and what dangerous?

That may be supposed.

And they will take them on the safe expeditions and be cautious about the dangerous ones?

True.

And they will give them as commanders experienced veterans [1] who will be their leaders and teachers?

Yes, that is very proper.

Still, the dangers of war cannot always be foreseen; there is a good deal of chance about them?

True.

Then against such chances the children must be at once furnished with wings, in order that in the hour of need they may fly away and escape.

What do you mean? he said.

I mean that we must mount them on horses in their earliest youth and take them on horseback to see war, in order that they may learn to ride; the horses must not be spirited and warlike, but the most tractable and yet the swiftest that can be had. In this way they will get an excellent view of what is hereafter to be their business; and if there is danger they have only to follow their elder leaders and escape.

I believe that you are right, he said.

Next, as to war; what are to be the relations of your sol-

---

[1] Instead of putting them in charge of slaves as was customary.

diers to one another and to their enemies? I should be inclined to propose that the soldier who leaves his rank or throws away his arms, or is guilty of any other act of cowardice,[2] should be degraded into the rank of a husbandman or artisan. What do you think?

By all means, I should say.

And he who allows himself to be taken prisoner may even be made a present of to his enemies; he is their prey and they may do as they like with him.

Certainly.

But the hero who has distinguished himself, what shall be done to him? In the first place, he shall receive honor in the army from his youthful comrades; every one of them in succession shall crown him. What do you say to that?

I approve.

And what do you say to his receiving the right hand of fellowship?

To that too, I agree.

But I suspect that you will hardly agree to my next proposal. What is that?

That he should kiss and be kissed by them.

That I entirely approve, and should be disposed to add another clause: Let no one whom he has a mind to kiss refuse to be kissed by him while the expedition lasts. So that if there be a lover in the army, whether his love be youth or maiden, he may be more eager to win the prize of valor.

That is good, I said. That the brave man is to have more wives than others has been already determined; and he is to have first choices in such matters more than others, in order that he may have as many children as possible.

That was agreed.

And the propriety of thus honoring brave youths may be proved out of Homer; who tells how Ajax,[3] after he had distinguished himself in battle, was rewarded with long chines, which seems to be a complement appropriate to a hero in the flower of his age, being not only a tribute of honor but also a very strengthening thing.

[2] The Greeks generally regarded an act of cowardice in battle as worse than death. It was in many cities punished by loss of citizenship. Bosanquet quotes the Athenian's oath: "I will not disgrace my sacred shield. I will not desert my fellow-soldier in the ranks."

[3] See Apology, note 56.

Very true, he said.

Then in this, I said, Homer will be our teacher; and we too, at sacrifices and on the like occasions, will honor the brave with hymns—

"And seats of precedence, and meats and flowing goblets;"

not only honoring them, but also exercising them in virtue.

That, he replied, is excellent.

Good, I said; and when a man dies gloriously in war shall we not say, in the first place, that he is of the golden race?[4]

To be sure.

Nay, have we not the authority of Hesiod for affirming that when they are dead—

"They are holy angels upon the earth, authors of good, averters of ill, the guardians of speaking men?"

And we shall believe him.

And suppose that we inquire of the god how we are to order the sepulture of divine and heroic personages, and do as he bids?[5]

By all means.

In ages to come we will do service to them and worship at their shrines as heroes. And not only they but all other benefactors who die from age, or in any other way, shall be admitted to the same honors.

That is very right, he said.

Next, how shall our soldiers treat their enemies? What do you say about this?

In what respect do you mean?

I mean, shall they be made slaves? Do you think that Hellenes ought to enslave Hellenes,[6] or allow others to enslave them, as far as they can help? Should not their custom be to spare them, considering the danger which there is that the whole race may one day fall under the yoke of the barbarians?

To spare them is infinitely better.

Then no Hellene should be owned by them as a slave; that is a rule which they will observe and advise the other Hellenes to observe.

Certainly, he said; that is the way to unite them against

---

[4] Compare myth at close of Book III.
[5] See Book IV., 427.
[6] At this time the Spartans held fellow Greeks in slavery.

the barbarians, and make them keep their hands off one another. Next as to the slain; ought the conquerors, I said, to take anything but their armor? Does not the practice of despoiling an enemy afford an excuse for not facing the battle? They skulk about the dead, pretending to be executing a duty, and many an army before now has been lost from this love of plunder.

Very true.

And is there not illiberality and avarice, and a degree of meanness and womanishness, in robbing a corpse, and making the dead body an enemy when the real enemy has walked away and left only his fighting gear behind him,—is not this rather like a dog who cannot get at his assailant, quarreling with the stones which strike him instead?

That is exactly parallel, he said.

Then we must abstain from spoiling the dead or hindering their burial?

Yes, he replied, that we must.

Neither, as our object is to preserve good feeling among the Hellenes, shall we offer up the arms of Hellenes at any rate, at the temples of the gods; nay, we have some reason to be afraid that such an offering may be a pollution unless commanded by the god himself.

Very true.

Again, as to the devastation of an Hellenic territory or the burning of houses, what is to be the practice?

Will you let me have the pleasure, he said, of hearing your opinion upon this?

Both should be forbidden, in my judgment; I would take the annual produce and no more. Would you wish to know why I say this?

Very much.

Why, I imagine that as there is a difference in the names "discord" and "war," there is also a difference in their natures; the one is expressive of what is internal and domestic, the other of what is external and foreign; and the first of these is properly termed discord, and only the second, war.

That is a very just distinction, he replied.

Shall I further add that the Hellenic race is all united by ties of blood and friendship, and alien and strange to the barbarians?

Very good, he said.

And therefore when Hellenes fight with barbarians and barbarians with Hellenes, they will be described by us as being at war when they fight, and by nature in a state of war, and this kind of antagonism is to be called war; but when Hellenes fight with one another we shall say that they are by nature friends, and at such a time Hellas is in a state of disorder and distraction, and enmity of that sort is to be called discord.

In that view, I agree.

Consider then, I said, when that which is now acknowledged by us to be discord occurs, and a city is divided, if both parties destroy the lands and burn the houses of one another, how wicked does the strife appear,—how can either of them be a lover of his country? for no true lover of his country would tear in pieces his nurse and mother: there might be reason in the conqueror depriving the conquered of their harvest, but still they would have the idea of peace in their hearts, and not of everlasting war.

Yes, he said, that is a better temper than the other.

And when you found a State, are you not intending to found an Hellenic State?

Of course, he replied.

Then will not the citizens be good and civilized?

To be sure.

And will they not be lovers of Hellas, and think of Hellas as their own land, and share in the common temples?

Most certainly.

And any difference that arises among Hellenes will be regarded by them as discord only,—a quarrel among friends, which is not to be called a war?

Certainly not.

Then they will quarrel as those who intend some day to make up their quarrel?

Certainly.

Correcting them in love, not punishing them with a view to enslaving or destroying them; as correctors, not as enemies?

That is very true.

And as they are Hellenes themselves they will not devastate Hellas, nor will they burn houses, nor ever suppose that the whole population of a city—men, women, and children—are equally their enemies, for they know that the guilt of war is always confined to a few persons, and that the many are their friends. And for all these reasons they will be unwilling to waste their lands and raze their houses; their enmity to them will only last until the many innocent sufferers have compelled the guilty few to give satisfaction?

I agree, he said, in thinking that these are the sort of rules which our citizens ought to observe towards their (Hellenic) adversaries; in their wars with barbarians the present practice of the Hellenes to one another will afford a sufficient rule.

Let this then be enacted for the observance of our guardians; that they are neither to devastate the ground nor to burn houses.

Yes, let that be enacted; and we may safely maintain that this and all our previous enactments are excellent.

But still, Socrates, I must say, that if you are allowed to go on in this way you will entirely forget the other question which in entering on this discussion you put aside, namely: the inquiry as to whether such an order of things is possible, and if possible, in what way possible? For, admitting the possibility, I am quite ready to acknowledge that the plan has every sort of advantage. I will add what you have omitted, that they will be the bravest of warriors, ever exhorting one another by the names of fathers, brothers, and sons, and therefore never leaving their ranks; and if you suppose the women to join their armies, whether in the same rank or in the rear, either as a terror to the enemy, or as auxiliaries in case of need, I know that this will make them altogether invincible; and there are many domestic advantages which might be mentioned as well, and these also I fully acknowledge. But, as I admit all these advantages and as many more as you please, if this State of yours were to come into being, say no more of that; and let us now come to the question of possibility and ways and means—all the rest may be left.

If I loiter for a moment, you instantly make a raid upon me, I said, and have no mercy; I have hardly escaped the first and second waves, and you don't seem to be aware that you are now bringing upon me the third, which is the greatest.[7] When you have seen this, and heard the roar,

---

[7] In Republic V. Socrates puts forth three propositions which he humorously calls waves, as though the company were likely to be overwhelmed by them. These propositions are: 1. The sexes should have all occupations in common and therefore the same education. 2. Wives and children should be in common. 3. The State should be ruled by philosophers.

I think you will acknowledge that some fear and hesitation was natural, considering the marvelous nature of the proposal which I have to offer for consideration.

The more appeals of this sort which you make, he said, the more determined are we that you should tell us how such a State is possible: speak out, and at once.

Let me begin by reminding you that we found our way hither in the search after justice and injustice.

True, he replied; but what makes you say this?

I was only going to ask whether, if we have discovered them, we are to require that the just man should in nothing fail of absolute justice; or may we be satisfied with an approximation, and the attainment of a higher degree of justice than is to be found in other men?

The approximation will be enough.

Then the nature of justice and the perfectly just man, and of injustice and the perfectly unjust, was only an ideal? We were to look at them in order that we might judge of our own happiness and unhappiness according to the standard which they exhibited and the degree in which we resembled them, not with any view of demonstrating the possibility of their existence?

That is true, he said.

How would a painter be the worse painter because, after having minutely painted an ideal of a perfectly beautiful man, he was unable to show that any such man could ever have existed?

He would not.

Well, and were we not creating an ideal of a perfect State?

To be sure.

And is our theory a worse theory because we are unable to prove the possibility of a city being ordered in the manner described?

Surely not, he replied.

That must be acknowledged, I said. But if, at your request, I am to try and show how and under what condition the possibility is highest, I must ask you, having this in view, to repeat your former admissions.

What admissions?

I want to know whether words do not surpass realities; **473** and whether the actual, whatever a man may think, does not fall short of the truth? What do you say?

I admit that.

Then you must not insist on my proving that the actual State will in every respect agree with the description of the ideal: if we are only able to discover how a city may be governed nearly in the way that we propose, you will admit that we have discovered the possibility which you demand; and that will content you. I am sure that I should be contented with that—will not you?

Yes, I will.

Then let me next endeavor to show what is that fault in States which is the cause of their present maladministration, and what is the least change which will enable a State to pass into the truer form; and let the change, if possible, be of one thing only, or, if not, of two; at any rate, let the changes be as few and slight as possible.

Certainly, he replied.

I think then, I said, that there might be a revolution if there were just one change, which is not a slight or easy though still a possible one.

What is that? he said.

Now then, I said, I go to meet that which I liken to the greatest of waves, yet shall the word be spoken, even though the running over of the laughter of the wave shall just sink me beneath the waters of laughter and dishonor; and do you attend to me.

Proceed, he said.

I said: Until, then, philosophers are kings, or the kings and princes of this world have the spirit and power of philosophy, and political greatness and wisdom meet in one, and those commoner natures who follow either to the exclusion of the other are compelled to stand aside, cities will never cease from ill—no, nor the human race, as I believe—and then only will this our State have a possibility of life and behold the light of day: this was what I wanted but was afraid to say, my dear Glaucon; for to see that there is no other way either of private or public happiness is indeed a hard thing.

Socrates, he said, what a speech is this? I would have you consider that the word which you have uttered is one at which numerous persons, and very respectable persons too, will in a moment pull off their coats, as I may in a figure say, and in light array, taking up any weapon that comes to hand, they will run at you might and main, intending to do heaven knows what ; and if you don't prepare an answer, and put yourself in motion, you will be " pared by their fine wits," and no mistake. **474-479**

You got me into the scrape, I said.

And I was quite right, he said ; however, I will do all I can to get you out ; but I can only give you wishes and exhortations, and also, perhaps, I may be able to fit answers into your questions better than another—that is all. And now having such an auxiliary, you must do your best to show the unbelievers that you are right.

I ought to try, I said, as I have an offer of such valuable assistance. And I think that, if there is to be a chance of our escaping, we must define who these philosophers are who, as we say, are to rule in the State ; then we shall be able to defend ourselves : there will be discovered to be some natures who ought to rule and to study philosophy ; and others who are not born to be philosophers, and are meant to be followers rather than leaders.

Then now for a definition, he said.

Follow me, I said, and I hope that I may somehow or other be able to give you a satisfactory explanation.

Proceed, he replied.

[The true philosopher is one who loves all wisdom. He alone distinguishes between the changing world of the senses and the eternal world of absolute truth. In contrast with him, the many have no true knowledge but only the appearance of knowledge which may be called opinion.]

Those who see the many beautiful, and who yet neither see, nor can be taught to see, absolute beauty ; who see the many just, and not absolute justice, and the like,—such persons may be said to have opinion but not knowledge?

That is certain.

But those who see the absolute and eternal and immutable may be said to know, and not to have opinion only?

Neither can that be denied.

The one love and embrace the subjects of knowledge, **480** the other those of opinion? The latter are the same, as I dare say you will remember, who listened to sweet sounds and gazed upon fair colors, but would not tolerate the existence of absolute beauty?

Yes, I remember.

Shall we then be guilty of any impropriety in calling them lovers of opinion rather than lovers of wisdom, and will they be very angry with us for thus describing them?

I shall tell them that they ought not to be angry at a description of themselves which is true.

But those who embrace the absolute are to be called lovers of wisdom and not lovers of opinion?

Assuredly.

BOOK VI

AND thus, Glaucon, after the argument has gone a weary way, the true and the false philosophers have at length appeared in view.   484

I do not think, he said, that the way could have been shortened.

I suppose not, I said; and yet I believe that the contrast might be made still more striking if there were not many other questions awaiting us, which he who desires to see in what the life of the just differs from that of the unjust must consider.

And what question is next in order? he asked.

Surely, I said, there can be no doubt about that. Inasmuch as philosophers only are able to grasp the eternal and unchangeable, and those who wander in the region of the many and variable are not philosophers, I must ask you which of the two kinds should be the rulers of our State?

And what would be a fair answer to that question? he said.

Ask yourself, I replied, which of the two are better able to guard the laws and institutions of our State; and let them be our guardians.

Very good, he said.

Neither, I said, can there be any question that the guardian who is to keep anything should have eyes rather than no eyes?

There can be no question of that.

And are not those who are deprived of the knowledge of the true being of each thing, and have in their souls no clear pattern,[1] and are unable as with a painter's eye to look at the very truth and to that original to repair, and having perfect vision of the other world to order the laws about beauty, goodness, justice in this, and to guard and preserve the order of them—are they not, I say, simply blind?

Indeed, he replied, they are much in that condition.

And shall these be our guardians when there are others who, besides being their equals in experience and not inferior to them in any particular of virtue, have also the knowledge of the true being of everything?

[1] See Book IX., 592.

There can be no reason, he said, for rejecting those who have this great and preëminent quality, if they do not fail in any other respect.

485

Suppose then, I said, that we determine how far they can unite this and the other excellences.

By all means.

First of all, as we began by observing, their nature will have to be ascertained; and if we are agreed about that, then, if I am not mistaken, we shall also be agreed that such an union of qualities is possible, and that those in whom they are united, and those only, should be rulers in the State. Let us begin by assuming that philosophical minds always love that sort of knowledge which shows them the eternal nature in which is no variableness from generation and corruption.

Let that be acknowledged.

And further, I said, let us admit that they are lovers of all being; there is no part whether greater or less, or more or less honorable, which they are willing to renounce; that has been already illustrated by the example of the lover and the man of ambition.[2]

True.

There is another quality which they will also need if they are to be what we were saying.

What quality is that?

Truthfulness: they will never intentionally receive falsehood, which is their detestation, and they will love the truth.

Yes, he said, that may be affirmed.

"May be," my friend, I replied, that is not the word; say rather, "must be affirmed:" for he whose nature is amorous of anything cannot help loving all that belongs or is akin to the object of his affections.

Right, he said.

And is there anything more akin to wisdom than truth?

Impossible, he said.

Or can the same nature be a lover of wisdom and a lover of falsehood?

Never.

The true lover of learning then must from his earliest youth, as far as in him lies, desire all truth?

Assuredly.

[2] This refers to a passage in Book V., 474, which has been omitted.

But then again, he whose desires are strong in one direction will have them weaker in others; they will be like a stream which has been drawn off into another channel.

True.

He whose desires are drawn toward knowledge in every form will be absorbed in the pleasures of the soul, and will hardly feel bodily pleasure—I mean, if he be a true philosopher and not a sham one.

That is most certain.

Such an one is sure to be temperate and the reverse of covetous; for the motives which make another man covetous and also profuse in expenditure, are no part of his character. There is another criterion of the philosophical nature which has also to be considered. 486

What is that?

There should be no secret corner of meanness; for meanness is entirely opposed to a soul that is always longing after the whole of things both divine and human.

Most true, he replied.

Can the soul then, which has magnificence of conception and is the spectator of all time and all existence, think much of human life?

Impossible, he replied.

Or can such an one account death fearful?

No indeed.

Then the cowardly and mean nature has no part in true philosophy?

I should say not.

Or again: can he who is harmoniously constituted, who is not covetous or mean, or a boaster, or a coward—can he, I say, ever be unjust or hard in his dealings?

Impossible.

You will note also whether a man is righteous and gentle, or rude and unsociable; these are the signs which distinguish even in youth the philosophical nature from the unphilosophical.

True.

And there is another point which should be remarked.

What is that?

Whether he has or has not a pleasure in learning; for no one will love that which gives him pain, and in which after much toil he makes little progress.

Certainly not.

And again, if he is forgetful and retains nothing of what he learns, will he not be an empty vessel?

That is certain.

Laboring in vain, he must end in hating himself and his fruitless occupation?

Yes.

Then the forgetful soul cannot be ranked among philosophers; a philosopher ought to have a good memory?

Certainly.

But the inharmonious and unseemly nature can only tend to disproportion?

No doubt of that.

And do you consider truth to be akin to proportion or disproportion?

To proportion.

Then, besides other qualities, let us seek for a well-proportioned and gracious mind whose own nature will of herself be drawn to the true being of everything.

Certainly.

Well, and do not all these qualities go together, and are they not necessary to a soul, which is to have a full and perfect participation of being?

They are absolutely necessary, he replied.

487 And must not that be a blameless study which he only can pursue who has a good memory, and is quick to learn, noble, gracious, the friend of truth, justice, courage, temperance, who are his kindred?[3]

The god of jealousy himself, he said, could find no fault with such a study.

And to these, I said, when perfected by years and education, and to these only you will entrust the State.

Here Adeimantus interposed and said: To this, Socrates, no one can offer a reply; but there is a feeling which those who hear you talk as you are now doing often experience, and which I may describe in this way: they fancy that they are led astray a little at each step in the argument, owing to their own want of skill in asking and answering questions; these littles accumulate, and at the end of the discussion they are found to have sustained a dire reverse and to be at the antip-

---

[3] See Book II., 376; III., 412-414.

odes of their former selves. And as unskillful players of draughts are at last shut up by their skilled adversaries and have no piece to move, so they find themselves at last shut up and have no word to say in this new game of which words are the counters; and yet all the time they are in the right. This observation is suggested to me by what is now occurring. For at this instant any one will say, that although in words he is not able to meet you at each step in the argument, as a fact he sees that the votaries of philosophy who carry on the study, not only in youth with a view to education, but as the pursuit of their maturer years,—that these men, I say, for the most part grow into very strange beings, not to say utter rogues, and that the result with those who may be considered the best of them is, that they are made useless to the world by the very study which you extol.

Well, I said; and do you think that they are wrong?

I cannot tell, he replied; but I should like to know what is your opinion.

Let me tell you then that I think they are quite right.

Then how can you be justified in saying that cities will not cease from evil until philosophers rule in them, when philosophers are acknowledged by us to be of no use to them?

You ask a question, I said, which I can only answer in a parable.

Yes, said he; and that is a way of speaking to which you are not accustomed, I suppose.

I perceive, I said, that you are vastly amused at having got me to speak on such an impossible theme; and now you shall hear the parable in order that you may judge better of the meagreness of my imagination: for the treatment which the best men experience from their States is so grievous that no single thing on earth can be compared with them; and therefore in defending them I must have recourse to fiction, and make a compound of many things, like the fabulous unions of goats and stags which are found in pictures. Imagine then a fleet or a ship in which there is a captain who is taller and stronger than any of the crew, but he is a little deaf and has a similar infirmity in sight, and his knowledge of navigation is not much better. Now the sailors are quarrelling with one another about the steering; every one is of opinion that he ought to steer, though he has never learned and cannot tell who taught him or when he learned, and will even assert that the art of navigation cannot be taught, and is ready to cut in pieces him who says the contrary. They throng about the captain, and do all that they can to make him commit the helm to them; and then, if they fail on some occasion and others prevail, they kill the others or throw them overboard, and having first chained up the noble captain's senses with drink or some narcotic drug, they mutiny and take possession of the ship and make themselves at home with the stores; and thus, eating and drinking, they continue their voyage with such success as might be expected of them. Him who is their partisan and zealous in the design of getting the ship out of the captain's hands into their own, whether by force or persuasion, they compliment with the name of sailor, pilot, able seaman, and abuse the other sort of man and call him a good-for-nothing; but they have not even a notion that the true pilot must pay attention to the year and seasons and sky and stars and winds, and whatever else belongs to his art, if he intends to be really qualified for the command of a ship; at the same time that he must and will be the steerer, whether people like him to steer or not; and they think that the combination of this with the art of navigation is impossible. Now in vessels and among sailors, whose condition is such as this, how will the true pilot be regarded? Will he not be called by the mutineers useless, prater, star-gazer?

489

Of course, said Adeimantus.

I do not suppose, I said, that you would care to hear the interpretation of the figure, which is an allegory of the true philosopher in his relation to the State[4]; for you understand already.

Certainly.

Then suppose you now take the parable to the gentleman who is surprised at finding that philosophers have no honor in their cities, and explain to him and try to convince him that their having honor would be far more extraordinary.

I will.

Say to him, that, in deeming the best of the votaries of philosophy to be useless to the rest of the world, he is right; but

---

[4] The captain personifies the people as Uncle Sam stands for the American people. The sailors represent the politicians; the true pilot represents the philosopher.

he ought to attribute their uselessness to the fault of those who will not use them, and not to themselves. The pilot should not humbly beg the sailors to be commanded by him—that is not the order of nature; neither are the wise to go to the doors of the rich (the ingenious author of this told a lie), for the truth is, that, when a man is ill, whether he be rich or poor, he must go to the physician's door—the physician will not come to him, and he who is asking to be governed, to the door of him who is able to govern. No ruler who is good for anything ought to ask his subjects to obey him; he is not like the present governors of mankind who may be compared to the mutinous sailors, and the true helmsman to those whom they call useless and star-gazers.

Precisely, he said.

For these reasons, and among men like these, the noblest pursuit of all is not likely to be much esteemed by those who are of the opposite persuasion; not that the greatest and most lasting injury is done to philosophy by them, but by her own professing followers, the same of whom you suppose the accuser to say, that the greater number of them are arrant rogues, and the best are useless; in which opinion I agreed.

Yes.

And the reason why the good are useless has been now explained?

True.

Then shall we now endeavor to show that the corruption of the greater number is also unavoidable, and that this is not to be laid to the charge of philosophy any more than the other?

By all means.

And let us ask and answer in turn, first going back to the description of the gentle and noble nature. Truth, as you will remember, was his captain, whom he followed always and in all things; failing in this, he was an impostor, and had no part or lot in true philosophy.

Yes, that was said.

Well, and is not this quality alone greatly at variance with our present notions of him?

Certainly, he said.

And have we not a right to say, in his defense, that the true lover of knowledge is always striving after being—that is his nature; he will not rest in the fanciful multiplicity of individuals, but will go on—the keen edge will not be blunted, neither the force of his desire abate until he have attained the knowledge of the true nature of every essence by a kindred power in the soul, and by that power drawing near and mingling incorporate with very being, having begotten mind and truth, he will know and live and grow truly, and then, and not till then, will he cease from his travail.

Nothing, he said, can be more just than such a description of him.

And will the love of a lie be any part of a philosopher's nature? Will he not utterly hate a lie?

That he will.

And when truth is the captain, we cannot suspect any evil of the band which he leads?

Impossible.

Justice and health will be of the company, and temperance will follow after.

True, he replied.

Neither is there any reason why I should again set in array the philosopher's virtues, as you will doubtless remember that courage, magnanimity, apprehension, memory, were his natural gifts. And you objected that, although no one could deny what I then said, still, if you leave words and look at facts, the persons who are thus described are some of them useless, and the greater number wholly depraved; and this led us to inquire into the grounds of these accusations, and we had arrived at the point of asking why are the many bad, which question of necessity brought us back to the examination and definition of the true philosopher.

Exactly.

And now we have to consider the corruptions of this nature, why so many are spoiled and so few escape spoiling—those, I mean, whom you call useless but not wicked; and after that we will consider the imitators who turn into philosophers, what manner of natures are they who aspire after a profession which is above them and of which they are unworthy, and then, by their manifold inconsistencies, bring upon philosophy, and upon all philosophers, that universal reprobation of which we speak.

But what, he said, is the nature of these corruptions?

That I will try to explain to you, I said, if I can. Every one will admit that a nature thus gifted, and having all the supposed conditions of the philosophic nature perfect, is a plant that rarely grows among men—there are not many of them.

They are very rare.

And what numberless causes may tend utterly to destroy these rare natures!

What causes?

In the first place there are their own virtues, their courage, temperance, and the rest of them, every one of which praiseworthy qualities (and this is a most singular circumstance) destroys and distracts from philosophy the soul which is the possessor of them.[5]

That is very singular, he replied.

Then there are all the ordinary goods of life—beauty, wealth, strength, rank, and great connections in the State—on which I need not enlarge, having given you a general outline of them; these also have the effect of corrupting and distracting them.

I know the goods which you mean, and I should like to know what you mean about them.

Grasp the truth, then, as a whole, I said, and in the right way, and you will have no difficulty in understanding the preceding remarks, and they will not appear strange to you.

And how am I to do that? he asked.

Why, I said, we know that when any seed or plant, whether vegetable or animal, fails to meet with proper nutriment or climate or soil, the greater the vigor, the greater the need also of suitable conditions, because, as I imagine, evil is a greater enemy to good than to the not-good.

Very true.

There is reason in supposing that the finest natures, when under alien conditions, receive more injury than the inferior, because the contrast is greater.

That is true.

And may we not say, Adeimantus, that the most gifted minds, when they are ill-educated, become the worst? Do not great crimes and the spirit of pure evil spring out of a fullness of nature ruined by education rather than from any

[5] Compare 495.

inferiority, whereas weak natures are scarcely capable of any very great good or very great evil?

There I think that you are right.

And our philosopher follows the same analogy—he is like a plant which, having proper nurture, grows and matures into all virtue, but, if sowed and planted in an alien soil, becomes the most noxious of all weeds, unless saved by some divine help. Do you really think, as people are fond of saying, that our youth are corrupted by the Sophists, or that individual Sophisters corrupt them in any degree worth speaking of? Are not the public who say these things the greatest of all Sophists? And do they not educate to perfection alike young and old, men and women, and fashion them after their own hearts?

492

When is this accomplished? he said.

When they meet together, and the world sits down at an assembly, or in a court of law, or a theatre, or a camp, or at some other place of resort, and there is a great uproar, and they praise some things which are being said or done, and blame other things, equally exaggerating in both, shouting and clapping their hands, and the echo of the rocks and the place in which they are assembled redoubles the sound of the praise or blame—at such a time will not a young man's heart leap within him? Will the influences of education stem the tide of praise or blame, and not rather be carried away in the stream? And will he not have the notions of good and evil which the public in general have—he will do as they do; and as they are, such will he be?

Yes, Socrates; necessity will compel him.

And yet, I said, there is a still greater necessity, which has not been mentioned.

What is that?

The "gentler force" of attainder or exile or death, which, as you are aware, these new Sophists and educators, who are the public, apply when their words are powerless.

Indeed they do, and no mistake.

Now what opinion of any other Sophist, or of any private man, can be expected to overcome in such an unequal contest?

None, he replied.

No, indeed, I said, even to make the attempt is a piece of folly; for there neither is, has been, nor ever can be, as I think, another type of character, trained to virtue independently of them—I speak, my friend, of man only; what is more than man, as the proverb says, is not included: for I would not have you ignorant that, in the present evil state of governments, whatever is saved and comes to good is saved by the power of God, as you may truly say. 493

To that I quite assent, he replied.

Then let me beg your assent also to a further observation.

What is that?

Why, that all those mercenary adventurers, whom the world calls Sophists and rivals, do but teach the collective opinion of the many, which are the opinions of their assemblies; and this is their wisdom. I might compare them to a man who should study the tempers and desires of a mighty strong beast who is fed by him—he would learn how to approach and handle him, also at what times and from what causes he is dangerous or the reverse, and what is the meaning of his several cries, and by what sounds, when another utters them, he is soothed or infuriated; and you may suppose further that when, by constantly living with him, he has become perfect in all this which he calls wisdom, he makes a system or art, which he proceeds to teach, not that he has any real notion of what he is teaching, but he names this honorable and that dishonorable, or good or evil, or just or unjust, all in accordance with the tastes and tempers of the great brute, when he has learnt the meaning of his inarticulate grunts. Good he pronounces to be what pleases him, and evil what he dislikes; and he can give no other account of them except that the just and noble are the necessary, having never himself seen, and having no power of explaining to others, the nature of either, or the immense difference between them. Would not he be a rare educator?

Indeed, I think that he would.

And in what respect does he differ from him who thinks that wisdom is the discernment of the tastes and pleasures of the assembled multitude, whether in painting or music, or, finally, in politics? For I suppose you will agree that he who associates with the many, and exhibits to them his poem or other work of art or political service, making them his judges, except under potest, will also experience the fatal necessity of producing whatever they praise. And yet the reasons are utterly ludicrous which they give in confirmation of their notions about the honorable and good. Did you ever hear any of them which were not?

No, nor am I likely to hear.

You recognize the truth of what has been said? Then let me ask you to consider further whether the world will ever be induced to believe in the existence of absolute beauty rather than of the many beautiful, or of the absolute in each kind rather than of the many in each kind?

494

Certainly not.

Then the world cannot possibly be a philosopher?

Impossible.

And therefore philosophers must inevitably fall under the censure of the world?

They must.

And of individuals who consort with the mob and seek to please them?

That is evident.

Then, do you see any way in which the philosopher can be preserved in his calling to the end? and remember what we were saying of him, that he was to have knowledge and memory and courage and magnanimity—these were admitted by us to be the true philosopher's gifts.

Yes.

Now, will not such an one be, from the first, in all things first among all, especially if his bodily endowments are like his mental ones?

Certainly, he said.

And his friends and fellow-citizens will want to use them as he gets older for their own purposes?

No question.

Falling at his feet, they will make requests to him and do him honor and flatter him, because they want to get into their hands the power which he will one day possess.

That is often the way, he said.

And what will he do under such circumstances, especially if he be a citizen of a great city, rich and noble, and a tall proper youth?[6] Will he not be full of boundless aspirations, and fancy himself able to manage the affairs of Hellenes and of bar-

[6] Bosanquet thinks this passage refers to Alcibiades. See Protagoras, note 1.

barians, and in the thought of this he will dilate and elevate himself in the fullness of vain pomp and senseless pride?

Very true, he said.

Now, when he is in this state of mind, if some one gently comes to him and tells him that he is without sense, which he must have, and that the missing sense is not to be had without serving an apprenticeship, do you think that, under such adverse circumstances, he will be easily induced to listen to him?

That would be very unlikely.

But suppose further that there is one person who has feeling, and who, either from some excellence of disposition or natural affinity, is inclined or drawn towards philosophy, and his friends think that they are likely to lose the advantages which they were going to reap from his friendship, what will be the effect upon them? Will they not do and say anything to prevent his learning and to render the teacher powerless, using to this end private intrigues as well as public prosecutions?

There can be no doubt of that.

And how can one who is thus circumstanced ever become a philosopher?

Impossible.

Then, were we not right in saying that even the very qualities which make a man a philosopher may, if he be ill-educated, serve to divert him from philosophy, no less than riches and their accompaniments and the other so-called goods of life?[7]

That was quite true.

Thus, my excellent friend, is brought about the ruin and failure of the natures best adapted to the best of all pursuits, who, as we assert, are rare at any time; and this is the class out of whom come those who are the authors of the greatest evil to States and individuals; and also of the greatest good when the tide carries them in the direction of good; but a small man never was the doer of any great thing either to individuals or States.

That is most true, he said.

They fall away, and philosophy is left desolate, with her marriage rite incomplete:[8] for her own have forsaken her, and

---

[7] Compare 491.
[8] Here, as so often, Plato represents the relation between the good soul and the truth by the figure of love and marriage.

while they are leading a false and unbecoming life, she, like an orphan bereft of her kindred, is dishonored by other unworthy persons, who enter in and fasten upon her the reproaches which her reprovers utter; by whom, as you say, her votaries are affirmed, some of them to be good for nothing, and the greater number deserving of everything that is bad.

That is certainly what is said.

Yes; and what else would you expect, I said, when you think of the puny creatures who, seeing this land open to them —a land well stocked with fair names and showy titles—like prisoners who run away out of prison into a sanctuary, take a leap out of the arts into philosophy; those who do so being probably the cleverest hands at their own miserable crafts? for, although philosophy be in this evil case, still there remains a dignity about her which is not found in the other arts. And many are thus attracted by her whose natures are imperfect and whose souls are marred and enervated by their meannesses, as their bodies also are disfigured by their arts and crafts. Is not that true?

Yes.

Are they not exactly like a bald little tinker who has just got out of durance and come into a fortune; he washes the dirt off him and has a new coat, and is decked out as a bridegroom going to marry his master's daughter, who is left poor and desolate?

The figure is exact.

496 And what will be the issue of such marriages? Will they not be vile and bastard?

There can be no question of that.

And when persons who are unworthy of education approach philosophy and make an alliance with her who is in a rank above them, what sort of ideas and opinions are likely to be generated? Will they not be sophisms captivating to the ear, yet having nothing in them genuine or worthy of or akin to true wisdom?

No doubt, he said.

Then there is a very small remnant, Adeimantus, I said, of worthy disciples of philosophy: perchance some noble nature, brought up under good influences, and in the absence of temptation, who is detained by exile in her service, which he refuses to quit; or some lofty soul born in a mean city, the politics of which he contemns or neglects; and perhaps there may be a few who, having a gift for philosophy, leave other arts, which they justly despise [9] and come to her; and peradventure there are some who are restrained by our friend Theages' bridle (for Theages,[10] you know, had everything to divert him from philosophy; but his ill-health kept him from politics). My own case of the internal sign [11] is indeed hardly worth mentioning, as very rarely, if ever, has such a monitor been vouchsafed to any one else. Those who belong to this small class have tasted how sweet and blessed a possession philosophy is, and have also seen and been satisfied of the madness of the multitude, and known that there is no one who ever acts honestly in the administration of States, nor any helper who will save any one who maintains the cause of the just. Such a saviour would be like a man who has fallen among wild beasts—unable to join in the wickedness of his fellows, neither would he be able alone to resist all their fierce natures, and therefore he would be of no use to the State or to his friends, and would have to throw away his life before he had done any good to himself or others.[12] And he reflects upon all this, and holds his peace, and does his own business. He is like one who retires under the shelter of a wall in the storm of dust and sleet which the driving wind hurries along; and when he sees the rest of mankind full of wickedness, he is content if only he can live his own life and be pure from evil or unrighteousness, and depart in peace and good will, with bright hopes.

And he who does this, he said, will have done a great work before he departs.

Yes, I said, a great work, but not the greatest, unless he find a State suitable to him; for in a State which is suitable to him he will have a larger growth, and be the saviour of his country as well as of himself.

497

Enough, then, of the causes why philosophy is in such an evil name; how unjustly, has been explained: and now is there anything more which you wish to say?

[9] See Book IX., 590.
[10] Mentioned in Apology, 33.
[11] See Apology, 31 and 40.
[12] Plato had personal experiences upon which to base this passage. His master Socrates had been martyred (see Apology, 31, where Socrates tells why he took no part in public affairs). Plato himself had been sold as a slave by the tyrant of Syracuse. His painful experiences in endeavoring to reform the government of Syracuse probably occurred after the writing of the Republic.

Nothing more of that, he replied; but I should like to know which of the existing governments you deem suitable to philosophy.

Not any of them, I said; and that is the very accusation which I bring against them: not one of them is worthy of the philosophic nature: and hence that nature is warped and alienated from them; as the exotic seed which is sown in a foreign land becomes denaturalized, and assimilates to the character of the soil, which gets the better, even so this growth of philosophy, instead of persisting, receives another character. But if philosophy ever finds that perfection in the State which she herself is, then will be seen that she is in truth divine, and that all other things, whether natures of men or institutions, are but human; and now, I know, that you are going to ask what that State is.

No, he said; there you are wrong, for I was going to ask another question—whether this is the State of which we are the founders and inventors, or another?

Yes, I replied, ours in most respects; but you may remember our saying before that some living authority would always be required in the State, whose idea of the constitution would be the same which guided you originally when laying down the laws.

That was said, he replied.

Yes, but imperfectly said; you frightened us with objections, which certainly showed that the discussion would be long and difficult; and even what remains is the reverse of easy.

What is that?

The question how the study of philosophy may be so ordered as to be consistent with the preservation of the State; for all great things are attended with risk; as the saying is, "Hard is the good."

Still, he said, let us clear that point up, and the inquiry will then be complete.

I shall not be hindered, I said, by any want of will, but, if at all, by a want of power: of my zeal you shall have ocular demonstration; and please to remark how bold I am just now in venturing to assert that a State ought not to have philosophy studied after the present fashion.

How do you mean?

At present, I said, even those who study philosophy in early youth, and in the intervals of money-making and housekeeping, do but make an approach to the most difficult branch of the study, and then take themselves off (I am speaking of those who have the most training, and by the most difficult branch I mean dialectic); and in after life they perhaps go to a discussion which is held by others, and to which they are invited, and this they deem a great matter, as the study of philosophy is not regarded by them as their proper business: then, as years advance, in most cases their light is quenched more truly than Heracleitus' sun, for they never rise again.[13]

But what ought to be their course?

Just the opposite. In childhood and youth their study, and what philosophy they learn, should be suited to their tender age: let them take care of their bodies during the period of growth, and thus philosophy will have her instruments ready; as the man advances to mature intelligence, increasing the gymnastics of the soul; but when their strength fails, and is past civil and military duties, then let them range at will and have no other serious employment, as we intend them to live happily here, and, this life ended, to have a similar happy destiny in another.

How truly in earnest you are, Socrates! he said; I am sure of that; and yet I believe that most of your hearers are likely to be still more in earnest in their opposition to you, and will never be converted; Thrasymachus least of all.

Don't raise a quarrel, I said, between Thrasymachus and me, who have just become friends, although, indeed, we were never enemies; for I shall go on using every effort until I either convert him and other men, or do something which avails against the day when they live again, and hold the like discourse in another existence.

That will be a long time hence.

Say rather, I replied, a time which is not to be reckoned in comparison with eternity. That the world will not believe my words is quite natural; for they never saw that of which we are now speaking realized; what they saw was a conven-

---

[13] Heracleitus (hĕr'a-klī'tus): a great philosopher, living in Ephesus in Asia Minor about 500 B.C. Heracleitus said the sun was extinguished every evening and new every morning.

tional imitation of philosophy, which consisted of words artificially brought together, not like these agreeing of their own accord; but a human being who in word and work is perfectly moulded, as far as he can be, into the proportion and likeness of virtue, such an one ruling in a city which bears the same image they have never yet seen, in the case of one any more than of many—do you think they ever did?

499

No, indeed.

No, my friend, nor have they often heard the words of beauty and freedom; such words as those which men use when they are earnestly and in every way seeking after truth, for the sake of knowledge, while they look coldly on the subtleties of controversy, the end of which is opinion and strife, whether they meet with them in the courts of law or in society.

They are strangers, he said, to the words of which you speak.

And this was what we foresaw, and this was the reason why truth forced us to admit that there is no chance of perfection, either in cities or governments or individuals, until a necessity was laid upon the second small class of philosophers (not the rogues, but those whom we termed useless), of taking care of the State and obeying the call of the State; or until kings themselves, or the sons of kings or potentates, were inspired with a true love of philosophy. Now I maintain that there is no reason in saying that either of these alternatives, or both of them, is impossible; if they were, we might indeed be justly ridiculed as dreamers and visionaries. Am I not right?

Quite right.

If then, in the countless ages of the past, or at the present hour in some foreign clime which is far away and beyond our ken, the perfected philosopher is or has been or shall be hereafter compelled by a superior power to have the charge of the State, we are ready to assert to the death, that this our constitution has been, is, yea, and will be at any time, when the Muse of Philosophy is queen. Neither is there any impossibility in this; the difficulty is not denied by us.

I agree with you, he said.

But you will say that mankind in general are not agreed?

That is what I should say, he replied.

O my friend, I said, do not have such a bad opinion of mankind: they will surely be of another mind, if gently and with the view of soothing them and removing the evil name of too much learning, you show them the philosopher as just now described, according to his true character and profession, and then they will see that you are not speaking of those whom they supposed; if they view him in this light, they will surely change their mind, and answer in another strain. Who can be at enmity with one who loves them; who that is himself gentle and free from envy will be jealous of one in whom there is no jealousy? Nay, let me answer for you, that a few such there may be, but not many who have so harsh a temper.

500

I entirely agree with you, he said.

And do you not agree with me also as to the cause of the harsh feeling which the many have towards philosophy? This originates in the pretenders, who enter in, like a band of revelers, where they have no business, and are always abusing and quarreling with them, who make persons instead of things the theme of their conversation; and this is most unbecoming in philosophers.

Most unbecoming.

For he, Adeimantus, whose mind is fixed upon true being has no time to look down upon the affairs of men, or to be filled with jealousy and enmity in the struggle against them; his eye is ever directed towards fixed and immutable principles, which he sees neither injuring nor injured by one another, but all in order moving according to reason; these he imitates, and to these he would, as far as he can, conform himself. Can a man help imitating that with which he holds reverential converse?

Impossible.

And the philosopher also, conversing with the divine and immutable, becomes a part of that divine and immutable order,[14] as far as nature allows; but all things are liable to detraction.

Certainly.

And if a necessity be laid upon him of fashioning, not

---

[14] The thought that if we lovingly attend to the divine, we shall imitate the divine, and that if we lovingly imitate the divine we shall become divine and eternal is the argument of S. John xv.

only himself but human nature generally, whether in States or individuals, into that which he there beholds, think you that he will be an unskillful artificer of justice, temperance, and every civil virtue?

Anything but unskillful.

And if the world perceives that we are speaking the truth about him, will they be angry with philosophy? Will they disbelieve us, when we tell them that the State can only be happy which is planned by artists who make use of the heavenly pattern?

They will not be angry if they only understand, he replied. But what do you mean about the plan?

I mean, I replied, that they will take a State and human nature for their tablet and begin by making a clean surface. Now this is not an easy thing to do; and this is the mark which at once distinguishes them from every other legislator,—they will have nothing to do, either with individual or State, and will inscribe no laws, until they have either found, or themselves made, a clean surface.

They will be very right, he said.

Having effected this, they will proceed to make an outline of the constitution.

No doubt.

And in the course of the work, as I conceive, they will often turn their eyes first towards one, then towards the other. I mean that they will look at justice and beauty and temperance as they are in nature, and again at the corresponding quality in mankind, and they will inlay the true human image, moulding and selecting out of the various forms of life; and this they will conceive according to that other image, which, when existing among men, Homer calls the form and likeness of God.

That is true, he said.

And one feature they will erase, and another they will inscribe, until they have made the ways of men, as far as possible, agreeable to the ways of God?

Indeed, he said, in no other way could they make a fairer picture.

And now, I said, do you think that we are beginning to persuade those whom you said were rushing at us with might and main, that the painter of constitutions is such an one as we were praising,—he, I mean, at whom they were so much infuriated, because into his hands we committed the State, or are they growing calmer at what they hear?

Much calmer, if there is any sense in them.

Why, where can they still find any ground for objection? Will they doubt that the philosopher is a lover of truth and being?

That would be monstrous.

Or that his nature, being such as we have delineated, is akin to the highest good?

Neither can they doubt that.

But again, will they tell us that such a nature, if properly trained, will not be perfectly good and wise as much as any that ever was? Or will they prefer those whom we have set aside?

Surely not.

Then will they still be angry at our saying, that until philosophers bear rule in States, the evils of States and individuals will never cease, nor will this our imaginary State ever be realized?

I think that they will be less angry.

Shall we assume that they are not only less angry but quite gentle, and that they have been converted and for very shame cannot refuse to come to terms?

Certainly, he said.

Then now we may assume that they have been converted. And will any one deny the other point, that there may be sons of kings who are philosophers?

No one will doubt that, he said.

And when they have come into being will any one say that they must of necessity be destroyed; for that they can hardly be saved is not denied even by us, but all will allow that, in the whole course of ages, peradventure a single one may be saved?

Surely.

But, said I, one is enough; let there be one man who has a city obedient to his will, and he might bring the ideal polity into being.

Yes, one is enough.

When the ruler has framed these laws and institutions, the citizens may possibly be willing to obey them?

Certainly.

And that others should approve of what we approve, is no miracle or impossibility?

I think not.

But we have sufficiently shown, in what has preceded, that all this, if only possible, is assuredly for the best.

Yes, that has been proved.

The conclusion is, then, that our laws are best, and, though difficult of attainment, are not wholly unattainable.

Very good.

And now that this difficulty is ended another arises; how and by what studies and pursuits will saviours of the constitution be formed, and at what ages are they to apply themselves to their several studies?—that has now to be discussed.

Yes, certainly.

I omitted the troublesome business of the possession of women, and the procreation of children, and the appointment of the rulers, because I knew that the perfect State would be eyed with jealousy and was difficult of attainment; but that piece of cleverness was not of much use to me, for I had to discuss them all the same. And now, having done with the women and children, I must pursue the other question of the rulers, beginning at the beginning. We were saying, as you will remember, that they were to be lovers of their country, tried amid the influences of pleasures and pains, and

503 neither in labors, nor fears, nor any other change of circumstances were to lose their patriotism; and he who failed in this was to be rejected, but he who always came forth pure, like gold tried in the refiners' fire, was to be made a ruler, and to receive honors and rewards in life and after death. That was the sort of thing which was being said, and then the argument turned aside and veiled her face; not liking to stir the question which has now arisen.

I perfectly remember that, he said.

Yes, my friend, I said, and I then shrank from hazarding the bold word; but now let me dare to say,—that the perfect guardian must be a philosopher.

Yes, he said, let that be proclaimed.

And consider, I said, that there will not be many of them,—that is not to be expected; for the gifts which we said were essential rarely grow together; they are mostly found in shreds and patches.

What do you mean? he said.

You are aware, I replied, that persons who have quick intelligence, memory, sagacity, shrewdness, and all that sort of thing, are not often of a nature which is willing at the same time to live orderly and in a peaceful and settled manner; and this is equally true of the high-spirited and magnanimous; they are driven any way by their impetuosity, and all their solid principle goes out of them.

That is true, he said.

On the other hand, those steadfast, immovable natures upon which you can rely, and which have not the wit to run away in a battle, are equally immovable when there is anything to be learned; they seem to be in a torpid state, and are apt to yawn and go to sleep over any intellectual toil.

That is true.

And yet we were saying that both qualities were necessary in those to whom the higher education is to be imparted, and who are to share in any office or command.

True, he said.

And will they be a class which is rarely found?

Yes, indeed.

Then the aspirant must be tested in those labors and dangers and pleasures which we mentioned before; and there is another kind of probation which we did not mention,—they must be exercised also in many kinds of knowledge, to see whether the soul will be able to endure the highest of all, or will faint under them, as many do amid the toils of the games.

Yes, he said, that is the way in which we ought to regard them. But what do you mean by the highest of all knowledge?

You may remember, I said, that we divided the soul into three parts,[15] and the several natures of justice, temperance, courage, and wisdom were compared and defined by us?

Indeed, he said, if I had forgotten that, I should not deserve to hear more.

And do you remember, I said, what preceded the discussion of them?

---

[16] See Book IV., 435-442.

What was that?

We spoke, if I am not mistaken, of a perfect way, which was longer and more circuitous, at the end of which they were to appear in full view; this however, as we said, need not prevent our offering an exposition of a popular sort, in character like what had preceded. And you replied that such an exposition would be enough for you, and so the inquiry was continued in what appeared to me to be a very imperfect manner; but whether you were satisfied or not is for you to say.

Yes, he said, I thought and the others thought that you gave us a fair measure of truth.

But, my friend, I said, a measure of such things which in any degree falls short of the truth is not fair measure; for nothing imperfect is the measure of anything, although persons are too apt to be contented and think that they need search no further.

Yes, that is not uncommon when people are indolent.

Yes, I said; and there cannot be any worse fault in the guardian of a State and the laws.

True.

The guardian then, I said, must be required to take the longer route, and toil at learning as well as at gymnastics, or he will never reach the height of that knowledge which is his proper calling.

What, he said, is there a knowledge still higher than these —higher than justice and the other virtues?

Yes, I said, there is. And of these too we must behold not the outline merely, as at present—nothing short of the most perfect representation should satisfy us. When little things are elaborated with an infinity of pains, in order that they may appear in full clearness and precision, how ridiculous that the highest truths should not be held worthy of the greatest exactness!

Yes, said he, and that is a right noble thought; but do you suppose that we shall refrain from asking you which are the highest?

Nay, I said, ask if you will; but I am certain that you have often heard the answer, and now you either do not understand or you are disposed to be troublesome; I incline to think the latter, for you have been often told that the idea of good is the highest knowledge, and that all other things become useful and advantageous only by their use of this. And you must be quite aware that of this I am about to speak, concerning which, as I shall say, we know so little; and, wanting which, any other knowledge or possession of any kind will profit us nothing. Do you think that the possession of the whole world is of any value without the good? or of all wisdom, without the beautiful and good?[16]

No, indeed, he said.

You are doubtless aware that most people call pleasure good, and the finer sort of wits say wisdom? And you are aware that the latter cannot explain the nature of wisdom, but are obliged after all to say that wisdom is of the good?

That is very ridiculous, he said.

Yes, I said, that they should begin by reproaching us with our ignorance, and then presume our knowledge of good—for wisdom, as they say, is of the good, which implies that we understand them when they use the term "good"—is certainly ridiculous.

Most true, he said.

And those who make pleasure their good are in equal perplexity; for they are compelled to admit that there are bad pleasures as well as good.

Certainly.

And therefore to acknowledge that bad and good are the same?

True.

There can be no doubt about the numerous difficulties in which this question is involved.

There can be none.

Well, and is not this an obvious fact, that many are willing to possess, or to do, or to wear the appearance of the just and honorable without the reality; but no one is satisfied to possess the appearance of good—the reality is what they seek; the appearance in the case of the good is despised by every one.

Very true, he said.

This, then, which every man pursues and makes his end, having a presentiment that there is such an end, and yet hesitating because neither knowing the nature nor having the same

---

[16] "What is a man profited if he gain the whole world and lose his own soul."—Matthew xvi. 26.

sure proof of this as of other things, and therefore having no profit in other things,—is this, I would ask, a principle about which those who are called the best men in the State, and to whom everything is to be entrusted, ought to be in such darkness?

506.

Certainly not, he said.

I am sure, I said, that he who does not know how the beautiful and the just are likewise good will not be worth much as a guardian of them: and I suspect that no one will have a true knowledge of them without this knowledge.

That, he said, is a shrewd suspicion of yours.

And if we only have a guardian who has this knowledge our State will be perfectly ordered?

Of course, he replied; but I wish you would tell me whether you conceive this supreme principle of the good to be knowledge or pleasure, or different from either?

Aye, I said, I knew quite well that a fine gentleman like you would not be contented with the thoughts of other men.

True, Socrates; and I must say that you have no right to be always repeating the opinions of others, and never to tell your own, and this after having passed a lifetime in the study of philosophy.

Well, but has any one a right to say, positively, what he does not know?

Not, he said, with the positiveness of knowledge; he has no right to do that: but he ought to say what he thinks, as a matter of opinion.

But do you not know, I said, that opinions are bad all, and the best of them blind? You would not deny that those who have any true notion without intelligence are only like blind men finding their way along a straight road?

Very true.

And do you wish to behold what is blind and crooked and base, when brightness and beauty are within your reach?

Still, I must implore you, Socrates, said Glaucon, not to turn away just as you are reaching the goal; if you will only give such an explanation of the good as you have already given about justice and temperance and the other virtues, that will satisfy us.

Yes, my friend, I said, and that will satisfy me too, extremely well, but I cannot help fearing that I shall fail, and that in my zeal I shall make a fool of myself. No, sweet sirs, let us not at present ask what is the actual nature of the good, for to reach what is in my thoughts now is too much for me in my present mood. But of the child of the good who is likest him, I would fain speak, if I could be sure that you wished to hear —otherwise, not.

Nay, he said, speak; the child shall be the interest, and you shall remain in our debt for an account of the parent or principal.

I do indeed wish, I replied, that I could pay, and you receive, the parent or principal account, and not, as now, the interest or child only; take, however, the child, which is the interest, and at the same time have a care that I do not render a false account, although I have no intention of deceiving you.

507-511

Yes, we will take all the care that we can: proceed.

Yes, I said, but I must first come to an understanding with you, and remind you of what I have mentioned in the course of this discussion, and at many other times.

What is that? he said.

The old story, that there is a many beautiful and a many good, and so of other things which we describe and define; to all of them the term "many" is applied.

True, he said.

And there is an absolute beauty and an absolute good, and so of other things to which the term "many" is applied; they may be brought under a single idea, which is called the essence of each.

That is true.

The many, as we say, are seen but not known, and the ideas are known but not seen.

[There is an analogy between material vision and intellectual vision. The material sun generates and nourishes the things in the world which we see, and also gives us light by which to see them. In like manner the good is the true creator of the essence of things and also the author of all knowledge of the essence of things. It may be said that material vision gives two degrees of imperfect knowledge or opinion, the more imperfect being the perception of shadows, and the less imperfect being the perception of material objects; also that intellectual vision gives two degrees of more perfect knowledge, the lower being such knowledge as we have in the pure sciences of arithmetic, geometry and the like, while the highest of all knowledge is dialectic, which brings us to a pure insight into pure truth.]

BOOK VII

AFTER this, I said, imagine the enlightenment or ignorance of our nature in a figure: Behold! human beings living in a sort of underground den, which has a mouth open towards the light and reaching all across the den; they have been here from their childhood, and have their legs and necks chained so that they cannot move, and can only see before them; for the chains are arranged in such a manner as to prevent them from turning round their heads. At a distance above and behind them the light of a fire is blazing, and between the fire and the prisoners there is a raised way; and you will see, if you look, a low wall built along the way, like the screen which marionette players have before them, over which they show the puppets.

I see, he said.

And do you see, I said, men passing along the wall carrying vessels, which appear over the wall; also figures of men and animals, made of wood and stone and various materials; and some of the passengers, as you would expect, are talking, and some of them are silent?

That is a strange image, he said, and they are strange prisoners.

Like ourselves, I replied; and they see only their own shadows, or the shadows of one another, which the fire throws on the opposite wall of the cave?

True, he said; how could they see anything but the shadows if they were never allowed to move their heads?

And of the objects which are being carried in like manner they would only see the shadows?

Yes, he said.

And if they were able to talk with one another, would they not suppose that they were naming what was actually before them?

Very true.

And suppose further that the prison had an echo which came from the other side, would they not be sure to fancy that the voice which they heard was that of a passing shadow?

No question, he replied.

There can be no question, I said, that the truth would be to them just nothing but the shadows of the images.

That is certain.

And now look again, and see how they are released and cured of their folly. At first, when any one of them is liberated and compelled suddenly to go up and turn his neck round and walk and look at the light, he will suffer sharp pains; the glare will distress him, and he will be unable to see the realities of which in his former state he had seen the shadows; and then imagine some one saying to him, that what he saw before was an illusion, but that now he is approaching real being and has a truer sight and vision of more real things,—what will be his reply? And you may further imagine that his instructor is pointing to the objects as they pass and requiring him to name them,—will he not be in a difficulty? Will he not fancy that the shadows which he formerly saw are truer than the objects which are now shown to him?

Far truer.

And if he is compelled to look at the light, will he not have a pain in his eyes which will make him turn away to take refuge in the object of vision which he can see, and which he will conceive to be clearer than the things which are now being shown to him?

True, he said.

And suppose once more, that he is reluctantly dragged up a steep and rugged ascent, and held fast and forced into the presence of the sun himself, do you not think that he will be pained and irritated, and when he approaches the light he will have his eyes dazzled, and will not be able to see any of the realities which are now affirmed to be the truth?

516

Not all in a moment, he said.

He will require to get accustomed to the sight of the upper world. And first he will see the shadows best, next the reflections of men and other objects in the water, and then the objects themselves; next he will gaze upon the light of the moon and the stars; and he will see the sky and the stars by night, better than the sun, or the light of the sun, by day?

Certainly.

And at last he will be able to see the sun, and not mere reflections of him in the water, but he will see him as he is in his own proper place, and not in another, and he will contemplate his nature.

Certainly.

And after this he will reason that the sun is he who gives the seasons and the years, and is the guardian of all that is in the visible world, and in a certain way the cause of all things which he and his fellows have been accustomed to behold?

Clearly, he said, he would come to the other first and to this afterwards.

And when he remembered his old habitation, and the wisdom of the den and his fellow-prisoners, do you not suppose that he would felicitate himself on the change, and pity them?

Certainly, he would.

And if they were in the habit of conferring honors on those who were quickest to observe and remember and foretell which of the shadows went before, and which followed after, and which were together, do you think that he would care for such honors and glories, or envy the possessors of them? Would he not say with Homer,—

" Better to be a poor man, and have a poor master,"

and endure anything, rather than to think and live after their manner?

Yes, he said, I think that he would rather suffer anything than live after their manner.

Imagine once more, I said, that such an one coming suddenly out of the sun were to be replaced in his old situation, is he not certain to have his eyes full of darkness?

Very true, he said.

And if there were a contest, and he had to compete in measuring the shadows with the prisoners who have never moved out of the den, during the time that his sight is weak, and before his eyes are steady (and the time which would be needed to acquire this new habit of sight might be very considerable), would he not be ridiculous? Men would say of him that up he went and down he comes without his eyes ; and that there was no use in even thinking of ascending : and if any one tried to loose another and lead him up to the light, let them only catch the offender in the act, and they would put him to death.

No question, he said.

This allegory, I said, you may now append to the previous argument; the prison is the world of sight, the light of the fire is the sun, the ascent and vision of the things above you may truly regard as the upward progress of the soul into the intellectual world; that is my poor belief, to which, at your desire, I have given expression. Whether I am right or not God only knows; but, whether true or false, my opinion is that in the world of knowledge the idea of good appears last of all, and is seen only with an effort; and, when seen, is also inferred to be the universal author of all things beautiful and right, parent of light and the lord of light in this world, and the source of truth and reason in the other: this is the first great cause which he who would act rationally either in public or private life must behold.

I agree, he said, as far as I am able to understand you.

I should like to have your agreement in another matter, I said. For I would not have you marvel that those who attain to this beatific vision are unwilling to descend to human affairs; but their souls are ever hastening into the upper world in which they desire to dwell; and this is very natural, if our allegory may be trusted.

Certainly, that is quite natural.

And is there anything surprising in one who passes from divine contemplations to human things, misbehaving himself in a ridiculous manner; if, while his eyes are blinking and before he has become accustomed to the darkness visible, he is compelled to fight in courts of law, or in other places, about the images or shadows of images of justice, and is endeavoring to meet the conceptions of those who have never yet seen the absolute justice?

There is nothing surprising in that, he replied.

Any one who has common sense will remember that the bewilderments of the eyes are of two kinds, and arise from two causes, either from coming out of the light or from going into the light, which is true of the mind's eye, quite as much as of the bodily eye; and he who remembers this when he sees the soul of any one whose vision is perplexed and weak, will not be too ready to laugh; he will first ask whether that soul has come out of the brighter life, and is unable to see because unaccustomed to the dark, or having turned from darkness to the day is dazzled by excess of light. And then he will count the one happy in his condition and state of being, and he will pity the other; or, if he have a mind to laugh at the soul which comes from below into the light, there will be more reason in this than in the laugh which greets the other from the den.

That, he said, is a very just remark.

But if this is true, then certain professors of education must be mistaken in saying that they can put a knowledge into the soul which was not there before, like giving eyes to the blind.

Yes, that is what they say, he replied.

Whereas, I said, our argument shows that the power is already in the soul; and that as the eye cannot turn from darkness to light without the whole body, so too, when the eye of the soul is turned round, the whole soul must be turned from the world of generation into that of being, and become able to endure the sight of being, and of the brightest and best of being—that is to say, of the good.

Very true.

And this is conversion; and the art will be how to accomplish this as easily and completely as possible; not implanting eyes, for they exist already, but giving them a right direction, which they have not.

Yes, he said, that may be assumed.

And hence while the other qualities seem to be akin to the body, being infused by habit and exercise and not originally innate, the virtue of wisdom is part of a divine essence, and has a power which is everlasting, and by this conversion is rendered useful and profitable, and is also capable of becoming hurtful and useless. Did you never observe the narrow intelligence flashing from the keen eye of a clever rogue —how eager he is, how clearly his paltry soul sees the way to his end; he is the reverse of blind, but his keen eyesight is taken into the service of evil, and he is dangerous in proportion to his intelligence?

Very true, he said.

But what if there had been a circumcision of such natures in the days of their youth; and they had been severed from the leaden weights, as I may call them, with which they are born into the world, which hang on to sensual pleasures, such as those of eating and drinking, and drag them down and turn the vision of their souls about the things that are below,—if, I say, they had been released from them and turned round to the truth, the very same faculty in these very same persons would have seen the other as keenly as they now see that on which their eye is fixed.

That is very likely.

Yes, I said; and there is another thing which is likely, or rather a necessary inference from what has preceded, that neither the uneducated and uninformed of the truth, nor yet those who never make an end of their education, will be able ministers of State: not the former, because they have no single aim of duty which is the rule of their actions, private as well as public; nor the latter, because they will not act at all except upon compulsion, fancying that they are already in the islands of the blest.

Very true, he replied.

Then, I said, the business of us who are the founders of the State will be to compel the best minds to attain that knowledge which has been already declared by us to be the greatest of all,—to that eminence they must ascend and arrive at the good, and when they have ascended and seen enough we must not allow them to do as they do now.

What do you mean?

I mean that they remain in the upper world: but this must not be allowed; they must be made to descend again among the prisoners in the den, and partake of their labors and honors, whether they are worth having or not.[1]

But is not this unjust? he said; ought we to give them an inferior life, when they might have a superior one?

You have again forgotten, my friend, I said, the intention of the legislator; he did not aim at making any one class in the State happy above the rest; the happiness was to be in the whole State, and he held the citizens together by persuasion and necessity, making them benefactors of the State, and therefore benefactors of one another; to this end he created them, not that they should please them-

---

[1] On the Mount of Transfiguration (Luke ix. 33) Peter said, "Master, it is good for us to be here: and let us make three tabernacles." Luke adds the phrase—"not knowing what he said." Christ made no reply in words, but presently led them back to work and to die for the saving of the world.

selves, but they were to be his instruments in binding up the State.

True, he said, I had forgotten that.

Observe then, I said, Glaucon, that there will be no injustice in compelling our philosophers to have a care and providence of others; we shall explain to them that in other States, men of their class are not obliged to share in the toils of politics: and this is reasonable, for they grow up at their own sweet will, and the government would rather not have them. Now the wild plant which owes culture to nobody, has nothing to pay for culture; but we have brought you into the world expressly for this end, that you may be rulers of the hive, kings of yourselves and of the other citizens. And you have been educated far better and more perfectly than they have, and are better able to share in the double duty. And therefore each of you, when his turn comes, must go down to the general underground abode, and get the habit of seeing in the dark; for all is habit; and when you are accustomed you will see ten thousand times better than those in the den, and you will know what the images are, and of what they are images, because you have seen the beautiful and just and good in their truth. And thus the order of our State will be a waking reality, and not a dream, as is commonly the manner of States; in most of them men are fighting with one another about shadows and are distracted in the struggle for power, which in their eyes is a great good. But the truth is, that the State in which the rulers are most reluctant to govern is best and most quietly governed, and that in which they are most willing, the worst.

Quite true, he replied.

And will our pupils, when they hear this, refuse to share in turn the toils of State, when they are allowed to spend the greater part of their time with one another in the heaven of ideas?

Impossible, he answered; for they are just men, and the commands which we impose upon them are just; there can be no doubt that every one of them will take office as a stern necessity and not like our present ministers of State.

Yes, my friend, I said; and that is just the truth of the case. If you contrive for your future rulers another and a better life than that of a ruler, then you may have a well-ordered State; for only in the State which offers this will they rule who are truly rich, not in silver and gold, but in virtue and wisdom, which are the true blessings of life. Whereas if they go to the administration of public affairs, poor and hungering after their own private advantage, thinking that hence they are to snatch the good of life, order there can never be; for they will be fighting about office, and the civil and domestic broils which thus arise will be the ruin of the rulers themselves and of the whole State.

Most true, he replied.

And the only life which looks down upon the life of political ambition is that of true philosophy? Do you know of any other?

No, indeed, he said.

And those who govern ought not to be lovers of the task?

If they are there will be rival lovers, and they will fight.

No question.

Whom then would you choose rather than those who are wisest about affairs of State, and who at the same time have other honors and another and a better life?

They are the men, and I will choose them, he replied.

Would you like us then to consider in what way such guardians may be called into existence, and how they are to be brought from darkness to light,—as some are said to have ascended from the world below to the gods?

Certainly I should, he replied.

The process, I said, is not the spinning round of an oyster-shell,[2] but the conversion of a soul out of night-like day to the real ascent of true being, which is true philosophy. Now what sort of knowledge has the power of effecting this? that is a question which has to be considered.

Certainly.

Then what sort of knowledge is there which would draw the soul from becoming to being? At the same time there is another thing which occurs to me. You will remember that our young men are to be warrior athletes?

Yes, that was said.

Then this new kind of knowledge must have another quality?

---

[2] In allusion to "a game in which a shell black on one side and white on the other was thrown on a line and according as the black or white turned up one party was obliged to fly and the other pursued." (L. and S.)

What quality?

Usefulness in war.

Yes, if possible.

There were two parts in our former scheme of education, were there not?

True.

There was gymnastic which presided over the growth and decay of the body, and may therefore be regarded as having to do with generation and corruption?

True.

Then that is not the knowledge which we are seeking to discover?

No.

But what do you say of music, as far as that entered into our scheme?

That, he said, as you will remember, was the counterpart of gymnastic, and trained the guardians by the influences of habit, giving them, not science, but a sort of harmonical composition, and a kind of rhythmical movement; and the words, whether true or false, had kindred elements of rhythm and harmony in them; but musical knowledge was not of a kind which tended to that good which you are now seeking.

You are most accurate, I said, in your recollection; for there certainly was nothing of that kind in our previous education. But then what branch of knowledge is there, my dear friend, which is of the desired nature? For the useful arts were rejected by us as mean.

Undoubtedly; and yet if music and gymnastic are excluded, and the arts are also excluded, what remains?

Well, I said, there may be nothing left; and then we shall have to take something which is of universal application.

What is that?

A something which all arts and sciences and intelligences use in common, and which every one ought to learn among the elements of education.

What is that?

The little matter of distinguishing one, two, and three, which I may sum up under the name of number and calculation,—of that all arts and sciences are necessarily partakers.

Very true.

Then the art of war partakes of them?

To be sure.

Then Palamedes,[3] when he appears in the play, proves Agamemnon[4] ridiculously unfit to be a general. Did you never remark how he declares that he had invented number, and had numbered and set in array the ranks of the army at Troy; which implies that they had never been numbered before, and Agamemnon must be supposed literally to have been incapable of counting his own feet—how could he, if he was ignorant of number? And if that is true, what sort of a general must he have been?

I should say a very strange one, certainly.

Must not a warrior then, I said, in addition to his military skill, have a knowledge of arithmetic?

Certainly he must, if he is to have the slightest knowledge of military tactics, or indeed, I should rather say, if he is to be a man at all.

I should like to know whether you have the same notion which I have of this study?

What is that?

I am of opinion that this is a study of the kind which we are seeking, and which leads naturally to reflection, but one which has never been rightly used as simply conducting towards being.

Will you explain your meaning? he said.

I will try, I said; and I wish you would consider and help me, and say "yes" or "no" when I attempt to distinguish in my own mind what branches of knowledge have this conducting power, in order that we may have clearer proof that this is one of them.

[Some objects we seem able to know sufficiently with the senses alone. Others demand further investigation. In making this investigation we find it profitable to count and calculate. But besides this practical value, "arithmetic has a very great and elevating effect, compelling the soul to reason about abstract number, and if visible or tangible objects are obtruding upon the argument, refusing to be satisfied."]

That is very true.

Now, suppose a person were to say to the arithmeticians:

---

[3] See Apology, note 55.   [4] See Apology, note 21.

O my friends, what are these wonderful numbers about which you are reasoning, in which, as you say, there is a unity such as you require, and each unit is equal, invariable, indivisible, what would they answer?

They would answer, as I suppose, that they are speaking of those numbers which are only realized in thought.

Then you see that this knowledge may be truly called necessary, as necessitating the use of the pure intelligence in the attainment of pure truth?

Yes; that is a marked characteristic.

And have you further remarked that those who have a natural talent for calculation are generally quick at every other kind of knowledge; and even the dull, if they have had an arithmetical training, gain in quickness, if not in any other way?

That is true, he said.

And indeed, you will not easily find a more difficult study, and not many as difficult.

You will not.

And, for all these reasons, arithmetic must not be given up; and this is a kind of knowledge in which the best natures should be trained.

I agree.

Let this then be made one of our subjects of education. And next, shall we inquire whether the kindred science also concerns us?

You mean geometry?

Yes.

Certainly, he said; that part of geometry which relates to war is clearly our concern; for in pitching a camp, or taking up a position, or closing or extending the lines of an army, or any other military manœuvre, whether in actual battle or on a march, there will be a great difference in a general, according as he is or is not a geometrician.

Yes, I said, but for that purpose a very little of either geometry or calculation will be enough; the question is rather of the higher and greater part of geometry, whether that tends towards the great end—I mean towards the vision of the idea of good; and thither, as I was saying, all things tend which compel the soul to turn her gaze towards that place, where is the full perfection of being, of which she ought, by all means, to attain the vision.

True, he said.

Then if geometry compels us to view essence, it concerns us; if generation only, it does not concern us?

Yes, that is what we assert.

Yet, at present, I said, the science is in flat contradiction to the language which geometricians use, as will hardly be denied by those who have any acquaintance with their study; for they speak of finding the side of a square, and applying and adding as though they were doing something and had a practical end in view; their "necessity" is the necessity to get a living, which is ridiculous; whereas knowledge is the real object of the whole science.

Certainly, he said.

Then must not a further admission be made?

What admission?

The admission that this knowledge at which geometry aims is of the eternal, and not of the perishing and transient.

That, he replied, may be readily allowed, and is true.

Then, my noble friend, geometry will draw the soul towards truth, and create the mind of philosophy, and raise up that which is now unhappily allowed to fall down.

Nothing will be more effectual.

Then nothing should be more effectually enacted, than that the inhabitants of your fair city should learn goemetry. Moreover the science has indirect effects, which are not small.

Of what kind are they? he said.

There are the military advantages of which you spoke, I said; and in all departments of study, as experience proves, any one who has studied geometry is infinitely quicker of apprehension.

Yes, he said, the difference between a geometrician and one who is not a geometrician is very great indeed.

Then shall we propose this as a second branch of knowledge which our youth will study?

Let us make the proposal, he replied.

And suppose we make astronomy the third,—what do you say?

I am strongly inclined to that, he said; the observation of the seasons and of months and years is quite essential to husbandry and navigation, and not less essential to military tactics.

I am amused, I said, at your fear of the world, which makes

you guard against the appearance of insisting upon useless studies; and I quite admit the difficulty of convincing men that in every soul there is an organ which is purified and illumined by these studies, when by other pursuits lost and dimmed; and this eye of the soul is more precious far than ten thousand bodily ones, for this alone beholds the vision of truth. Now there are two classes of persons: one class who will agree in this and will take your words as a revelation; another class who have no perception of the thing meant, to whom they will naturally seem to be idle and unprofitable tales. And you had better decide at once with which of the two you are arguing, or whether without regard to either you would not prefer to carry on the argument chiefly for your own sake; not that you have any jealousy of others, who may benefit if they please.

I think that I should prefer to carry on the argument on my own behalf.

Then take a step backward, for we have gone wrong in the order of the sciences.

What was the mistake? he said.

After plane geometry, I said, we took solids in revolution, instead of taking solids in themselves; whereas after the second dimension the third, which is concerned with cubes and dimensions of depth, ought to have followed.

That is true, Socrates; but these subjects seem to be as yet hardly explored.

Why, yes, I said, and for two reasons: in the first place, no government patronizes them, which leads to a want of energy in the study of them, and they are difficult; in the second place, students cannot learn them unless they have a teacher. But then a teacher is hardly to be found, and even if one could be found, as matters now stand, the students of these subjects, who are very conceited, would not mind him. That, however, would be otherwise if the whole State patronized and honored them; then they would listen, and there would be continuous and earnest search, and discoveries would be made; since even now, disregarded as they are by the world, and maimed of their fair proportions, and although none of their votaries can tell the use of them, still these studies force their way by their natural charm, and very likely they may emerge into light.

Yes, he said, there is a remarkable charm in them. But I

do not clearly understand the change in the order. First you began with a geometry of plane surfaces?

Yes, I said.

And you placed astronomy next, and then you made a step backward?

Yes, I said, the more haste the less speed; the ludicrous state of solid geometry made me pass over this branch and go on to astronomy, or motion of solids.

True, he said.

Then regarding the science now omitted as supplied, if only encouraged by the State, let us go on to astronomy.

That is the natural order, he said. And now, Socrates, as you rebuked the vulgar manner in which I praised astronomy before, my praises shall accord with the method of your inquiry. For every one, as I think, must feel that astronomy compels the soul to look upwards, and leads us from this world to another.

529-534

I am an exception then, for I should rather say that those who elevate astronomy into philosophy make us look downwards and not upwards.

Why, how is that? he asked.

You, I replied, have evidently a sublime conception of the knowledge of the things above. And I dare say that if a person were to throw his head back and study the fretted ceiling, you would still think that his mind was the percipient, and not his eyes. And you are very likely right, and I may be a simpleton: for, in my opinion, only that knowledge which is of being and the unseen can make the soul look upwards, and whether a man gapes at the heavens or blinks on the ground, seeking to learn some particular of sense, I would deny that he can learn, for nothing of that sort is matter of science; his soul is looking, not upwards, but downwards, whether his way to knowledge is by water or by land, and he may float on his back in either element.

I acknowledge, he said, the justice of your rebuke. Still, I should like to know how astronomy can be learned in any other way more conducive to that knowledge of which we speak?

[The true object of astronomy is not the starry heavens, beautiful as they are to the eyes, but the laws of pure motion. And astronomy must be pursued as an abstract science if "it is to become a real part of education, improving the natural use of reason." In like manner the true science of harmony does not concern itself with sounds and consonances that appear to the ear, nor even with the numerical relations between such sounds, but with the "natural harmonies of number." Such study seems to some a thing of "more than mortal knowledge" but it is in the highest degree useful, "if pursued with a view to the beautiful and good." Socrates continues:]

Now, when all these studies reach the point of intercommunion and connection with one another, and come to be considered in their mutual affinities, then, I think, but not till then, will the pursuit of them have a value for our objects; otherwise they are useless.

That, Socrates, is also my own notion; but it is a vast work of which you speak.

[Socrates says: The science for which pure arithmetic, geometry, astronomy, and harmony prepare the way is dialectic. Those sciences only prepare the way and do not themselves attain to the highest truth; but no one can understand dialectic who has not been prepared by the proper study of the preliminary sciences. The bodily eye, according to the story of the den, rose from seeing shadows to seeing images, and then objects, and lastly the sun.]

In like manner, when a person begins dialectics, and starts on the discovery of the absolute by the light of reason only, and without any assistance of sense, and does not rest until by pure intelligence he attains pure good, he finds himself at the end of the intellectual world, as in the other case at the end of the visible.

[As in Book VI., it is shown that there are four degrees of knowledge: (1) "The knowledge of shadows;" (2) "belief," or the perception of objects; (3) "understanding," or the knowledge of the abstract sciences, such as arithmetic, geometry, etc.; (4) "science," or "reason," which alone, by dialectic, arrives at the absolute truth. If dialectic is thus the "coping-stone of the sciences," then surely the children of the State who are to be its future rulers should be led to the acquisition of this science. Socrates now asks :]

535 But to whom are we to assign these studies, and in what way are they to be assigned?—that is a question which remains to be considered.

Yes, plainly.

You remember, I said, how the rulers were chosen before?

Certainly, he said.

The same natures must still be chosen, and the preference again given to the surest and the bravest, and, if possible, to the fairest; and, having noble and manly tempers, they should also have the natural gifts which accord with their education.

And what are they?

Such gifts as keenness and ready powers of acquisition; for the mind more often faints from the severity of study than from the severity of gymnastics : the toil is more entirely the mind's own, and is not shared with the body.

Very true, he replied.

Further, he of whom we are in search should have a good memory, and be an unwearied, solid man, who is a lover of labor in any line, or he will never be able to undergo the double toil and trouble of body and mind.

Certainly, he said; a man must have some natural gifts.

The mistake at present is, I said, that those who study philosophy have no vocation, and this, as I was before saying, is the reason why she has fallen into disrepute: her true sons should study her and not bastards.

How do you mean?

In the first place, her votary should not have a lame or one legged industry. I mean, that he should not be half industrious and half idle: as, for example, when a man is a lover of gymnastic and hunting, and all other bodily exercises, but a hater rather than a lover of the labor of learning or hearing or inquiry. Or a man may be lame in another way, and the love of labor may take an opposite form.

That is quite true, he said.

And as to truth, I said, is not a soul to be deemed halt and lame who hates voluntary falsehood and is extremely indignant at himself and others when they tell lies, and yet receives involuntary falsehood, and does not mind wallowing like a swinish beast in the mire of ignorance, and has no shame at being detected?

Most certainly, he said.

And, again, as to temperance and courage and magnanimity, and every other virtue, should they not observe the ways of the true son and of the bastard? for wherever States and individuals have no eye for this sort of qualities, they unconsciously make a friend or perhaps a ruler of one who is in a figure a lame man or a bastard, from a defect in some one of these qualities. 536

That is very true, he said.

All these things, then, will have to be carefully considered, and those whom we introduce to this vast system of education and training must be sound in limb and mind, and then justice herself will have nothing to say against us, and we shall be the saviours of the State; but, if our pupils are men of another stamp, the reverse will happen, and we shall pour a still greater flood of ridicule on philosophy.

That would be discreditable.

Yes, I said, that is quite true; and yet, perhaps, in thus turning jest into earnest I am equally ridiculous.

In what respect?

I had forgotten, I said, that we were not in earnest, and spoke with too much excitement. For when I saw philosophy trampled under foot of men I could not help feeling a sort of indignation at the authors of her disgrace: and my anger made me vehement.

Indeed; I did not observe that you were more vehement than was right.

But I felt that I was. And now let me remind you that, although in our former selection we chose old men, that will not do in this. Solon was under a delusion when he said that a man as he is growing older may learn many things,—for he can no more learn than he can run; youth is the time of toil.

That is certainly true.

And, therefore, calculation and geometry, and all the other elements of instruction, which are a preparation for dialectic, should be presented to the mind in childhood; not, however, under any notion of forcing them.

Why not?

Because a freeman ought to be a freeman in the acquisition of knowledge. Bodily exercise, when compulsory, does no harm; but knowledge which is acquired under compulsion has no hold on the mind.

Very true, he said.

Then, my good friend, I said, do not use compulsion, but let early education be a sort of amusement; that will better enable you to find out the natural bent.

537

There is reason in that, he said.

Do you remember our saying that the children, too, must be taken to see the battle on horseback; and if there were no danger they might be led close up, and, like young hounds, have a taste of blood given them?

Yes, I remember.

Now that may be practiced, I said, in other things—labors, lessons, dangers—and he who appears to be most ready ought to be enrolled in a select number.

At what age?

At the age when the necessary gymnastics are over : the period whether of two or three years which passes in this sort of training is useless for any other purpose; for sleep and exercise are unpropitious to learning : and the trial of who is first in gymnastic exercises is one of the most important tests to which they are subjected.

Certainly, he replied.

After that time those who are selected from the class of twenty years old will be promoted to higher honor, and the sciences which they learned without any order in their early education will now be brought together, and they will be able to see the correlation of them to one another and to true being.

Yes, he said, that is the only kind of knowledge which is everlasting.

Yes, I said; and the capacity for such knowledge is the great criterion of dialectical talent : the speculative or comprehensive mind is always the dialectical.

I agree in that, he said.

These, I said, are the points which you must consider; and those who have most of this comprehension, and who are most steadfast in their learning, and in their military, and generally in their public duties, when they arrive at the age of thirty will have to be chosen by you out of the select class, and elevated to higher honor; and you will have to prove them by the help of dialectic, in order to learn which of them is able to give up the use of sight and other senses, and in company with truth to attain absolute being. And here, my friend, great caution is required.

Why great caution?

Do you not remark, I said, how great the evil is which dialectic has introduced?

What is that? he said.

The lawlessness of which the professors of the art [5] are full.

That is true, he said.

Do you think that there is anything unnatural in their case? or shall I ask you to make allowance for them?

What sort of allowance?

I want you, I said, by way of parallel, to imagine a supposititious son who is brought up in great wealth; he is one of a large and numerous family, and has many flatterers. When grown up he learns that his alleged are not his real parents; but who the real ones are he is unable to discover. Can you tell me how he will be likely to behave towards his flatterers and his supposed parents, first of all during the period when he was ignorant of the false relation, and then again when he knew? Or would you like to hear my suspicion?

Very much.

I suspect, then, that while he was ignorant of the truth he would be likely to honor his father and his mother and his supposed relations more than the flatterers; he would be less willing to see them in want, or to do any violence to them, or say anything evil of them, and in important matters less willing to disobey them.

That might be expected.

But when he has made the discovery, I should imagine that he would diminish his honor and regard for them, and would become more devoted to the flatterers; their influence over him would greatly increase; he would now live after their ways, and openly associate with them, and unless he were of an unusually good disposition, he would think no more of his parents or other supposed friends.

[5] In reference to the Sophists, see General Introduction, p. xxvii.

Well, that is extremely probable. But how is the image applicable to the disciples of philosophy?

In this way: you know that there are certain principles about justice and good, which were taught us in childhood, and under their parental authority we have been brought up, obeying and honoring them.

That is true.

And there are also opposite maxims and habits of pleasure which flatter and attract our soul, but they do not influence those who have any sense of right, and who continue to honor the maxims of their fathers and obey them.

True.

Now, when a man is in this state, and the questioning spirit asks what is fair or honorable, and he answers as the law directs, and then arguments come and refute the word of the legislator, and he is driven into believing that nothing is fair any more than foul, or just and good any more than the opposite, and the same of all his time-honored notions, do you think that he will still honor and obey them?

That is impossible.

And when he ceases to think them honorable and natural as heretofore, and he fails to discover the true, can he be expected to pursue any life other than that which flatters his desires?

He cannot.

And from being an observer of the law he is converted into a lawless person?

Unquestionably.

Now all this is very natural in those who study philosophy in this manner, and also, as I was just now saying, most excusable.

Yes, he said, and, as I may add, pitiable.

Therefore, that your feelings may not be moved to pity about our thirty-years-old citizens, every care must be taken in introducing them to dialectic.

Certainly.

They must not be allowed to taste the dear delight too early; that is one thing specially to be avoided; for young men, as you may have observed, when they first get the taste in their mouths, argue for amusement, and are always contradicting and refuting others in imitation of those who refute them;

they are like puppy-dogs, who delight to tear and pull at all who come near them.

Yes, he said, that is their great delight.

And when they have made many conquests and received defeats at the hands of many, they violently and speedily get into a way of not believing anything that they believed before, and hence, not only they, but philosophy generally, has a bad name with the rest of the world.

That is very true, he said.

But when a man begins to get older, he will no longer be guilty of that sort of insanity; he will follow the example of the dialectician who is seeking for truth, and not of the eristic,[6] who is contradicting for the sake of amusement; and the greater moderation of his character will increase and not diminish the honor of the pursuit.

Very true, he said.

And did we not make special provision for this, when we said that the natures of those to whom philosophy was to be imparted were to be orderly and steadfast, not, as now, any chance aspirant or intruder?

Very true, he said.

Suppose, I said, that the study of philosophy be continued diligently and earnestly and exclusively for twice the number of years which were passed in bodily exercise—will that be enough?

Would you say six or four years? he asked.

Suppose five years to be the time fixed, I replied; after that they must be sent down into the den and compelled to hold any military or other office which young men are qualified to hold: in this way they will get their experience of life, and there will be an opportunity of trying whether, when they are drawn all manner of ways by temptation, they will stand firm or stir at all.

And how long is this stage of their lives to last?

Fifteen years, I answered; and when they have reached fifty years of age, then let those who still survive and have distinguished themselves in every deed and in all knowledge come at last to their consummation: the time has now arrived at which they must raise the eye of the soul to the universal light which lightens all things, and behold the ab-

---

[6] Eristic: one who is fond of dispute.

solute good; for that is the pattern according to which they are to order the State and the lives of individuals, and the remainder of their own lives also, making philosophy their chief pursuit; but, when their turn comes, also toiling at politics and ruling for the public good, not as if they were doing some great thing, but of necessity; and when they have brought up others like them and left them in their place to be governors of the State, then they will depart to the Islands of the Blest [7] and dwell there; and the city will give them public memorials and sacrifices and honor them, if the Pythian oracle consent,[8] as demigods, and at any rate as blessed and divine.

You are a statuary, Socrates, and have made our governors perfect in beauty.

Yes, I said, Glaucon, and our governesses too; for you must not suppose that what I have been saying applies to men only and not to women as far as their natures can go.

There you are right, he said, if, as we described, they are to have all things in common with the men.

Well, I said, and you would agree (would you not?) that what has been said about the State and the government is not a mere dream, and although difficult not impossible, but only possible in the way that has been supposed; that is to say when the true philosopher kings, one or more of them, are born in a State, despising the honors of this present world which they deem mean and worthless, above all esteeming right and the honor that springs from right, and regarding justice as the greatest and most necessary of all things, whose ministers they are, and whose principles will be extended by them when they set in order their own city?

How will they do that? he said.

They will begin by sending out into the country all the inhabitants of the city who are more than ten years old, and will take possession of their children, who will be unaffected by the habits of their parents; they will then train them in their own habits and laws, that is to say, in those which we have given them; and in this way the State and constitution of which we were speaking will soonest and most easily succeed, and the nation which has such a constitution will be most benefited.

[7] See Apology, note 23.   [8] See Rep., IV., 427 and note 9.

Yes, that will be the best way. And I think, Socrates, that you have very well described the way in which such a constitution might come into being.

And have we not said enough of the State, and of the man who corresponds to the State, for there is no difficulty in seeing how we shall describe him?

There is no difficulty, he replied, and I say with you, enough.

BOOK VIII

AND so, Glaucon, we have arrived at the conclusion that in the perfect State wives and children are to be in common; and education and the arts of war and peace are also to be common, and the best philosophers and the bravest warriors are to be their kings?[1]

543

That, replied Glaucon, is acknowledged.

Yes, I said; and we have further acknowledged that the governors, when appointed themselves, would take their soldiers and place them in houses such as we were describing; nor would any one say that anything which he had was his own—their houses were to be common; and as for their property, you remember about that?

Yes, I remember that no one was to have any of the ordinary possessions of mankind; they were to be a sort of warrior athletes and guardians, receiving from the other citizens, in lieu of annual payment, only their maintenance, and they were to take care of themselves and of the whole State.

True, I said; and now that this division of our work is concluded, let us find the point at which we digressed, that we may return into the old path.

There is no difficulty in doing that, he replied; you appeared then, as now, to have finished the description of the State; and you said that such a State was good, and the man was good who answered to the State, although you had more excellent things to relate both of State and man. And you said further, that if this was the true form, then the others were false; and of the false forms, you said, as I remember, that there were four principal ones,[2] and that the defects of them, and of the individuals corresponding to them, were worth examining: when we had seen them all, and finally agreed as to who was the best and who was the worst of them, we might consider, as you said, whether the best was not also the happiest, and the worst the most miserable. And when I asked you what the four forms of government

544

---

[1] The proof of these three propositions occupies Books V., VI., and VII.
[2] For definition of the five forms of government see Introduction to Republic, p. 184.

were of which you spoke, then Polemarchus and Adeimantus put in their word; and you began again, and have found your way to the point at which we have now arrived.

Your recollection, I said, is most exact.

Then, like a wrestler, he replied, you must put yourself again in the same position; and let me ask the same questions, and do give me the same answer which you were about to give me then.

Yes, if I can, I will, I said.

I shall particularly wish to hear what were the four constitutions of which you were speaking.

That, I said, is easily answered: the four governments of which I spoke, so far as they have distinct names, are, first, the Cretan and Spartan,[3] which are generally applauded: next, there is oligarchy; this is not equally approved, and is a form of government which has many evils: thirdly, democracy, which naturally follows oligarchy, although different: and lastly comes tyranny, great and famous, which is different from them all, and is the fourth and worst disorder of a State. I do not know of any other constitution which can be said to have a distinct form, but there are lordships and principalities which are bought and sold, and some other intermediate forms of government; and these nondescripts are found among barbarians oftener than among Hellenes.

Yes, he replied, there are said to be many curious forms of government among them.

Do you know, I said, that governments vary as the characters of men vary, and that there must be as many of the one as there are of the other? Or perhaps you suppose that States are made of "oak and rock,"[4] and not out of the human natures which are in them, and which turn the scale and draw other things after them?

Nay, he said, the States are as the men are; they do but grow out of human characters.

Then if the constitutions of States are five, the disposition of individual minds will also be five?

---

[3] Crete: a large island in the Ægean, southeast of Greece. Sparta: one of the most powerful states of Greece, situated at the southern extremity. The governments of these states Plato regards as the timocratic form.

[4] See Apology, note 38.

Certainly.

Him who answers to aristocracy and whom we rightly call just and good, we have already described[5]; and now we have to describe the inferior sort of natures, being the contentious and ambitious, who answer to the Spartan polity; also the oligarchical, democratical, and tyrannical man. Let us place the most just by the side of the most unjust, and then we shall be able to compare the relative happiness or unhappiness of pure justice and pure injustice: this will complete the inquiry. And then we shall know whether we are to pursue injustice, as Thrasymachus advises, or justice, as the present argument counsels.

Certainly, he replied, that will be the way.

Suppose, then, following our old plan, which we adopted as being clearer, of taking the State first and then proceeding to the individual, we begin with the government of honor (for I know of no name for such a government other than timocracy, or perhaps timarchy); and then we will view the like character in the individual; and, after that, consider oligarchy and the oligarchical man; and then again we will turn our attention to democracy and the democratical man; and lastly, we will go and view the city of tyranny, and there take a look into the tyrant's soul, and try to arrive at the final decision.

That way of viewing and judging of the matter will be very rational.

First, then, I said, let us inquire how timocracy (or the government of honor) arises out of aristocracy (or the government of the best). Clearly, all political changes originate in divisions of the actual governing power; for a government which is united, however small, cannot be moved.

That is true, he said.

In what way, then, will our city be moved, and in what manner will the two classes of auxiliaries and rulers disagree among themselves or with one another? Shall we, after the manner of Homer, pray the Muses to tell us "how strife was first kindled?" Shall we imagine them, in tragic style, pretending to be in earnest, playing with us as with children in solemn words?

How would they address us?

[5] The philosopher.

After this manner: A city which is thus constituted can hardly be shaken; but, seeing that everything which has a beginning has also an end, even this constitution will in time perish and come to dissolution.

[It is explained how guardians who are good and wise may have children who possess none of the qualities which a guardian should have. So, though the guardians appoint the best of the youth to be their successors,]

still they will be unworthy to hold their father's places, and when they come into power as guardians, they will soon be found to fail in taking care of us, the Muses, first by undervaluing music, and secondly gymnastic; and hence our young men will be less cultivated. In the succeeding generation rulers will be appointed who have none of the qualities of guardians. In order to put to the test the metal of your different races, which, like Hesiod's, are of gold, and silver, and brass, and iron,[a] iron will be mingled with silver, and brass with gold, and hence there will arise inequality and irregularity, which always and in all places are causes of enmity and war. Such is the origin of strife, wherever arising; and this is the answer of the Muses to us.

Yes, he said, and we may assume that they answer truly.

Why, yes, I said, of course they answer truly: the Muses cannot do otherwise.

And what do the Muses say next?

When strife arose, then the two races were drawn different ways: the iron and brass fell to acquiring money and land and houses and gold and silver; but the gold and silver races, having the true riches in their own nature, inclined towards virtue and the ancient order of things. There was a battle between them, and at last they agreed to assign their land and houses to the possession of individuals; and they enslaved their friends and maintainers, whom they had formerly protected in the condition of freemen, and made of them subjects and servants; while they themselves were occupied with war and the watching of them.

That, he replied, will probably be the origin of the change.

---

[a] Compare myth, close of Book III.

And the new government which thus arises will be of a form intermediate between oligarchy and aristocracy.

Very true.

And now, after the change has been made, what will be their way of life? Clearly, the new State, being in a mean between oligarchy and the perfect State, will partly follow one and partly the other, and will also have some peculiarities.

That is true, he said.

In the honor given to rulers, in the abstinence of the warrior class from agriculture, handicrafts, and other trades, in the institution of common meals, attention to gymnastics and military training—in all these the citizen will resemble the perfect State.

True.

But in the fear of admitting philosophers to power, because their philosophy is no longer simple and earnest, but made up of mixed elements; and in turning from them to passionate and simpler characters, who are by nature fitted for war rather than peace; and in the value which they set upon military stratagems and contrivances, and in their everlasting wars—this State will be for the most part peculiar.

Yes.

Yes, I said; and men of this stamp will be covetous of money, like those who live in oligarchies; they will have a fierce secret longing after gold and silver, which they will hoard in dark places, having magazines and treasures of their own for the deposit and concealment of them; also castles which are just nests for their eggs, and in which they will spend large sums on their wives, or on any others whom they please.

That is most true, he said.

And they are miserly because they have no means of openly acquiring the money which they prize; they will spend that which is another man's in their lust; stealing their pleasures and running away like children from the law, their father: they have been schooled not by gentle influences but by force; for they have no thought of the true muse of reason and philosophy, and gymnastic is preferred by them to music.

Undoubtedly, he said, the form of government which you describe is a mixture of good and evil.

Why, there is a mixture, I said; but one thing, and one thing only, is predominantly seen,—the spirit of contention and ambition; and these are due to the prevalence of the passionate or spirited element.[7]

Assuredly, he said.

Such is the origin and such the character of this State, of which the outline only has been given; the more perfect execution of the sketch was not required, because the outline is enough to show the type of the most perfectly just and unjust; and to go through all the States and all the characters of men, leaving none of them out, would be an interminable labor.

Very true, he replied.

Who answers to this form of government—how did he come into being, and what is he like?

I think, said Adeimantus, that in the spirit of contention which characterizes him, he is not unlike our friend Glaucon.

Perhaps, I said, he may be like him in that one point; but there are other respects in which he is very different.

In what respects?

He should have more of self-assertion and be somewhat less favored by the Muses, yet not other than a lover of the Muses; and he should be a good listener, but not a speaker. A man of this sort may be imagined to be rough with slaves, not like the educated man, who is too proud for that; and he will also be courteous to freemen, and remarkably obedient to authority; he is a lover of power and a lover of honor; claiming to be a ruler, not because he is a speaker, or on any ground of that sort, but because he is a soldier, and, as a soldier, has performed feats of arms: he is also a lover of gymnastic exercises and of the chase.

Yes, he said, that is the character of timocracy.

Such an one will despise riches only when he is young; but as he gets older he will be more and more attracted to them, because he has a piece of the avaricious nature in him, and is not single-minded towards virtue, having lost his best guardian.

Who is that? said Adeimantus.

Philosophy, I said, tempered with music,[8] who comes and

---

[7] See Book IV., 439 and following.
[8] This sentence embraces Plato's entire scheme of education. In early life the soul should be compassed by influences in art form, which have been determined in accordance with absolute truth by the philosopher. Later, the soul which is properly educated through such influences should rise to clear knowledge of the absolute truth by means of philosophic reflection.

takes up her abode in a man through life, and is the only saviour of his virtue.

Good, he said.

Such, I said, is the timocratical youth, and he is like the timocratical State.

Exactly.

His origin is as follows: He is often the son of a brave father, who dwells in an ill-governed city, the honors and offices of which he declines, and will not go to law, but is ready to waive his rights in order that he may escape trouble.

And how does the son come into being?

The character of the son begins to develop when he hears his mother grumbling at her husband for not having a seat in the government, the consequence of which is that she loses precedence among other women. Further, when she sees her husband not very eager about money, and instead of battling and railing in the law courts or assembly, taking everything of that sort quietly; and when she observes that his thoughts always centre in himself, while he treats her with very considerable indifference, she is annoyed at all this, and says to her son that his father is only half a man and far too easy-going: not to mention other similar complaints which women love to utter.

Yes, said Adeimantus, they give us plenty of them, and in their own characteristic style.

And you know, I said, that the old servants of the family, who are supposed to be attached, talk privately in the same strain to the sons; and if they see any one who owes money to their father, or is wronging him in any way, and he fails to prosecute them, they tell the youth that when he grows up he must retaliate upon his injurers, and be more of a man than his father. He has only to walk abroad and he hears and sees the same sort of thing: those who do their own business in the city are called simple, and held in no esteem, while the busybodies are honored and applauded. The result is that the young man, hearing and seeing all these things,—hearing, too, the words of his father, and having a nearer view of his way of life, and making comparisons of him and others,—is drawn opposite ways: while his father is watering and nourishing the rational principle in his soul, the others are encouraging the passionate and appetitive; and he being not originally of a bad nature, but having kept bad company, is brought by their joint influence to a middle point, and gives up the kingdom which is within him to the middle principle of contentiousness and passion,[9] and becomes proud and ambitious.

You seem to me to have described his origin perfectly.

Then we have now, I said, the second form of government and the second type of character?

We have.

Next, let us look at another man who, as Æschylus says, is set over against another State; or rather, as our plan requires, begin with the State.

By all means.

I believe that oligarchy follows next in order.

And what manner of government do you term oligarchy?

A government resting on a valuation of property, in which the rich have power and the poor are deprived of power.

I understand, he replied.

Shall I describe how the change from timocracy to oligarchy arises?

Yes.

Well, I said, no eyes are required in order to see how that comes about.

How?

That private hoard of theirs is the source of the evil; the accumulation of gold ruins timocracy: they invent some extravagance which is in open contravention of the law, but neither they nor their wives care about this.

That might be expected.

And then one seeing another prepares to rival him, and thus the whole body of the citizens acquires a similar character.

Likely enough.

After that they get on in trade, and the more they think of this the less they think of virtue; for when riches and virtue are placed together in the scales of the balance, the one always rises as the other falls.

True.

And in proportion as riches and rich men are honored in the State, virtue and the virtuous are dishonored.

Clearly.

[9] See Book IV., 435-442.

And what is honored is cultivated, and that which has no honor is neglected.

That is the case.

And so at last, instead of loving contention and glory, men become lovers of trade and money, and they honor and reverence the rich man, and make a ruler of him, and dishonor the poor man.

Certainly.

Then they proceed to make a law which fixes a sum of money as the qualification of citizenship; the money fixed is more or less as the oligarchy is more or less exclusive; and they forbid any one whose property is below the amount fixed to share in the government: these changes in the constitution they effect by force of arms, if intimidation has not already done the work.

Very true.

And this, speaking generally, is the way in which oligarchy is established.

Yes, he said; but what are the characteristics of this form of government, and what are the supposed defects?

First of all, I said, consider the nature of the qualification. Just think what would happen if the pilots were to be chosen according to their property, and a poor man refused permission to steer, even though he were a better pilot?

You mean that they would shipwreck?

Yes; and is not this true of the government of anything?

Yes, that is what I should imagine.

And would you say this of a city also, or do you make an exception in favor of a city?

Nay, he said, the case of a city is still stronger, in proportion as the rule of a city is greater and more difficult.

This, then, will be the first great defect of oligarchy?

Clearly.

And here is another defect which is quite as bad.

What defect?

The inevitable division; such a State is not one, but two States, the one of poor men, the other of rich men, who are living on the same spot and ever conspiring against one another.

Yes, that is equally bad.

Another discreditable feature is the impossibility of carrying on any war, because if they arm and use the multitude they are more afraid of them than of the enemy: that is unavoidable. If they do not use them, then, in the hour of battle, they appear oligarchs indeed, few to fight and few to rule: and at the same time their fondness for money makes them unwilling to pay taxes.

That is not creditable.

And what do you say of our former charge that, under such a constitution, the same persons are busy at many things, and are husbandmen, tradesmen, warriors, all in one? Does that seem well?

552

Anything but well.

There is another evil which is, perhaps, the greatest of all, and to which this State first begins to be liable.

What is the evil?

The evil is that a man may sell all that he has, and another may possess his property, yet after the sale he may dwell in the city of which he is no longer a part, being neither trader, nor artisan, nor horseman, nor hoplite,[10] but only poor and helpless.

Yes, that begins in this State.

An oligarchy offers no security against this; for oligarchies have both the extremes of great wealth and utter poverty.

True.

But think again: what sort of a gentleman is this? In his wealthy days, while he was spending his money, was he a whit more good to the State for the purposes of which we were just now speaking? Or did he only seem to be a member of the ruling body, being really no more a ruler than he was a subject, but just a spendthrift?

As you say, he seemed to be a ruler, but was only a spendthrift.

May we not say that this is the drone in the house who is like the drone in the honeycomb, and that the one is the plague of the city as the other is of the hive?

Just so, Socrates.

And God has made the flying drones, Adeimantus, all without stings, whereas of the walking drones he has made some without stings and others with dreadful stings: of the stingless class are those who in their old age end by dying paupers; of the stingers come all the criminal class, as they are termed.

[10] Heavy-armed soldier.

Most true, he said.

Clearly then, whenever you see paupers in a State, somewhere in that neighborhood there are hidden away thieves and cut purses, and robbers of temples, and other malefactors.

That is clear.

Well, I said, and in oligarchical States do you not find paupers?

Yes, he said; nearly everybody is a pauper who is not a ruler.

And may we be so bold as to suppose that there are also many criminals to be found in them, rogues who have stings, and whom the authorities are careful to restrain by force?

Certainly, we may be so bold.

The existence of such persons is to be attributed to want of education, ill-training, and an evil constitution of the State?

True.

Such, then, is the form and such are the evils of oligarchy; and there may be other evils.

That is pretty much the truth.

Then now oligarchy, or the form of government in which the rulers are elected for their wealth, may be regarded as dismissed. Let us next proceed to consider the nature and origin of the individual who answers to the State.

Yes, by all means.

Is not this the manner of the change from the timocratical to the oligarchical? Suppose the representative of timocracy to have a son: at first he begins by emulating his father and walking in his footsteps, but presently he sees him strike all in a moment on a sunken reef, which is the State, and he and all that he has are lost; he may have been a general or some other high officer who is brought to trial under a prejudice raised by informers, and either put to death, or exiled, or deprived of the privileges of a citizen, and all his property taken from him.

That is very likely to happen.

And the son has seen and known all this—he is a ruined man, and his fear has taught him to knock ambition and passion headforemost from his bosom's throne: humbled by poverty he takes to money-making, and by mean and small savings and doings gets a fortune together. Is not this man likely to seat the concupiscent and covetous elements on that vacant throne? They will play the great king within him, and he will array them with tiara and collar and scimitar.

Likely! Yes, he replied.

And when he has made the reasoning and passionate faculties sit on the ground obediently on either side, and taught them to know their place, he compels the one to think only of the method by which lesser sums may be converted into larger ones, and schools the other into the worship and admiration of riches and rich men; no ambition will he tolerate except the ambition of getting rich and the means which lead to this.

Of all conversions, he said, there is none so speedy or so sure as when the ambitious youth changes into the avaricious one.

And the avaricious, I said, is the oligarchical youth?

Yes, he said; at any rate the individual out of whom he came is like the State out of which oligarchy came.

Let us then consider whether there is any likeness between them.

Very good.

First, then, they resemble one another in the value 554 which they set upon wealth?

Certainly.

Also in their penurious, laborious character; the individual only satisfies his necessary appetites, and confines his expenditure to them; his other desires he subdues, under the idea that there is no use in them?

True.

He is a shabby fellow, I said, who saves something out of everything and makes a purse for himself; and this is the sort of man whom the vulgar applaud. Is he not like the State which he represents?

That would be my view of him, he replied; at any rate, money is highly valued by him as well as by the State.

Why, he is not a man of cultivation, I said.

I imagine not, he said; had he been educated he would never have made a blind god director of his chorus, or given him chief honor.[11]

Excellent! I said. Yet consider this: Will there not be

---

[11] Plutus, god of wealth (identified with Hades or Pluto, god of the lower world): according to one myth blinded by Zeus in order that he might distribute his wealth impartially. Jowett paraphrases the passage thus: " He would never have allowed the blind god of riches to lead the dance within him."

found in him, owing to his want of cultivation, dronelike desires as of pauper and rogue, which are forcibly kept down by his general habit of life?

True.

Do you know where you will have to look if you want to discover his rogueries?

Where must I look?

Let him be the guardian of an orphan, or have some other great opportunity of acting dishonestly, and then he will show that, in sustaining the reputation of uprightness which attaches to him in his dealings generally, he coerces his other bad passions by an effort of virtue; not that he convinces them of evil, or exerts over them the gentle influence of reason, but he acts upon them by necessity and fear, and because he trembles for his possessions.

That is clear.

Yes, indeed, I said, my dear friend, you will find that the natural desires of the drone commonly exist in him all the same, whenever he has the spending of another's goods.

No mistake about that.

This sort of man, then, will be at war with himself; he will be two men, and not one; but, in general, his better desires will be found to prevail over his inferior ones.

True.

For these reasons such an one will be more decent than many are; yet the true virtue of a unanimous and harmonious soul will be far out of his reach.

That I believe.

And surely, in his private capacity, the miser will be an ignoble competitor in a State for any prize of victory, or other object of honorable ambition; he is too much afraid of awakening his expensive appetites and inviting them to help and join in the struggle; in true oligarchical fashion he fights with a small part only of his resources, and the result commonly is that he loses the prize and saves his money.

Very true.

Can we any longer doubt, then, that the miser and money-maker answers to the oligarchical State?

Certainly not.

Next comes democracy and the democratical man: the

origin and nature of them we have still to learn, that we may compare the individual and the State, and so pronounce upon them.

That, he said, is our method.

Well, I said, is not this the way in which the change from oligarchy into democracy arises?—they are insatiable of wealth which they propose to themselves as their end; and the rulers, who are aware that their own power rests upon property, refuse to curtail by law the extravagance of the spendthrift youth because they will gain by their ruin; they lend them money, and buy them out of their land, and grow in wealth and honor?

Exactly.

There can be no doubt that in a State you cannot have in the citizens the love of wealth and the spirit of moderation; one or the other will have to be disregarded.

That is tolerably clear.

And in oligarchical States, from carelessness and the indulgence of their extravagance, men of good family have often been reduced to beggary?

Yes, often.

And still they remain in the city; there they are, and they have stings and arms, and some of them owe money, some are no longer citizens[12]: a third class are in both predicaments, and they hate and conspire against those who have got their property, and anybody else, and are eager for revolution.

That is true.

On the other hand, the men of business, stooping as they walk, and pretending never so much as to see those whom they have already ruined, insert the sting—that is, their money—into anybody else who is not on his guard against them, and recover the parent or principal sum many times over multiplied into a family of children: this is the way in which they make drone and pauper to abound in the State.

Yes, he said, there are plenty of them, that is certain.

The evil is like a fire which is blazing up, and which they will not extinguish either by placing restriction on the disposition of property or—

What is the other solution of the difficulty?

[12] Literally some are dishonored, *i.e.*, officially deprived of citizenship.

One which is about as good, and has the advantage of compelling the citizens to look to their characters: Let there be an ordinance that every one shall enter into voluntary contracts at his own risk, and there will be less of this scandalous money-making, and the evils of which we were speaking will be greatly lessened in the State.

Yes, they will be greatly lessened.

At present the governors, induced by the motives which I have named, treat their subjects badly; while they and their adherents, especially the young men of the governing class, lead a life of luxury and idleness both of body and mind; they do nothing, and are incapable of holding out against pleasure and pain.

Very true.

They care only for making money, and are as indifferent as the pauper to the cultivation of virtue.

Yes, quite indifferent.

Now in this state of things the rulers and their subjects come in one another's way, whether on a journey or some other occasion of meeting, or on a pilgrimage or march as fellow-soldiers or fellow-sailors; they observe each other in the moment of danger (and where danger is there is no fear that the poor will be despised by the rich), and very likely the wiry, sunburnt poor man may be placed in battle at the side of a wealthy one who has never spoilt his complexion, and has plenty of superfluous flesh—when he sees such an one puffing and at his wits'-end, can he avoid drawing the conclusion that men of this sort are only rich because no one has the courage to despoil them? And when they meet in private will they not be saying to one another that our " warriors are nothing worth?"

Yes, he said, I am quite aware that this is their way of talking.

And, as where a body is weak the addition of a touch from without may bring on illness, and sometimes even when there is no external provocation a commotion may arise within, in the same way where there is weakness in the State there is also likely to be illness, the occasion of which may be very slight, one party introducing their democratical, the other their oligarchical allies, and the State may fall sick, and be at war with herself and in a state of distraction, even when there is no external cause.

Yes, surely.

And then democracy comes into being after the poor have conquered their opponents, slaughtering some and banishing some, while to the remainder they give an equal share of freedom and power; and this is the form of government in which the magistrates are commonly elected by lot.[13]

Yes, he said, that is the nature of democracy, whether established by arms or by fear, and the withdrawal of the opposite party.

And now what is their manner of life, and what sort of a government is this? For as the government is, such will be the man.

Clearly, he said.

In the first place, are they not free? and the city is full of freedom and frankness—there a man may do as he likes.

Yes, that is often said, he replied.

And where this freedom is, there every man is clearly able to order his life as he pleases?

Clearly.

Then in this kind of State there will be the greatest variety of human natures?

There will.

This, then, is likely to be the fairest of States, and may be compared to an embroidered robe which is spangled with flowers; and being in like manner spangled with the manners and characters of mankind will appear to be the fairest of them all. And just as women and children think variety charming, so there are many men who will deem this the fairest of States.

Yes.

Yes, I said, my noble sir, and a good place in which to go and look for a government.

Why?

Because of the liberty which reigns there: they have a complete assortment of constitutions; and if a man has a mind to establish a State, as we are doing, he must go to a democracy as he would go to a bazaar, where they sell them, and pick out one that suits him; then, when he has made his choice, he may lay the foundation of his State.

He will be sure, he said, to have patterns enough.

[13] In Athens at that time many offices were assigned by lot.

And there being no necessity, I said, for you to govern in this State, even if you have the capacity, or to be governed unless you like, or to go to war when the others go to war, or to be at peace when others are at peace, unless you are disposed—there being no necessity also because some law forbids you to hold office or be a dicast,[14] that you should not hold office or be a dicast, if you have a mind yourself—is not that a way of life which for the moment is supremely delightful?

Yes, for the moment, that is true.

And is not the calmness of those against whom sentence has been given often quite charming? Under a government of this sort there are men who, when they have been condemned to death or exile, stay where they are and walk about the world; the gentleman parades like a hero, as though nobody saw or cared.

Yes, he replied, I have often remarked that.

Yes, I said; and the forgiving spirit of democracy, and the "don't care" about trifles, and the disregard which she shows of all the fine principles which we were solemnly affirming at the foundation of the city—as when we said that, except in the case of some rare natures, never will there be a good man who from his early youth has not made things of beauty an amusement and also a study—how grandly does she trample all that under foot, never giving a thought to the pursuits which make a statesman, and is satisfied to honor a man who says that he is the people's friend.

Yes, he said, that is glorious.

These and other kindred characteristics are proper to democracy, which is a charming form of government, full of variety and diversity, and dispensing equality to equals and unequals alike.

That, he said, is sufficiently well-known.

Consider now, I said, what manner of man the individual is, or rather consider, as in the case of the State, how he is created.

Very good, he said.

Is not this the way,—he is the son of the miserly and oligarchical father who has trained him in his own habits?

Exactly.

[14] An Athenian judicial officer corresponding somewhat to our juryman.

And, like his father, he keeps under the pleasures which are of the spending and not of the getting sort, being those which are called by us unnecessary. The argument will be clearer if we here distinguish which are the necessary and which are the unnecessary pleasures.

I should like to do that.

Necessary pleasures are those of which we cannot get rid, and which benefit us when they are satisfied; both kinds are rightly called necessary, because our nature is necessarily attracted to them.

True.

And therefore we are not wrong in calling them necessary? 559

We are not.

Again, as to the desires which a man may get rid of, if he makes that his object when young, the presence of which, moreover, does no good, and in some cases the reverse of good,—shall we not be right in saying that all these are unnecessary?

Yes, certainly.

Suppose we select an example of either kind, in order that we may have a general notion of them?

Very good.

Will not the desire of eating, that is, of simple food and condiments, as far as they are required for health and strength, be of the necessary class?

That is what I should suppose.

The pleasure of eating is necessary in two ways,—first as beneficial, and also as needed for the support of life?

Yes.

But the condiments are only necessary as being good for health?

Certainly.

And the desire which goes beyond this of viands of a less simple kind, which might generally be got rid of, if controlled and trained in youth, and is hurtful to the body and hurtful to the soul in the pursuit of wisdom and virtue, may be rightly called unnecessary?

Very right.

May we not say that these spend and the other desires make money, because they are of use with a view to production?

Certainly.

And of the pleasures of love, and all other pleasures, the same holds good?

True.

And the drone of which we were speaking meant him who was surfeited in pleasures and desires of this sort, and was governed by the unnecessary desires, whereas he who was governed by the necessary was miserly and oligarchical?

Very true, he said.

Again, I said, let us see how the democratical man grows out of the oligarchical: the following, as I suspect, is commonly the process.

What?

When a young man who has been brought up as we were just now describing, in a vulgar and miserly way, has tasted drones' honey and has come to associate with fierce and cunning natures who are able to provide for him all sorts of refinements and varieties of pleasure,—then, as you may imagine, the change will begin of the oligarchical principle within him into the democratical.

That, he said, is the inevitable result.

And as in the city like was helping like, and the change was effected by an alliance from without assisting one division of the citizens, so the young man also changes by a class of desires from without assisting a class of those within, that which is akin and alike again helping that which is akin and alike.

Certainly.

And if there be any ally which aids the oligarchical side, whether the influence of friends or kindred, advising or rebuking him, then there arises a faction and an opposite faction, and the result is a civil war.

Certainly.

And there are times when the democratical principle gives way to the oligarchical, and some of his desires die, and others are banished; a spirit of reverence enters into the young man's soul and order is restored.

Yes, he said, that sometimes happens.

And then, again, after the old desires have been driven out fresh ones spring up, which are like them; they have never known a parent's discipline, and this makes them fierce and numerous.

Yes, he said, that often occurs.

They draw him to his old associates, and holding secret intercourse with him, breed and muster in him? [15]

Very true.

At length they seize upon the citadel of the young man's soul, which they perceive to be void of all fair accomplishments and pursuits and of every true word, which are the best guardians and sentinels in the minds of men dear to the gods.

None better.

False and boastful words and conceits grow up instead of them, and take the same position in him?

Yes, he said; indeed they do.

And so the young man returns into the country of the lotus-eaters,[16] and takes up his abode there in the face of all men, and if any help be sent by his friends to the oligarchical part of him, the vain conceits shut the gate of the king's fastness; they will not allow the new ally to pass. And if ambassadors, venerable for their age, come and parley, they refuse to listen to them; there is a battle and they win: then modesty, which they call silliness, is ignominiously thrust into exile by them. They affirm temperance to be unmanliness, and her also they contemptuously eject; and they pretend that moderation and orderly expenditure are vulgarity and meanness; and, with a company of vain appetites at their heels, they drive them beyond the border.

Yes, with right good will.

And when they have made a sweep of the soul of him who is now in their power, and is being initiated by them in great

---

[15] "When the unclean spirit is gone out of a man, he walketh through dry places, seeking rest; and finding none, he saith, I will return unto my house whence I came out. And when he cometh, he findeth it swept and garnished. Then goeth he and taketh to him seven other spirits more wicked than himself; and they enter in and dwell there; and the last state of that man is worse than the first."—Luke xi. 24-26.

[16] According to Homeric legend, Odysseus in his wanderings came to a land whose people ate only the fruit and blossom of a plant called the lotus. Those who tasted this food wished to remain there forever and lost all desire for home.

> " Whoever tasted once of that sweet food
> Wished not to see his native country more,
> Nor give his friends the knowledge of his fate.
> And then my messengers desired to dwell
> Among the Lotus-eaters, and to feed
> Upon the lotus, never to return."
> —BRYANT'S HOMER.

See Tennyson's " Lotus Eaters."

mysteries,[17] the next thing is to bring back to their house insolence and anarchy and waste and impudence in bright array, having garlands on their heads, with a great company, while they hymn their praises and call them by sweet names; insolence they term breeding, and anarchy liberty, and waste magnificence, and impudence courage. In this way the young man passes out of his original nature, which was trained in the school of necessity, into the freedom and libertinism of useless and unnecessary pleasures.

561

Yes, he said, that is obviously the way.

When the change has been made he lives on, spending his money and labor and time on unnecessary pleasures quite as much as on necessary ones; but if he be fortunate, and is not too much intoxicated with passion, when he gets older, after the tumult of freedom has mostly passed away—supposing that he then re-admits into the city some part of the exiled virtues, and does not wholly give himself up to their successors—in that case he balances his pleasures and lives in a sort of equilibrium, putting the government of himself into the hands of the one that offers and wins the turn; and when he has had enough of that, then into the hands of another, and is very impartial in his encouragement of them all.

Very true, he said.

Neither does he receive or admit into the fortress any true word of advice; if any one says to him that some pleasures are the satisfactions of good and noble desires, and others of evil desires, and that he ought to use and honor some and curtail and reduce others—whenever this is repeated to him he shakes his head and says that they are all alike, and that one is as honorable as another.

Why, yes, he said; that is the sort of man, and that is his way of behaving.

Yes, I said, he lives through the day indulging the appetite of the hour; and sometimes he is lapped in drink and strains of the flute; then he is for total abstinence, and tries to get thin; then, again, he is at gymnastics; sometimes idling and neglecting everything, then once more living the life of a philosopher; often he is at politics, and starts to his feet and says and does anything that may turn up; and, if he is emulous of any one who is a warrior, off he is in that direction, or

---

[17] In allusion to the religious mysteries. See Symposium, note 32.

of men of business, once more in that. His life has neither order nor law; and this is the way of him—this he terms joy and freedom and happiness.

Yes, he said, there is liberty, equality, and fraternity enough in him.

Yes, I said; he may be described as—

> "A man so various that he seems to be
> Not one, but all mankind's epitome."

He is, like the State, a rare being, and has many forms. And many a man and many a woman will emulate him, and many a constitution and many an example of life is contained in him.

That is true.

Let him then be set over against democracy; he may truly be called the democratic man.

Let that be his place, he said.

And now comes the most beautiful of all, man and State alike, tyranny and the tyrant; these we have to consider.

Quite true, he said.

Say then, my friend, how does tyranny arise—out of democracy of course?

Clearly.

And does not tyranny spring from democracy in the same way as democracy from oligarchy—I mean, after a sort?

How is that?

The good which oligarchy proposed was excess of wealth; in this oligarchy originated. Am I not right?

Yes.

And the insatiable desire of wealth, and the neglect of all other things for the sake of money-getting, was also the ruin of oligarchy?

True.

And democracy has a notion of good, the insatiable desire of which also brought her to an end?

What notion of good?

Freedom, I replied; that, as people often say, is best in a democracy—and, therefore, in a democracy only will the freedom of nature deign to dwell.

Why, said he, that is very often said.

And, I was going to observe, that the insatiable desire of

this and the neglect of other things, introduces the change in democracy, which occasions a demand for tyranny.

How is that?

When a democracy which is thirsting for freedom has evil cup-bearers presiding over the feast, and has drunk too deeply of the strong wine of freedom, then, unless her rulers are very amenable and give a plentiful draught, she calls them to account and punishes them, and says that they are cursed oligarchs.

Yes, he replied, that is a very common thing.

Yes, I said; and loyal citizens are insulted by her as lovers of slavery and men of naught; she would have subjects who are like rulers, and rulers who are like subjects: these are men after her own heart, whom she praises and honors both in private and public. Now, in such a State, can liberty have any limit?

Certainly not.

Nay, I said, the anarchy grows and finds a way into private houses, and ends by getting among the animals and infecting them.

How do you mean?

I mean that the father gets accustomed to descend to the level of his sons and to fear them, and the son to be on a level with his father, he having no shame or fear of either of his parents; and this is his freedom, and the metic [18] is equal with the citizen and the citizen with the metic, and the stranger on a level with either.

Yes, he said, that is true.

That is true, I said; and, moreover, little things of this sort happen: the master fears and flatters his scholars, and the scholars despise their masters and tutors; and, in general, young and old are alike, and the young man is on a level with the old, and is ready to compete with him in word or deed; and old men condescend to the young, and are full of pleasantry and gayety; they do not like to be thought morose and authoritative, and therefore they imitate the young.

Quite true, he said.

The last extreme of popular liberty is when the slave bought with money, whether male or female, is just as free as his or

---

[18] Metic (mē'tĭc): In Athens, a resident alien who paid a certain tax but had no civic rights. (L. and S.)

her purchaser; nor must I forget to tell of the liberty and equality of the two sexes in relation to each other.

Why not, he said, as Æschylus remarks, utter the word which rises to our lips?

Yes, I replied; that is what I am now doing; and I must say that no one who does not know would believe, how much greater is the liberty which animals who are under the dominion of men have in a democracy than in any other State: for truly, the she-dogs, as the proverb says, are as good as their she-mistresses, and the horses and asses come to have a way of marching along with all the rights and dignities of freemen; and they will run at anybody whom they meet in the street if he does not get out of their way: and all things are just ready to burst with liberty.

You tell me, he said, my own dream; for that which you describe often happens to me when I am taking a country walk.

And above all, I said, and as the result of all, see how sensitive the citizens become; they chafe impatiently at the least touch of authority, and at length, as you know, they cease to care even for the laws, written or unwritten; for they will have no one over them.

Yes, he said, that I know quite well.

And this, my friend, I said, is the fair and glorious beginning out of which springs tyranny.

Glorious indeed, he said. But what is the next step?

The ruin of oligarchy is the ruin of democracy; the same disorder intensified by liberty dominates over democracy, the truth being that the excessive increase of anything often causes a reaction in the opposite direction; and this is the case not only in the seasons and in vegetable and animal forms, but above all in forms of government.

564

That is very likely.

For excess of liberty, whether in States or individuals, seems only to pass into excess of slavery.

Yes, that is the natural order.

Then tyranny naturally arises out of democracy, and the most aggravated form of tyranny and slavery out of the most extreme form of liberty.

Yes, he said, there is reason in all that.

That, however, was not, as I believe, your question,—you

rather desired to know what is that disorder which is generated alike in oligarchy and democracy, and enslaves both?

True, he replied.

Well, I said, I meant to refer to the class of idle spendthrifts, of whom the more courageous are the leaders and the more timid the followers, the same whom we were comparing to drones, some stingless, and others having stings.

A very just comparison, he said.

These two classes are the plagues of every city in which they are generated, being what phlegm and bile are to the body. And the good physician and lawgiver of the State ought, like the wise bee-master, to keep them at a distance and prevent, if possible, their ever coming in; and if they have anyhow found a way in, then he should have them and their cells cut out as speedily as possible.

Yes, indeed, he said, that he should.

Then, in order that we may see more clearly what we are doing, let us imagine democracy to be divided into three classes, which also exist in fact; for liberty creates drones quite as much in the democratic as in the oligarchical State.

That is true.

But in the democracy they are more intensified.

How is that?

The reason is, that in the oligarchical State, as they are disqualified and driven from power, they cannot train or gather strength; whereas in a democracy they are almost the entire ruling power, and the keener sort speak and act, while the rest sit buzzing about the bema [19] and will not suffer a word to be said on the other side; and hence there is hardly anything in these States which is not their doing.

Very true, he said.

Then there is another class which is divided from the multitude.

What is that?

The richest class, which in a nation of traders is generally the most orderly.

That may be assumed.

They are the most squeezable persons and yield the largest amount of honey to the drones.

[19] The platform from which a speaker addressed an assembly.

Why, he said, there is little to be squeezed out of people who have little.

And this is called the wealthy class, and the drones feed upon them.

That is pretty much the case, he said.

565

There is also a third class, consisting of working men, who are not politicians, and have little to live upon. And this, when assembled, is the largest and most powerful class in a democracy.

Why, that is true, he said; but then the multitude is seldom willing to meet unless they get a little honey.

And do they not share? I said. Do not their leaders take the estates of the rich, and give to the people as much of them as they can, consistently with keeping the greater part themselves?

Why, yes, he said, to that extent the people do share.

And the persons whose property is taken from them are compelled to defend themselves as they best can.

Of course.

And then, although they may have no desire of change, the others charge them with plotting against the State and being friends of oligarchy?

True.

And the end is that when they see the people, not of their own accord, but through ignorance, and because they are deceived by slanderers, seeking to do them wrong, then at last they are forced to become oligarchs in reality, and this is occasioned by the stings of the drones goading them?

Exactly.

Then come impeachments and judgments and trials of one another.

True.

The people have always some one as a champion whom they nurse into greatness.

Yes, that is their way.

And this is the very root from which a tyrant springs; when he first appears above ground he is a protector.

Yes, that is quite clear.

How then does a protector begin to change into a tyrant?

Clearly when he does what the man is said to do in the tale of the Arcadian temple of Lycæan Zeus.[20]

[20] Lycæus (ly-sē'us): a lofty mountain of Arcadia in southern Greece, was one of the chief seats of the worship of Zeus.

What tale?

The tale is that he who has tasted the entrails of a single human victim minced up with the entrails of other victims is destined to become a wolf. Did you never hear that?

O yes.

And the protector of the people is like him, having a mob entirely at his disposal, he is not restrained from shedding the blood of kinsmen; by the favorite method of false accusation he brings them into court and murders them, making the life of man to disappear, and with unholy tongue and lips tasting the blood of kindred; some he kills and others he banishes, at the same time proclaiming abolition of debts and partition of lands; and after this, what can be his destiny but either to perish at the hands of his enemies, or from being a man to become a wolf—that is a "tyrant?"

566

That is inevitable.

This, I said, is he who begins to make a party against the rich.

The same.

And then he is driven out, and comes back, in spite of his enemies, a tyrant full made.

That is clear.

And if they are unable to drive him out, or get him condemned to death by public opinion, they form the design of putting him out of the way secretly.

Yes, he said, that is the usual plan.

Then comes the famous request of a body-guard, which is made by all those who have got thus far in their career, "Let not the people's friend," as they say, "be lost to them."

Exactly.

This the people readily grant; all their fears are for him—they have no fear for themselves.

Very true.

And when a man who is wealthy and is also accused of being an enemy of the people sees this, then, my friend, as the oracle said to Crœsus,—

"By pebbly Hermas' shore he flees and rests not, and is not ashamed to be a coward." [21]

[21] Part of the reply made by the oracle of Apollo at Delphi to Crœsus, king of Lydia, when he inquired of the god whether he should go to war with Cyrus, king of Persia.

And quite right too, said he, for, if he were ashamed, he would never be ashamed again.

Yes, I said, and he who is caught is put to death.[22]

Inevitably.

And he, the protector of whom we spake, is not fallen in his might, but himself the overthrower of many, is to be seen standing up in the chariot of State with the reins in his hand, no longer protector, but tyrant absolute.

No doubt, he said.

And now let us tell of the happiness of the man, and also of the State, in which this sort of creature is generated.

Yes, he said, let us tell of that.

At first, in the early days of his power, he smiles upon every one and salutes every one; he to be called a tyrant, who is making promises in public and also in private! liberating debtors, and distributing land to the people and to his followers, and wanting to be kind and good to every one.

That is the regular thing.

But when he has got rid of foreign enemies, and is reconciled with some of them and has destroyed others, and there is nothing to fear from them, then he is always stirring up some war or other, in order that the people may require a leader.

Yes, that may be expected of him.

Has he not also another object, which is that they may be impoverished by payment of taxes, and thus compelled to devote themselves to their daily wants, and therefore less likely to plot against him?

Clearly.

Yes, and if he suspects any of them of having notions of freedom, and of being disloyal to him, he has a good pretext for destroying them by giving them up to the enemy; and for all these reasons the tyrant is always compelled to be getting up a war.

That is inevitable.

Now he begins to grow unpopular.

That is the necessary result.

Then some of those who joined in setting him up, and who are in power—that is to say, the most courageous of them—speak their minds to him and to one another, and cast in his teeth the things which are being done.

[22] Note the fate of Polemarchus, Republic, I., note 1.

Yes, that is to be expected.

And the tyrant, if he means to rule, must get rid of them; he cannot stop while he has a friend or an enemy who is good for anything.

That is plain.

And therefore he must use his eyes and see who is valiant, who is high-minded, who is wise, who wealthy; happy man, he is the enemy of them all, and must seek occasion against them whether he will or no, until he has made a purgation of the State.

Yes, he said, and a rare purgation.

Yes, I said, not the sort of purgation which the physicians make of the body; for they take away the worse and leave the better part, but he does the opposite.

I suppose that he cannot help himself, he replied.

What a blessed alternative, I said, to be compelled to dwell only with the many bad, and hated by them, or not to live at all.

Yes, that is the alternative.

And the more detestable he is in his actions the more body-guards and the greater devotion in them will he require?

Certainly.

And who are the devoted band, and where will he procure them?

They will flock to him, he said, of their own accord, if he pays them.

By the dog! I said, you are again introducing drones out of other lands and of every sort.

Yes, he said, that I am.

But will he not desire to get them on the spot?

How do you mean?

He will emancipate the slaves and enroll them in his body-guard?

To be sure, he said, and he will be able to trust them best of all.

What a blessed fellow, I said, must this tyrant be; when he has put to death the others he has only these for his trusted friends.

Yes, he said, and they are his friends.

Yes, I said, and these are the new citizens whom he has called into existence, who admire him and live with him, while the good hate and avoid him.

Of course.

Verily, then, tragedy is a wise thing and Euripides a great tragedian.

Why do you say that?

Why, because he is the author of that rare saying,—

"Tyrants are wise by living with the wise;"

and he clearly meant to say that they are the wise with whom the tyrant lives.

Yes, he said, and he also praises tyranny as godlike: this and many other things of the same kind are said by him and the other poets.

And therefore, I said, the tragic poets in their wisdom will forgive us and others who have a similar form of government, if we object to having them in our State, because they are the eulogists of tyranny.

Yes, he said, those who have the wit will doubtless forgive us.

Yes, I said, and they go about to other cities and attract mobs; and have voices fair and loud and persuasive, and draw the cities over to tyrannies and democracies.

Very true.

Moreover, they are paid for this and receive honor—the greatest honor from tyrants, and the next greatest from democracies; but the higher they ascend our constitution hill, the more their reputation fails, and seems unable from shortness of breath to proceed further.

True.

But we are digressing. Let us therefore return and inquire how the tyrant will maintain that fair and numerous and various and ever-changing army of his.

If, he said, there are sacred treasures in the city, he will spend them as far as they go; that is obvious. And he will then be able to diminish the taxes which he would otherwise have to impose.

And when these fail?

Why, clearly, he said, then he and his boon companions, whether male or female, will be maintained out of his father's estate.

I see your meaning, I said. You mean that the people who begat him will maintain him and his companions?

Yes, he said; he cannot get on without that.

But what if the people go into a passion, and aver that a grown-up son ought not to be supported by his father, but that the father should be supported by the son? He did not bring his son into the world and establish him in order that when he was grown up he himself might serve his own servants, and maintain him and his rabble of slaves and companions; but that, having such a protector, he might be emancipated from the government of the rich and aristocratic, as they are termed. And now, here is this son of his, bidding him and his companions pack, just as a father might drive out of his house a riotous son and his party of revelers.

In the end, he said, the parent will be certain to discover what a monster he has been fostering in his bosom; and when he wants to drive him out, he will find that he is weak and his son strong.

Why, you do not mean to say that the tyrant will use violence? What! beat his father if he resists?

Yes, he will; and he will begin by taking away his arms.

Then he is a parricide, and a cruel unnatural son to an aged parent whom he ought to cherish; and this is real tyranny, about which there is no mistake: as the saying is, the people who would avoid the slavery of freemen, which is smoke and appearance, has fallen under the tyranny of slaves, which is fire. Thus liberty, getting out of all order and reason, passes into the harshest and bitterest form of slavery.

Yes, he said, that is true.

Very well, I said; and may we not say that we have discussed enough the nature of tyranny, and the manner of the transition from democracy to tyranny?

Yes, quite enough, he said.

BOOK IX

LAST of all comes the tyrannical man; about whom we have once more to ask how is he formed out of the democratical? and how does he live, in happiness or in misery? 571

Yes, he said, he is the only one remaining.

There is, however, I said, a previous question which I should like to consider.

What is that?

I do not think that we have adequately determined the nature and number of the appetites, and until this is accomplished the inquiry will always be perplexed.

Well, but you may supply the omission.

Very true, I said; and observe the point which I want to understand. Certain of the unnecessary pleasures and appetites are deemed to be unlawful; every man appears to have them, only in some persons they are controlled by the laws and by reason, and the better desires prevail over them, and either they are wholly banished or are few and weak: while in the case of others they are stronger, and there are more of them.

Which appetites do you mean?

I mean those which are awake when the reasoning and taming and ruling power is asleep; the wild beast in our nature, gorged with meat or drink, starts up and walks about naked, and surfeits after his manner, and there is no conceivable folly or crime, however shameless or unnatural—not excepting incest or parricide, or the eating of forbidden food—of which such a nature may not be guilty.

That is most true, he said.

But when a man's pulse is healthy and temperate, and he goes to sleep cool and rational, after having supped on a feast of reason and speculation, and come to a knowledge of himself, having indulged appetites neither too much nor too little, but just enough to lay them to sleep, and prevent them and their enjoyments and pains from interfering with the higher principle—leaving that in the solitude of pure abstraction, free to contemplate and aspire to the knowledge of the unknown, whether in past, present, or future: when, again, 572

he has allayed the passionate element, if
 ...nst any one—I say, when, after pacifying
 ...rinciples, he rouses up the third or rational
 ... takes his rest, then, as you know, he attains
 ...y, and is least likely to be the sport of fanciful
 ...ions.

 ...nion I entirely agree.

this I have been running into a digression; but
the po... which I desire to note is that in all of us, even in
good men, there is such a latent wild-beast nature, which peers
out in sleep. Pray, consider whether I am right, and you
agree with me in this view.

Yes, I agree.

Remember then the character which we assigned to the democratic man. He was supposed from his youth upwards to have been trained under a miserly parent, and to have encouraged the saving appetites, and discountenanced the lighter and more ornamental ones?

True.

And then he got into the company of a more refined, licentious sort of people, and he took to wantonness, and began to have a dislike of his father's narrow ways. At last, being a better man than his corruptors, he came to a mean, and led a life, not of lawless and slavish passion, but of regular and successive indulgence. That was our view of the way in which the democrat was generated out of the oligarch?

Yes, he said; and that is still our view.

And now, I said, years will have passed away, and you must imagine this man, such as he is, to have a son, who is brought up in his father's principles; and then further imagine the same thing to happen to the son which has already happened to the father—he is seduced into a perfectly lawless life, which is termed perfect liberty; and his father and friends take part with his moderate desires, while others assist the opposite ones. At length, these dire magicians and tyrant-makers begin to fear that they will be unable to hold the youth, and then they contrive to implant in him a master passion, to be lord over his idle and spendthrift desires—like a monster drone having wings. That is the only image which will depict him and his lusts.

Yes, he said, that is the best, the only image of him.

And while the other lusts amid clouds of incense and perfumes and garlands and wines, and all the dissoluteness of social life are buzzing around him and flattering him to the utmost, there is implanted in him the sting of desire, and then this lord of the soul is in a frenzy—madness is the captain of the guard —and if he discerns in his soul any opinions or appetites which may be regarded as good, and which have any sense of shame remaining, he puts an end to them, and casts them forth until he has purged away temperance and brought in madness to the full.

Yes, he said, that is the way in which the tyrannical man is generated.

And is not this the reason why of old love has been called a tyrant?

Yes, perhaps.

Further, I said, has not a drunken man also the spirit of a tyrant?

True.

And you know that a man who is deranged and not right in his mind, will fancy that he is able to rule, not only over men, but also over the gods?

True.

And the tyrannical man comes into being just at that point when either under the influence of nature, or habit, or both, he becomes drunken, lustful, passionate?

Exactly.

Such is the man and such is his origin. And next, how does he live?

That, as people facetiously say, you may as well tell me.

I imagine, I said, as the next step in his progress, that there will be feasts and carousals and revellings, and courtesans, and all that sort of thing; love is the lord of the house within him, who orders all the concerns of the soul.

That is certain.

Yes; and every day and every night desires grow up many and formidable, and their demands are many.

They are indeed, he said.

His revenues, if he has any, are soon spent.

True.

Then he borrows money, and his estate is taken from him.

Of course.

When he has nothing left, must not his desires, crowding in the nest like young ravens, be crying aloud for food ; he, goaded on by them, and especially by love himself on whom they dance attendance, is at his wits' end to discover whom he can defraud or despoil of his property, in order that he may gratify them?

Yes, that is sure to be the case.

He must have money, and no matter how, if he is to escape horrid pangs and pains.

He must.

And as in himself there was a succession of pleasures, and the new got the better of the old and took away their rights, so he being younger will claim to have more than his father and his mother, and if he has spent his own property, he will take a slice out of theirs.

No doubt of that.

And if his parents will not suffer this, then he will try to cheat and deceive them.

Very true.

And if he cannot, then he will plunder and force them.

Yes, probably.

And if the old man and the old woman hold out against him, will he be very careful of doing anything which is tyrannical?

Nay, he said, I should not feel at all comfortable about his parents.

But, O heavens! Adeimantus, on account of some newfangled love of a harlot, who is anything but a necessary connection, can you believe that he would strike the mother who is his ancient friend and necessary to his very existence, and would place her under the authority of the other, when she is brought under the same roof with her ; or that, under like circumstances, he would do the same to his withered old father, first and most indispensable of friends, for the sake of some blooming love of a youth who is the reverse of indispensable?

Yes, indeed, he said ; I believe that he would.

Truly, then, I said, a tyrannical son is a blessing to his father and mother.

Yes, indeed, he replied.

He first takes their property, and when that fails, and pleasures are beginning to swarm in the hive of his soul, then he breaks into a house, or steals the garments of some nightly wayfarer, and the next thing is that he lifts a temple; and while all this is going on, the old opinions about good and evil which he had when a child, and which were thought by him to be right, are overthrown by those others which have just been emancipated, and are now the guard and associates of love, being those which in former days, when he was a partisan of democracy and subject to the laws and to his father, were only let loose in the dreams of sleep. But now that he is under the tyranny of love, he becomes always and in waking reality what he was then very rarely and in a dream only; he will commit the foulest murder, or eat forbidden food, or be guilty of any other horrid act. Love is his tyrant, and lives lordly in him, and being himself a king emancipated from all control, he leads him on—like man like State—into the performance of reckless deeds in order to maintain himself and his rabble, which evil communications have brought in from without, or which he himself has allowed to break loose within him by reason of a similar character in himself. Is not this a picture of his way of life? 575

Yes, indeed, he said.

And if there are only a few of them, and the rest of the people are well disposed, they go away and become the bodyguard or mercenary soldiers of some other tyrant who may probably want them for a war; and if there is no war, they stay at home and do mischief in the city.

What sort of mischief?

For example, they are the thieves, burglars, cutpurses, footpads, robbers of temples, man-stealers of the community, and if they are able to speak they play the part of informers, and bear false witness, and take bribes.

And these, he replied, are not very small evils, even if the perpetrators of them are a few in number.

Yes, I said; but small and great are comparative terms, and all these things, in the misery and evil which they inflict upon a State, do not come within a thousand miles of the tyrant: the people are fools, and this class and their followers grow numerous and are aware of their numbers, and they take him who has most of the tyrant in his soul, and make him their leader.

Yes, he said, that is natural; for he will be the most tyrannically disposed.

If the people yield, well and good; but if they resist him, as he began by beating his own father and mother, so now, if he has the power, he beats his dear old fatherland and motherland, as the Cretans say, and brings in his young retainers to be their rulers and masters. And this is the end of his passions and desires.

Exactly.

Even in early days and before they get power, this is the way of them; they associate only with their own flatterers or ready tools; or, if they want anything from anybody, they themselves are equally ready to fall down before them; there is no attitude into which they will not throw themselves, but when they have gained their point they know them no more.

576

Yes, truly.

They are always either the masters or servants and never the friends of anybody; the tyrant never tastes of true freedom or true friendship.

Certainly not.

And may we not call such men treacherous?

No question.

Also they are utterly unjust, if we were right in our notion of justice?

Yes, he said, and in that we were perfectly right.

Let us then sum up in a word, I said, the character of the worst man: he is the waking reality of what we dreamed.

Most true.

And this is he who being most of a tyrant by nature bears rule, and the longer he lives the more of a tyrant he becomes.

That is certain, said Glaucon, taking his turn to answer.

And will not he who has been shown to be the wickedest, be also the most miserable? and he most of all and longest of all who has tyrannized longest and most, and is most of a tyrant—although this may not be the opinion of men in general?

Yes, he said, that is inevitable.

And must not the tyrannical man be like the tyrannical State, and the democratical man like the democratical State; and the same of the others?

Certainly

And as State is to State in virtue and happiness, man is to man?

To be sure.

Then comparing the former city which was under a king and the city which was under a tyrant, how do they stand as to virtue?

They are the opposite extremes, he said, for one is the very best and the other is the very worst.

There can be no mistake, I said, as to which is which, and therefore I will at once inquire whether you would arrive at a similar decision about their relative happiness and misery. And here we must not allow ourselves to be panic-stricken at the apparition of the tyrant, who is only a unit and may perhaps have a few retainers about him; but let us go as we ought and view the whole city and look all around, and then we will give our opinion.

A fair invitation, he replied; and I see, as every one must, that a tyranny is the wretchedest form of government, and monarchy the happiest.

And may I not fairly ask in like manner to have a judge of the men whose mind can enter into and see through human nature; he must not be a child who looks at the outside and is dazzled at the pompous aspect which tyranny assumes to the beholder, but let him be one who has a clear insight. May I suppose that the judgment is given in the hearing of us all by one who is able to judge, and has dwelt in the same place with him, and been present at his daily life and known him in his family, in which he is seen stripped of his tragedy attire, and again in the hour of public danger; he shall tell us about the happiness and misery of the tyrant when compared with other men?

That again, he said, is a very fair proposal.

Let us now assume this able and experienced judge to be ourselves, and then we shall have some one who will answer our inquiries.

By all means.

Let us ask you not to forget the parallel of the individual and the State; bearing this in mind, and glancing in turn from one to the other of them, will you tell me their respective conditions?

In what points? he asked.

Beginning with the State, I replied, would you say that a city which is governed by a tyrant is free or enslaved?

Nothing, he said, can be more completely enslaved.

And yet, as you see, there are masters and there are freemen in such a State?

Yes, he said, I see that there are,—a few; but the people as a whole (speaking generally) and the best of them are disgracefully and miserably enslaved.

Then if the man is like the State, I said, must not the same hold of the man? his soul is full of meanness and serfdom,—the best elements in him are enslaved; and there is a small ruling part which is also the worst and maddest.

That is inevitable.

And would you say that the soul of such an one is the soul of a freeman or of a slave?

He has the soul of a slave, in my judgment.

And the State which is enslaved under a tyrant is very far from acting voluntarily?

Very far, indeed.

And also the soul which is under a tyrant (I am speaking of the soul taken as a whole) is very far from doing as she desires; there is a gadfly which goads her, and she is full of trouble and remorse?

Certainly.

And is the city which is under a tyrant rich or poor?

Poor.

And the tyrannical soul must be always poor and insatiable?

True.

578 And must not such a State and such a man be always full of fear?

Yes, indeed.

Is there any State in which you will find more of lamentation and sorrow and groaning and pain?

Certainly not.

And is there any man in whom you will find more misery of the same kind than in the tyrannical man, who is in a fury of passions and desires?

Impossible.

Reflecting then upon these and similar evils, you held the tyrannical State to be the most miserable of States?

And I was right, he said.

Certainly, I said. And when you see the same evils in the tyrannical man, what do you say of him?

I say that he is by far the most miserable of all men.

There, I said, I think that you are wrong.

How is that? he said.

I do not think that he has as yet reached the utmost extreme of misery.

Then who is more miserable?

One of whom I am about to speak.

Who is that?

He who is of a tyrannical nature, and instead of leading a private life is cursed with the further misfortune of being a public tyrant.

I should conjecture from the previous remarks that you are right.

Yes, I said; but in this high argument of good and evil you should not conjecture only—you should have a certainty.

That is very true, he said.

Let me then offer you an illustration, which may, I think, have an application to this subject.

What is your illustration?

The case of rich individuals in cities who possess many slaves: from them you may form an idea of the tyrant's State, for they both have slaves; the only difference is that he has more slaves.

Yes, that is the difference.

You know that they live securely and have no fear of their servants?

What should they fear?

Nothing. But do you observe the reason of this?

Yes; the reason is, that the whole city is leagued together for the protection of each individual.

That is quite true, I said. But imagine that one of these owners is carried off by a god into the wilderness, where there are no freemen to help him—he and his household, and he is the master say of about fifty slaves—will he not be in an agony of apprehension lest he and his wife and children should be put to death by his slaves?

Yes, he said, he will be in the utmost alarm.

Will he not be compelled to flatter divers of his slaves, and make many promises to them of freedom and other things much against his will?—he will become the servant of his servants.

Yes, he said, that will be the only way of saving his life.

And suppose that the same god who carries him off puts him down among neighbors who will not allow a man to be the master of another, and, if they catch him, are ready to inflict capital punishment upon him?

Then his case will be even worse, he said, when he is surrounded and watched by enemies.

And is not this the sort of prison in which the tyrant will be bound?—he being by nature such as we have described, is full of all sorts of fears and lusts. His soul is dainty and greedy, and yet he only, of all men, is never allowed to go on a journey, or to see the things which other freemen desire to see, but he lives in his hole like a woman hidden in the house, and is jealous of any other citizen who goes into foreign parts and sees anything of interest.

Very true, he said.

Such being his evil condition, am I not right in saying that the tyrannical man, ill-governed in his own person, whom you just now described as the most miserable of all, will be yet more miserable in a public station, when, instead of leading a private life, he is constrained by fortune to be a tyrant? He has to be master of others when he is not master of himself: he is like a diseased or paralytic man who is compelled to pass his life, not in retirement, but fighting and combating with other men.

Yes, he said, that is very true, and the similitude is most exact.

Is not his case utterly miserable? and does not the actual tyrant lead a worse life than him whom you determined to be worst?

Certainly.

He who is the real tyrant, whatever men may think, is the real slave, and is obliged to practice the greatest adulation and servility, and to be the flatterer of the vilest of mankind. He has desires which he is utterly unable to satisfy, and has more wants than any one, and is truly poor, if you know how to inspect the whole soul of him: all his life long he is beset with fear and is full of convulsions and distractions, even as the State which he resembles; and surely the resemblance holds?

True, he said.

Moreover, as we were saying, he grows worse from having power: he becomes of necessity more jealous, more faithless, more unjust, more friendless, more impious; he entertains and nurtures every evil sentiment, and the consequence is that he is supremely miserable, and thus he makes everybody else equally miserable.

No man of any sense will dispute that.

Come then, I said, and as the umpire gives sentence in the games, do you also decide who in your opinion is first in the scale of happiness, and who second, and in what order the others follow: there are five of them in all—they are the royal, timocratical, oligarchical, democratical, tyrannical.

The judgment will be easily given, he replied; they shall be choruses entering on the stage, and I will decide the place of each of them by the criterion of virtue and vice, happiness and misery.

Need we hire a herald, or shall I proclaim the result—that the son of the best (Ariston)[1] is of opinion that the best and justest man is also the happiest, and that this is he who is the most royal master of himself; and that the worst and most unjust man is also the most miserable, and that this is he who is the greatest tyrant of himself and of his State?

Make the proclamation, he said.

And shall I proclaim further, "whether seen or unseen by gods and men?"

Yes, he said, you had better add that.

Then this, I said, will be the first proof; and there is another, which may also have some weight.

What is that?

The second proof is derived from the nature of the soul, seeing that the individual soul, like the State, has been divided by us into three principles,[2] the division may furnish a new demonstration.

Of what nature?

There are three pleasures which correspond to the three principles, and also three desires and governing powers.

How do you mean? he said.

There is one principle with which a man learns, another

---

[1] Glaucon, to whom Socrates was talking, was the son of Ariston. Ariston means literally *best*.
[2] See Book IV., 435-442.

with which he is angry; the third, having many forms, has no single name, but is termed appetitive, from the extraordinary strength and vehemence of the pleasures of eating and drinking and the other sensual appetites; also money loving, because this sort of desires can only be gratified by the help of money.

581

That is true, he said.

If we were to say that the loves and pleasures of this third part of the soul were concerned with gain, we should then be able to fall back on a single class; and might truly describe this part of the soul as loving gain or money.

Yes, I should say that.

Again, is not the passionate element wholly set on ruling and conquering and getting fame?

True.

Suppose we call that contentious or ambitious—would the term be suitable?

Extremely suitable.

On the other hand, every one sees that the principle of knowledge is wholly directed to the truth, and cares less than any of the others for gain or fame?

Far less.

"True lover of wisdom," "lover of knowledge," are titles which are rightly applicable to that part of the soul?

Certainly.

One principle prevails in the souls of one class of men, another in others, just as may happen?

Yes.

Then we may assume that there are three classes of men—lovers of wisdom, lovers of ambition, lovers of gain?

Exactly.

And there are three kinds of pleasures, which are their several objects?

Very true.

Now, if you examine the three classes, and ask of them in turn which of their lives is pleasantest, each of them will be found praising his own and depreciating that of others: the money-maker will contrast the vanity of honor or of learning with the solid advantages of gold and silver?

True, he said.

And the lover of honor—what will be his opinion? Will

he not think that the pleasure of riches is vulgar, while the pleasure of learning, which has no meed of honor, he regards as all smoke and nonsense?

True, he said.

But may we not suppose, I said, that philosophy estimates other pleasures as nothing in comparison with the pleasure of knowing the truth, and in that abiding, ever learning, in the pursuit of truth, not far indeed from the heaven of pleasure? The other pleasures the philosopher disparages by calling them necessary, meaning that if there were no necessity for them, he would not have them.

There ought to be no doubt about that, he replied.

Since, then, the pleasures of each class and the life of each are in dispute, and the question is not which life is more or less honorable, or better or worse, but which is the more pleasant or painless—how shall we know?

I cannot tell, he said.

Well, but what ought to be the criterion? Is any better than experience and wisdom and reason?

There cannot be a better, he said.

Then, I said, reflect. Of the three individuals, which has the greatest experience of all the pleasures which we enumerated? Has the lover of gain greater experience of the pleasure of knowledge derived from learning the nature of the truth than the philosopher has of the pleasure of gain?

The philosopher, he replied, has greatly the advantage; for he has always known the taste of the other pleasures from his youth upwards: but the lover of gain in all his experience has not of necessity tasted—or, I should rather say, could hardly have tasted by any process of learning the nature of things—the sweetness of intellectual pleasures.

Then the lover of wisdom has a great advantage over the lover of gain, for he has a double experience?

Very great indeed.

Again, has the philosopher greater experience of the pleasures of honor, or the lover of honor of the pleasures of knowledge?

Nay, he said, they are all honored in proportion as they attain their object; for the rich man and the brave man and the wise man alike have their crowd of worshippers, and as they all receive honor they all have experience of the pleasures of honor, but the delight which is to be found in the knowledge of true being is known to the philosopher only.

His experience, then, will enable him to judge better than any one?

Far better.

And he is the only one who has wisdom as well as experience?

Certainly.

The very faculty which is the instrument of judgment is not possessed by the covetous or avaricious man, but only by the philosopher?

What faculty?

Reason, which, as we were saying, ought to have the decision.

Yes.

And reasoning is peculiarly his instrument?

Certainly.

If wealth and gain were the criterion, then what the lover of gain praised and blamed would surely be truest?

Assuredly.

Or if honor or victory or courage, in that case the ambitious or contentious would decide best?

Clearly.

But since experience and wisdom and reason are the judges, the inference of course is, that the truest pleasures are those which are approved by the lover of wisdom and reason. And so we arrive at the result, that the pleasure of the intelligent part of the soul is the pleasantest of the three, and that he in whom this is the ruling principle has the pleasantest life?

583-585

Unquestionably, he said, the wise man has the fullest right to approve of his own life.

And what does the judge affirm to be the life which is next, and the pleasure which is next?

Clearly that of the soldier and lover of honor: that is nearer to himself than that of the trader.

Last comes the lover of gain.

Very true, he said.

Twice, then, has the just man overthrown the unjust; and now comes the third trial, which is sacred to the Olympic saviour Zeus[3] : a sage whispers in my ear that no pleasure except that of the wise is quite true and pure—all others are a shadow only; and this will surely prove the greatest and most decisive of falls?

Yes, the greatest; but will you explain how this is?

[Socrates leads a discussion intended to prove that the pleasures of the sensual and also of the spirited part of man's nature are less real and less satisfying than those of the rational part. He continues:]

Those then who know not wisdom and virtue, and are always busy with gluttony and sensuality, go down and up again as far as the mean; and in this space they move at random throughout life, but they never pass into the true upper world; thither they neither look, nor do they ever find their way, neither are they truly filled with true being, nor do they taste of true and abiding pleasure. Like brute animals, with their eyes down and bodies bent to the earth or leaning on the dining-table, they fatten and feed and breed, and, in their excessive love of these delights, they kick and butt at one another with horns and hoofs which are made of iron; and they kill one another by reason of their insatiable lust. For they fill themselves with that which is not substantial, and the part of themselves which they fill is also unsubstantial and incontinent.

586

Verily, Socrates, said Glaucon, you describe the life of the many like an oracle.

Their pleasures are mixed with pains. How can they be otherwise? For they are mere images and shadows of the true, and are colored only by contrast, and this way of looking at them doubly exaggerates them, and implants in the minds of fools insane desires of them; and they are fought about as Stesichorus says that the Greeks fought about the shadow of Helen at Troy[4] in ignorance of the truth.

Yes, inevitably, he said; that is the way.

---

[3] One of the titles of Zeus was saviour. The third cup of wine was dedicated to him. To drink this cup came to be a symbol of good luck, and the third time came to mean the lucky time. In allusion to this Socrates says the third victory of the just man should be dedicated to the Olympian saviour.

[4] See Phædrus, note 37. According to Stesichorus, Paris did not carry to Troy the real Helen, but only a phantom of her created by the goddess Hera (hē′ra), the Roman Juno.

And must not the like happen with the spirited or passionate element of the soul? Will not the passionate man be in the like case, if he carries his passion into act, either because he is envious and ambitious, or violent and contentious, or angry and discontented, and is seeking to attain honor and victory and the satisfaction of his anger without reason or sense?

Yes, he said, the same will happen with the spirited element also.

Then may we not confidently assert that the lovers of money and honor, when they seek their pleasures under the guidance and in the company of reason, and pursue after and win the pleasures which wisdom shows them, will also have the truest pleasures in the highest degree which is attainable to them, inasmuch as they follow truth; and they will also have those which are natural to them, if that which is best to each one is also most natural to him?

Yes, certainly; the best is the most natural.

Then, when the whole soul follows the philosophical principle, and there is no division, the several parts each of them do their own business, and are just, and each of them enjoy their own best and truest pleasures?

587

Exactly.

But when either of the other principles prevails, it fails in attaining its own pleasure, and compels the others to pursue after a shadow of pleasure which is not theirs?

True.

And the greater the interval which separates them from philosophy and reason, the more strange and illusive will be the pleasure?

Yes.

And that is farthest from reason which is at the greatest distance from law and order.

Clearly.

And the lustful and tyrannical desires are at the greatest distance?

Yes.

And the royal and orderly desires are nearest?

Yes.

Then the tyrant will live most unpleasantly, and the king most pleasantly?

Yes.

Would you know the measure of the interval between them? If you will tell me.

There appear to be three pleasures, one genuine and two spurious; now the transgression of the tyrant reaches a point beyond the spurious; he has run away from the region of law and reason, and taken up his abode with certain slave pleasures which are his satellites, and the measure of his inferiority can only be expressed in a figure.

[Here follows a curious, perhaps humorous, calculation to prove that the good king is 729 times happier than the tyrant.]

What a wonderful calculation! And how enormous is the interval which separates the just from the unjust in regard to pleasure and pain!

588

Yet a true calculation, I said, and a number which nearly concerns human life, if human life is concerned with days and nights and months and years.

Yes, he said, human life is certainly concerned with them.

Then if the good and just man be thus superior in pleasure to the evil and unjust, his superiority will be infinitely greater in propriety of life and in beauty and virtue?

Immeasurably greater, indeed, he said.

Well, I said, and now we have arrived at this point I may resume the beginning of the argument, which arose out of some one saying that injustice was a gain to the perfectly unjust who was reputed to be just. Was not that said?

Yes, that was said.

Come then, I said, and now that we have determined the power and quality of justice and injustice, let us have a word with him.

What shall we say to him?

Let us make an image of the soul, that he may have his own words presented before his eyes.

What sort of an image?

An ideal image of the soul, like the creations of ancient mythology, such as the Chimera [5] or Scylla [6] or Cerberus,[7] or

---

[5] See Phædrus, note 16.

[6] Scylla (sỹl'la): a sea-monster, variously described, usually with six heads, and lower limbs of barking dogs and serpents.

[7] Cerberus (sĕr'be-rus), a many-headed dog with serpents about his neck, stationed at the entrance to Hades. Different poets describe him differently.

any other in which two or more different natures are said to grow into one.

There are said to have been such unions.

Then do you now model the form of a multitudinous, polycephalous [a] beast, having a ring of heads of all manner of beasts, tame and wild, which he is able to generate and metamorphose at will.

That, he said, implies marvelous powers in the artist; but, as language is more pliable than wax or similar substances, I have done as you say.

Suppose now that you make a second form as of a lion, and a third of a man, the second smaller than the first, and the third smaller than the second.

That, he said, is an easier task; and I have made them as you say.

Then now join them, and let the three grow into one.

That has been accomplished.

Now fashion the outside into a single image, as of a man, so that he who is not able to look within, and sees only the outer hull or vessel, may believe the beast to be a single human creature.

That is completed, he said.

And now let us say to him who maintains the profitableness of justice and the unprofitableness of injustice, that his doctrine amounts to this: he is asserting that his interest is to feast and strengthen the lion and the lion-like qualities and to starve and weaken the man; who in consequence of this is at the mercy of either of the other two, and he is not to attempt to familiarize or harmonize them with one another: he ought rather to suffer them to fight and bite and devour one another.

Certainly, he said; that is what the approver of injustice says.

To him the supporter of justice makes answer that he ought rather to aim in all he says and does at strengthening the man within him, in order that he may be able to govern the many-headed monster. Like a good husbandman he should be watching and tending the gentle shoots, and preventing the wild ones from growing; making a treaty with the lion-heart, and uniting the several parts with one another and with themselves.

[a] Many-headed.

Yes, he said, that is quite what the maintainer of justice will say.

And in every point of view, whether of pleasure, honor, or advantage, the approver of justice is right and speaks the truth, and the disapprover is wrong, and false, and ignorant?

Yes, truly.

Come, now, and let us reason with the unjust, who is not intentionally in error. "Sweet Sir," we will say to him, "what think you of the noble and ignoble? Is not the noble that which subjects the beast to the man, or rather to the god in man; and the ignoble that which subjects the man to the beast?" He can hardly avoid admitting this,—can he now?

Not if he has any regard for my opinion.

But, if he admit this, we may ask him another question: How would a man profit if he received gold and silver on the condition that he was to enslave the noblest part of him to the worst? Who can imagine that a man who sold his son or daughter into slavery for money, especially if he sold them into the hands of fierce and evil men, would be the gainer, however large might be the sum which he received? And will any one say that he is not a miserable caitiff who sells his own divine being to that which is most atheistical and detestable, and has no pity? Eriphyle[9] took the necklace as the price of her husband's life, but he is taking a bribe in order to compass a worse ruin.

590

Yes, said Glaucon, far worse, I will answer for him.

Is not intemperance censured, I said, because in this condition that huge multiform monster is allowed to be too much at large?

Clearly.

And pride and sullenness are blamed, as occasioning the growth and increase of the lion and serpent element out of proportion?

Yes.

And luxury and softness are blamed, because they relax and weaken this same element, and make a man a coward?

Very true.

---

[9] Eriphyle (ĕr'ĭ-fȳ'le): according to legend, the sister of King Adrastus of Argos, and wife of Amphiarus, a sooth-sayer. It was agreed that when husband and brother differed in opinion, Eriphyle should decide between them. Once when the question was whether Amphiarus should go to a war, Eriphyle, for the bribe of a precious necklace, decided that he must go, though she knew from her husband's prophecy that he could not return alive.

And is not a man reproached for flattery and meanness who subordinates the spirited animal to the unruly monster, and, for the sake of money, of which he can never have enough, habituates him in the days of his youth to be trampled in the mud, and from being a lion to become a monkey?

True, he said.

And why are vulgarity and handicraft arts a reproach? Only because they imply a natural weakness of the higher principle, and the individual is unable to control the creatures within him, but has to court them, and his only study is how to flatter them?[10]

That appears to be true.

And, therefore, that he may be under the same rule as the best, we say that he ought to be the servant of the best; not, as Thrasymachus supposed, to the injury of him who served, but because every one had better be ruled by divine wisdom dwelling within him; or, if that be impossible, then by an external authority, in order that we may be all, as far as possible, under the same government?

True, he said.

And this is clearly seen to be the intention of the law, which is the ally of the whole city; and is seen also in the authority which is exerted over children, and the refusal to allow them to be free until the time when, as in a State, we have given them a constitution, and by cultivation of the higher element have established in their hearts a watchman and ruler like our own, and when this is done they may go their ways.

Yes, he said, that is a further proof.

In what point of view, then, and on what ground shall a man be profited by injustice or intemperance or other baseness, even though he acquire money or power?

There is no ground on which this can be maintained?

What shall he profit, if his injustice be undetected? for he who is undetected only gets worse, whereas he who is detected and punished has the brutal part of his nature silenced and humanized; the gentler element in him is liberated, and his whole soul is perfected and ennobled by the acquirement of justice and temperance and wisdom, more than the body ever is by receiving gifts of beauty, strength, and health, in proportion as the soul is more honorable than the body.

[10] See Book VI., 496.

Certainly, he said.

The man of understanding will concentrate himself on this as the work of life. And in the first place, he will honor studies which impress these qualities on his soul, and will disregard others?

Clearly, he said.

In the next place, he will keep under his body, and so far will he be from yielding to brutal and irrational pleasures, that he will regard even health as quite a secondary matter; his first object will be not that he may be fair or strong or well, unless he is likely thereby to gain temperance, but he will be always desirous of preserving the harmony of the body for the sake of the concord of the soul?

Certainly, he replied, that he will, if he has true music in him.

And there is a principle of order and harmony in the acquisition of wealth; this also he will observe, and will not allow himself to be dazzled by the opinion of the world, and heap up riches to his own infinite harm?

I think not, he said.

He will look at the city which is within him, and take care to avoid any change of his own institutions, such as might arise either from abundance or from want; and he will duly regulate his acquisition and expense, in so far as he is able?

Very true.

And for the same reason, he will accept such honors as he deems likely to make him a better man; but those which are likely to disorder his constitution, whether private or public honors, he will avoid?

Then, if this be his chief care, he will not be a politician.

By the dog of Egypt, he will! in the city which is his own, though in his native country perhaps not, unless some providential accident should occur.

I understand; you speak of that city of which we are the founders, and which exists in idea only; for I do not think that there is such an one anywhere on earth?

In heaven, I replied, there is laid up a pattern of such a city, and he who desires may behold this, and beholding, govern himself accordingly. But whether there really is or ever will be such an one is of no importance to him; for he will act according to the laws of that city and of no other?

True, he said.

BOOK X

Of the many excellences which I perceive in the order of our State, there is none which upon reflection pleases me better than the rule about poetry.

What rule?

The rule about rejecting imitative poetry, which certainly ought not to be received; as I see far more clearly now that the parts of the soul have been distinguished.

What do you mean by that?

Speaking in confidence, for I should not like to have my words repeated to the tragedians and the rest of the imitative tribe—but I do not mind saying to you that all poetical imitations are a sort of outrage on the understanding of the hearers, and that the only cure of this is the knowledge of their true nature.

Explain the purport of your remark.

Well, I will tell you: although I have always from my earliest youth had an awe and love of Homer, which even now makes the words falter on my lips, for he is the great captain and teacher of all that goodly band of Tragic writers; but a man is not to be reverenced before the truth, and therefore I will speak out.

Very good, he said.

Listen to me then, or rather, answer me.

Put your question.

Can you tell me what imitation is?

[Glaucon is afraid to reply and Socrates undertakes to explain as follows:

There are many beds in the world. They are all different, but all conform to a common plan or idea of what a bed should be. The makers of the beds have this idea in mind, but they themselves do not create the idea. The idea or perfect type is created by God. The beds which the carpenter makes are imperfect copies of the one perfect type. All carpenters are therefore imitators.

Again, the painter makes a picture of the bed. In so doing he imitates not the original bed or type made by God, but the imperfect copy made by the carpenter. Moreover a bed may be looked at from many points of view and appears different from each. The painter represents it as it appears from one point only. To take another instance, a painter may paint a cobbler or a carpenter, though he knows nothing of their arts. Therefore we see the art of painting is an imitation of appearances and the creations of the painter are far removed from reality or truth. In this sense any one may be a creator who catches in a mirror the reflection of the sun, or earth or anything else.

The poets are likewise imitators. They write charmingly about all the arts and virtues, but it is impossible from the very nature of knowledge for one person to know all these things. Moreover, any one who is able to make the original surely would not devote himself to making copies. The poet who had true knowledge of the arts and virtues, would leave many fair works as memorials of himself, instead of singing the praises of others who do accomplish these works. Homer, in his poems, deals with politics, education, military tactics, and the like. If he had had a knowledge of his subjects, if, for example, he had been a legislator or general, he would have made laws for the better government of some State or given his counsel in war. In reality, he did no public service nor did he act as guide and teacher to his friends. If Homer or Hesiod had been able to educate and improve mankind, they would have had many loving disciples who would not have allowed them to go about begging, or else would have followed them about in order to get an education. Now since none of these good works or good counsels may be ascribed to the poets, we may infer that they all, beginning with Homer, have been imitators. As a painter who understands nothing of cobbling may make the likeness of a cobbler, so the poets, in the color of language, present images of virtue and many arts whose nature they understand only enough to imitate them; and by the beauty of their melody they deceive the ignorant.

It may indeed be shown that "imitation is concerned with that which is thrice removed from the truth" as follows: The excellence or beauty of anything depends upon the use for which it is intended. The user of the flute alone knows what are the good and bad qualities of a flute, and must instruct the artificer how to make the flute. The imitator who paints or describes the flute, has neither the more perfect knowledge which the user possesses nor the less perfect knowledge which the artificer has gained from the user. He is, therefore, as said, thrice removed from true knowledge. "Imitation is a kind of sport or play, and the epic and tragic writers are imitators in the highest degree."

Now that the nature of imitation has been discovered, the next inquiry is—to what faculty in man does imitation appeal? Take first the case of painting. Objects in the world about us look different at different times. For example, the same object appears straight when out of water and crooked in water. Thus do our senses deceive us by various kinds of illusion. We should be greatly confused by this variety of appearance, were it not that by measuring, weighing, and numbering, we can determine the fact. That part of the soul which trusts to measuring and calculation is the highest and best part, or the rational principle of the soul. That part of the soul which is deceived by appearance and does not rely on measuring, is one of the inferior principles of the soul. Now the imitations of painting, which, as we have seen, are far removed from the truth, address themselves not to reason, but to an inferior part of the soul which is capable of being imposed upon.

We shall find that poetry is analogous to painting in that it appeals to another inferior principle in man's soul. When a man meets with misfortune, his first impulse is to moan and lament. This impulse is prompted by an irrational or cowardly part of his soul. The highest or rational principle bids him resist the desire to bewail his sufferings. It bids him find a cure or endure with patience. Now the calm wise temperament in which the rational principle prevails is not easy to imitate; nor would it be appreciated by the mixed multitude which form the audience of the poets. The multitude understand best the fitful and passionate temper of man. Therefore in order to be popular, the imitative poet does not try to please or affect the rational principle in the soul of his hearers. Instead, he appeals to their feelings and represents men in trouble, weeping and wailing over misfortunes. We are right then in refusing to admit the poet to the State, for he awakens and nourishes the feelings, but he impairs the reason.

The most serious charge against poetry is its power of harming even the good. Even those of us who with pride restrain ourselves from outcry over suffering, delight in giving way to sympathy with the weeping and wailing heroes of tragedy. Can it be right for us to admire in another what we would be ashamed of in ourselves? If we indulge in pity for others, we become weak ourselves and will end by weeping over our own sorrows. The same is true of comedy. We laugh at jests on the stage, which we should be ashamed to utter ourselves. If we continue to be amused by coarse merriment we shall ourselves become buffoons. In like manner anger and all the other passions are fed and watered by poetry. But since law and reason are to be rulers in our State, not pain and pleasure, we must expel all poetry except hymns to the Gods and praises of famous men.

We are conscious of the charm of poetry and we should gladly admit her to the State could she make a defense of herself and prove that she is not only delightful but "useful to States and to human life."]

But so long as she is unable to make good her defense, even though our ears may listen, our soul will be charmed against her by repeating this discourse of ours, and into the childish love which the many have of her we shall take care not to fall again, for we see that poetry being such as she is, is not to be pursued in earnest or regarded seriously as attaining to the truth; and he who listens to her will be on his guard against her seductions, fearing for the safety of the city which is within him, and he will attend to our words.

Yes, he said, I quite agree with you.

Yes, I said, my dear Glaucon, for great is the issue at stake, greater than appears, whether a man is to be good or bad. Neither under the influence of honor or money or power, aye, or under the excitement of poetry, ought he to fail in the observance of justice and virtue.

I agree, he said; and I think that any one would agree who heard the argument.

And yet, I said, no mention has been made of the greatest prizes and rewards of virtue.

If, he said, there are others greater than these they must be of an inconceivable greatness.

Why, I said, what was ever great in a short time? The whole period of threescore years and ten is surely but a little thing in comparison with eternity?

Say rather "nothing," he replied.

And should an immortal being seriously think of this little space rather than of the whole?

Yes, he said, I think that he should. But what do you mean?

Are you not aware, I said, that the soul is immortal and imperishable?

He looked at me in astonishment, and said: No, indeed; you do not mean to say that you are able to prove that?

Yes, I said, I ought to be able, and you too, for there is no difficulty.

I do not see that, he said; and I should like to hear this argument of which you make no difficulty.

Listen then, I said.

[In almost everything there is an inherent evil or disease. For example, the evil of corn is mildew, of iron, rust. The evil which is inherent in a thing may destroy it; or if this does not, nothing else can. The soul has its evils,—injustice, intemperance, cowardice, and the like; but these evils do not destroy the soul as disease destroys the body. Now it is unreasonable to suppose that a thing which cannot be destroyed from within by its own corruption, can be destroyed by some external evil. Bad food cannot destroy the body unless the corruption of the food is communicated to the body. In this case disease arises and this disease, not the food, destroys the body. On the same principle, unless some bodily evil can produce an evil of the soul, the bodily evil cannot destroy the soul. No bodily evil can infect the soul for no one can prove that even death makes a man more unholy or unjust. As no bodily evil can infect the soul none can destroy the soul. Now the soul which cannot be destroyed by any evil, whether inherent or external, must exist forever and so be immortal.]

Socrates continues:]

Her immortality may be proven by the previous argument and by other arguments; and you should also see her original nature, not as we now behold her, marred by communion with the body and other miseries, but you should look upon her with the eye of reason, pure as at birth, and then her beauty would be discovered, and in her image justice would be more clearly seen, and injustice, and all the things which we have described. But now, although we have spoken the truth concerning her as she appears at present, we must remember that we have seen her only in a condition which may be compared to that of the sea-god Glaucus, whose original image can hardly be discerned because his natural members are broken off and crushed and in many ways damaged by the waves, and incrustations have grown over them of seaweed and shells and stones so that he is liker to some sea-monster than to his natural form. And the soul is in a similar condition, disfigured by ten thousand ills. But not there, Glaucon, not there must we look.

Where then?

At her love of wisdom. Let us see whom she affects, and what converse she seeks in virtue of her near kindred with the immortal and eternal and divine; also how different she would become if wholly following this superior principle, and borne by a divine impulse out of the ocean in which she now is, and disengaged from the stones and shells and things of earth and rock which in wild variety grow around her because she feeds upon earth, and is crusted over by the good things of this life as they are termed: then you would see her as she is, and know whether she have one form only or many, or what her nature is. Of her form and affections in this present life I have said enough.

True, he said.

Thus, I said, have we followed out the argument, putting aside the rewards and glories of justice, such as you were saying that Homer and Hesiod introduced; and justice in her own nature has been shown to be best for the soul in her nature; let her do what is just, whether she have the ring of Gyges[1] or not, and, besides the ring of Gyges, the helmet of Hades.[2]

That is very true.

[1] See Book II., 359
[2] Hades (Roman Pluto), sovereign of the lower world, possessed a helmet or cap, the symbol of his invisible empire, which rendered the wearer invisible.

And now, Glaucon, there will be no harm in further enumerating how many and how great are the rewards which justice and the other virtues procure to the soul from gods and men, both in life and after death.

Certainly, he said.

Will you repay me, then, what you borrowed in the argument?

What was that?

I granted that the just man should appear unjust and the unjust just: for you were of opinion that even if the true state of the case could not possibly escape the eyes of gods and men, still this ought to be admitted for the sake of the argument, in order that pure justice might be weighed against pure injustice. Do you not remember?

You would have reason to complain of me if I had forgotten.

Then, as the cause is decided, I demand on behalf of justice that the glory which she receives from gods and men be also allowed to her by you; having been shown to have reality, and not to deceive those who truly possess her, she may also have appearance restored to her, and thus obtain the other crown of victory which is hers also.

The demand, he said, is just.

In the first place, I said—and this is the first point which you will have to give back—the nature both of just and unjust is truly known to the gods?

I am willing to restore that.

And if they are both known to them, one must be the friend and the other the enemy of the gods, as we admitted at first?

True.

And the friend of the gods may be supposed to receive from them every good, excepting only such evil as is the necessary consequence of former sins?

Certainly.

Then this must be our notion of the just man, that even when he is in poverty or sickness, or any other seeming misfortune, all things will in the end work together for good to him in life and death [3]: for the gods have a care of any one

---

[3] "And we know that all things work together for good to them that love God."—Romans viii. 28.

whose desire is to become just and to be like God, as far as man can attain his likeness, by the pursuit of virtue?

Yes, he said; if he is like God he will surely not be neglected by him.

And of the unjust may not the opposite be assumed?

Certainly.

Such, then, is the prize of victory which the gods give the just?

Yes, he said, that is my belief.

And what do they receive of men? Look at things as they really are and you will see that the clever unjust are in the case of runners, who run well from the starting-place to the goal, but not back again from the goal: they start off at a great pace, but in the end only look foolish, slinking away with their ears draggling on their shoulders, and without a crown; but the true runner comes to the finish and receives the prize and is crowned. And this is the way with the just; he who endures to the end of every action and occasion of his entire life has a good report and carries off the prize which men bestow.

True.

And now you must allow me to repeat the blessings which you attributed to the fortunate unjust. I shall say of the just as you were saying of the unjust, that as they grow older, if that is their desire, they become rulers in their own city; they marry whom they like and give in marriage to whomsoever they like; all that you said of the others I now say of these. And, on the other hand, I say of the unjust that the greater number, even though they escape in their youth, are found out at last and look foolish at the end of their course, and when they come to be old and miserable are flouted alike by stranger and citizen; they are beaten and then come those things unfit for ears polite, as you truly term them; they will be racked and burned, as you were saying; I shall ask you to suppose that you have heard all that. Will you allow me to assume that much?

Certainly, he said, for what you say is true.

These, then, are the prizes and rewards and gifts which are bestowed upon the just by gods and men in this present life, in addition to those other good things which justice of herself gives.

Yes, he said; and they are fair and lasting.

And yet, I said, all these things are as nothing, either in number or greatness, in comparison with those other recompenses which await both just and unjust after death, which are more and greater far. And you ought to hear them, and then both of them will have received the perfect meed of words due to them.

Speak, he said; there are few things which I would more gladly hear.

Well, I said, I will tell you a tale; not one of the tales which Odysseus tells to Alcinous,[4] yet this too is a tale of a brave man, Er the son of Armenius, a Pamphylian by birth. He was slain in battle, and ten days afterwards, when the bodies of the dead were brought in already in a state of corruption, he was brought in with them undecayed, and carried home to be buried. And on the twelfth day, as he was lying on the funeral pile, he returned to life and told them what he had seen in the other world. He said that when his soul departed he went on a journey with a great company, and that they came to a mysterious place at which there were two chasms in the earth; they were near together, and over against them were two other chasms in the heaven above. In the intermediate space there were judges seated, who bade the just, after they had judged them, ascend by the heavenly way on the right hand, having the signs of the judgment bound on their foreheads; and in like manner the unjust were commanded by them to descend by the lower way on the left hand; these also had the symbols of their deeds fastened on their backs. He drew near, and they told him that he was to be the messenger of the other world to men, and they bade him hear and see all that was to be heard and seen in that place. Then he beheld and saw on one side the souls departing at either chasm of heaven and earth when sentence had been given on them; and at the two other openings other souls, some ascending out of the earth dusty and worn with travel, some descending out of heaven, clean and bright. And always, on their arrival, they seemed as if they had come from a long journey, and they went out into the meadow with joy and there encamped as at a festival, and those who knew one

---

[4] Alcinous (ăl-sĭn′o-us): a mythical king whom Odysseus met in his journeys.

another embraced and conversed, the souls which came from earth curiously inquiring about the things of heaven, and the souls which came from heaven of the things of earth. And they told one another of what had happened by the way, some weeping and sorrowing at the remembrance of the things which they had endured and seen in their journey beneath the earth (now the journey lasted a thousand years), while others were describing heavenly blessings and visions of inconceivable beauty. There is not time, Glaucon, to tell all; but the sum was this: He said that for every wrong which they had done to any one they suffered tenfold; the thousand years answering to the hundred years which are reckoned as the life of man. If, for example, there were any who had committed murders, or had betrayed or enslaved cities or armies, or been guilty of any other evil behavior, for each and all of these they received punishment ten times over, and the rewards of beneficence and justice and holiness were in the same proportion. Not to repeat what he had to say concerning young children dying almost as soon as they were born; of piety and impiety to gods and parents, and of murderers, there were retributions yet greater which he narrated. He mentioned that he was present when one of the spirits asked another, "Where is Ardiæus[5] the Great?" (Now this Ardiæus was the tyrant of some city of Pamphylia, who had murdered his aged father and his elder brother, and had committed many other abominable crimes, and he lived a thousand years before the time of Er.) The answer was: "He comes not hither, and will never come." And "indeed," he said, "this was one of the terrible sights which was witnessed by us. For we were approaching the mouth of the cave, and having seen all, were about to re-ascend, when of a sudden Ardiæus appeared and several others, most of whom were tyrants; and there were also besides the tyrants private individuals who had been great criminals; they were just at the mouth, being, as they fancied, about to return into the upper world, but the opening, instead of receiving them, gave a roar, as was the case when any incurable or unpunished sinner tried to ascend; and then wild men of fiery aspect, who knew the meaning of the sound, came up and seized and carried off several of them, and Ardiæus and others they bound

* Ardiæus (är′di-ē′us).

head and foot and hand, and threw them down and flayed them with scourges, and dragged them along the road at the side, carding them on thorns like wool, and declaring to the pilgrims as they passed what were their crimes, and that they were being taken away to be cast into hell. And of all the terrors of the place there was no terror like this of hearing the voice ; and when there was silence they ascended with joy." These were the penalties and retributions, and there were blessings as great.

Now when the spirits that were in the meadow had tarried seven days, on the eighth day they were obliged to proceed on their journey, and on the fourth day from that time they came to a place where they looked down from above upon a line of light, like a column extending right through the whole heaven and earth, in color not unlike the rainbow, only brighter and purer ; another day's journey brought them to the place, and there, in the midst of the light, they saw reaching from heaven the extremities of the chains of it : for this light is the belt of heaven, and holds together the circle of the universe, like the undergirders of a trireme.[6] And from the extremities of the chains is extended the spindle of Necessity, on which all the revolutions turn. The shaft and hook of this spindle are made of steel, and the whorl is made partly of steel and also partly of other materials. Now the whorl is in form like the whorl used on earth ; and you are to suppose, as he described, that there is one large hollow whorl which is scooped out, and into this is fitted another lesser one, and another, and another, and four others, making eight in all, like boxes which fit into one another ; their edges are turned upwards, and all together form one continuous whorl. This is pierced by the spindle, which is driven home through the center of the eighth. The first and outermost whorl has the rim broadest, and the seven inner whorls narrow, in the following proportions—the sixth is next to the first in size, the fourth next to the sixth ; then comes the eighth ; the seventh is fifth, the fifth is sixth, the third is seventh, last and eighth comes the second. The largest [or fixed stars] is spangled, and the seventh [or sun] is brightest ; the eighth [or moon] colored by the reflected light of the seventh ; the second and fifth [Mercury and Saturn] are like one another, and of a yellower color than the preceding ; the

---

[6] A kind of boat with three rows of oars on a side.

third [Venus] has the whitest light; the fourth [Mars] is reddish; the sixth [Jupiter] is in whiteness second. Now the whole spindle has the same motion; but, as the whole revolves in one direction, the seven inner circles move slowly in the other, and of these the swiftest is the eighth; next in swiftness are the seventh, sixth, and fifth, which move together; third in swiftness appeared to them to move in reversed orbit the fourth; the third appeared fourth, and the second fifth. The spindle turns on the knees of Necessity; and on the upper surface of each circle is a siren, who goes round with them, hymning a single sound and note. The eight together form one harmony; and round about, at equal intervals, there is another band, three in number, each sitting upon her throne: these are the Fates, daughters of Necessity, who are clothed in white raiment and have garlands upon their heads, Lachesis and Clotho and Atropos,[7] who accompany with their voices the harmony of the sirens—Lachesis singing of the past, Clotho of the present, Atropos of the future; Clotho now and then assisting with a touch of her right hand the motion of the outer circle or whorl of the spindle, and Atropos with her left hand touching and guiding the inner ones, and Lachesis laying hold of either in turn, first with one hand and then with the other.

Now when the spirits arrived, their duty was to go to Lachesis; but first a prophet came and arranged them in order; then he took from the knees of Lachesis lots and samples of lives, and going up to a high place, spoke as follows: "Hear the word of Lachesis, the daughter of Necessity. Mortal souls, behold a new cycle of mortal life. Your genius will not choose you, but you will choose your genius; and let him who draws the first lot have the first choice of life, which shall be his destiny. Virtue is free, and as a man honors or dishonors her he will have more or less of her; the chooser is answerable—God is justified." When the Interpreter had thus spoken he cast the lots among them, and each one took up the lot which fell near him, all but Er himself (he was not allowed), and each as he took his lot perceived the number which he had drawn. Then the Interpreter placed on the ground before them the samples of life; and there were many more lives than the souls present, and there were all sorts of lives—of every animal and every condition of man. And

---

[7] Lachesis (lăk′e-sĭs). Clotho (klō′thō). Atropos (ăt′ro-pos).

there were tyrannies among them, some continuing while the tyrant lived, others which broke off in the middle and came to an end in poverty and exile and beggary; and there were lives of famous men, some who were famous for their form and beauty as well as for their strength and success in games, or, again, for their birth and the qualities of their ancestors; and some who were the reverse of famous for the opposite qualities. And of women likewise; there was not, however, any definite character among them, because the soul must of necessity choose another life, and become another. But there were many elements mingling with one another, and also with elements of wealth and poverty, and disease and health; and there were mean states also. And this, my dear Glaucon, is the great danger of man; and therefore the utmost care should be taken. Let each one of us leave every other kind of knowledge and seek and follow one thing only, if peradventure he may be able to learn and find who there is who can and will teach him to distinguish the life of good and evil, and to choose always and everywhere the better life as far as possible. He should consider the bearing of all these things which have been mentioned severally and collectively upon a virtuous life; he should know what the effect of beauty is when compounded with poverty or wealth in a particular soul, and what are the good and evil consequences of noble and humble birth, of private and public station, of strength and weakness, of cleverness and dullness, and of all the natural and acquired gifts of the soul, and study the composition of them; then he will look at the nature of the soul, and from the consideration of all this he will determine which is the better and which is the worse life, and at last he will choose, giving the name of evil to the life which will make his soul more unjust, and good to the life which will make his soul more just; all else he will disregard. For this, as we have seen, is the best choice both for this life and after death. Such an iron sense of truth and right must a man take with him into the world below, that there too he may be undazzled by the desire of wealth or the other allurements of evil, lest, coming upon tyrannies and similar villainies, he do irremediable wrongs to others and suffer yet worse himself; but let him know how to choose the mean and avoid the extremes on either side, as far as in him lies, not only in this life but in all that which is to come. For this is the way of happiness.

And this was what the Interpreter said at the time, as the messenger from the other world reported him to have spoken: "Even for the last comer, if he chooses wisely and will live diligently, there is appointed a happy and not undesirable existence. Let not the first be careless in his choice, and let not the last despair." As he spoke these words he who had the first choice drew near and at once chose the greatest tyranny; his mind, having been darkened by folly and sensuality, he did not well consider, and therefore did not see at first that he was fated, among other evils, to devour his own children. But, when he came to himself and saw what was in the lot, he began to beat his breast and lament over his choice, forgetting the proclamation of the Interpreter; for, instead of blaming himself as the author of his calamity, he accused chance and the gods, and everything rather than himself. Now he was one of those who came from heaven, and in a former life had dwelt in a well-ordered State, but his virtue was a matter of habit only, and he had no philosophy. And this was more often the fortune of those who came from heaven, because they had no experience of life; whereas, in general, the dwellers upon earth, who had seen and known trouble, were not in a hurry to choose. And owing to this inexperience of theirs, and also because the lot was a chance, many of the souls exchanged a good destiny for an evil or an evil for a good. For if a man had always from the first dedicated himself to sound philosophy, and had been moderately fortunate in the number of the lot, he might, as the messenger reported, be happy in this life, and also his passage to another life and return to this, instead of being rugged and underground, would be smooth and heavenly. Most curious, he said, was the spectacle of the election—sad and laughable and strange; the souls generally choosing according to their condition in a previous life. There he saw the soul that was once Orpheus[b] choosing the life of a swan out of enmity to the race of women, hating to be born of a woman

620

---

[b] See Apology, note 51. By the power of his music Orpheus succeeded in entering the world of the dead and regaining his beautiful young wife Eurydice (ŭ-rў'dĭ-ce) on condition that he should not turn back to see if she were following until they reached the upper air. He looked back, however, and Eurydice was taken from him. In his grief he is said to have hated all women and repelled the advances of those who tried to captivate him. Angered by this, the Thracian women, under the excitement of certain religious rites, tore him to pieces.

because they had been his murderers; he saw also the soul of Thamyris [9] choosing the life of a nightingale; birds, on the other hand, like the swan and other musicians, choosing to be men. The soul which obtained the twentieth lot chose the life of a lion, and this was the soul of Ajax [10] the son of Telamon, who would not be a man, remembering the injustice which was done him in the judgment of the arms. The next was Agamemnon,[11] who took the life of an eagle, because, like Ajax, he hated human nature on account of his sufferings. About the middle was the lot of Atalanta,[12] she seeing the great fame of an athlete, was unable to resist the temptation; and after her there came the soul of Epeus [13] the son of Panopeus passing into the nature of a woman cunning in the arts; and far away among the last who chose, the soul of the jester Thersites [14] was putting on the form of a monkey. There came also the soul of Odysseus [15] having yet to make a choice, and his lot happened to be the last of them all. Now the recollection of former toils had disenchanted him of ambition, and he went about for a considerable time in search of the life of a private man who had nothing to do; he had some difficulty in finding this which was lying about and had been neglected by everybody else; and when he saw it he said that he would have done the same had he been first instead of last, and that he was delighted at his choice. And not only did men pass into animals, but I must also mention that there were animals tame and wild who changed into one another and into corresponding human natures, the good into the gentle and the evil into the savage, in all sorts of combinations.

[9] Thamyris (thăm'y̆-ris): a legendary Thracian bard. He challenged the Muses to a trial of skill, was defeated, and deprived by them of sight and the power of song.

[10] See Apology, note 56. He is said to have killed himself because of his defeat in the contest with Odysseus for the armor of Achilles.

[11] Leader in the expedition of the Greeks against Troy. See Apology, note 21.

[12] Atalanta (ăt'a-lăn'ta): a huntress, beautiful and swift of foot.

[13] Epeus [(e-pē'us), son of Panopeus (păn'o-peŭs)]: maker of the famous wooden horse, which, filled with armed Greeks, was carried by the unsuspecting Trojans within their walls and proved their destruction. For at night the men concealed within, opened the gates of Troy to the Greeks. See Apology, note 21.

[14] Thersites (ther-sī'-tēz): one of the Greeks who went to Troy; noted for his impudent talk and insolent brawling; said to have been killed by Achilles because he ridiculed that hero's lament over a fallen foe.

[15] See Apology, note 58.

All the souls had now chosen their lives, and they went in the order of their choice to Lachesis, who sent with them the genius whom they had severally chosen, to be the guardian of their lives and the fulfiller of the choice; this genius led the souls first to Clotho, and drew them within the revolution of the spindle impelled by her hand, thus ratifying the destiny of each; and then, when they were fastened, carried them to Atropos, who spun the threads and made them irreversible; whence without turning round they passed beneath the throne of Necessity; and when they had all passed, they marched on in a scorching heat to the plain of Forgetfulness, which was a barren waste destitute of trees and verdure; and then towards evening they encamped by the river of Negligence, the water of which no vessel can hold; of this they were all obliged to drink a certain quantity, and those who were not saved by wisdom drank more than was necessary; and those who drank forgot all things. Now after they had gone to rest, about the middle of the night there was a thunderstorm and earthquake, and then in an instant they were driven all manner of ways like stars shooting to their birth. He himself was hindered from drinking the water. But in what manner or by what means he returned to the body he could not say; only, in the morning awaking suddenly, he saw himself lying on the pyre.

And thus, Glaucon, the tale has been saved and has not perished, and may be our salvation if we are obedient to the word spoken; and we shall pass safely over the river of Forgetfulness and our soul will not be defiled. Wherefore my counsel is, that we hold fast to the heavenly way and follow after justice and virtue always, considering that the soul is immortal and able to endure every sort of good and every sort of evil. Thus shall we live dear to one another and to the gods, both while remaining here and when, like conquerors in the games who go round to gather gifts, we receive our reward. And it shall be well with us both in this life and in the pilgrimage of a thousand years which we have been reciting.

PHÆDO

SUGGESTIONS ON THE STUDY OF THE PHÆDO

INSTEAD of the ordinary form of Introduction the following suggestions on the study of the Phædo are submitted.

I. Do not study the dialogue first of all to see whether you agree with the arguments or conclusions of Socrates. Try first to hear him out, just as if you were with him in the prison, and to appreciate sympathetically the course and the spirit of his argument about immortality.

II. Do not begin by a formal study of the dialogue. Read it through at least once just as you would read a novel, to get the story, and general sense and spirit of the whole.

III. Study of the formal arguments for immortality: Read first very thoughtfully the account of the doctrine of ideas, the doctrine of the pre-existence of the soul, and the doctrine of reminiscence in the Introduction, page xxvi. If you have other books to read on these subjects, so much the better. Then write out as briefly and clearly as possible the five formal arguments for immortality, as they are given in the text and summaries.

Note: The first and fifth arguments seemed to one of the hearers (103) inconsistent. Jowett thinks them really inconsistent.

Note on the argument from reminiscence: How we get pure abstract ideas, such as those found in pure mathematics, has been a standing question in philosophy. Plato held, as we see, that we remember such ideas from a former existence. Some modern philosophers have held that we are born with these ideas or with natural capacities which always lead us to them. Others have held that all such ideas are gained by experience. Some hold that the experiences of our ancestors are born in us as instinctive tendencies which give rise to these ideas. The last view has more in common with that of Plato than may at first appear; for, according to this view, the individual has a kind of pre-existence in his ancestors, and his most abstract ideas are organic memories from that ancestral pre-existence. The modern theory does not, however, represent the soul as having existed individually before birth and so does not suggest an individual existence after death.

IV. Besides working out the formal arguments for immortality, Plato suggests his belief in respect to it by many incidents of the story. In some cases the connection between the incident and the argument is plain, in other cases, less so.

(1.) Consider each of the following incidents to see what, if any, connection it has with Socrates' belief as shown in the dialogue as a whole. (*a*) The message to Evenus (61 and following); (*b*) The direction about the care of his sons (115); (*c*) The answer to Crito about his burial (115); (*d*) The answer to Crito's proposal that he postpone his death to the last legal moment (116).

(2.) Collect a series of quotations from the dialogue which show the state of Socrates' feeling, and consider the connection of this feeling in presence of death, with his professed belief.

(3.) More difficult points: (*a*) Read 89, 90, and 91, to where the argument is resumed. Note Socrates' advice against misology or despair of reason. Read with special care the paragraph beginning, " Yes, Phædo, he replied," etc., in 90. What connection do you find between Socrates' reason why we should not be misologists and his belief as shown in the dialogue as a whole? (*b*) Read the paragraph in 91 beginning " Let us then," etc. This paragraph appears to be a confession of doubt and of willingness to have his arguments for immortality overthrown. Is this confession real or affected? If it is affected, is it consistent with Socrates' character and professions? If it is real, is it consistent with the rest of the dialogue? (*c*) Read from 78 to the end of 83. What is the deepest reason given here for loving good and for not loving evil?

Note: Taking the dialogue as a whole, it is evident that Plato's belief in immortality rests upon his conviction that beyond the world which appears to our senses, which is full of change, of illusion, and of evil, there is a world which is eternal and good; that the soul belongs by its deepest nature to that eternal and good world; and that by purging the soul from thoughts of this present evil world, and by feeding the soul upon that which is eternal and good, we may escape from this miserable changing existence, into our true estate with God. To know the divine is to embrace it and to assimilate the divine

—is to *be* divine; and to be divine is to be eternal. "This is life eternal that ye might know God and Jesus Christ whom he hath sent." Plato comes nearer to seeing this than does many a Christian.

PHÆDO

PERSONS OF THE DIALOGUE.[1]

PHÆDO, *who is the narrator of*   APOLLODORUS.
the Dialogue to   SIMMIAS.
ECHECRATES *of Phlius.*   CEBES.
SOCRATES.   CRITO.
ATTENDANT OF THE PRISON.

SCENE:—The Prison of Socrates.
PLACE OF THE NARRATION:—Phlius.[2]

Echecrates. Were you yourself, Phædo, in the prison with Socrates on the day when he drank the poison?[3]   **Steph. 57**

Phædo. Yes, Echecrates, I was.

Ech. I wish that you would tell me about his death. What did he say in his last hours? We were informed that he died by taking poison, but no one knew anything more; for no Phliasian ever goes to Athens now, and a long time has elapsed since any Athenian found his way to Phlius, and therefore we had no clear account.

Phæd. Did you not hear of the proceedings at the trial?   **58**

[1] Phædo (fē'dō): a Greek philosopher, said to have been brought to Athens as a slave in his youth and ransomed by one of the friends of Socrates. Later he founded a school of philosophy.
 Echecrates (e-kĕk'ra-tēz): not mentioned elsewhere in Plato.
 Apollodorus. See Symposium, note 1.
 Simmias (sĭm'mĭ-as): a native of Thebes, educated in the Pythagorean philosophy, which taught the doctrine of the pre-existence of the soul. Hence his readiness to accept Socrates' argument based on that doctrine. He is said to have written twenty-three dialogues, all of which are lost.
 Cebes (sē'bēz): a Greek philosopher, native of Thebes. He wrote three dialogues, one of which, called Pinax, or The Picture, has been preserved.
 Crito: see Apology, note 35.
[2] Phlius (flī'us): a town about sixty miles west of Athens.
[3] Hemlock.

Ech. Yes; some one told us about the trial, and we could not understand why, having been condemned, he was put to death, as appeared, not at the time, but long afterwards. What was the reason of this?

Phæd. An accident, Echecrates. The reason was that the stern of the ship which the Athenians sent to Delos happened to have been crowned on the day before he was tried.

Ech. What is this ship?

Phæd. This is the ship in which, as the Athenians say, Theseus[4] went to Crete when he took with him the fourteen youths, and was the saviour of them and of himself. And they were said to have vowed to Apollo at the time, that if they were saved they would make an annual pilgrimage to Delos. Now this custom still continues, and the whole period of the voyage to and from Delos, beginning when the priest of Apollo crowns the stern of the ship, is a holy season, during which the city is not allowed to be polluted by public executions; and often, when the vessel is detained by adverse winds, there may be a very considerable delay. As I was saying, the ship was crowned on the day before the trial, and this was the reason why Socrates lay in prison and was not put to death until long after he was condemned.

Ech. What was the manner of his death, Phædo? What was said or done? And which of his friends had he with him? Or were they not allowed by the authorities to be present? And did he die alone?

Phæd. No; there were several of his friends with him.

Ech. If you have nothing to do, I wish that you would tell me what passed, as exactly as you can.

Phæd. I have nothing to do, and will try to gratify your wish. For to me too there is no greater pleasure than to have

---

[4] Theseus (thē'sŭs): a legendary Greek hero, one of whose exploits was the slaying of a monster called the Minotaur (mĭn'o-taur). To this monster, imprisoned in a cave of Crete, Athens had to send a yearly sacrifice of seven youths and seven maidens. Theseus went voluntarily as one of these victims to Crete and with the help of Ariadne (à'rĭ-ăd'ne), the king's daughter, succeeded in slaying the Minotaur. The grateful Athenians preserved the ship in which Theseus made his voyage and sent in it every year envoys and a sacrifice to Delos.

Delos (dē'los), a small island of the Ægean, was sacred to the worship of Apollo, one of the greatest and most beneficent of the Greek gods, who is said to have been born there. The priest of Apollo decked the stern of the vessel with garlands before it left port.

Socrates brought to my recollection; whether I speak myself or hear another speak of him.

Ech. You will have listeners who are of the same mind with you, and I hope that you will be as exact as you can.

Phæd. I remember the strange feeling which came over me at being with him. For I could hardly believe that I was present at the death of a friend, and therefore I did not pity him, Echecrates; his mien and his language were so noble and fearless in the hour of death that to me he appeared blessed. I thought that in going to the other world he could not be without a divine call, and that he would be happy, if any man ever was, when he arrived there; and therefore I did not pity him as might seem natural at such a time. But neither could I feel the pleasure which I usually felt in philosophical discourse (for philosophy was the theme of which we spoke). I was pleased and I was also pained, because I knew that he was soon to die, and this strange mixture of feeling was shared by us all; we were laughing and weeping by turns, especially the excitable Apollodorus—you know the sort of man?

Ech. Yes.

Phæd. He was quite overcome; and I myself, and all of us were greatly moved.

Ech. Who were present?

Phæd. Of native Athenians there were, besides Apollodorus, Critobulus and his father Crito, Hermogenes, Epigenes, Æschines, and Antisthenes; likewise Ctesippus of the deme of Pæania, Menexenus, and some others; but Plato, if I am not mistaken, was ill.

Ech. Were there any strangers?

Phæd. Yes, there were; Simmias the Theban, and Cebes, and Phædondes; Euclid and Terpsion, who came from Megara.

Ech. And was Aristippus there, and Cleombrotus?[5]

[5] Hermogenes (hĕr-mŏj′e-nēz); Epigenes and Æschines: mentioned in Apology, 33. Antisthenes (ăn-tĭs′the-nēz); Ctesippus: speaker in Euthydemus; Menexenus (mē-nĕx′e·nus); Phædondes (fē-dŏn′dēz); Euclid (ū′klĭd); Terpsion (tĕrp′sĭ-on); Aristippus (ăr-ĭs-tĭp′us); Cleombrotus (klē-ŏm′brō-tus). Of these the most important are Euclid, Aristippus and Antisthenes, each of whom founded a school of philosophy. These are called minor Socratic schools, because each of them partially represents the teaching and spirit of Socrates. Plato perhaps means to censure Cleombrotus and Aristippus for not being present, although so near (the island Ægina (ē-jī′na) and its city of that name being but twenty miles from Athens, southwest). Cicero says that Cleombrotus after reading this dialogue killed himself by throwing himself into the sea.

Phæd. No, they were said to be in Ægina.

Ech. Any one else?

Phæd. I think that these were about all.

Ech. And what was the discourse of which you spoke?

Phæd. I will begin at the beginning, and endeavor to repeat the entire conversation. You must understand that we had been previously in the habit of assembling early in the morning at the court in which the trial was held, and which is not far from the prison. There we remained talking with one another until the opening of the prison doors (for they were not opened very early), and then went in and generally passed the day with Socrates. On the last morning the meeting was earlier than usual; this was owing to our having heard on the previous evening that the sacred ship had arrived from Delos, and therefore we agreed to meet very early at the accustomed place. On our going to the prison, the jailer who answered the door, instead of admitting us, came out and bade us wait and he would call us. "For the eleven,"[6] he said, "are now with Socrates; they are taking off his chains, and giving orders that he is to die to-day." He soon returned and said that we might come in. On entering we found Socrates just released from chains, and Xanthippe,[7] whom you know, sitting by him, and holding his child in her arms. When she saw us she uttered a cry and said, as women will: "O Socrates, this is the last time that either you will converse with your friends, or they with you." Socrates turned to Crito and said: "Crito, let some one take her home." Some of Crito's people accordingly led her away, crying out and beating herself. And when she was gone, Socrates, sitting up on the couch, began to bend and rub his leg, saying, as he rubbed: How singular is the thing called pleasure, and how curiously related to pain, which might be thought to be the opposite of it; for they

60

---

[6] See Apology, note 45.

[7] Xanthippe (zăn-tĭp'pe): wife of Socrates. Her name has been proverbial in ancient and modern times as that of a shrew. Some find excuse for her in her husband's neglect of his private affairs. Xenophon says that her son became embittered on account of his mother's severity and that Socrates reasoned with the son, reminding him of the mother's many acts of self-sacrifice for her children. In the incident here related, her grief seems to us much more creditable than the indifference of Socrates. Compare John xix. 26 and 27: "When Jesus therefore saw his mother and the disciple standing by whom he loved, he saith to his mother, Woman, behold thy son! Then saith he to the disciple, Behold thy mother! And from that hour that disciple took her unto his own home."

never come to a man together, and yet he who pursues either of them is generally compelled to take the other. They are two, and yet they grow together out of one head or stem; and I cannot help thinking that if Æsop[8] had noticed them, he would have made a fable about God trying to reconcile their strife, and when he could not, he fastened their heads together; and this is the reason why when one comes the other follows, as I find in my own case pleasure comes following after the pain in my leg which was caused by the chain.

Upon this Cebes said: I am very glad indeed, Socrates, that you mentioned the name of Æsop. For that reminds me of a question which had been asked by others, and was asked of me only the day before yesterday by Evenus[9] the poet, and as he will be sure to ask again, you may as well tell me what I should say to him, if you would like him to have an answer. He wanted to know why you who never before wrote a line of poetry, now that you are in prison are putting Æsop into verse, and also composing that hymn in honor of Apollo.

Tell him, Cebes, he replied, that I had no idea of rivaling him or his poems; which is the truth, for I knew that I could not do that. But I wanted to see whether I could purge away a scruple which I felt about certain dreams. In the course of my life I have often had intimations in dreams "that I should make music." The same dream came to me sometimes in one form, and sometimes in another, but always saying the same or nearly the same words: Make and cultivate music, said the dream. And hitherto I had imagined that this was only intended to exhort and encourage me in the study of philosophy, which has always been the pursuit of my life, and is the noblest and best of music.[10] The dream was bidding me do what I was already doing, in the same way that the competitor in a race is bidden by the spectators to run when he is already running. But I was not certain of this, as the dream might have meant music in the popular sense of the word, and being under sentence of death, and the festival giving me a respite, I thought that I should be safer if I satisfied the scruple, and, in obedience to the

---

[8] A famous writer of fables, who lived about 600 B.C.; probably a native of Phrygia in Asia Minor.
[9] See Apology, note 8.
[10] See Republic, II., note 17.

dream, composed a few verses before I departed. And first I made a hymn in honor of the god of the festival, and then considering that a poet, if he is really to be a poet or maker,[11] should not only put words together but make stories, and as I have no invention, I took some fables of Æsop, which I had ready at hand and knew, and turned them into verse. Tell Evenus this, and bid him be of good cheer; say that I would have him come after me if he be a wise man, and not tarry; and that to-day I am likely to be going, for the Athenians say that I must.

Simmias said: What a message for such a man! having been a frequent companion of his I should say that, as far as I know him, he will never take your advice unless he is obliged.

Why, said Socrates. Is not Evenus a philosopher?

I think that he is, said Simmias.

Then he, or any man who has the spirit of philosophy, will be willing to die, though he will not take his own life, for that is held not to be right.

Here he changed his position, and put his legs off the couch on to the ground, and during the rest of the conversation he remained sitting.

Why do you say, inquired Cebes, that a man ought not to take his own life, but that the philosopher will be ready to follow the dying?

Socrates replied: And have you, Cebes and Simmias, who are acquainted with Philolaus,[12] never heard him speak of this?

I never understood him, Socrates.

My words, too, are only an echo; but I am very willing to say what I have heard: and indeed, as I am going to another place, I ought to be thinking and talking of the nature of the pilgrimage which I am about to make. What can I do better in the interval between this and the setting of the sun?[13]

Then tell me, Socrates, why is suicide held not to be right? as I have certainly heard Philolaus affirm when he was staying

---

[11] The Greek word for poet means, literally, *maker*.
[12] Philolaus (fĭl-o-lā′us): a distinguished philosopher, a disciple of Pythagoras and the instructor of Simmias and Cebes. See Phædo, note 1, on Simmias.
[13] Athenian law permitted no executions in the day-time.

with us at Thebes [14]; and there are others who say the same, although none of them has ever made me understand him.

62

But do your best, replied Socrates, and the day may come when you will understand. I suppose that you wonder why, as most things which are evil may be accidentally good, this is to be the only exception (for may not death, too, be better than life in some cases?), and why, when a man is better dead, he is not permitted to be his own benefactor, but must wait for the hand of another.

By Jupiter! [15] yes, indeed, said Cebes laughing, and speaking in his native Doric. [16]

I admit the appearance of inconsistency, replied Socrates, but there may not be any real inconsistency after all in this. There is a doctrine uttered in secret [17] that man is a prisoner who has no right to open the door of his prison and run away; this is a great mystery which I do not quite understand. Yet I too believe that the gods are our guardians, and that we are a possession of theirs. Do you not agree?

Yes, I agree to that, said Cebes.

And if one of your own possessions, an ox or an ass, for example, took the liberty of putting himself out of the way when you had given no intimation of your wish that he should die, would you not be angry with him, and would you not punish him if you could?

Certainly, replied Cebes.

Then there may be reason in saying that a man should wait, and not take his own life until God summons him, as he is now summoning me.

Yes, Socrates, said Cebes, there is surely reason in that. And yet how can you reconcile this seemingly true belief that God is our guardian and we his possessions, with that willingness to die which we were attributing to the philosopher? That the wisest of men should be willing to leave this service in which they are ruled by the gods who are the best of rulers, is not reasonable, for surely no wise man thinks that when set at liberty he can take better care of himself than

---

[14] See Protagoras, note 34.
[15] Jupiter: the chief Roman deity, corresponding to the Greek Zeus.
[16] Doric (dŏr'ĭk): a dialect of the Greek language.
[17] This probably refers to a saying of Pythagoras, whose more important teachings were kept secret from all except his disciples.

the gods take of him. A fool may perhaps think this—he may argue that he had better run away from his master, not considering that his duty is to remain to the end, and not to run away from the good, and that there is no sense in his running away. But the wise man will want to be ever with him who is better than himself. Now this, Socrates, is the reverse of what was just now said; for upon this view the wise man should sorrow and the fool rejoice at passing out of life.

The earnestness of Cebes seemed to please Socrates. Here, said he, turning to us, is a man who is always inquiring, and is not to be convinced all in a moment, nor by every argument.

63

And in this case, added Simmias, his objection does appear to me to have some force. For what can be the meaning of a truly wise man wanting to fly away and lightly leave a master who is better than himself. And I rather imagine that Cebes is referring to you; he thinks that you are too ready to leave us, and too ready to leave the gods who, as you acknowledge, are our good rulers.

Yes, replied Socrates; there is reason in that. And this indictment you think that I ought to answer as if I were in court?

That is what we should like, said Simmias.

Then I must try to make a better impression upon you than I did when defending myself before the judges. For I am quite ready to acknowledge, Simmias and Cebes, that I ought to be grieved at death, if I were not persuaded that I am going to other gods who are wise and good (of this I am as certain as I can be of anything of the sort), and to men departed (though I am not so certain of this) who are better than those whom I leave behind; and therefore I do not grieve as I might have done, for I have good hope that there is yet something remaining for the dead, and as has been said of old, some far better thing for the good than for the evil.

But do you mean to take away your thoughts with you, Socrates, said Simmias? Will you not communicate them to us?—the benefit is one in which we too may hope to share. Moreover, if you succeed in convincing us, that will be an answer to the charge against yourself.

I will do my best, replied Socrates. But you must first let

me hear what Crito wants ; he was going to say something to me.

Only this, Socrates, replied Crito : the attendant who is to give you the poison has been telling me that you are not to talk much, and he wants me to let you know this ; for that by talking, heat is increased, and this interferes with the action of the poison ; those who excite themselves are sometimes obliged to drink the poison two or three times.

Then, said Socrates, let him mind his business and be prepared to give the poison two or three times, if necessary ; that is all.

I was almost certain that you would say that, replied Crito ; but I was obliged to satisfy him.

Never mind him, he said.

And now I will make answer to you, O my judges, and show that he who has lived as a true philosopher has reason to be of good cheer when he is about to die, and that after death he may hope to receive the greatest good in the other world. And how this may be, Simmias and Cebes, I will endeavor to explain. For I deem that the true disciple of philosophy is likely to be misunderstood by other men ; they do not perceive that he is ever pursuing death and dying ; and if this is true, why, having had the desire of death all his life long, should he repine at the arrival of that which he has been always pursuing and desiring ?

Simmias laughed and said : Though not in a laughing humor, I swear that I cannot help laughing, when I think what the wicked world will say when they hear this. They will say that this is very true, and our people at home will agree with them in saying that the life which philosophers desire is truly death, and that they have found them out to be deserving of the death which they desire.

And they are right, Simmias, in saying this, with the exception of the words " They have found them out," for they have not found out what is the nature of this death which the true philosopher desires, or how he deserves or desires death. But let us leave them and have a word with ourselves : Do we believe that there is such a thing as death ?

To be sure, replied Simmias.

And is this anything but the separation of soul and body ? And being dead is the attainment of this separation when the soul exists in herself, and is parted from the body and the body is parted from the soul—that is death?

Exactly: that and nothing else, he replied.

And what do you say of another question, my friend, about which I should like to have your opinion, and the answer to which will probably throw light on our present inquiry: Do you think that the philosopher ought to care about the pleasures—if they are to be called pleasures—of eating and drinking?

Certainly not, answered Simmias.

And what do you say of the pleasures of love—should he care about them?

By no means.

And will he think much of the other ways of indulging the body, for example, the acquisition of costly raiment, or sandals, or other adornments of the body? Instead of caring about them, does he not rather despise anything more than nature needs? What do you say?

I should say that the true philosopher would despise them.

Would you not say that he is entirely concerned with the soul and not with the body? He would like, as far as he can, to be quit of the body and turn to the soul.

That is true.

In matters of this sort philosophers, above all other men, may be observed in every sort of way to dissever the soul from the body.

That is true.

Whereas, Simmias, the rest of the world are of opinion that a life which has no bodily pleasures and no part in them is not worth having; but that he who thinks nothing of bodily pleasures is almost as though he were dead.

That is quite true.

What again shall we say of the actual acquirement of knowledge?—is the body, if invited to share in the inquiry, a hinderer or a helper? I mean to say, have sight and hearing any truth in them? Are they not, as the poets are always telling us, inaccurate witnesses? and yet, if even they are inaccurate and indistinct, what is to be said of the other senses? —for you will allow that they are the best of them?

Certainly, he replied.

Then when does the soul attain truth?—for in attempting

to consider anything in company with the body she is obviously deceived.

Yes, that is true.

Then must not existence be revealed to her in thought, if at all?

Yes.

And thought is best when the mind is gathered into herself and none of these things trouble her—neither sounds nor sights nor pain nor any pleasure,—when she has as little as possible to do with the body, and has no bodily sense or feeling, but is aspiring after being?

That is true.

And in this the philosopher dishonors the body; his soul runs away from the body and desires to be alone and by herself?

That is true.

Well, but there is another thing, Simmias: Is there or is there not an absolute justice?

Assuredly there is.

And an absolute beauty and absolute good?

Of course.

But did you ever behold any of them with your eyes?

Certainly not.

Or did you ever reach them with any other bodily sense? (and I speak not of these alone, but of absolute greatness, and health, and strength, and of the essence or true nature of everything). Has the reality of them ever been perceived by you through the bodily organs? or rather, is not the nearest approach to the knowledge of their several natures made by him who so orders his intellectual vision as to have the most exact conception of the essence of that which he considers?

Certainly.

And he attains to the knowledge of them in their highest purity who goes to each of them with the mind alone, not allowing when in the act of thought the intrusion or introduction of sight or any other sense in the company of reason, but with the very light of the mind in her clearness penetrates into the very light of truth in each; he has got rid, as far as he can, of eyes and ears and of the whole body, which he conceives of only as a disturbing element, hindering the soul from the acquisition of knowledge when in company with her—is not this the sort of man who, if ever man did, is likely to attain the knowledge of existence?

There is admirable truth in that, Socrates, replied Simmias.

And when they consider all this, must not true philosophers make a reflection, of which they will speak to one another in such words as these: We have found, they will say, a path of speculation which seems to bring us and the argument to the conclusion, that while we are in the body, and while the soul is mingled with this mass of evil, our desire will not be satisfied, and our desire is of the truth. For the body is a source of endless trouble to us by reason of the mere requirement of food; and also is liable to diseases which overtake and impede us in the search after truth: and by filling us so full of loves, and lusts, and fears, and fancies, and idols, and every sort of folly, prevents our ever having, as people say, so much as a thought. For whence come wars, and fightings, and factions? whence but from the body and the lusts of the body? For wars are occasioned by the love of money, and money has to be acquired for the sake and in the service of the body; and in consequence of all these things the time which ought to be given to philosophy is lost. Moreover, if there is time and an inclination toward philosophy, yet the body introduces a turmoil and confusion and fear into the course of speculation, and hinders us from seeing the truth; and all experience shows that if we would have pure knowledge of anything we must be quit of the body, and the soul in herself must behold all things in themselves: then I suppose that we shall attain that which we desire, and of which we say that we are lovers, and that is wisdom; not while we live, but after death, as the argument shows; for if while in company with the body, the soul cannot have pure knowledge, one of two things seems to follow—either knowledge is not to be attained at all, or, if at all, after death. For then, and not till then, the soul will be in herself alone and without the body. In this present life, I reckon that we make the nearest approach to knowledge when we have the least possible concern or interest in the body, and are not saturated with the bodily nature, but remain pure until the hour when God himself is pleased to release us. And then the foolishness of the body will be cleared away and we shall be pure and hold converse with other pure souls, and know of ourselves the clear light everywhere; and this is surely the light of truth. For no impure thing is allowed to approach the pure. These are the sort of words, Simmias, which the true lovers of wisdom cannot help saying to one another, and thinking. You will agree with me in that?

Certainly, Socrates.

But if this is true, O my friend, then there is great hope that, going whither I go, I shall there be satisfied with that which has been the chief concern of you and me in our past lives. And now that the hour of departure is appointed to me, this is the hope with which I depart, and not I only, but every man who believes that he has his mind purified.

Certainly, replied Simmias.

And what is purification but the separation of the soul from the body, as I was saying before; the habit of the soul gathering and collecting herself into herself, out of all the courses of the body; the dwelling in her own place alone, as in another life, so also in this, as far as she can; the release of the soul from the chains of the body?

Very true, he said.

And what is that which is termed death, but this very separation and release of the soul from the body?

To be sure, he said.

And the true philosophers, and they only, study and are eager to release the soul. Is not the separation and release of the soul from the body their especial study?

That is true.

And as I was saying at first, there would be a ridiculous contradiction in men studying to live as nearly as they can in a state of death, and yet repining when death comes.

Certainly.

Then Simmias, as the true philosophers are ever studying death, to them, of all men, death is the least terrible. Look at the matter in this way: how inconsistent of them to have been always enemies of the body, and wanting to have the soul alone, and when this is granted to them, to be trembling and repining; instead of rejoicing at their departing to that place where, when they arrive, they hope to gain that which in life they loved (and this was wisdom), and at the same time to be rid of the company of their enemy.

Many a man has been willing to go to the world below in the hope of seeing there an earthly love, or wife, or son, and conversing with them. And will he who is a true lover of wisdom, and is persuaded in like manner that only in the world below he can worthily enjoy her, still repine at death? Will he not depart with joy? Surely, he will, my friend, if he be a true philosopher. For he will have a firm conviction that there only, and nowhere else, he can find wisdom in her purity. And if this be true, he would be very absurd, as I was saying, if he were to fear death.

He would indeed, replied Simmias.

And when you see a man who is repining at the approach of death, is not his reluctance a sufficient proof that he is not a lover of wisdom, but a lover of the body, and probably at the same time a lover of either money or power, or both?

That is very true, he replied.

There is a virtue, Simmias, which is named courage. Is not that a special attribute of the philosopher?

Certainly.

Again, there is temperance. Is not the calm, and control, and disdain of the passions which even the many call temperance, a quality belonging only to those who despise the body, and live in philosophy?

That is not to be denied.

For the courage and temperance of other men, if you will consider them, are really a contradiction.

How is that, Socrates?

Well, he said, you are aware that death is regarded by men in general as a great evil.

That is true, he said.

And do not courageous men endure death because they are afraid of yet greater evils?

That is true.

Then all but the philosophers are courageous only from fear, and because they are afraid; and yet that a man should be courageous from fear, and because he is a coward, is surely a strange thing.

Very true.

And are not the temperate exactly in the same case? They are temperate because they are intemperate,—which may seem to be a contradiction, but is nevertheless the sort of thing which happens with this foolish temperance. For there are pleasures which they must have, and are afraid of losing; and therefore they abstain from one class of pleasures because they are overcome by another: and whereas intemperance is defined as "being under the dominion of pleasure," they overcome only because they are overcome by pleasure. And that is what I mean by saying that they are temperate through intemperance.

That appears to be true.

Yet the exchange of one fear or pleasure or pain for another fear or pleasure or pain, which are measured like coins, the greater with the less, is not the exchange of virtue. O my dear Simmias, is there not one true coin for which all things ought to exchange?—and that is wisdom[18]; and only in exchange for this, and in company with this, is anything truly bought or sold, whether courage or temperance or justice. And is not all true virtue the companion of wisdom, no matter what fears or pleasures or other similar goods or evils may or may not attend her? But the virtue which is made up of these goods, when they are severed from wisdom and exchanged with one another, is a shadow of virtue only, nor is there any freedom or health or truth in her; but in the true exchange there is a purging away of all these things, and temperance, and justice, and courage, and wisdom herself, are a purgation of them. And I conceive that the founders of the mysteries[19] had a real meaning and were not mere triflers when they intimated in a figure long ago that he who passed unsanctified and uninitiated into the world below will live in a slough, but that he who arrives there after initiation and purification will dwell with the gods. For "many," as they say in the mysteries, "are the thyrsus-bearers, but few are the mystics,"[20]—meaning, as I

[18] Compare Isaiah lv. 2: "Wherefore do ye spend money for that which is not bread and your labor for that which satisfieth not." Compare also Protagoras, 349-360.
Also Matt. xiii. 45 and 46: "Again the kingdom of heaven is like unto a merchantman, seeking goodly pearls: who, when he had found one pearl of great price, went and sold all that he had, and bought it."
[19] See Symposium, note 32.
[20] Dionysus or Bacchus, god of wine, was one of the gods in whose worship mysteries were employed. His devotees carried a wand or thyrsus. Among these wand-bearers were many whose participation in the rites was merely formal, in comparison with whom the true worshippers were few. Hence arose the proverb quoted by Socrates. According to his interpretation, only philosophers are completely purified and initiated into an understanding of divine things. Compare Matt. xxii. 14: "For many are called but few are chosen."

interpret the words, the true philosophers. In the number of whom I have been seeking, according to my ability, to find a place during my whole life; whether I have sought in a right way or not, and whether I have succeeded or not, I shall truly know in a little while, if God will, when I myself arrive in the other world: that is my belief. And now Simmias and Cebes, I have answered those who charge me with not grieving or repining at parting from you and my masters in this world; and I am right in not repining, for I believe that I shall find other masters and friends who are as good in the world below. But all men cannot receive this, and I shall be glad if my words have any more success with you than with the judges of Athenians.

Cebes answered: I agree, Socrates, in the greater part of what you say. But in what relates to the soul, men are apt to be incredulous; they fear that when she leaves the body her place may be nowhere, and that on the very day of death she may be destroyed and perish,—immediately on her release from the body, issuing forth like smoke or air and vanishing away into nothingness. For if she could only hold together and be herself after she was released from the evils of the body, there would be good reason to hope, Socrates, that what you say is true. But much persuasion and many arguments are required in order to prove that when the man is dead the soul yet exists, and has any force or intelligence.

True, Cebes, said Socrates; and shall I suggest that we talk a little of the probabilities of these things?

I am sure, said Cebes, that I should greatly like to know your opinion about them.

I reckon, said Socrates, that no one who heard me now, not even if he were one of my old enemies, the comic poets,[21] could accuse me of idle talking about matters in which I have no concern. Let us then, if you please, proceed with the inquiry.

[Socrates recalls an ancient doctrine that the souls of men pass after death into the other world, whence they return and

---

[21] See Apology, note 5. Eupolis (ū'pŏ-lis), another comic poet of the day, said of Socrates: "I hate Socrates, that prating beggar, who pays great attention, forsooth, to all these other things, but as to how withal he shall be fed, to this he gives no heed at all." Other instances also are known of the enmity of the poets for Socrates.

are born again into this world. This generation of the living from the dead is analogous to other processes in nature. Just as sleeping passes into waking and waking into sleeping, as the greater becomes the less and the less grows into the greater, as all opposites pass, the one into the other, so life passes into death and death again becomes life. To complete the circle of nature it is necessary that death should generate life.]

70-
72

My dear Cebes, if all things which partook of life were to die, and after they were dead remained in the form of death, and did not come to life again, all would at last die, and nothing would be alive—how could this be otherwise? For if the living spring from any others who are not the dead, and they die, must not all things at last be swallowed up in death?

There is no escape from that, Socrates, said Cebes; and I think that what you say is entirely true.

Yes, he said, Cebes, I entirely think so too; and we are not walking in a vain imagination: but I am confident in the belief that there truly is such a thing as living again, and that the living spring from the dead, and that the souls of the dead are in existence, and that the good souls have a better portion than the evil.

Cebes added: Your favorite doctrine, Socrates, that knowledge is simply recollection, if true, also necessarily implies a previous time in which we learned that which we now recollect. But this would be impossible unless our soul was in some place before existing in the human form [22]; here then is another argument of the soul's immortality.

73

But tell me, Cebes, said Simmias interposing, what proofs are given of this doctrine of recollection? I am not very sure at this moment that I remember them.

One excellent proof, said Cebes, is afforded by questions. If you put a question to a person in a right way, he will give

[22] " Our birth is but a sleep and a forgetting;
The soul that rises with us, our life's star,
Hath had elsewhere its setting,
And cometh from afar.
Not in entire forgetfulness,
And not in utter nakedness,
But trailing clouds of glory, do we come
From God, who is our home."
—*Wordsworth's* " Intimations of Immortality."

a true answer of himself, but how could he do this unless there were knowledge and right reason already in him? And this is most clearly shown when he is taken to a diagram [23] or to anything of that sort.

But if, said Socrates, you are still incredulous, Simmias, I would ask you whether you may not agree with me when you look at the matter in another way; I mean, if you are still incredulous as to whether knowledge is recollection?

Incredulous, I am not, said Simmias; but I want to have this doctrine of recollection brought to my own recollection, and, from what Cebes has said, I am beginning to recollect and be convinced: but I should still like to hear what more you have to say.

[Socrates gives a proof of the doctrine as follows: What we recollect we must have known at some previous time. This recollection is due to a power of mind called association. For example, a lyre or a garment may remind us of the person who has used the one or worn the other. Simmias may make us think of Cebes because they are frequently in one another's company. Likewise, the imperfect equality of two pieces of wood or stone suggests the idea of perfect equality. Indeed we must have the standard of perfect equality before we can compare two things. Now where did we get our idea of perfect equality. Surely not through our experience with material objects in this life, for no two material objects are absolutely alike. Their appearance is changing and they serve only to recall the idea of absolute likeness which is ever the same. Moreover the knowledge of perfect equality is not given to us at birth, for all men do not possess it. It comes to none save by a process of remembering, and what we call learning is only recollection. Clearly then, our knowledge of perfect equality and likewise of perfect beauty, perfect goodness, perfect justice, and the like must have been acquired by us before we came into this world. Therefore our souls must have existed and had intelligence before birth.]

73-76

[23] In a passage from Plato's Meno, which is often quoted in educational journals to illustrate the Socratic method of questioning, a slave boy who cannot read, answers "of himself," a series of simple questions about a geometrical diagram. The boy is led in this way to see for himself the truth of a certain geometrical proposition. Socrates argues that since the boy has not learned these things in this life, he must be remembering them from a former life.

Then may we not say, Simmias, that if, as we are always repeating, there is an absolute beauty, and goodness, and essence in general, and to this, which is now discovered to be a previous condition of our being, we refer all our sensations, and with this compare them—assuming this to have a prior existence, then our souls must have had a prior existence, but if not, there would be no force in the argument. There can be no doubt that if these absolute ideas existed before we were born, then our souls must have existed before we were born, and if not the ideas, then not the souls.

Yes, Socrates; I am convinced that there is precisely the same necessity for the existence of the soul before birth, and of the essence of which you are speaking: and the argument arrives at a result which happily agrees with my own notion. For there is nothing which to my mind is so evident as that beauty, good, and other notions of which you were just now speaking, have a most real and absolute existence; and I am satisfied with the proof.

Well, but is Cebes equally satisfied? for I must convince him too.

I think, said Simmias, that Cebes is satisfied: although he is the most incredulous of mortals, yet I believe that he is convinced of the existence of the soul before birth. But that after death the soul will continue to exist is not yet proven even to my own satisfaction. I cannot get rid of the feeling of the many to which Cebes was referring—the feeling that when the man dies the soul may be scattered, and that this may be the end of her. For admitting that she may be generated and created in some other place, and may have existed before entering the human body, why after having entered in and gone out again may she not herself be destroyed and come to an end?

Very true, Simmias, said Cebes; that our soul existed before we were born was the first half of the argument, and this appears to have been proven; that the soul will exist after death as well as before birth is the other half of which the proof is still wanting, and has to be supplied.

But that proof, Simmias and Cebes, has been already given, said Socrates, if you put the two arguments together—I mean this and the former one, in which we admitted that everything living is born of the dead. For if the soul existed before birth, and in coming to life and being born can be born only from death and dying, must she not after death continue to exist, since she has to be born again? surely the proof which you desire has been already furnished. Still I suspect that you and Simmias would be glad to probe the argument further; like children, you are haunted with a fear that when the soul leaves the body, the wind may really blow her away and scatter her; especially if a man should happen to die in stormy weather and not when the sky is calm.

Cebes answered with a smile: Then, Socrates, you must argue us out of our fears—and yet, strictly speaking, they are not our fears, but there is a child within us to whom death is a sort of hobgoblin; him too we must persuade not to be afraid when he is alone with him in the dark.

Socrates said: Let the voice of the charmer [24] be applied daily until you have charmed him away.

And where shall we find a good charmer of our fears, Socrates, when you are gone?

78 Hellas, he replied, is a large place, Cebes, and has many good men, and there are barbarous races not a few: seek for him among them all, far and wide, sparing neither pains nor money; for there is no better way of using your money. And you must not forget to seek for him among yourselves too; for he is nowhere more likely to be found.

The search, replied Cebes, shall certainly be made. And now, if you please, let us return to the point of the argument at which we digressed.

[Socrates leads the discussion. Another argument against the dissolution of the soul at death is found in the nature of the soul itself. Only those things which are compound 78-80 or composite, like the objects of sense, are naturally capable of being dissolved and changed. But the soul, not being compound is indivisible and therefore indestructible. It belongs to that class of unchanging things which are also invisible like the essence of beauty or equality. It is only when the soul makes use of the senses that she is dragged by the body down into the region of changeable things.]

---

[24] As incantations are employed against hobgoblins, wise words must be the charm against foolish fears. In another dialogue Plato speaks of the soul being healed by the charm of fair words.

But when returning into herself she reflects ; then she passes into the realm of purity, and eternity, and immortality, and unchangeableness, which are her kindred, and with them she ever lives, when she is by herself and is not let or hindered ; then she ceases from her erring ways, and being in communion with the unchanging is unchanging. And this state of the soul is called wisdom ?

[Again when we compare the functions of the soul and body we find that the soul is akin to the divine and the body to the mortal. For the soul rules and governs, the body obeys and serves.]

The soul is in the very likeness of the divine, and immortal, and intelligible, and uniform, and indissoluble, and unchangeable ; and the body is in the very likeness of the human, and mortal, and unintelligible, and multiform, and dissoluble, and changeable.

[Even the body may be preserved almost entire for ages by the embalmer's art.]

And are we to suppose that the soul, which is invisible, in passing to the true Hades, which like her is invisible, and pure, and noble, and on her way to the good and wise God,[25] whither, if God will, my soul is also soon to go,—that the soul, I repeat, if this be her nature and origin, is blown away and perishes immediately on quitting the body, as the many say ? That can never be, my dear Simmias and Cebes. The truth rather is, that the soul which is pure at departing draws after her no bodily taint, having never voluntarily had connection with the body, which she is ever avoiding, herself gathered into herself (for such abstraction has been the study of her life). And what does this mean but that she has been a true disciple of philosophy, and has practiced how to die easily ? And is not philosophy the practice of death ?
Certainly.

That soul, I say, herself invisible, departs to the invisible world,—to the divine and immortal and rational : thither arriving, she lives in bliss and is released from the error and folly

---

[25] " And the spirit shall return unto God who gave it."—Eccl. xii. 7.

of men, their fears and wild passions and all other human ills, and forever dwells, as they say of the initiated, in company with the gods? Is not this true, Cebes?

Yes, said Cebes, beyond a doubt.

But the soul which has been polluted, and is impure at the time of her departure, and is the companion and servant of the body always, and is in love with and fascinated by the body and by the desires and pleasures of the body, until she is led to believe that the truth only exists in a bodily form, which a man may touch and see and taste and use for the purposes of his lusts,—the soul, I mean, accustomed to hate and fear and avoid the intellectual principle, which to the bodily eye is dark and invisible, and can be attained only by philosophy; do you suppose that such a soul as this will depart pure and unalloyed?

That is impossible, he replied.

She is engrossed by the corporeal, which the continual association and constant care of the body have made natural to her.

81-82

[The souls of the wicked, loath to leave the body and fearful of the world below, must wander about tombs[26] until they are imprisoned in another body. And some enter the bodies of birds or animals which have natures like their own. Others which are less evil pass again into the forms of men.]

But he who is a philosopher or lover of learning, and is entirely pure at departing, is alone permitted to reach the gods.[27] And this is the reason, Simmias and Cebes, why the true votaries of philosophy abstain from all fleshly lusts, and endure and refuse to give themselves up to them,—not because they fear poverty or the ruin of their families, like the lovers of

[26] " The soul grows clotted by contagion,
Imbodies, and imbrutes, till she quite lose
The divine property of her first being.
Such are those thick and gloomy shadows damp
Oft seen in charnel vaults and sepulchres
Lingering and sitting by a new-made grave
As loath to leave the body that it loved,
And linked itself by carnal sensuality
To a degenerate and degraded state."
—*Milton's* " Comus."

[27] Compare Phædrus, 249.

money, and the world in general; nor like the lovers of power and honor, because they dread the dishonor or disgrace of evil deeds.

No, Socrates, that would not become them, said Cebes.

No indeed, he replied; and therefore they who have a care of their souls, and do not merely live in the fashions of the body, say farewell to all this; they will not walk in the ways of the blind: and when Philosophy offers them purification and release from evil, they feel that they ought not to resist her influence, and to her they incline, and whither she leads they follow her.

What do you mean, Socrates?

I will tell you, he said. The lovers of knowledge are conscious that their souls, when philosophy receives them, are simply fastened and glued to their bodies: the soul is only able to view existence through the bars of a prison,[28] and not in her own nature; she is wallowing in the mire of all ignorance; and philosophy, seeing the terrible nature of her confinement, and that the captive through desire is led to conspire in her own captivity (for the lovers of knowledge are aware that this was the original state of the soul, and that when she was in this state philosophy received and gently counseled her, and wanted to release her, pointing out to her that the eye is full of deceit, and also the ear and the other senses, and persuading her to retire from them in all but the necessary use of them, and to be gathered up and collected into herself, and to trust only to herself and her own intuitions of absolute existence, and mistrust that which comes to her through others and is subject to vicissitude)—philosophy shows her that this is visible and tangible, but that what she sees in her own nature is intellectual and invisible. And the soul of the true philosopher thinks that she ought not to resist this deliverance, and therefore abstains from pleasures and desires and pains and fears, as far as she is able; reflecting that when a man has great joys or sorrows or fears or desires, he suffers from them, not the sort of evil which might be anticipated—as for example, the loss of his health or property which he has sacrificed to his lusts—but he has suffered an evil greater far, which is the greatest and worst of all evils, and one of which he never thinks.

[28] "For now we see through a glass darkly."—1 Cor. xiii. 12. Compare Rep., VII., 514 and following.

And what is that, Socrates? said Cebes.

Why this: When the feeling of pleasure or pain in the soul is most intense, all of us naturally suppose that the object of this intense feeling is then plainest and truest: but this is not the case.

Very true.

And this is the state in which the soul is most inthralled by the body.

How is that?

Why, because each pleasure and pain is a sort of nail which nails and rivets the soul to the body, and engrosses her and makes her believe that to be true which the body affirms to be true; and from agreeing with the body and having the same delights she is obliged to have the same habits and ways, and is not likely ever to be pure at her departure to the world below, but is always saturated with the body; so that she soon sinks into another body and there germinates and grows, and has therefore no part in the communion of the divine and pure and simple.

That is most true, Socrates, answered Cebes.

And this, Cebes, is the reason why the true lovers of knowledge are temperate and brave; and not for the reason which the world gives.

Certainly not.

84 Certainly not! For not in that way does the soul of a philosopher reason; she will not ask philosophy to release her in order that when released she may deliver herself up again to the thralldom of pleasures and pains, doing a work only to be undone again, weaving instead of unweaving her Penelope's web.[29] But she will make herself a calm of passion, and follow Reason, and dwell in her, beholding the true and divine (which is not matter of opinion), and thence derive nourishment. Thus she seeks to live while she lives, and after death she hopes to go to her own kindred and to be freed from human ills. Never fear, Simmias and Cebes, that a soul which has been thus nourished and has had these pursuits, will at her departure from the body be scattered and blown away by the winds and be nowhere and nothing.

---

[29] Penelope (pē-nĕl'ō-pe): wife of the legendary hero Odysseus. During his absence at the Trojan War she was beset by many suitors. To put them off, she promised to make choice as soon as she finished a web she was weaving; but each night she unraveled what she wove during the day.

When Socrates had done speaking, for a considerable time there was silence; he himself and most of us appeared to be meditating on what had been said; only Cebes and Simmias spoke a few words to one another. And Socrates observing this asked them what they thought of the argument, and whether there was anything wanting? For, said he, much is still open to suspicion and attack, if any one were disposed to sift the matter thoroughly. If you are talking of something else I would rather not interrupt you, but if you are still doubtful about the argument do not hesitate to say exactly what you think, and let us have anything better which you can suggest; and if I am likely to be of any use, allow me to help you.

Simmias said: I must confess, Socrates, that doubts did arise in our minds, and each of us was urging and inciting the other to put the question which we wanted to have answered and which neither of us liked to ask, fearing that our importunity might be troublesome under present circumstances.

Socrates smiled, and said: O Simmias, how strange that is; I am not very likely to persuade other men that I do not regard my present situation as a misfortune, if I am unable to persuade you, and you will keep fancying that I am at all more troubled now than at any other time. Will you not allow that I have as much of the spirit of prophecy in me as the swans?[30] For they, when they perceive that they must die, having sung all their life long, do then sing more than ever, rejoicing in the thought that they are about to go away to the god whose ministers they are. But men, because they are themselves afraid of death, slanderously affirm of the swans that they sing a lament at the last, not considering that no bird sings when cold, or hungry, or in pain, not even the nightingale, nor the swallow, nor yet the hoopoe; which are said indeed to tune a lay of sorrow, although I do not believe this to be true of them any more than of the swans. But because they are sacred to Apollo and have the gift of prophecy and anticipate the good things of another world, therefore they sing and rejoice in that day more than they ever did before. And I too, believing myself to be the consecrated

85

---

[30] The swan was sacred to Apollo and said to be gifted with the power of song and of prophecy. The myth of the swan's dying song has come down to modern times.

servant of the same God, and the fellow-servant of the swans, and thinking that I have received from my master gifts of prophecy which are not inferior to theirs, would not go out of life less merrily than the swans. Cease to mind then about this, but speak and ask anything which you like, while the eleven magistrates of Athens allow.

[Since Socrates is so willing to continue the discussion, Simmias and Cebes state their difficulties,—Simmias first as follows: One may say that harmony is invisible, incorporeal, perfect, and divine; yet when the lyre is destroyed, the harmony ceases. How then can the soul which has the same relation to the body as harmony to the lyre, survive the body?

85-88

Cebes also uses a figure to express his doubt. It is reasonable to say that a man lasts longer than the garment which he wears. And yet a wearer, though he may make and wear out many coats is himself outlived by the last. Now the body is the garment of the soul; and the soul may wear out many bodies in one life and many more in the successive lives into which it is born. But how can we prove that the soul may not become weary and at last utterly perish in one of its deaths, and so be outlived by the last body?

Here Phædo interrupts the narration of his story to say to Echecrates:]

All of us, as we afterwards remarked to one another, had an unpleasant feeling at hearing them say this. When we had been so firmly convinced before, now to have our faith shaken seemed to introduce a confusion and uncertainty, not only into the previous argument, but into any future one; either we were not good judges, or there were no real grounds of belief.

Ech. There I feel with you—indeed I do, Phædo, and when you were speaking, I was beginning to ask myself the same question: What argument can I ever trust again? For what could be more convincing than the argument of Socrates, which has now fallen into discredit? That the soul is a harmony is a doctrine which has always had a wonderful attraction for me, and, when mentioned, came back to me at once, as my own original conviction. And now I must begin again and find another argument which will assure me that when the man is dead the soul dies not with him. Tell me, I beg, how did Socrates proceed? Did he appear to share the unpleasant feeling which you mention? or did he receive the interruption calmly and give a sufficient answer? Tell us, as exactly as you can, what passed.

Phæd. Often, Echecrates, as I have admired Socrates, I never admired him more than at that moment. That he should be able to answer was nothing, but what astonished me was, first, the gentle and pleasant and approving manner in which he regarded the words of the young men, and then his quick sense of the wound which had been inflicted by the argument, and his ready application of the healing art. He might be compared to a general rallying his defeated and broken army, urging them to follow him and return to the field of argument.

Ech. How was that?

Phæd. You shall hear, for I was close to him on his right hand, seated on a sort of stool, and he on a couch which was a good deal higher. Now he had a way of playing with my hair, and then he smoothed my head, and pressed the hair upon my neck, and said: To-morrow, Phædo, I suppose that these fair locks of yours will be severed.[31]

Yes, Socrates, I suppose that they will, I replied.

Not so, if you will take my advice.

What shall I do with them? I said.

To-day, he replied, and not to-morrow, if this argument dies and cannot be brought to life again by us, you and I will both shave our locks: and if I were you, and could not maintain my ground against Simmias and Cebes, I would myself take an oath, like the Argives, not to wear hair any more until I had renewed the conflict and defeated them.[32]

Yes, I said, but Heracles himself is said not to be a match for two.[33]

---

[31] As a token of mourning, according to the custom.

[32] Argives (är'jĭvz): a branch of the Greek people inhabiting a small district of Greece, south-west of Athens. Herodicus tells how once when the Argives were defeated, and lost a city in war, they took an oath not to cut their hair till their loss had been retrieved.

[33] See Euthydemus, note 20. One of his labors was the destroying of the Hydra, a monstrous water-snake. While fighting with this he was attacked by a crab and was compelled to call on Iolaus (Ĭ'o-lāus), his nephew, for help. Hence the proverb—Heracles is not a match for two.

Summon me then, he said, and I will be your Iolaus until the sun goes down.

I summon you rather, I said, not as Heracles summoning Iolaus, but as Iolaus might summon Heracles.

That will be all the same, he said. But first let us take care that we avoid a danger.

And what is that? I said.

The danger of becoming misologists, he replied, which is one of the very worst things that can happen to us. For as there are misanthropists or haters of men, there are also misologists or haters of ideas, and both spring from the same cause, which is ignorance of the world. Misanthropy arises from the too great confidence of inexperience; you trust a man and think him altogether true and good and faithful, and then in a little while he turns out to be false and knavish; and then another and another, and when this has happened several times to a man, especially within the circle of his own most trusted friends, as he deems them, and he has often quarreled with them, he at last hates all men, and believes that no one has any good in him at all. I dare say that you must have observed this.

Yes, I said.

And is not this discreditable? The reason is, that a man, having to deal with other men, has no knowledge of them; for if he had knowledge, he would have known the true state of the case, that few are the good and few the evil, and that the great majority are in the interval between them.

How do you mean? I said.

I mean, he replied, as you might say of the very large and very small, that nothing is more uncommon than a very large or very small man; and this applies generally to all extremes, whether of great and small, or swift and slow, or fair and foul, or black and white: and whether the instances you select be men or dogs or anything else, few are the extremes, but many are in the mean between them. Did you never observe this?

Yes, I said, I have.

And do you not imagine, he said, that if there were a competition of evil, the first in evil would be found to be very few?

Yes, that is very likely, I said.

Yes, that is very likely, he replied; not that in this respect arguments are like men—there I was led on by you to say more than I had intended; but the point of comparison was, that when a simple man who has no skill in dialectics believes an argument to be true which he afterward imagines to be false, whether really false or not, and then another and another, he has no longer any faith left, and great disputers, as you know, come to think at last that they have grown to be the wisest of mankind; for they alone perceive the utter unsoundness and instability of all arguments, or indeed, of all things, which, like the currents in the Euripus,[31] are going up and down in never-ceasing ebb and flow.

That is quite true, I said.

Yes, Phædo, he replied, and very melancholy too, if there be such a thing as truth or certainty or power of knowing at all, that a man should have lighted upon some argument or other which at first seemed true and then turned out to be false, and instead of blaming himself and his own want of wit, because he is annoyed, should at last be too glad to transfer the blame from himself to arguments in general; and forever afterwards should hate and revile them, and lose the truth and knowledge of existence.

Yes, indeed, I said; that is very melancholy.

Let us then, in the first place, he said, be careful of admitting into our souls the notion that there is no truth or health or soundness in any arguments at all; but let us rather say that there is as yet no health in us, and that we must quit ourselves like men and do our best to gain health,—you and all other men with a view to the whole of your future life, and I myself with a view to death. For at this moment I am sensible that I have not the temper of a philosopher; like the vulgar, I am only a partisan. For the partisan, when he is engaged in a dispute, cares nothing about the rights of the question, but is anxious only to convince his hearers of his own assertions. And the difference between him and me at the present moment is only this,—that whereas he seeks to convince his hearers that what he says is true, I am rather seeking to convince myself; to convince my hearers is a secondary matter with me. And do but see how

---

[31] Euripus (ū-rī′pus): the narrow strait which separates Bœotia (bē-ŏ′shĭ-a), a province of Greece, from the island Eubœa (ū-bē′a), where the ancients believed that the current changed seven times a day.

much I gain by this. For if what I say is true, then I do well to be persuaded of the truth, but if there be nothing after death, still, during the short time that remains, I shall save my friends from lamentations, and my ignorance will not last, and therefore no harm will be done. This is the state of mind, Simmias and Cebes, in which I approach the argument. And I would ask you to be thinking of the truth and not of Socrates: agree with me, if I seem to you to be speaking the truth; or if not, withstand me might and main, that I may not deceive you as well as myself in my enthusiasm, and like the bee, leave my sting in you before I die.

And now let us proceed, he said.

[Socrates returns to the objection of Simmias which he answers very easily. Harmony cannot exist prior to the instrument with which it is made. We must first have the lyre and strings. Harmony follows last of all as an effect. Now does the soul follow as an effect of the body? Has it not been proved that the soul existed before birth, and that all our knowledge is but recollection of what we experienced before the soul entered the body? Simmias acknowledged that his theory of the soul as a harmony must be rejected because it is inconsistent with the doctrine of preëxistence which to his mind has been proved beyond a doubt.

91-98

Again, Socrates says, while one harmony may be more or less completely a harmony than another, one soul is no more or no less a soul than another. That is, a harmony admits of degrees, a soul does not, and therefore a soul is not a harmony. Lastly, how can the soul be the harmony of the body when it continually opposes and constrains the passions? Harmony is subject to the lyre, but the soul is leader and master of the body—" a far diviner thing than any harmony."

Socrates turns next to discuss and answer the objection of Cebes, which he says involves one of the most important questions of philosophy, namely, how things come into being and perish, or the nature of generation and corruption. Here he digresses to tell of his own experience when, as a young man, he sought to know the causes of all things—why they are created and why destroyed. His investigations and speculations led him into many perplexities, so that he began to doubt even the most commonplace facts. Then he heard of the philosopher Anaxagoras,[35] who claimed that Mind was the cause and disposer of all things. Socrates was greatly delighted at this notion, and thought if mind were the disposer, surely mind would dispose all for the best. He had great hopes that the new teacher would satisfactorily explain to him in detail all that he had been seeking to understand and prove how everything was for the best in nature and in man. He continues:]

What hopes I had formed, and how grievously was I disappointed! As I proceeded, I found my philosopher altogether forsaking mind or any other principle of order, but having recourse to air, and ether, and water, and other eccentricities. I might compare him to a person who began by maintaining generally that mind is the cause of the actions of Socrates, but who, when he endeavored to explain the causes of my several actions in detail, went on to show that I sit here because my body is made up of bones and muscles; and the bones, as he would say, are hard and have ligaments which divide them, and the muscles are elastic, and they cover the bones, which have also a covering or environment of flesh and skin which contains them; and as the bones are lifted at their joints by the contraction or relaxation of the muscles, I am able to bend my limbs, and this is why I am sitting here in a curved posture: that is what he would say, and he would have a similar explanation of my talking to you, which he would attribute to sound, and air, and hearing, and he would assign ten thousand other causes of the same sort, forgetting to mention the true cause, which is, that the Athenians have thought fit to condemn me, and accordingly I have thought it better and more right to remain here and undergo my sentence; for I am inclined to think that these muscles and bones of mine would have gone off to Megara or Bœotia,[36]— by the dog of Egypt they would, if they had been guided only by their own idea of what was best, and if I had not chosen as the better and nobler part, instead of playing truant and running away, to undergo any punishment which the state inflicts. There is surely a

[35] See Phædrus, note 55.
[36] Megara (měg'á-rá): a town twenty miles west of Athens.

strange confusion of causes and conditions in all this. It may be said, indeed, that without bones and muscles and the other parts of the body I cannot execute my purposes. But to say that I do as I do because of them, and that this is the way in which mind acts, and not from the choice of the best, is a very careless and idle mode of speaking. I wonder that they cannot distinguish the cause from the condition, which the many feeling about in the dark, are always mistaking and misnaming. And thus one man makes a vortex all round and steadies the earth by the heaven; another gives the air as a support to the earth, which is a sort of broad trough. Any power which in disposing them as they are disposes them for the best never enters into their minds, nor do they imagine that there is any superhuman strength in that; they rather expect to find another Atlas[37] of the world who is stronger and more everlasting and more containing than the good is, and are clearly of opinion that the obligatory and containing power of the good is as nothing; and yet this is the principle which I would fain learn if any one would teach me. But as I have failed either to discover myself, or to learn of any one else, the nature of the best, I will exhibit to you, if you like, what I have found to be the second best mode of inquiring into the cause.

[Failing in his endeavor to comprehend the world by means of the senses, Socrates took refuge in the world of thought. By reflection he arrived at a principle which he regarded

99-107

as indisputable. Whatever agreed with this he assumed to be true, whatever disagreed, false. He wishes now to explain what he means by this principle although it is nothing new. It is what he has always been repeating in his doctrine of ideas. He believes that corresponding to every class of material objects or qualities, there is a perfect and eternal being which he calls an idea. These ideas exist independently of the world of sense, apart from and above it. They are the perfect types of which the things in this world are imperfect copies. These perfect types are the causes of the existence of their earthly copies. For example, there is an

---

[37] Atlas: An ancient Greek divinity, who was supposed to support the heavens on his shoulders. Socrates says that the philosophers referred to expect to supplant the legendary Atlas by a physical principle. He believes that the true Atlas which supports all things is the Good.

absolute beauty, an absolute greatness, an absolute good, and the like. Now a thing can be beautiful only by reason of its participation in the absolute or perfect beauty, that is, the idea of beauty. A thing is made good or great only by the indwelling of the idea of goodness or greatness. Socrates now applies his doctrine of ideas to the question of the soul's immortality, as follows: Ideas which are opposite in character never co-exist. They mutually exclude one another and never pass over the one into the other. Moreover, things in which a certain idea forever abides, will never admit the opposite of that idea. For example, no odd number will ever admit the idea of the even, because the ideas of the odd and the even are essentially opposed. So the soul, whose inseparable attribute is life, will never admit life's opposite, death. Thus the soul is shown to be immortal, and since immortal, indestructible.]

But then, O my friends, he said, if the soul is really immortal, what care should be taken of her, not only in respect of the portion of time which is called life, but of eternity! And the danger of neglecting her from this point of view does indeed appear to be awful.[38] If death had only been the end of all, the wicked would have had a good bargain in dying, for they would have been happily quit not only of their body, but of their own evil together with their souls. But now, as the soul plainly appears to be immortal, there is no release or salvation from evil except the attainment of the highest virtue and wisdom. For the soul when on her progress to the world below takes nothing with her but nurture and education; which are indeed said greatly to benefit or greatly to injure the departed, at the very beginning of his pilgrimage in the other world.

For after death, as they say, the genius of each individual, to whom he belonged in life, leads him to a certain place in which the dead are gathered together for judgment, whence they go into the world below, following the guide, who is appointed to conduct them from this world to the other: and when they have there received their due and remained their

---

[38] "For what is a man profited if he shall gain the whole world and lose his own soul."—Matt. xvi. 26.
"Seeing then that all these things shall be dissolved, what manner of persons ought ye to be in all holy conversation and godliness."—II. Peter iii. 11.

108

time, another guide brings them back again after many revolutions of ages. Now this journey to the other world is not, as Æschylus says in the Telephus,[39] a single and straight path,—no guide would be wanted for that, and no one could miss a single path; but there are many partings of the road, and windings, as I must infer from the rites and sacrifices which are offered to the gods below in places where three ways meet on earth.[40] The wise and orderly soul is conscious of her situation, and follows in the path; but the soul which desires the body, and which, as I was relating before, has long been fluttering about the lifeless frame and the world of sight, is after many struggles and many sufferings hardly and with violence carried away by her attendant genius, and when she arrives at the place where the other souls are gathered, if she be impure and have done impure deeds, or been concerned in foul murders or other crimes which are the brothers of these, and the works of brothers in crime,—from that soul every one flees and turns away; no one will be her companion, no one her guide, but alone she wanders in extremity of evil until certain times are fulfilled, and when they are fulfilled, she is borne irresistibly to her own fitting habitation; as every pure and just soul which has passed through life in the company and under the guidance of the gods has also her own proper home.

108-114

[Socrates gives a mythical description of the earth, the heavens, and the interior of the earth with its seas and rivers. This is followed by an account of how the dead are judged. Those who have committed the greatest crimes are hurled into Tartarus never to return. Those who have lived neither well nor ill, are punished for their wrong deeds and rewarded for the good. Those who have led holy lives, especially those who have been purified by philosophy, live forever in mansions fair beyond description.

Socrates continues thus:]

Wherefore, Simmias, seeing all these things, what ought not we to do in order to obtain virtue and wisdom in this life? Fair is the prize, and the hope great.

---

[39] Telephus (tĕl'e-fus): a lost tragedy by Æschylus. See Rep., II., note 3.
[40] It was customary to perform rites once a month in honor of certain gods of the lower world. These ceremonies took place at road crossings.

I do not mean to affirm that the description which I have given of the soul and her mansions is exactly true—a man of sense ought hardly to say that. But I do say that, inasmuch as the soul is shown to be immortal, he may venture to think, not improperly or unworthily, that something of the kind is true. The venture is a glorious one, and he ought to comfort himself with words like these, which is the reason why I lengthen out the tale. Wherefore, I say, let a man be of good cheer about his soul, who has cast away the pleasures and ornaments of the body as alien to him, and rather hurtful in their effects, and has followed after the pleasures of knowledge in this life; who has adorned the soul in her own proper jewels, which are temperance, and justice, and courage, and nobility, and truth—in these arrayed she is ready to go on her journey to the world below, when her time comes. You, Simmias and Cebes, and all other men, will depart at some time or other. Me already, as the tragic poet would say, the voice of fate calls. Soon I must drink the poison; and I think that I had better repair to the bath first, in order that the women may not have the trouble of washing my body after I am dead.

115

When he had done speaking, Crito said: And have you any commands for us, Socrates—anything to say about your children, or any other matter in which we can serve you?

Nothing particular, he said: only, as I have always told you, I would have you to look to yourselves; that is a service which you may always be doing to me and mine as well as to yourselves. And you need not make professions; for if you take no thought for yourselves, and walk not according to the precepts which I have given you, not now for the first time, the warmth of your professions will be of no avail.

We will do our best, said Crito. But in what way would you have us bury you?

In any way that you like; only you must get hold of me, and take care that I do not walk away from you. Then he turned to us, and added with a smile: I cannot make Crito believe that I am the same Socrates who have been talking and conducting the argument; he fancies that I am the other Socrates whom he will soon see, a dead body—and he asks, How shall he bury me? And though I have spoken many words in the endeavor to show that when I have drunk the poison I shall leave you and go to the joys of the blessed,

—these words of mine, with which I comforted you and myself, have had, as I perceive, no effect upon Crito. And therefore I want you to be surety for me now, as he was surety for me at the trial: but let the promise be of another sort; for he was my surety to the judges that I would remain, but you must be my surety to him that I shall not remain, but go away and depart; and then he will suffer less at my death, and not be grieved when he sees my body being burned or buried. I would not have him sorrow at my hard lot, or say at the burial, Thus we lay out Socrates, or, Thus we follow him to the grave or bury him; for false words are not only evil in themselves, but they infect the soul with evil. Be of good cheer then, my dear Crito, and say that you are burying my body only, and do with that as is usual, and as you think best.

116

When he had spoken these words, he arose and went into the bath-chamber with Crito, who bid us wait; and we waited, talking and thinking of the subject of discourse, and also of the greatness of our sorrow; he was like the father of whom we were being bereaved, and we were about to pass the rest of our lives as orphans. When he had taken the bath his children were brought to him—(he had two young sons and an elder one); and the women of his family also came, and he talked to them and gave them a few directions in the presence of Crito; and he then dismissed them and returned to us.

Now the hour of sunset was near, for a good deal of time had passed while he was within. When he came out, he sat down with us again after his bath, but not much was said. Soon the jailer, who was the servant of the eleven, entered and stood by him, saying: To you, Socrates, whom I know to be the noblest and gentlest and best of all who ever came to this place, I will not impute the angry feelings of other men, who rage and swear at me when, in obedience to the authorities, I bid them drink the poison—indeed I am sure that you will not be angry with me; for others, as you are aware, and not I, are the guilty cause. And so fare you well, and try to bear lightly what must needs be; you know my errand. Then bursting into tears he turned away and went out.

Socrates looked at him and said: I return your good wishes,

and will do as you bid. Then turning to us, he said, How charming the man is: since I have been in prison he has always been coming to see me, and at times he would talk to me, and was as good as could be to me, and now see how generously he sorrows for me. But we must do as he says, Crito; let the cup be brought, if the poison is prepared: if not, let the attendant prepare some.

Yet, said Crito, the sun is still upon the hill-tops, and many a one has taken the draught late, and after the announcement has been made to him, he has eaten and drunk, and indulged in sensual delights; do not hasten then, there is still time.

Socrates said: Yes, Crito, and they of whom you speak are right in doing thus, for they think that they will gain by the delay; but I am right in not doing thus, for I do not think that I should gain anything by drinking the poison a little later; I should be sparing and saving a life which is already gone: I could only laugh at myself for this. Please then to do as I say, and not to refuse me.

Crito, when he heard this, made a sign to the servant; and the servant went in, and remained for some time, and then returned with the jailer carrying the cup of poison. Socrates said: You, my good friend, who are experienced in these matters, shall give me directions how I am to proceed. The man answered: You have only to walk about until your legs are heavy, and then to lie down, and the poison will act. At the same time he handed the cup to Socrates, who in the easiest and gentlest manner, without the least fear or change of color or feature, looking at the man with all his eyes, Echecrates, as his manner was, took the cup and said: What do you say about making a libation out of this cup to any god? May I, or not? The man answered: We only prepare, Socrates, just so much as we deem enough. I understand, he said: yet I may and must pray to the gods to prosper my journey from this to that other world—may this then, which is my prayer, be granted to me. Then holding the cup to his lips, quite readily and cheerfully he drank off the poison. And hitherto most of us had been able to control our sorrow; but now when we saw him drinking, and saw too that he had finished the draught, we could no longer forbear, and in spite of myself my own tears were flowing fast; so that I covered my face and wept over myself, for certainly I was not weeping over him, but at the thought of my own calamity in having lost such a companion. Nor was I the first, for Crito, when he found himself unable to restrain his tears, had got up and moved away, and I followed; and at that moment, Apollodorus, who had been weeping all the time, broke out into a loud cry which made cowards of us all. Socrates alone retained his calmness: What is this strange outcry? he said. I sent away the women mainly in order that they might not offend in this way, for I have heard that a man should die in peace. Be quiet then, and have patience. When we heard that, we were ashamed, and refrained our tears; and he walked about until, as he said, his legs began to fail, and then he lay on his back, according to the directions, and the man who gave him the poison now and then looked at his feet and legs; and after a while he pressed his foot hard and asked him if he could feel; and he said, No; and then his leg, and so upwards and upwards, and showed us that he was cold and stiff.

118 And he felt them himself, and said: When the poison reaches the heart, that will be the end. He was beginning to grow cold about the groin, when he uncovered his face, for he had covered himself up, and said (they were his last words) —he said: Crito, I owe a cock to Asclepius; will you remember to pay the debt?[41] The debt shall be paid, said Crito; is there anything else? There was no answer to this question; but in a minute or two a movement was heard, and the attendants uncovered him; his eyes were set, and Crito closed his eyes and mouth.

Such was the end, Echecrates, of our friend, whom I may truly call the wisest, and justest, and best of all the men whom I have ever known.

[41] See Protagoras, note 8. What Socrates meant by this his last speech is doubtful. Some hold that he believed literally in Æsculapius as a god, that he had actually made a vow to him, and that he did not wish to die with any religious duty unfulfilled. Others hold that he used the language of the popular religion figuratively, that he meant to say that he was now cured of the worst possible malady, the earthly life, and that he owed thanks to God for this cure. In general, it remains doubtful how far Plato believed literally in the religion of his time and how far he used the language of that religion figuratively to express higher views.

www.ingramcontent.com/pod-product-compliance
Lightning Source LLC
Chambersburg PA
CBHW021418300426
44114CB00010B/553